Shakespeare, memory, and modern Irish literature

Manchester University Press

Shakespeare, memory, and modern Irish literature

Nicholas Taylor-Collins

MANCHESTER UNIVERSITY PRESS

Published by Manchester University Press
Oxford Road, Manchester M13 9PL

www.manchesteruniversitypress.co.uk

British Library Cataloguing-in-Publication Data
A catalogue record for this book is available from the British Library

ISBN 978 1 5261 4961 9 hardback

First published 2022

The publisher has no responsibility for the persistence or accuracy of URLs for any external or third-party internet websites referred to in this book, and does not guarantee that any content on such websites is, or will remain, accurate or appropriate.

Typeset by Deanta Global Publishing Services, Chennai, India

For Emma,
for Aryel

Contents

Acknowledgements   *page* ix
Note on the text   xii

Introduction: Remembering memory   1

Part I: Ghosts

Introduction   39
1 'Go on from this': J. M. Synge's *Playboy*   50
2 'Remember me': *Hamlet*, memory, and Leopold
     Bloom's *poiesis*   70
3 'Someone wholly other': John Banville's *Ghosts*   93

Part II: Bodies

Introduction   115
4 '[M]y genius for forgetting': Samuel Beckett's
     theatrical bodies   137
5 'Kate had herself sterilized': Edna O'Brien's
     self-disciplining bodies   169

Part III: Land

Introduction   205
6 '[R]ights of memory': W. B. Yeats, surface, and
     counter-memory   220

7   '[D]ithering, blathering': Seamus Heaney, the diseased
    word-hoard, and the Historian   252

Conclusion: 'I disremember'   278

References   285
Index   302

Acknowledgements

I owe thanks to many people who have known and helped me during the long gestation of this book. First to my teachers, especially the late Perry Keenlyside, whose energy spilled over into my own reading and thinking. Also to Michael Cook and Phillip Parr: their erudition and teaching led me towards teaching as a vocation. I hope to have done them all proud.

I also thank my university tutors, with whom I have had long conversations, and on whose advice, counsel, and knowledge I have often leant. I had many discussions with Thomas Docherty who encouraged me to think bigger, and to whom 'thank you' would seem too small, and this book would not have existed without the encouragement and boldness of Carol Rutter. I hope to have channelled some of her expertise. My thanks also to Anne Fogarty, and to Michael Gardiner who helped me to recognise what question this book could really attempt to answer. Thank you, too, to Declan Kiberd, for assisting me with Chapter 3, and to Stanley van der Ziel for supportive and enriching conversations for nearly ten years. A more recent discussion with Kaara L. Peterson was instructive.

To my colleagues at Hampton School and Highgate School: thank you for putting up with me wittering on about this project. Also to colleagues and friends in Swansea, I owe thanks for helping me on to the ladder. *Diolch* to Alice Barnaby, Kirsti Bohata, Georgie Lucas, Eoin Price, Richard Robinson, and Daniel Williams. Likewise to my English literature colleagues at Cardiff Met, Carmen Casaliggi and Elizabeth English, on whose welcome and support I have relied more than they are likely to know.

My eternal thanks to my students, many of whom were early audiences for my ideas (even without their realising). In this regard, I owe a special thanks to Katie FitzGerald, Ruby Gold, Anna Seale, Megan Sands, and Zara Shepherd-Brierley who happily read Seamus Heaney's poems with me (and maybe even liked them by the end). Also to Nadia Ash and Jimi-Dean Miller, whose own journeys are just beginning, but whose conversations have already proven enriching.

Thank you to the organisers of the conferences and symposia where I first presented these ideas: King's College, London; Queen's College, Belfast; St Mary's University; Swansea University; Trinity College, Dublin; Université Charles de Gaulle – Lille 3; University College Cork; University College, Dublin; University of Leeds; University of Stirling; University of Warwick; and University of York. I would also like to thank the librarians and archivists who have helped me. These include those at the British Library, the National Library of Ireland, the library of the University of Warwick, the library of Swansea University, and also the library of Cardiff Met, who were especially helpful during the recent COVID-19 pandemic when access to resources was extremely limited. The reference to Edna O'Brien's teleplay *The Wedding Dress* in Chapter 5 is courtesy of the Special Collections at the BFI National Archive. Chapter 2 first appeared as '"[R]emember me": Hamlet, memory and Bloom's *poiesis*' in *Irish Studies Review*, 25.2 (2017), 241–58, and is reprinted by permission of the publisher (Taylor & Francis). Likewise, small passages of Chapter 4 first appeared as 'Body and memory in *Coriolanus*' in *Notes and Queries*, 68.1 (2021), 119–21, and they are reprinted by permission of Oxford University Press. Thank you to those presses, and also to Matthew Frost and his team at Manchester University Press who have been encouraging and helpful throughout the publication process. I am grateful to the reviewers for their generous and helpful comments.

In the early periods of researching this book I spent much of my spare time with a small group of dear friends. They patiently listened to my travails with Shakespeare and never failed with their encouragement. My thanks to them: Max Archer, Michael Bow, Hannah Brenton, Edward Field, Gemma Field, Cathryn Moses-Stone, Aoife O'Donnell, and Joseph Stone. I also thank Chris Rawnsley, my longest-suffering companion on the road from there to here; and I thank Malwina Fojcik for the stunning cover wrapping these pages.

I could not have succeeded in the ways I have without the support of my family. Primarily my parents, Lindsay and Stephen, who have provided more than they could justly be expected to – I will be forever thankful for them letting me squirrel another book under the duvet after bedtime, and for taking me to see *A Midsummer Night's Dream* in Regent's Park. I was always accompanied there by my sisters, Lucy and Claudia, who have shown tremendous resilience in putting up with me all these years. Thank you. More recently I have been grateful for the support of the Taylor-Blunden clan, Berni, Phil, Charlotte, and Harry.

Words are insufficient – or, at least, I am a poor master of them – to explain properly how grateful I am to Emma. No idea recorded below has been thought and developed without her. No expression has gone untested. No moral unchallenged. I am better because of her, and this book is immeasurably improved after her scrutiny. Thank you. We are happily joined by our *petit lionceau*, Aryel Thomas, who has already wasted much of our time – though not nearly enough just yet. May he be interested enough to read this one day.

Though I have had this extraordinary support, errors may linger below; they are fully my own.

Note on the text

All references to Shakespeare's drama are to individual editions in The Arden Shakespeare Third Series, and I parenthetically reference the Shakespeare texts using standard notation.

My references to James Joyce's *Ulysses* (1922) use standard notation for the corrected, revised edition of that text.

References to poems cite line numbers only.

On a few occasions, I have silently amended the long -s from early modern texts.

Introduction: Remembering memory

This book is about the importance of literary memory, both on *general* and *particular* planes of examination. On the former, I am interested in the ways in which Shakespeare – 'our contemporary', in Jan Kott's (1964) idiom – is remembered and put to work by modern writers. What appears to become available through remembering Shakespeare – the Shakespeare-as-memory, the 'Shakespeare' who is shorthand for his literature, the 'Shakespeare' who becomes a byword for 'memory' itself – are not just narratives, characters, or (most importantly) language. Rather, constructed by all of these are also a society, politics, history, and morality – expressing a 'structure of feeling', in Raymond Williams's terminology (Williams, 2011: 104–5). One or other of these are prioritised by those who remember Shakespeare, though they are all equally available.

On the latter – the *particular* plane – I am motivated by the way that Irish writers specifically put Shakespeare to work by remembering his writing in their own modern Irish literature. The result of this work and these anamnestic processes is, I will argue, 'modern Ireland': a modern, sovereign nation that, through its writers and their literature, has been shaped culturally as much as juridically. This book is a contribution to what Oona Frawley has termed 'Irish cultural memory', an idea or object 'in the singular, [which] contains a multitude of conflicting, overlapping, contradictory and competing memories, in the plural' (Frawley, 2011: xvii). Richard Helgerson sketched the same culture–nation nexus in relation to early modern England, using as a launchpad Edmund Spenser's wish to create a kingdom of his own language (Spenser, 1970:

611). Helgerson begins his *Forms of Nationhood* by suggesting that Spenser's project was widespread among his contemporaries:

> To have the kingdom of their own language. To govern the very linguistic system, and perhaps more generally the whole cultural system, by which their own identity, and their own consciousness were constituted. To remake it, and presumably themselves as well, according to some ideal pattern. (Helgerson, 1992: 6–7)

Helgerson's vocabulary of idealism and patterning is near identical to Williams's when describing the structure of feeling, as though the means of expression and of expressing the self come close to expressing and fashioning the 'nation', newly formed – and whatever 'nation' might mean. Shakespeare was one of Helgerson's selected writers to exemplify this culture–nation expressionism, and my macro observation is that Shakespeare's preeminent national expressionism is deployed by modern Irish writers who are also fashioning their nation through cultural means.

Through the particular examination that nevertheless remains relatively broad – over a century of writing from the end of the nineteenth to the early twenty-first centuries, across seven writers, through three written forms (drama, the novel, poetry) – I will also show that whilst the anamnestic process is about *looking backwards*, these memories are transformed in a number of ways to help the Irish writers contribute their cultural manifesto to their nation – for the nation is always a promise, and all promises are future oriented.[1] And yet, the nature of remembering is in fact disruptive:[2] the nation is contested, ambiguous, up for grabs. Rather than merely remembering, these Irish writers are *dis*remembering. To disremember is not only to remember real historical events, but at the same time to construct artistic memories that configure an alternative to or substitution for the historical event – but in a way that disrupts or deconstructs coherence, rather than shoring up and consolidating the historical narrative.

This argument, when returned to the general plane of examination, also demands that we as critics reconsider the nature of literary intertextuality. Beyond both Julia Kristeva's 'mosaic of quotations' (Kristeva, 1986: 37) and Roland Barthes's 'quotations without inverted commas' (Barthes, 1977: 160), a theory of disremembering shows how borrowing (or stealing, *pace* T. S. Eliot

(1950: 125))[3] from any writer, including Shakespeare, is a metaphorically violent act that may incur further literary or represen-
tational distortions, however situated or manifested. At the very
least, any culture of remembrance and commemoration needs
another reckoning to appreciate fully what is at stake when we
remember, and what dangers or profit may follow, and my focus
is on a type of literary commemoration that is often suppressed
on a textual level – Shakespeare's words are not always tele-
graphed or acknowledged – or sometimes apparently neutered, as
if Shakespeare's language were an appendage detachable from its
texts and contexts. My use of dismemory (and disremembering)
therefore also builds on Guy Beiner's recent critical intervention in
Forgetful Remembrance, in which the historian uses a particular
Ulster definition of disremembering as 'impl[ying] a disinclination
to remember' or to 'pretend to forget' (Beiner, 2018: 30). My point
is that intertextuality exemplifies a pretence to forget – the artificial
nature of fiction demonstrates the pretence, and the lack of quotation marks enacts the forgetfulness – *and* that the failed element of
the forgetfulness is often disruptive; hence, 'dismemory'. Moreover,
if within the economy of memory 'remembrance is the abnormal
exception' and 'It is wrong to think of forgetting as a malfunction'
(Beiner, 2018: 26), then we as literary critics are obliged to search
more rigorously for the so-called 'forgotten' intertextual references.
This book is therefore both about a modern Ireland as a nation-
state that remembers Shakespeare and his early modern England
(even one with a fraught, emergent colonial practice in Ireland), *and*
offers practical examples of how to read 'dismemorially' to exca-
vate the buried secrets (Beiner, 2018: 30) of Shakespeare in modern
Irish letters.

The Republic of Ireland offers a significant space for this kind of
exploration because of the way that memory and commemoration
are practised on individual and national levels there. We are now
coming towards the end of a decade of centenaries, where 2016
represented the pinnacle of the decade – a commemorative practice common in Ireland that has its roots in Reformation England
(McBride, 2001: 16 ff.). The decade commemorates the Irish revolution from the labour controversies that culminated in the 1913
Dublin lockout, via the Easter Rising of 1916, to the end of the Irish
Civil War in 1923. The net result of these monumental events was

a partitioned Ireland with a Free State in the south; by 1947 the Irish Republic was formally born. To remember this central decade, from 1913 to 1923, is also to remember the birth of the modern Irish nation-state.

These commemorations were counterbalanced – albeit unevenly – by the commemoration of the quatercentenary of Shakespeare's death. In 2016, the *Irish Times* posed a series of questions to Irish 'writers, journalists and academics', and 'The results of this 2016 Irish Times survey were published under the heading "Shakespeare and Me: Irish Writers on the Bard's Best Bits" on the day of the quatercentenary' (Taylor-Collins and van der Ziel, 2018: 10). Remembering Shakespeare in this way and at that moment should not be overlooked, most importantly because 23 April 2016 (the four-hundredth anniversary of Shakespeare's death) was nigh-on 100 years to the day that the Rising took place – the Rising that was commemorated in the very same issue of the *Irish Times*.

But it would be foolhardy to suggest that these two iterations of commemoration or 'remembering' constitute a homogeneous act, either in relation to these particular events, or in relation to the practice of remembering at all. The decadeofcentenaries.com website records many of the activities held on to commemorate the revolutionary period;[4] it is noteworthy that these commemorate a range of events, including the Battle of the Somme – in which Irishmen died under the banner of the British Union Flag – and the War of Independence – in which Irishmen died under both the Union and the Irish Republican flags.[5] There was much controversy about the Irish nationalists who fought under the British Union Flag, often socially cast out on returning home to Ireland. To see both wars commemorated under the auspices of the same commemorative process therefore signals a paradigm shift in Irish nationalism today.

These commemorations move beyond just the traditional monument into a range of media and a diverse approach to commemoration. To mark the centenary of the beginning of the Battle of the Somme on 1 July 2016, for example, a 'riverside sound installation' by artist Christina Kubisch opened at the National War Memorial Gardens in Islandbridge, Dublin.[6] When it came to commemorating the Dublin Lockout of 1913 – both a labour action and 'also a power struggle in relation to who would control a self-governing Ireland' (Ferriter, 2015: 2) – the National Library of Ireland (NLI) was the site of the traditional approach to commemoration with its exhibition, while An Post, the Irish postal service, produced commemorative stamps. Meanwhile, an alliance between the Irish Heritage Trust, Dublin City Council, and the Irish Congress of Trade Unions (ICTU), led by Anu Productions, brought about the *Dublin Tenement Experience: Living the Lockout* during which a house on Dublin's Henrietta Street played host to an immersive, theatrical experience of the lockout. This commemoration is symptomatic of what Joep Leerssen labels 'community remembrancing' (Leerssen, 2001: 215), the type historically afforded only to Irish nationalists as a subaltern act in the face of more official memorialisations by the British Empire. In praise of the *Dublin Tenement Experience*, Fintan O'Toole wrote in the *Irish Times* that 'there needs to be a serious commitment to artistic engagement with the process of com-memoration' (O'Toole, 2013: para. 4), and that the Henrietta Street experience successfully achieved that. Education also has been at the forefront: there were competitions for school students, and pub-lic lecture series for interested citizens. In London, the local Easter Rising 1916 Committee hosted a walking tour through the centre of the city to point out sites of interest. Some have even suggested that people could begin to suffer from 'centenary fatigue' in light of the volume of events taking place.[7]

Perhaps the most vivid and visible of these commemorations was that of the Rising itself that took place at the General Post Office (GPO) building on O'Connell Street (formerly Sackville Street) – the site of the most famous of the occupations during Easter Week 1916. In 2016 Captain Peter Kelleher of the Irish Army re-read the Proclamation of the Provisional Irish Republic, as was originally pronounced by Pádraig Pearse (1879–1916) in 1916 from the GPO. The crowds of civilians watched on as the armed forces guarded the sacred site of the GPO during Capt Kelleher's performance, which was startling in its majesty and ostentation. It can only have been 100 years previously when that number of soldiers stood out-side the GPO, albeit serving under a different flag. Moreover, Capt Kelleher's oratorical prowess resembled that of Pearse himself who had first displayed his speechifying powers at the funeral of Fenian Jeremiah O'Donovan Rossa (1831–1915). Pearse's funeral oration was so compelling that it 'soon became the favourite recitation at concerts and social entertainments all over the country' (Tóibín,

2016: 18). However, Colm Tóibín also documents that when Pearse delivered the Proclamation oration, his 'oratorical skills seemed to fail him – or maybe it was the audience that was different' (Tóibín, 2016: 19). In which case, Capt Kelleher's re-enactment exceeded the original – approximating a simulacrum – in its commemorative practice. In this excess, we have an example of my 'disremembering' on the commemorative stage: the re-enactment both remembers and constructs the original differently through an artistic process – and does these things at the same time.

These commemorations constitute the most public and most concertedly organised form of memory in contemporary culture – but by no means the most prevalent. Instead, I argue that literature is itself the most prevalent form of commemoration: literary writing offers a mode of memory through which the writer and readers remember the past. The literary culture in Ireland is itself tied to the nationalist movement, from Yeats's nineteenth-century ideas about the Celtic Twilight, via Seamus Heaney's *North* (1975) that recalls centuries-old violence from northern Europe, to Seamus Deane's *Reading in the Dark* (1996), a fictionalised memoir that, among other things, questions the role of the border. In each of these cases, the texts enact a series of memories of the past, bringing them to bear on the contemporary moment of their publication. Literature, therefore, acts as both repository of memory and the anamnestic act itself.

My argument develops further. Just as there was an overlap in commemoration of 1916 between memories of the birth of the modern Irish nation-state and the quatercentenary of Shakespeare's death, so do I contend that much literature that contributed to the birth of modern Ireland also acted as a memorial conduit to Shakespeare's early modern English literature. From the representation of ghostly memories in J. M. Synge, James Joyce, and John Banville, through embodied memories in Samuel Beckett and Edna O'Brien, to territorial memories in Yeats and Heaney, these writers remember Shakespeare in each case. These texts contribute to the development of a modern national identity and consciousness, and they do so through memories of Shakespeare's writing. As we now commemorate the birth of modern Ireland, we must also remember Shakespeare as these authors do in and through their writing.

Much as acts of commemoration in recent years are heterogeneous, literature too does not 'remember' in any coherent, homogeneous way. The ways in which I chart the memories of Shakespeare's texts in modern and contemporary Irish literature vary: in some cases, it is a clear and explicit invocation of Shakespeare, whilst in other cases, it is through what Raymond Williams termed a 'structure of feeling': the 'practical consciousness of a present kind, in a living and interrelating continuity' (Williams, 1977: 132). Williams complicated and elaborated his theory of structures of feeling, and in *Politics and Letters* (1979) he suggested variously that it can characterise responses to a 'pre-emergent' ideology, last between a decade and a longer period, and mediate between the lived experience and its articulation (Williams, 2015: 160, 165, 168, 172). In this latter respect, I read Shakespeare as offering a vocabulary that helps Irish authors articulate 'the endless comparison that must occur in the process of consciousness between the articulated and the lived' (Williams, 2015: 172). As I detail below, Shakespeare's presence is concomitant with the authors' articulated contributions – however unwitting – to the lived Irish nation-building project. Shakespeare's is an awkward presence, coeval as he was with the birth of English colonialism, but one that a succession of Irish writers is able to remember and to speak through.

Another way I figure the memorial connection is through Renate Lachmann's ideas of intertextuality that develop Julia Kristeva's. Lachmann argues persuasively that '[w]riting is both an act of memory and new interpretation, by which every new text is etched into memory space' (Lachmann, 2008: 301). This entails a reconsideration of intertextuality as

> demonstrat[ing] the process by which a culture, where 'culture' is a book culture, continually rewrites and retranscribes itself, constantly redefining itself through its signs. Every concrete text, as a sketched-out memory space, connotes the macrospace of memory that either represents a culture or appears as that culture. (Lachmann, 2008: 301)

Lachmann's focus on book culture is eminently applicable to the Irish context, in which writing has long been at the heart of the national imaginary. Lachmann sees 'three models of intertextuality ...: participation, troping and transformation', each of which is integral to my following argument. The first is 'dialogical sharing in the texts of a culture that occurs in writing': talking or responding explicitly to Shakespeare's texts will signify this type of intertextuality that bears the closest resemblance to Kristeva's initial ideas about the intertextual 'mosaic of quotations' (Kristeva, 1986: 37). The second, 'troping', is a 'turning away from the precursor text, a tragic struggle against those other texts … and an attempt to surpass, defend against, and eradicate traces of a precursor's text': this is a kind of forgetfulness that nonetheless presupposes the existence of, for example, Shakespeare in the Irish literature – amnesia forced by the strength of memory. Finally, 'transformation' is the 'appropriation of other texts' that 'conceals [them], veils them, plays with them, renders them unrecognizable, irreverently overturns their oppositions'. This latter memorial form is prominently visible in satire and parody, in which the readerly game consists in *un*veiling and recognising the precursor texts. These are but the literary equivalents of Jan Assmann's 'mnemohistory' that also looks to 'survey … the webs of intertextuality' (Assmann, 1997: 9), but through the history–memory nexus, rather than the literature–memory node. I concentrate on the latter, in which, as Lachmann emphasises, 'All texts participate, repeat and constitute acts of memory' (Lachmann, 2008: 304–5).

In the preface to *Shakespeare's Ghost Writers* (1987), Marjorie Garber frames this argument in another way – and this time with specific reference to Shakespeare. Freud's theory of the uncanny, argues Garber, 'is very much part of the aura that surrounds the Shakespearean ghost, a figure that is always already somewhere else, always already gone, and yet, at the same time, always just around the corner'. This is how Shakespeare emerges in literature, becoming the 'transferential love-object of literary studies' (Garber, 2010: xxiv–xxv): in this way, Shakespeare can be figured as 'memory' itself. In what follows, I am arguing throughout that Shakespeare is the uncanny ghost in Irish literature, whose presence persists, even at those times least wanted or least expected: his texts are 'always just around the corner'. That uncanny appearance is often as surprising to the writer as it is to us readers. Certain Irish writers intertextually remember Shakespeare, in the terms provided by Lachmann, because his texts are uncannily available in culture. That his own writing contributed to the emergence of early modern England as a nation-state is one of his remembered legacies, as is the fact that early modern England contributed to the colonising of Ireland. Shakespeare's legacy in Ireland shares a twin value of both (English) glory and (Irish) humiliation – two words that will become

important below in my final chapter on Heaney. From this contra-
diction, the writers under examination use Shakespeare's writing
to enforce and underwrite their own contribution to the literary
nation-state, providing (on these occasions) Irish glory, albeit often
in terms antagonistic to establishment values or circumscriptions.
In my term that will gather new meanings and nuanced understand-
ings throughout the book, the Irish literary memory of Shakespeare
assumes the form of 'dismemory'. Dismemory, and its corollaries
'to disremember', enshrine a linear connection from Shakespeare
to twentieth-century Irish literature. However, the ways in which
this connection *dis*rupts linearity, and complicates the anamnestic
action of 'remembering', will become my interest.

I examine seven writers through close readings across three
parts. In Part I on 'Ghosts' – using Garber's focus on ghosts as a
viable site of departure – I explore Synge's *Playboy of the Western
World* (1907), 'Hades' in Joyce's *Ulysses* (1922), and John Banville's
Ghosts (1993). In Part II on 'Bodies', I explore Beckett's *Three
Novels* (1951–53) and Edna O'Brien's *The Country Girls Trilogy*
(1960–86). In the final part on Land, I explore a range of Yeats's
and Heaney's poetry. My interest throughout is in the ways in
which Shakespeare's texts ghost the modern/contemporary literature, explicitly and obliquely, and inform the way in which the
writers engage with or shape a modern Ireland in their writing.
Occasionally this process will entail examining Shakespeare's own
context, and even Shakespeare's own contemporaries who ghosted
his own world and writing; it will entail examining the *process* of
remembering in early modern culture that, as I discussed above, is
not homogeneous. Overall, I maintain that while Ireland and Irish
culture are interested and invested in a memorial culture, and in
remembering the birth of a nation, we must pay attention to what,
whom, and how these Irish writers are themselves remembering.

Irish memory

In Ciaran Carson's 'Queen's Gambit', from *Belfast Confetti* (1989),
the speaker riffs on the telephone number used to inform on illegal
activity during the Troubles in the North of Ireland. In the lines
that follow, it becomes possible to understand the nature of Irish
memory:

> She pushes buttons:
>
> Zero Eight Double Zero. Then the number of the Beast, the number
> of the Beast
> Turned upside down: Six Six Six, Nine Nine Nine ...
>
> The ambient light of yesterday is amplified by talk of might-have-beens,
> Making 69 – the year – look like quotation marks, commentators
> commentating on
>
> The flash-point of the current Trouble, though there's any God's amount
> Of Nines and Sixes: 1916, 1690, The Nine Hundred Years' War,
> whatever. (Carson, 1989: 34–5)

The speaker's turn to absurdity in 'The Nine Hundred Years' War' signals the almost unbelievable number of numbers that persist in Irish memory. These dates are all significant in the history of modern Ireland, but they are also sites for commemoration. Clearly 1916 offers the most keenly memorialised date during this decade of centenaries, but 1690 is commemorated annually in Northern Ireland especially, with the 12 July marches that celebrate – or counter-commemorate – William of Orange's victory at the Battle of the Boyne that apparently cemented the Protestant supremacy in Ireland. Key missing dates here include 1798, the year of Wolfe Tone's United Irishmen rebellion, and 1848, when the Young Irelanders' rebellion failed at Ballingarry. Linking each of these historical moments is the persistent Irish attempt to overthrow political control from the British island to the east. In all cases, the Irish cause failed.

As Carson's speaker signals, these numbers come to mind so readily partly because the dates are reminiscent of one another. This is but another way of saying that there are many dates to remember. Critically, given the litany of failures that Carson's speaker remembers, it must be asked why these are remembered over and above the successes. Roy Foster has written, specifically in relation to the Easter Rising and its aftermath, that 'For years afterwards, the revolutionary generation lived on their memories' (Foster, 2015: 289). Moreover, 'Commemoration, public remembrance and the manipulation of historic recollection had long been inseparable from Irish public life, creating a framework of activity which asserted national identity and underpinned the state'. To remember in Irish culture is to define and characterise Irishness itself, something that has been officially co-opted by the establishment in recent years. Vincent Cheng, for instance, has documented how

> In Ireland, poems (by poets such as Paul Muldoon and Eavan Boland), plays, performances, songs, films, documentaries, television programs, and so forth were all officially commissioned for the 1916 ballyhoo. Which is to say that the massive and coordinated weight of official, governmental publicity – and memory-making – were all thrown behind the effort to commemorate and memorialize the Easter 1916 Rising. (This has not always been true.) So it is in some ways quite remarkable, and rather startling, that a brief and aborted uprising – questionably planned, clumsily botched, and quite unpopular with the general populace at the time (indeed, when the captured rebels were led through the streets of a bombed-out Dublin, they were spat on by the Dubliners) – that it could have, 100 years later, reached this high canonical, iconic status of state-sponsored commemoration and historical memorialization. (Cheng, 2018: 78)

Not only is commemoration a distinctively Irish concern, but so is the amplification of what, in other historical narratives, might be considered negligible events. Emilie Pine, identifying the same phenomenon, recounts the erroneous inclusion of a photograph from 1952 at the earliest when the *Irish Times* released its 2006 supplement to commemorate ninety years since the 1916 Easter Rising. It was left to a keen-eyed reader to spot the identifying error (an anachronistic car licence plate) and alert the paper. Pine thereafter concludes that

> it is notable that the custodians of the Irish past, the heritage and archive community, were so keen (and so qualified) to correct the mistakes made by such a process. This keenness goes to show the extent to which the past matters within Ireland; indeed, the extent to which the past is still a current subject. And, if the Irish past is still a contested space, as this example illustrates, the act of contestation can be a positive force, helping us to know our past better. (Pine, 2011: 2)

Where Foster sees the space of Irish memory as intricately interwoven with the fabric of a national identity, Pine sees any contested memory as a positive phenomenon. Taken together, contesting memory will continue to produce and reproduce Ireland's identity anew, even if in a disruptive manner. This is a pattern I identify in the texts I examine.

And yet it has not always been this straightforward. Diarmaid Ferriter notes, for example, that 'Official and unofficial commemoration of the Irish revolution was also a thorny issue from the foundation of the Irish Free State' (Ferriter, 2015: 348). From 1922, commemoration of 1916 was 'problematic and a question' and 'frequently led to political disagreement, cantankerous debate and uncertainty'. This is because 'it provided an opportunity to create political capital out of the contested republican legacy and to emphasise the divisions that existed within the Irish body politic'. Through the language of 'contest' and 'divisions', it is evident that the single, unitary event described under the moniker 'Easter 1916' could in fact be remembered and commemorated in more than one way – that, through the phenomenon of remembering, it became plural. As Christopher Collins and Mary P. Caulfield make plain,[8] when thinking about the Irish theatre and performance in particular, 'What is peculiar to Ireland's relationship to modernity, memory and history is the pluralization of the historical consciousness' (Collins and Caulfield, 2014: 2–3).[9] The divisive pluralisation of Easter 1916 in its commemorations was reflective of the political landscape that produced it. These 'difficulties were obvious during the 1920s', writes Ferriter, noting that 'when CnG[10] hosted the first formal military ceremony to commemorate the Rising, invitations were issued to relatives of the executed 1916 leaders, but only one, Mrs Mallin (widow of Michael Mallin), attended'. By the 1930s, 'The question … was how the new Fianna Fáil[11] government would handle this issue', and this was complicated when 'the IRA [was] declared an illegal organisation in 1936, the year of the twentieth anniversary of the Rising'. It was therefore 'even more important for Fianna Fáil to claim sole right to the 1916 inheritance' (2015: 349–51). This absurd transmuting of memory into property that can be owned or disowned again reveals the controversy at the heart of remembering in modern culture, and will become a feature particularly of my exploration of Beckett's *Three Novels* in Chapter 4.

Shakespeare is a similar hot potato in the sense that there might be political controversy over how to remember his early modern legacy in Ireland. As I show in the following chapters, Shakespeare's

England was the same England that promoted a scorched earth policy in Ireland, advocated for a greater alien English population than native Irish population, and even sought to establish an English written rule of law in Ireland. These were considered civilising methods to bring the barbarous Irish under English control. It is perhaps no surprise that according to the Shakespeare400.org website – an internationally registered website set up to document commemorations of the quatercentenary of Shakespeare's death – only one event featured an Irish element. The *Shakespeare Lives in 2016* project included Terra Nova's *The Belfast Tempest* 'with special emphasis on Asia and the 56 nations of Africa and the Caribbean', and a community-focused project that presented performance artist Amanda Coogan's 'new multi-media work "You Turn Me On, I'm a Radio", a combination of sign language, performance, digital sound and live Instagram streaming' (Culture Northern Ireland, 30 October 2015). Additionally, the British Council website for Ireland (https://britishcouncil.ie) advertised performances of *Measure for Measure* by Fortune's Fool Productions, which included dates at Dublin Castle, the British government's outpost in Ireland until 1922. While these each positively remembered 'Shakespeare's works and his influence on culture, education and society', none of them considered the humiliating aspect of Shakespeare's legacy. In these memories, not only is the early modern English legacy forgotten but so is (Northern) Ireland's own history. Shakespeare's history is reoriented and co-opted as a global memory, and Ireland's turbulent history is disowned.

In memory, then, the past is plural and is co-opted, owned or disowned as part of competing narratives of the past. And, in the Irish context – a 'culture … obsessed with the past' (Pine, 2011: 3) – that memorial competition is constitutive of a national identity. Where nineteenth-century social theorist Ernest Renan (1882) argued that a nation was constituted by a 'daily plebiscite' complemented by a 'rich legacy of memories' (Renan, 1990: 9), Ireland's national consensus appears to emerge through a memorial *dissensus*. How then to treat this, and other pasts, with any sincerity? How to remember faithfully when plurality confounds singularity? The theories of memory I use in this book can help to answer these questions.

Theories of memory

In *Memory, History, Forgetting*, Paul Ricoeur likens the practice of memory to the ontic process of mourning. '[I]t is as a work of remembering', writes Ricoeur, 'that the work of mourning proves to be liberating, although at a certain cost, and that this relation is reciprocal. The work of mourning is the cost of the work of remembering, but the work of remembering is the benefit of the work of mourning' (Ricoeur, 2006: 72). Furthermore, citing Freud's divisions of the response to the loss of a cathected object – a loved one or the past, for instance – Ricoeur also distinguishes memorial practice according to the mourning/melancholia duality.[12] Mourning, Ricoeur recalls, is a process of successful de-cathecting, in which the lost object is accepted as lost; by contrast, melancholia takes place when the process of de-cathecting is unsuccessful. Consequently, the libidinal energy needs investing elsewhere, leading to a pathological feeling of melancholy. In social memorial practice, however, melancholic commemoration is characterised by libidinal investment in public ritual:

> Too much memory recalls especially the compulsion to repeat, which, Freud said, leads us to substitute acting out for the true recollection by which the present would be reconciled with the past: how much violence in the world stands as acting out 'in place of' remembering! We can, if we like, speak of repetition–memory for these funeral celebrations. (Ricoeur, 2006: 79)

These public rituals and commemorations – notably including the excessive memory at the GPO itself during Easter week – seem to fit this mould of melancholic, and therefore unreconciled, memory.

Developing his argument, Ricoeur cites the importance of 'the heritage of founding violence' (Ricoeur, 2006: 82). This also appears salient in the Irish case. 'It is a fact that there is no historical community that has not arisen out of what can be termed an original relation to war', he continues.

> What we celebrate under the heading of founding events are, essentially, violent acts legitimated after the fact by a precarious state of right, acts legitimated, at the limit, by their very antiquity, by their age. The same events are thus found to signify glory for some, humiliation for others. To their celebration, on the one hand, corresponds

their execration, on the other. It is in this way that real and symbolic wounds are stored in the archives of collective memory.

By delineating these processes of commemoration, the case for a specific Irish version of this takes hold. Note, for example, the pluralisation of the past – glory versus humiliation – in Ricoeur's schema, which matches Shakespeare's legacy: glory for England/Britain, humiliation for Ireland. Moreover, within the framework of establishing national sovereignty and demarcating an independent nation-state, it becomes clear: acted out, melancholic memory in the wake of a violent founding act – and any of the Lockout, the Rising, the Anglo-Irish war (1919–21), the Civil War (1922–23), or all of them plus other events that taken together constitute violent founding acts – accurately characterises not only the birth of modern Ireland, but the continued commemoration of its birth. Memory and public commemoration, as such, signify modern nation-states.

The shift from personal memory, as recorded in contemporary testimony, to public commemoration, needs some exploration. This poses no problem for Ricoeur, for whom proper memory includes in itself its possible ascription to any person, whether they experienced the original imprint, τύπος (*tupos*), or not. Following a necessary human idea that this memory happened to me, there is a cult of 'ownness', says Ricoeur; however, following Husserlian phenomenology, Ricoeur shows that the foreign-other underpins this cult, since 'it is indeed as foreign, that is as not-me, that the other is constituted, but it is "in" me that he is constituted' (Ricoeur, 2006: 118). The property and ownership/ownership discussion takes us back to Carson's poetic version of the same discussion and will reappear in my discussion of Beckett. For Ricoeur, this dual understanding of the other relies on 'the concept of "appresentation", held to be an exceptional mode of analogy'. That is to say, analogically the other is elided with the self. 'By reason of this analogical transfer', Ricoeur continues, 'we are authorized to use the first person in the plural form and ascribe to an us ... all the prerogatives of memory' (Ricoeur, 2006: 119). Thereafter,

> it is only by analogy, and in relation to individual consciousness and its memory, that collective memory is held to be a collection of traces left by the events that have affected the course of history of the groups concerned, and that it is accorded the power to place on

stage these common memories, on the occasion of holidays, rites, and public celebrations.

Finally, Ricoeur establishes that this analogical transfer is 'enough to give written history a point of anchorage in the phenomenological existence of groups' (120).

In *The Collective Memory* (1950), Maurice Halbwachs approaches the prospect of collective memory from a sociological, rather than phenomenological, perspective. Halbwachs urges that 'We appeal to witnesses to corroborate or invalidate as well as supplement what we somehow know already about an event' (Halbwachs, 1980: 22) when he argues that individual memory is a fallacy. Moreover, making another reference to an analogical transfer between the self and the other, he writes that when remembering collectively, 'It is *as if* we were comparing the testimony of several witnesses' (my emphasis). Halbwachs explains his rationale in greater detail: 'Our memories remain collective ... and are recalled to us through others even though only we were participants in the events or saw the things concerned. In reality, we are never alone'[13] (Halbwachs, 1980: 23). For example, 'Many impressions of my first visit to London ... reminded me of Dickens' novels read in childhood, so I took my walk with Dickens. In each of these moments I cannot say that I was alone, that I reflected alone'. Even when physically alone Halbwachs's individual is never sociologically isolated. These collective memories feed into written histories, though the two are distinct (Halbwachs, 1980: 78). It leaves a remaining tension for anyone writing history. Ferriter and Foster, for example, inherit the possibility of writing their respective histories because of the central factor of collective memory arising from necessarily contested individual memories; however, if collective memory accumulates into singular narratives of history, then at some point the historian must find a way of resolving the contest between the memories.

Given the primacy of collective remembrance in Ireland, it is evident that written histories – taking the contested memories as their initial εἰκών (*eikon*), via testimony and their documentation into archival form – will also offer up various versions of history. Or, 'it is hardly surprising and hardly troubling that different historians focus on different collections of documents or will interpret the same source material in different ways' (Ferriter, 2015: 95). To be accurate in writing history, therefore, is to be faithful to your chosen set of memories and archives: 'History, in this sense, constitutes a vast "heterology", a tracing of the "traces of the other"' (Ricoeur, 2006: 204). 'What we do need to look for, however', continues Ferriter, 'is honesty as opposed to myth and simplicity' (Ferriter, 2015: 95). In both cases, the historians are looking to flesh out and get nearer to the fleeting *eikon* that is at the foundation of the modern Irish nation-state. But perhaps that honesty could be achieved differently. Ricoeur severally explains that 'history alone retraces what actually happened' (Ricoeur, 2006: 204): its focus on the disappeared *eikon* that caused the original *tupos* distinguishes it from literature, for example. However, if that *eikon* had not disappeared in the first place, then the question of contested memories leading to competing histories could be obviated entirely. Rather than belatedly focusing on the act of remembering, surely it is more gainful to focus on the irretrievable object, the *eikon* itself. To do this, however, would require not a secure *practice* of commemoration, but rather an *art* of storing memory. Between the Middle Ages and the Renaissance, there emerged just such an art to attempt to store and later find the lost *eikon*. Its last heyday was in the early seventeenth century, just when one of the most effective writers of history, William Shakespeare, was himself becoming a memory, though Joyce arguably revived the art in *Ulysses*.[14] This focus on *art* over *practice* should be, and is, taken in this book as an acknowledged precedence of literary over historical narrative. After all, the art of memory is 'This true "alchemy of the imagination"', writes Ricoeur, quoting Frances Yates, which 'presides over a magical mnemotechnics which gives limitless power to the one who possesses it' (Ricoeur, 2006: 65). For an age that privileged memory, to be master of its art could make you master of modernity. In her *Art of Memory*, Yates (2005: 256) expressly argues that memory as a classical art was on the wane by the time of the English Renaissance. This classical art was characterised by several chief features: the use of psychic places to 'store' memories; different approaches to remembering 'words' and 'things'; the Aristotelian practice of repeated meditation on the item being remembered; and the importance of order in the process of memorising. This classical art, however, was not the memory practice that was flourishing in the later sixteenth century in England.

Instead, two chief strands of artistic memory emerged: the humanist and the hermetic-cabalist.

In the humanist strand, I will focus on Frenchman Peter Ramus (1515–72), whose memory practices used the process of dialectical thinking rather than the classical methods of memorising. The Ramist method helped students to learn their lines of Ovid at school, and therefore was immediately practicable. The Ramist method was dialectical in nature and was primed for the art of memory. It required first the proper organisation of the material being studied into general precepts prior to more specific characteristics. In 1564's *The Logike*, Ramus writes: '[I]n [s]etting forthe of an arte we gather only togeather that which dothe appartayne to the Arte whiche we intreate of, leauing to all other Artes that which is proper to them[;] this rule … maye be called the rule of Iu[s]tice' (Ramus, 1966: 8). Walter Ong, summarising Ramus's dialectic, finds the following analogy most serviceable: 'Ramus sums it all up by stating that the art of dialectic (*ars dialectica*) is related to "natural dialectic" as Apelles' picture of Alexander is to Alexander himself' (Ong, 1958: 180). The dialectical art is therefore some kind of secondary level of reality, in which primary reality is reflected or represented. By resolving questions through syllogism, the Ramist path to learning entails a repeatable method that requires singular dedication and focus of thought.

Whilst Ramus says nothing specifically in terms of memory, his 'topical classifications' nevertheless 'are classifications-for-recall, so that working with them is of itself working with a memory device' (Ong, 1958: 213). That is, once he has set out his Latin grammar, for example, simply learning the several dialectics that make up the various categories – Grammar that consists of two parts: Etymology (itself consisting of two further categories) and the Syntax of speech (again, comprising two further categories), etc. – constitutes an act of memorisation, leading to an act of anamnestic recall. Ong highlights the centrality of memory to Ramus's method, writing that 'the real reason why Ramus can dispense with memory is that his whole scheme of arts, based on a topically conceived logic, is a system of local memory' (Ong, 1958: 280). Memory *per se* is forgotten since it does not require a separate method, but the method itself hinges on the student's memory. Yates localises the success of the Ramist method, arguing that the Ramist approach to memory succeeded in

'Protestant countries like England ... [because] it provided a kind of inner iconoclasm, corresponding to the outer iconoclasm' (Yates, 2005: 731) of the Reformation. As if to prove this idea, more than a century ago Irishman Joseph Darlington associated Hamlet's philosophy of 'wilful doubt' with the break with Rome. 'It was a revolt', writes Darlington, 'from the dogmatic method of authority and faith' (Darlington, 1913: 478). In Darlington's reading, Hamlet becomes a successful advocate for the new faith and its accompanying philosophy. Critically, Darlington explains that this new philosophy was headed by a certain Peter Ramus: Darlington's Hamlet is a disciple of Ramus. Here the inner and outer worlds of character, and the private and public spheres of religion, share in the successes of a developing art of memory.

By contrast, the magical hermetic–cabalist element of the Renaissance also has a corresponding art of memory, attached to three key figures: Italians Giulio Camillo (c. 1480–1544) and Giordano Bruno (1548–1600), and Scottish Robert Fludd (1574–1637). Their theories of memory share a heritage in the primary hermetic, after whom the theory is named: Hermes Trismegistus, a syncretic figure combining the Egyptian god Thoth and Greek god Hermes. The Hermetic Corpus, supposedly authored by this mythical figure, was translated in the fifteenth century by Marsilio Ficino (1433–99), a Florentine humanist whose works hugely influenced the writings of Camillo and Bruno. This influence, Yates argues, eventually finds its way to Fludd, a controversial philosopher pining after James VI/I's patronage and, therefore, establishment support.

By using a model of a theatrical stage as his basis for storing and recalling memory, Fludd's memorial art concedes that the revelation of the divine *mens* within the sixteenth-century philosopher must take place in and through public spaces. Moreover, as Wilder shows, the theatre is a space for social memory, both individually and collectively. Robert Fludd was a turn-of-the-century scholar, pivoting between the Renaissance and the English Civil War. He 'lived at the very end of the era in which it was possible for one mind to encompass the whole of learning', and 'His was one of the last attempts to do so' (Godwin, 1979: 5). Fludd's interest was in macrocosms and microcosms, and unity of intellect was also Fludd's driving force; the vessel for his art was a theatre. In his memory treatise, Fludd uses a 'theatre as a memory place system for memory for words and

memory for things' (Yates, 2005: 319). This adheres to the classical memory treatises, such as the anonymous *Ad Herennium* that
sought to use imagined places as psychic memorial locations. To
this end, Fludd's memory theory looks backwards in time.

However, Fludd is also urgently contemporary. According to
Yates, the memory-theatre that Fludd designs is, in the first instance,
not a theatre, but just its stage. Furthermore, Yates painstakingly
shows (Yates, 2005: 336 ff.) that Fludd's stage is modelled on
the second Globe theatre on London's Southbank. The space of
Shakespeare's stage becomes a model for social memory, both in
the fleeting moments of the play's production – not just the theatre's
incineration in 1613 – and in a contemporary memory treatise. It
would be easy to dismiss this memory theatre, and its predeces-
sors,[15] as nothing other than a Renaissance version of counting
cards in a casino – that is, a parlour trick at best. However, when
we restore to theatrical practice itself the importance of memory,
and of the individual actors' remembering their lines, as well as the
Protestant practices that Ramus advanced, then it becomes clear
that newly Protestant England, with the theatre as its foremost
site of (long-lasting) cultural production, posits memory practices
such as these at the centre of the Renaissance modernity. As I will
show below, both theatrical memory (as practised in *Hamlet* (1600)
and explored in my opening three chapters) and forgetfulness (as
demonstrated in *Coriolanus* (1608), and explored in Chapter 4)
become central to early modern memorial discourses and to pro-
and antitheatrical invective.

The communal banner that is symbolically held aloft in the
theatre became, in 1642, a threat to the Puritans of the Long
Parliament. The fleeting memorial moments of the theatre were
viewed as profane acts that challenged divine authority and sullied
God's name. The Globe offered itself as a church whose god was
Shakespeare: in the beginning was his word. Christopher Balme
argues that the closure of the theatres in 1642 confirms that there
existed a 'functioning public sphere, where arguments ultimately
triumph over feudal whims, and where a substantial body of public opinion forces the passage of legislation resulting in the complete closure of playhouses' (Balme, 2014: 75). Balme also suggests
that the theatre as public agent is visible in the previous century:
'Between 1570 and 1642, roughly seventy years of Elizabethan,

Jacobean and Caroline theatrical activity were marked by ongoing discursive opposition, punctuated by a succession of "blasts" and "counterblasts"' (Balme, 2014: 76). The ideas that theatre is a space for collective (and collected individual) memory and that memory becomes communal through theatre are but a minor part of the emerging public sphere in early modern England – but a constitutive part nonetheless. Modernity and memory develop in parallel.

In sum, several ideas emerge from this discussion. First that an *art* of memory, rather than a practice of commemoration, may respond more honestly to the necessary plurality of memory – however foolish might be the endeavour to store an *eikon* purely. Second that in the early modern period, practising the art of memory was a fundamentally modern concern. Third that memory-practice in early modern England was both a public and private preoccupation; this proves the important link between the modern citizen, the nation-state to which they claim allegiance, and the art of memory. And fourth that two versions of the art of memory prevailed: the hermetic-cabalist with its systems and focus on a physical space in which to practise memory, and the humanist, which included a focus on Ramus's dialectical method that relied wholly on memory. Through the former, the Renaissance theatre offered itself as a *milieu de mémoire*, a 'setting in which memory [was] a real part of everyday experience' (Nora, 1996: 1). The early modern period is therefore important to a later reading of Ireland primarily because of the emergence of modernity. In my analysis, at the heart of that modernity is a private and a public memory practice that finds its paradigmatic presentation in the early modern theatre. Literature, therefore, may more adequately respond to the urgent pressures of memory and commemoration than history-writing.[16]

This turn to Shakespeare's theatre is critical, I believe, in understanding how Irish nationalists a century and more ago began to forge their own modern nation-state, primarily through establishing something that could be remembered in a literary framework. After all, there can be no commemoration without that founding act, as Ricoeur noted; and, moreover, if that founding act is to be remembered, then an art of memory that plans for future anamnesis is indispensable.

Irish literature

I suggested above that contested memories in the wake of the Irish revolution could be attributed to an absence of an art of memory, one which could attempt to fix, albeit fruitlessly, the original *eikon* more certainly in the memory of participants and witnesses in action. The early modern art of memory I have just sketched relied heavily on the theatre as a shared space of public and private experience, and the model that theatre provides is the legacy drawn upon by Irish nationalists. That is, the modern Irish art of memory – through the violent acts of the Easter Rising and Anglo-Irish War – also relied on a theatre of memory.

Only a few months after the Rising, W. J. Lawrence referred to the events in theatrical terms. Lawrence not only called the Rising a 'five-act tragedy', but he also conceded that though the Rising appeared to be 'Sheer madness', 'there was method in it' (Lawrence, 1916: 16).[17] This line of thought was developed by historian F. X. Martin who wrote that the Rising was staged as a drama (Martin, 1967: 9).[18] To this end, Ferriter quotes 'Stephen Gwynn, a serving British army officer and Nationalist MP' who alleged that the Rising had a built-in memorability because the Rising 'offered to Irishmen a stage for themselves' (Ferriter, 2015: 149). Moreover, Foster and Martin both point to the Rising's actors' prior experience in directing drama. For instance, Martin asserts that 'It is not without significance that [Pádraic] Pearse, [Joseph] Plunkett and [Thomas] MacDonagh had all directed plays in their time' (Martin, 1967: 10). These, and the rest of the Rising's architects, were 'playing in fact for the benefit and applause of future generations of Irishmen'. That is, their artistic theatricality was committed to fixing an Irish memory in perpetuity, turned toward the future promise of the nation. Foster additionally claims that 'The exhilaration experienced by some' of the actors 'was intensified by the theatricality of the whole affair': 'The insurgents kept a close eye on opportunities to historicize the event in the making' (Foster, 2015: 230).

Martin describes how the revolutionaries ensured a large audience for their drama. Though the selection of the GPO as headquarters of the Rising was 'disastrous', it nevertheless 'stood prominently on one side of the main thoroughfare of the city' and 'its seizure meant that not only would all normal activity in Dublin be disrupted but from it defiance would be trumpeted for everyone to hear' (Martin, 1967: 10–11). Moreover, the spectacular element of the Rising was important, since (and here Martin adopts his own level of poetic theatricality):

> The classical front of the G.P.O., with its Ionic pillars and portico, was to serve as an admirable background for Pearse reading the proclamation, as it was to be an awe-inspiring sight on Friday night, its pillars and roof wrapped in tongues of flame, amid the swelling orchestration of rifle-fire, machine-gun chatter, bursting hand-grenades and booming artillery, presenting a Wagnerian grand finale to Easter Week.

The Rising was not only staged as a drama, but as a Greek tragedy, festooned with the accoutrements of an ancient Greek *polis*.[19]

Foster writes of individual actors' behaviour, such as Constance Markievicz who 'was widely noted by the spectators, marching around Stephen's Green in a feathered hat and a characteristically *outré* uniform' (Foster, 2015: 234). The stage and its actors, he argues, were intimately aware of their own theatricality, and how that theatricality would continue to unfold over time. In language reminiscent of classical theories of memory being made of wax susceptible to printing, Foster adds that 'The expectation of taking part in a great symbolic act had been imprinted on their consciousness through years of conditioning. The insurrection at once actualized that moment, and brought them up against reality, changing everything that had gone before' (Foster, 2015: 222). Part of that change is the emergence of an imagined nation-state, *pace* Benedict Anderson, as proclaimed by Pearse during the Rising, and crystallised in the public Symbolic order through the political and martial wranglings that followed. Just as above, the Rising that was 'fixed' in the memory was coterminous with the modern Irish nation-state: theatre, memory, and nation conjoined at this point.

The Rising's architects had engaged in more traditional theatrical practice in several arenas:

> Some might claim that the Abbey Theatre was a theater of commemoration from its inception. The founding members were painstakingly aware of the importance of memorializing their work in order to spread the company's reputation at home and abroad. In their public and private letters, speeches, and declarations to the press,

Lady Gregory and Yeats represented the Abbey Theatre premieres as
moments in which history was being created. (Maples, 2011: 174)

Maples's comments identify Ricoeur's trajectory of memory-becom-
ing-history in the organisation of the Abbey. On a similar point,

> By 1907 the national theatre movement begun in 1899 by W. B.
> Yeats, Augusta Gregory and Edward Martyn had split and reformed.
> On one hand, there was the Abbey Theatre … which deliberately put
> art above politics. On the other, there was a burgeoning number of
> small companies which maintained a more directly political intent.
> (Foster, 2015: 76)

This division repeats that outlined by Walter Benjamin in his 1936
'The Work of Art in the Age of Mechanical Reproduction': 'The logical result of Fascism is the introduction of aesthetics into political
life. … Communism responds by politicizing art' (Benjamin, 1999:
234–5). Setting aside the particular political motivations that interest Benjamin, this contamination of the aesthetic with the political
fields appeals, not only because it appears to describe the theatrical
practice in Ireland, but also because of the idea of artistic reproduction in Benjamin's essay. Benjamin describes reproduction as a
process through which 'the original' artwork can 'meet the beholder
halfway'. This puts the 'copy of the original into situations which
would be out of reach for the original itself' (Benjamin, 1999: 214).
When I remove the idea of mechanical reproduction from this
description, Benjamin could equally be describing commemorative
practice, or the 'acting out' of memory in an attempt, however vain,
of fixing the *eikon*. The aestheticisation of politics, characteristic
of Yeats's Abbey Theatre according to Foster, constitutes part of
the artistic fixing in memory of that performance. Just as in early
modern England, where the transient moment of the theatre disappeared in the memories of its audience into the city,[20] so too did the
plays at the Abbey spread their memorial wings widely[21] – and so
too did the performance at the GPO during Easter 1916 stick in the
memory of Ireland's citizens, for at least a century until its 'dismemorial' re-creation by Capt Kelleher.

Though in the Abbey 'art' was placed 'above politics', it is
remembered most prominently in political terms. A national theatre was first conceived in 1897 when Yeats lunched with Gregory
and Martyn. Robert Welch notes that it was Yeats's observation of

Maud Gonne's oratorical exasperation at being unable to 'celebrate the centenary of the 1798 rebellion' while Queen Victoria's jubilee was being celebrated in Dublin. Gonne said 'slowly in a low voice: "must the graves of our dead go undecorated because Victoria has her Jubilee?", at which the crowd went wild' (Welch, 1999: 2). This 'anti-Jubilee demonstration was street theatre in the very most literal sense', notes Andrew Murphy (2015: 169). Although it was the ensuing riots that evening that played emotionally with Yeats, convincing him that 'an Irish appreciation of oratory could, by a theatrical movement, be turned towards more peaceful outcomes', it was also a failed commemorative act – an attempted act of anamnesis – that propelled Gonne's reaction and Yeats's dramatic aspirations. From its inception, the national, theatrical art of memory was inspired to set right a failure of commemoration.

Its first prominent production 'which was to be the great success of these early years' (Welch, 1999: 15) was Gregory's and Yeats's *Cathleen ni Houlihan* in 1902. This play 'cast the beautiful nationalist Maud Gonne in the part of a withered hag who would only walk again like a radiant young queen if young men were willing to kill and die for her' (Kiberd, 1996: 200). The character Michael is particularly compelled by the hag's talk of 'Four beautiful green fields' (Yeats, 2001b: 88), which reference the (colonised) four Irish provinces. The play is set in 1796, during the prelude to Wolf Tone's 1798 rebellion, and therefore remembers Ireland's past. 'The Rising, when it came', writes Kiberd, 'was therefore seen by many as a foredoomed classical tragedy, whose *dénouement* was both inevitable and unpredictable, prophesied and yet surprising' (Kiberd, 1996: 200). Again, the memorial focus carries within it a future orientation. Kiberd cements the idea that national theatre, even to contemporaries, was thought of as taking part in a national memory-making, all the while practising an anamnestic art of memory. Welch comments that 'What was enacted on stage was a scene of transformation; what the play accomplished was also an act of translation, whereby emblems and figures out of the Irish cultural memory were carried over into the twentieth century and given immediate and shocking relevance' (Welch, 1999: 16). In other words, the play commemorated the past, acting as a channel from the past to the present. Moreover, whilst 'The Easter rebels are sometimes depicted as martyrs to a text like *Cathleen ni Houlihan*', continues Kiberd, it is more complex than that: '[R]ather than reduce the living to a dead textuality, Yeats at his most daring asserts the power of texts to come to life' (Kiberd, 1996: 202). It becomes clear that memory was at the forefront of the national theatre.

There is clearly an abstract connection between Shakespeare's contemporary theatre of memory and the theatre of memory in the Abbey and at the GPO. But, notwithstanding that connection, 1916 was also the tercentenary of Shakespeare's death. Even during the Rising itself, the *Irish Times* asked its readers whether there were 'any better occasion' for reading Shakespeare 'than the coincidence of enforced domesticity with the poet's tercentenary' (*Irish Times*, 27 April 1916: 2). Rob Doggett notes that in the same newspaper issue, the 'British government ... announced ... a series of "Regulations To Be Observed Under Martial Law"' (Dogget, 2013: 217), crystallising how the memory of Shakespeare coincided easily with the memory-making of the revolutionaries. Murphy, also researching how the tercentenary of Shakespeare's death was commemorated, notes that the events proposed by the Dublin branch of the British Empire Shakespeare Society did not quite take place. Murphy records that 'Those involved in the Easter Rising can be said to have rejected almost everything that the British Empire Shakespeare Society – and the institutions in its orbit in Ireland – stood for' (Murphy, 2015: 163). The implication here is bleak for this study: perhaps Irish citizens in 1916 had neither awareness nor interest in celebrating Shakespeare, the paragon of English and British values. 'Crucially', however, 'the one thing they emphatically did *not* reject was Shakespeare himself.' Indeed, 'nationalists' embracing of Shakespeare was ... all of a piece with radical political appropriations of the playwright that had occurred on the other side of the Irish Sea during the course of the nineteenth century' (Murphy, 2015: 164). So not only did remembering Shakespeare in 1916 stand exceptional to the nationalists' response to the humiliation of British colonialism, but it was positively advocated as a revolutionary position.

Historical figures who held such opinions of Shakespeare ranged widely, including the (minor) figure of Joseph Darlington, S. J. Above I referenced his work on the Ramist philosophy in *Hamlet* and it is thought that he was the initial study for the dean of studies in Joyce's *A Portrait* – the tutor with whom Stephen discourses about Aquinas and, more importantly, the use of the Elizabethan English word 'tundish'.[22] This implies that in 1916 Joyce is remembering a tutor who himself remembered *Hamlet* and humanist memory practice: Shakespeare and memory are remembered in the literary landscape surrounding the Rising. Others who remembered Shakespeare positively include Pearse and Yeats – the former dying for the cause, the latter recording in poetry those deaths that served it. Murphy notes that 'Pearse recalled daydreaming himself into the world of the books that he read when he was young, including imagining himself as *Lear*'s Gloucester' (Murphy, 2015: 166). Moreover, in creating St Enda's, a school for boys with a Fenian ethos and Cuchulain as its mascot, Pearse said that 'The central purpose of [St Enda's] School is not so much the mere imparting of knowledge ... as the formation of its pupils' characters, eliciting and development of the individual bents and traits of each, the kindling of their imaginations' (Pearse, 1980: 317). To this end, Kiberd finds it noteworthy that 'Pearse's remedy was interesting: more, not less, English literature, as an instrument of liberation' (Kiberd, 1996: 283). Moreover, Joost Augusteijn (2010: 73–4 esp.) notes that Pearse's own literary education was underpinned by a love of Shakespeare, adding that at the meetings for the New Ireland Literary Society the seventeen-year-old Pearse – much to the consternation of his fellow members – would often quote Shakespeare in debates on the merits of Irish, and the demerits of British, literature. What becomes apparent after this, however, is that Shakespeare as a postmodern artist[23] is appropriable to (read: memorable for) anyone, for or against any purpose. In this, Shakespeare is analogous to memory itself: open to debate and interpretation, and therefore open to contested analyses.[24] He forms part of the collective memory bank.

Murphy concludes his examination of the tercentenary by recalling that, in London, 'the organisers of the Shakespeare tercentenary ... were keen to avoid even the faintest suggestion of blasphemy in celebrating Shakespeare on Easter Sunday, Shakespeare's birth/death day coinciding exactly, of course, with Easter in 1916' (Murphy, 2015: 178). The Rising and Shakespeare's tercentenary, in a small-scale examination, would appear to be linked by more than mere coincidence. But the link was not necessarily the commemoration of Shakespeare's death, but instead a continued remembrance of Shakespeare by those acting in a sequel to his bloody histories

– the chief actors in the Rising itself. Following the Rising, 'the process of re-assimilating Shakespeare to the cosy certainties of imperial Dublin continued' and 'In July, the Royal Hibernian Military
School mounted a Shakespeare Festival' (Murphy, 2015: 179). If
proof were needed that Shakespeare could be appropriated according to whichever agenda, it should be fact enough that a military
school hosted the festival only months after the military Rising was
planned by a host of Shakespeare-fascinated revolutionaries. The
memory of Shakespeare was not forgotten during the Rising, but
was bolstered by it, as it in turn bolstered the revolution. Here,
too, was the Shakespeare-inspired theatre of memory at work in
the Irish imaginary just when the modern nation was beginning to
emerge into the daylight.

I do not consider the theatre of memory model as restricted
either to Irish drama or to the revolutionary period itself. As Pine
has made clear,

> Performance is also an ongoing process, being re-shaped constantly,
> so that it is iterated and reiterated, a process of repetition that creates
> a ritual of the performance. However, in shaping the past for presen-
> tation, the forms of cultural remembrance – books, plays, art works,
> films, television, newspapers, museums, and memorials – are also acts
> of cultural mediation. (Pine, 2011: 4)

My concern is literary writing – dramatic, poetic, and prosaic – and
how those texts both store memory and provide ongoing access
to the past.[25] To this extent, reading Yeats's poems from the 1890s
today is both an act of memory for readers, and also gives access
to an 1890s act of memory for those readers. I am reframing Pine's
demand that audiences 'should not forget to interrogate those acts'
(Pine, 2011: 4) of remembrance with which they engage as 'remembering memory'.

*

Shakespeare symbolises England and Britain's glory, but England
and Britain represent Ireland's national humiliation. Dramatic literature and a theatrical art of memory helped modern Ireland shed
the shackles of Britain's colonialism a century ago, and given that
theatricality owes a memorial debt to Shakespeare, it is imperative

to remember how Shakespeare was remembered, just as it is imperative to remember how modern Ireland was born in its founding, violent acts.

Moreover, Ireland continues to be re-constructed as modern through repeated commemoration: the Easter Rising was stored via an artistic theatre of memory, but its continual recollection resituates Ireland as an independent nation-state. The same is true for all strands of nation-statism: Ireland's connection to the past, evidently, but also its establishment of sovereign law, of functioning private and public spheres through written constitution and biopolitical practice, and of control over territory. In the parts on 'Ghosts', 'Bodies', and 'Land' that follow, each of these strands is addressed in localised ways. However, given the impossible singularity of memory or of anamnesis – such as the memorial contests, heterological memory, the oscillation between opposites glory and humiliation – in each of the following cases I find that, rather than 'memory', these texts take part in what I term 'dismemory'. Dismemory is a productive art of memory – both memorial storage and anamnestic memorial access – that is future-oriented and more typically disruptive than it is unifying or mollifying.

I start by examining the linear connection that memory would seem to necessitate, doing so through the figuration of paternal ghosts that construct the apparent link between the present and the past. Starting appropriately with theatre, I examine the father–son motifs in Synge's *Playboy of the Western World* (1907), 'Hades' from Joyce's *Ulysses* (1922), and John Banville's *Ghosts* (1993). The spectral presence of the father analogises the memorial presence of Shakespeare. Moreover, both Shakespeare and *Hamlet* are explicitly evoked – Lachmann's 'dialogical sharing' – in these texts and remembered by these writers, almost as if the literary and colonial Father is spectrally present in the paternal characters. In these chapters, I demonstrate that the structure of memory cannot be constrained by linearity, and a spectrality of *disruptive* chronology must be considered: Shakespeare's ghost reappears in each literary generation – proving that the Shakespeare ghost is 'just around the corner', as Garber argues – and therefore remembered by these writers as they negotiate their place in modern Ireland.

After the evanescent and transcendent ghost, I then explore the immanent materiality of the Irish body whose biopower is harnessed in the course of the establishment of the modern Irish nation-state. In addition to the textual body – Samuel Beckett's testimonies; Edna O'Brien's memoirs – my focuses are, first, the male bodies in Samuel Beckett's *Three Novels* (1950–53), in which I examine the importance of theatricality. Molloy is only too aware of the somatic problems of lethargy and forgetfulness that accompany being a passive member of an audience – in accordance with early modern antitheatrical invectives, as also charted in Shakespeare's *Coriolanus* (1608) – and therefore he invents his own memories in response. Conversely, the Unnamable rather becomes an actor who 'forgets' the officials' language forced down his throat, thus destabilising his co-opted role as a citizen; Ben Jonson's satires are the model for this attitude. Meanwhile, in O'Brien's *The Country Girls Trilogy* (in which Beckett is also remembered), the intertextual memory of Shakespeare accords with Lachmann's 'troping', in which the reference to Shakespeare is suppressed or hidden. Rather than explicit intertextuality, instead, O'Brien's Caithleen Brady suffers from being beset by Othello- and Petruccio-like (*The Taming of the Shrew* (1594)) actions by Mr Gentleman and Eugene Gaillard. In turn, Caithleen becomes the *fille vièrge* Desdemona, and the 'tamed' Kate, respectively. However, when she elects to have a hysterectomy, she becomes a version of Hermione-as-statue from *The Winter's Tale* (1611), a depthless woman who loses her biopolitical future as Mother Ireland, but is conversely able to stymie fallacious, masculine narratives of Irish nationalisation. The result of both dismemories is a biopolitics that favours the citizen over the state, responding to – and disrupting – Ireland's constitutional biopolitics.

My final chapters focus on the longitudinal metaphor of land that constitutes another material object that, in a modern environment, is recast as 'territory'. Through an exploration of W. B. Yeats's and Seamus Heaney's poetry, I show how Yeats's concern with surface resolves into a discussion of dancing. I see Yeats remembering Shakespeare's *As You Like It* (1599), a drama wholly concerned with territorial inheritance, which ends with a forest dance to celebrate a new relationship with the land. John Davies's poem *Orchestra* (1596) supports this discussion, in which the intermittent (or disrupted) contact with the land characterises the memorial interaction. Whilst the critical commonplace is that Yeats is driven by a Lear-like fascination with old age, Duke Senior from *As*

You Like It offers a more productive sense of ageing that ties into Yeats's preoccupation with theosophy and Celtic myth. I see this as a 'counter-memorial' strategy, *pace* Foucault. In Heaney's poetry, by contrast, I delineate a 'counter-historical' strategy. Heaney offers a greater emphasis on the land's depth and the underground. In this, Heaney explicitly remembers *Hamlet*, in which the hero jumps into a grave in a bid to remember his father properly. There, Heaney's persona interrogates the sunken archive; however, rather than restore the memories as historical narrative, he re-archives them as poetic memories. Across both Yeats and Heaney, their territorial engagement paradoxically reveals their memories of Shakespeare whose literature underwrote an English proto-colonialism and settler practice that forced native Irish women and men off their own land. And yet, in that engagement, both Irish poets engage an irredentist politics that reclaims the Irish territorial advantage – restoring glory over colonial humiliation.

The selection of these writers is not to be overlooked. They each are canonical, white, predominantly male, and (for the most part) establishment figures for Irish nationalism. The sometime exception, Edna O'Brien, was considered scandalous when she wrote *The Country Girls*, but is by now considered a central figure in Irish letters. Three of them (thus far) have won Nobel Prizes, and one of the others was mentioned in another victor's speech. These writers are known as Irish, whether or not they always chose or choose to wear that identification heavily.[26] Moreover, by virtue of being canonical – and therefore of being well known – these writers remember one another in their intertextuality. It could be said, therefore, that these writers constitute an Irish memorial literature – or *dis*memorial, as I will show. There are other writers of course who number among them. Nevertheless, by curating them in this volume I am arguing that their collective writing, just as it represents Irish literature as a whole, also proves the indelible legacy that Shakespeare's early modern English writing has had and continues to have, in shaping modern Ireland.

There may be a lingering question as to the drawbacks of focusing solely on writers from the south of Ireland (either by birth or citizenship). For example, the motif of the 'partition' in Irish writing might appear less pressing when no consideration is given to the north. Instances below include Beckett's Unnamable (Chapter 4) who declares that he is the 'partition', 'neither one side nor the either. … I don't belong to either' (Beckett, 2009: 376), while in Heaney's 'Act of Union' (Chapter 7) the partition becomes visible in the line demarcating the two sonnets, as well as the implied line that, once crossed, designates (implicitly British) authority and control as rape. We could also think through these iterations in relation to Helena's complaint in *A Midsummer Night's Dream* to her 'sister', Hermia, who appears to have 'forgot' that, though they were 'seeming parted', they were 'yet an union in partition' (III.ii.199, 201, 209–10). Whilst this approach would be beneficial, it would lead to a different book altogether – one which would include writers from the north. I choose not to do this, but not because I do not believe in it; rather because my approach (on this occasion) is to focus on southern writers. In Taylor-Collins (2020b), by contrast, I examine Northern Irish poet Ciaran Carson, and how his 1989 *Belfast Confetti* 'remembers' Shakespeare's *Coriolanus*. It requires a different approach to that used in this book, and in the article I pose a difficult question about how any polity with competing hosts – Loyalist/Unionist and Republican in one; plebeian and patrician in the other – can sustain a practice of hospitality. Thus, I reserve the political question of the partition in this book, but neither dismiss nor ignore it.

Nevertheless, as the reader of the Shakespeare memories I see in my selected writers' texts, I am 'performing a memorial activity' (Pine, 2011: 4) myself, and in doing so I recognise the plurality of legacies that make up this space and nation called 'modern Ireland'. The stories I tell in the remainder of the book serve to place modern Irish literature as both a special case (on the particular plane) and as a test case (on the general) for how literary memory – 'intertextuality' – actually interacts with the formation of nationhood, identity, and a national body of letters. The case can surely be proven elsewhere in the same mode.

Notes

1 I am adding a dimension to Ian McBride's thesis that 'what we choose to remember is dictated by our contemporary concerns' (McBride, 2001: 6) by suggesting that what we do today is dictated by our concern for what we will remember tomorrow.

2 Cf. Oona Frawley: '[M]emory is both a disruptive and generative force that reacts to what is around it' (2011: xx–xxi).

3 Eliot's dictum that 'mature poets steal' is expressed in an essay about the early modern dramatist, Philip Massinger, concerned with comparing Massinger's verse with Shakespeare's. It is, in other words, an essay about intertextuality *avant la lettre*.

4 'To commemorate' and 'to remember' share a meaning, though differ in their etymology. The former is Latinate and the latter Anglo-Saxon via Middle French. See *OED* for full details. Though he later complicates his position, Paul Ricoeur (2006: 43, 42n.) initially writes that 'Commemorations are … reminders of a sort, in the sense of actualizations, of founding events supported by the "call" to remember which solemnizes the ceremony'.

5 Though the green-white-orange tricolour was one of the flags of the Republic, even from the nineteenth century, it was a green flag that was raised above the Dublin General Post Office (GPO) after the Proclamation of the Irish State during the 1916 Rising. For the list of commemorative events, see www.decadeofcentenaries.com/com memorations/ [accessed 1 June 2017].

6 See www.decadeofcentenaries.com/29-june-2016-opening-of-voices -of-memory-national-war-memorial-gardens-islandbridge-dublin-8/ [accessed 1 June 2017] for more information.

7 See, for example, Northern Vision TV's magazine programme *Focal Point* from 7 July 2016, when the interviewer asked representatives of the John Hewitt Society whether there had been too many commemorative events.

8 Collins and Caulfield's collection triangulates the power of history, memory, and forgetting, arguing that critics should be less hasty to oppose memory with forgetting, when in fact forgetting is built upon the logic of remembering. I find it interesting that their introduction hides two references to Shakespeare. Its subtitle, 'The Rest is History', draws on Hamlet's last line before his death (V.ii.342), and they also use the phrase 'cheek-by-jowl' (*MND* III.ii.338). Shakespeare appears, in some way, to be submerged even in a text that seeks to bring forgotten stories to consciousness.

9 For Collins and Caulfield, this pluralisation is a fundamental consequence of capitalism. I do not dispute that aspect of their argument, but I also see its own consequences more broadly than in the economic realm.

10 CnG = Cumann na nGaedheal, a pro-Treaty party that led the first government of the Free State until 1932. CnG became Fine Gael in 1933.

11 Fianna Fáil was Eamon de Valera's anti-Treaty party that headed the Irish government for several decades in the twentieth century. Aside

from four general elections – the country's first two, and the two during the 2010s – Fianna Fáil has received the highest number of votes in
every other election.

12 For Freud's explanation of mourning and melancholia, see 'Mourning
and Melancholia' (1915) in Freud (2001b: 243–58).

13 Could this act as a riposte to Sinn Féin, the phrase (and political party)
that translates as 'Ourselves Alone'? It certainly gives the lie to the
nationalist idea that Ireland can ever be thought of outside a relationship with Britain.

14 Luke Gibbons recalls that James Joyce undertook a 'systematic cultivation of the art of memory, based on his classical and scholastic training and his fascination with the mnemonic system of Giordano Bruno'
(Gibbons, 2014: 196). I consider Leopold Bloom's own *ars memoriae* in
Chapter 2.

15 Q.v. Yates (2005: 163 ff.).

16 For an example of this, consider Holinshed's *Chronicles* (1577–87),
which document English history. Holinshed's descriptions of King Henry
V returning from Agincourt to England and, ultimately, London, are recy-
cled by Shakespeare in the choric introduction to Act V. Shakespeare's
play is also called *The Chronicle History of Henry V* on the frontispiece
of the 1600 quarto. However, the Chorus in Act V also refers, more
or less explicitly, to the Earl of Essex's return to England 'from Ireland
coming, / Bringing rebellion broachèd on his sword' (V.0.32–3) in 1599.
Given Shakespeare's clear place in the memorial firmament over and
above Holinshed's, it is evident that Shakespeare's 'Chronicle' is far
more memorable and, crucially, far more contemporary: the past is in
dialogue with Shakespeare's present politics. For a greater discussion on
this, see Christopher Butler and Willy Maley (2013).

17 My thanks to Stephen O'Neill for drawing my attention to this valuable
source.

18 Cf. Andrew Murphy (2015: 177).

19 Cf. Foster (2015: 227).

20 Q.v. Tiffany Stern: 'Plays often indicate that an actor has privately learnt
his role, but does not know what parts his fellow actors are playing …,
or whom he is supposed to be addressing. … [M]any actors, having
learnt to deal primarily with their own parts in private study, had not
learnt to think of the play as a unity' (Stern, 2007: 64, 98).

21 It is no accident, I think, that the smaller theatres that prioritised political statement over artistic integrity have not received the level of critical
response equal to that of the Abbey Theatre.

22 Q.v. Joyce (2008b: 158–9). The word 'tundish' now exists in contemporary English in a different context.

23 Q.v. Thomas Docherty (1990: 17).
24 It is possible to see this practice forerunning Jan Kott's important arguments in Soviet Poland about Shakespeare's contemporaneity. See Kott (1964: passim).
25 As I have shown already, the stored memory is not identical to 'what happened', and access to the past is contested and competitive: nonetheless, memory and remembering continue to aspire to absolute immanence.
26 Banville, for example, has declared in interview that 'I don't see myself expressing Irish concerns' (Banville, 2000: para. 48).

Part I

Ghosts

The agent of repetition here, clearly, is the ghost. And what is a ghost? It is a memory trace. It is the sign of something missing, something omitted, something undone. It is itself at once a question, and the sign of putting things in question.

– from *Shakespeare's Ghost Writers*
by Marjorie Garber

Introduction

I devote the chapters in this part to three texts from authors across the twentieth century: J. M. Synge's *The Playboy of the Western World*, James Joyce's *Ulysses*, and John Banville's *Ghosts*. I not only connect the three texts in a genealogical connection, as if from father to son, but I also argue that they bear individual connections to Shakespeare through ghostly memory. Underpinning the individual arguments is a general tenet that ghosts come to represent some version of memory, underlining Garber's idea that a 'ghost is a memory trace' (Garber, 2010: 173). Alice Rayner has underscored this principle in her reflections on Herbert Blau's theatrical manifesto, commenting that he sought truth onstage, which etymologically returns us to the

> Greek words *aletheia* or *alethes*, which relate to the sense of 'unconcealed', which is to say visible. Those words also represent the negative of *lethe*, or 'forgetting', as in Lethe, the river of oblivion in the Greek Hades, and hence are connected to the idea of a remembering that is contingent on forgetting. The 'truth' of the practice of ghosting suggests that the actors are in some sense unconcealing and making visible what otherwise is invisible. They are unforgetting the presence of something absent, whether that be called a text or a character, history or the past. (Rayner, 2006: xvi)

For Rayner, all actors are ghosts in that they uncannily give vital force to non-living characters and words. Both for Rayner and for Garber, ghosts are memories, and ghosts compel the living's turn toward memory.

In the first instance, ghosts resemble the memories as described by the ancients. In the metaphor of the *eikon*'s imprint as *tupos* on the wax block ('Theatetus' in Plato, 2015: 191c–e), there is a clear separation of the memory from itself: *eikon* and *tupos* are distinct objects, both reflecting the same 'original' moment or idea. Their separation reminds us that even at the moment of perception, memory is separate from itself, let alone separate from the original idea that instigated the memory. It is little wonder that memories of a singular event will inevitably be plural. The distance between the remembered idea and the idea itself is notable because of its simulacrum-like nature. It is not dissimilar to *Hamlet*'s Ghost who declares that 'I am thy father's spirit' (I.v.9). Though a subtle distinction, the Ghost confirms that he is not identical to King Hamlet, but instead his simulacrum-like representation. Moreover, given that memories are implied to be of the past, the Ghost's reference to a king now dead shows how ghosts, too, represent past – now absent – beings. In this crucial sense, ghosts are kinds of memories.

In their turn, memories too are ghostly. W. B. Yeats, who had his own fascination with the occult and the theosophical, writes in *Per Amica Silentia Lunae* (1917) about reaching his own conception of ghosts. He started from a position of thinking about memory, writing that 'I came to believe in a great memory passing on from generation to generation'.[1] However, Yeats moves on from this position: 'But that was not enough, for these images showed intention and choice. They had a relation to what one knew and yet were an extension of one's knowledge' (Yeats, 1994: 18). The 'images' of the 'great memory' were insufficient because they were too passive: they were prostheses of the mind's memory, and yet the images that Yeats was mentally accessing were filled with a far greater agency. If these were memories, then they were livelier than any memory that had been called that word before.

Yeats's agent-memory develops into a plastic soul. For instance, Yeats describes how a soul that migrates from a dying body remembers the final thought that entered its mind. For this reason, 'when Hamlet refused the bare bodkin because of what dreams may come, it was from no mere literary fancy' (Yeats, 1994: 24). By way of example, Yeats cites his co-occultist, Madame Blavatsky, who said that when a man was dying he 'smelt the odour of the grave … and now that he is dead [he] cannot throw off that imagination'

(Yeats, 1994: 24). The soul is shaped by the memory of life. In this, it might be said that the soul is conditioned and created by memory, particularly at the moment when no more memories can be created. Yeats's final stage of development in this thinking seems inevitable: 'Communication with *Anima Mundi* is through the association of thoughts or images or objects; and the famous dead and those of whom but a faint memory lingers, can still – and it is for no other end that, all unknowing, we value posthumous fame – tread the corridor and take the empty chair' (Yeats, 1994: 27). Here are Yeats's ghosts who most famously make contact with him via his wife, as recorded in *A Vision B* (1937).[2] Ghosts emerge as a by-product of the memorial process: ghosts are the birth-children of memory and death.

Memories are also ghostly because they linger and they haunt: they refuse to leave the living alone. This lingering and haunting can be considered in two distinct categories: the inescapable, fearful haunting typical of demonic ghosts; and the soothing accompaniment, as with an angelic or divine spirit. The ghosts that haunt this chapter are both of these. In Synge's *Playboy*, Old Mahon is twice thought killed, only to return to the stage to haunt – albeit lively and physically – his son Christy Mahon. Old Mahon is the ghostly problem, symbolic of an older, lingering, and atavistic pre-modern Ireland. As such, the modern Christy is faced with a decision: either to keep attempting the patricide that would kill off the haunting, older generation, or to abide his father in some other way. Christy chooses the latter, going offstage to conquer his father, albeit by letting him haunt him still as a living, breathing ghost.

In 'Hades', the sixth chapter of Joyce's *Ulysses*, Leopold Bloom is haunted by memories and ghosts of generations on either side of him: both his father, Rudolf Virág, and his son, Rudy. Whilst the memory of his father's suicide and subsequent inquest worries and embarrasses Bloom, the memory and imagined future ghost of Rudy (himself a nominative memory of Bloom's father) excites and energises him. Bloom leaves Glasnevin cemetery looking forward to re-engaging with the Dublin community from which he has previously felt detached.

Finally, in Banville's *Ghosts*, Freddie is haunted by his own past and *alter ego*, Bunter, the agent of the theft and murder that led to Freddie's incarceration. Now that he is free, Freddie seeks isolation on an island full of misfits and stranded guests. Between the prison and the island, however, Freddie seeks to lay Bunter's ghost to rest. He does so by offering a metaphysical suicide, in which he lets his son live his life unencumbered by Freddie and his past; meanwhile, Freddie progresses into the shadows where he lives in the nether-world of ghosts: Freddie avoids the problem of haunting by becoming the ghost himself. It frees him from reality, and lets him approach the future with confidence. Freddie haunts the living world, for (as Banville writes in a recent memoir), 'the present is where we live, [but] the past is where we dream. Yet if it is a dream, it is substantial and sustaining. The past buoys us up, a tethered and ever-expanding hot-air balloon' (Banville, 2016: 4).

I see Shakespeare's *Hamlet* as the literary-cultural memory at the heart of each of these hauntings. *Hamlet* is a play of memory. Even prior to meeting the Ghost, Hamlet is proud to wear the mourning weeds that signal his bereavement for his father (I.ii.76–86). By Act One Scene Five, this memory play is spurred on by the Ghost's explicit injunction to Hamlet: 'Adieu, adieu, adieu, remember me' (I.v.91). Whilst Garber and I agree that, in relation to this command, 'the Name-of-the-Father is the dead father [and *t*]*his* father – the Ghost – isn't dead enough. The injunction to "Remember me" suggests that he is not quite dead', I disagree with her Lacanian assessment that 'Hamlet must renounce him, must internalize the Law by forgetting, not by remembering' (Garber, 2010: 176). Rather, this injunction compels Hamlet to erase and write his commonplace book anew, perhaps, as I argued above, through a Protestant and humanist Ramist strategy for learning that has memory at its heart:

Remember thee?
Yea, from the table of my memory
I'll wipe away all trivial fond records,
All saws of books, all forms, all pressures past
That youth and observation copied there
And thy commandment all alone shall live
Within the book and volume of my brain
Unmixed with baser matter. Yes, by heaven,
O most pernicious woman,
O villain, villain, smiling damned villain,
My tables! Meet it is I set it down
That one may smile and smile and be a villain – (I.v.97–108)[3]

Based on this soliloquy, Knecht argues that Hamlet 'forswears' his humanist training when he bids to wipe his memory clean in order to use his 'tables' to record the Ghost's story. This insults those who make use of commonplace books to store their various experiences, particularly because 'the commonplaces and *sententiae* of Humanist pedagogy have been rendered irrelevant by a being beyond human comprehension. The existence of the ghost demands a radical revaluation of all learning' (Knecht, 2015: 49). However, there may yet be another reading available. Darlington draws our attention to the Ramist practice of table-writing:

> As the system of dogmatism required a deliberate will to believe, so the reaction headed by Ramus demanded a deliberate will to doubt; never to assent to a statement on authority, until the doubter had made the requisite collection of instances in experience: these had to be arranged in lists called 'tables'. (Darlington, 1913: 479)

Rather than a confusing forswearing of the humanist method, followed by its reinstatement, Hamlet's memory might better be thought of as Ramist, and his tables the practice of the Ramist dialectic, with particular reference to the practice of memory. The Ramist method looks to resolve questions through syllogism by finding the means of joining the subject with its predicate. Ong gives the following example: 'Is man dialectical?' Here 'man' is the subject, 'dialectical' the predicate. The Ramist method proceeds through the stages of the argument, including 'causes, effects, subjects, adjuncts, disagreings'. From these five descend nine further 'derived arguments': genus form, name, notations, conjugates, testimonies, contraries, distributions, and definitions – until the term 'rational' emerges as a 'cause' of dialectical and the difference between 'man' and 'animal'. Thereafter comes the argument: 'Whatever is rational is dialectical, But every man is rational. Therefore every man is dialectical' (Ong, 1958: 182–3). These dialectical answers stress that the Ramist path to learning is through a repeatable method that requires singular dedication and focus of thought. The largest danger to a successful dialectic is its contamination with other subjects. Memory as an art must not be contaminated.

As I described in the Introduction, Ramus says nothing specifically in terms of memory, and yet, to recapitulate, his 'topical classifications … are classifications-for-recall, so that working with them is of itself working with a memory device' (Ong, 1958: 213). Hamlet's postulated focus on the method is a clear strategy for fulfilling the Ghost's injunction. Hence Hamlet's 'table' recording the Ghost's story in Act One Scene Five. The philosophical question to which Hamlet is directed is quite clear: 'Did Claudius kill my father?' With memory the original impetus – 'Adieu, adieu, adieu, remember me' (I.v.91) – Hamlet sets about his Ramist method. The first task is to begin the dialectical table, which he does immediately – 'Meet it is I set it down / That one may smile and smile and be a villain' (I.v.107–8) – before adopting the method completely. Indeed, Hamlet even stresses the Ramist diktat not to mix the categories of argument, explaining that 'thy commandment *all alone* shall live / Within the book and volume of my brain / *Unmixed with baser matter*' (I.v.102–4; my emphasis). Hamlet's method, much as Ramus's 'Apelles portrait of Alexander' is conditioned by a relation of representation, is also conditioned by artistry and mimicry or representation. Indeed, the following comment from Polonius, often dismissed as a reflection of Polonius's inadequate intelligence, can be reread as a worried comment on the new philosophy: 'Though this be madness yet there is method in't' (II.ii.201–2). Perhaps Polonius is referring directly to the new method as outlined by Ramus's theories, rather than an abstract idea. Indeed, method's etymology would suggest the former, given that it bore a particularly medical inflection up until the fifteenth century, when it was defined as 'rational procedure' (*OED*).[4]

If Hamlet is remembering his father and working towards answering his argument through a Ramist dialectic, then surely 'put[ting] on an antic disposition' (I.v.170) as a methodic representation fits the task. In fact, Hamlet's decision to use the play as a mousetrap to prick and catch sight of Claudius's guilt could also be seen as part of the artistic dialectical method. By the time the players arrive onstage, when Hamlet is interrogating them about Dido, Priam, and Aeneas, he praises one line's composition for resulting from 'an honest method' (II.ii.381). It is then that Hamlet asks the player if a line 'live in your memory' (I.ii.385–6) before embarking on his own memorial feats. Memory, method and artistry all intertwine for Hamlet as he bids to solve his dialectical problem.

However, Hamlet's inconsistent passion makes him a bad Ramist, unlike the sanguine Horatio. As Horatio takes on his role as memorial to Hamlet, he begins with the general causes, as Ramus advised, telling Fortinbras:

> And let me speak to th' yet unknowing world
> How these things came about. So shall you hear
> Of carnal, bloody and unnatural acts,
> Of accidental judgements, casual slaughters,
> Of deaths put on by cunning, and for no cause,
> And in this upshot purposes mistook
> Fallen on th'inventors' heads. All this I can
> Truly deliver. (V.ii.363–9)

The general cause – Hamlet's death – leads dialectically on to this catalogue of reasons, each preposed with 'of'. Hereafter, Horatio will give further reasons which will help to answer Fortinbras's determining question: 'What feast is toward in thine eternal cell / That thou so many princes at a shot / So bloodily hast struck?' (V.ii.349–51).

Fortinbras, like Hamlet, is driven by memory. He asks for Horatio's memory of Hamlet and the events that resulted in the bloody scene he comes across in Elsinore; but he also announces a few lines later that 'I have some rights of memory in this kingdom' (V.ii.373): Fortinbras's own narrative starts with a set of private memories. If Hamlet's connection to Ramus is to take hold, that does not mean that it is attributable to Fortinbras as well. Instead, we might add Fortinbras's name to the litany of educational models on offer in the play: Hamlet's/Horatio's Wittenbergian Protestantism; Polonius's/Laertes's Parisian Catholicism; and Fortinbras's military and monarchic education. These three types might be seen as triangulating English politics for the nearly 100 years that followed *Hamlet*'s scripting and first performances. These competing educational priorities add to the set of parallels that at once link and distinguish Hamlet, Laertes, and Fortinbras. For the purposes of the argument here, it is apparent that Hamlet is not purely a modern mind contemplating his own mortality while securing another's death. *Hamlet* is always more than that, and in this case, it is the working through of a Ramist dialectic, seeking an answer to the question: 'Did Claudius kill my father?' That this question responds to a command to 'remember' proves the work of *Hamlet* to be bound up on one level with memory: a personal memory that, through the

Ramist method, drives the tragic plot. As the play unfolds, Hamlet's bid to 'Revenge [his father's] foul and unnatural murder' (I.v.25) is therefore inextricably tied to Hamlet's memory of the Ghost: '[W]hat is at stake in the shift of emphasis from vengeance to remembrance is nothing less than the whole play' (Greenblatt, 2013: 208). When Hamlet speaks with Gertrude in her closet, the Ghost returns to make sure that Hamlet is on the right path to vengeance: 'Do not *forget*! This visitation / Is but to whet thy almost blunted purpose' (III.iv.107–8; my emphasis). Evidently, remembering and revenging amount to the same thing for Hamlet. There is no *Hamlet* without memory: '[T]he whole of Hamlet is an act of memory made visible' (Rayner, 2006: xx).

Hamlet's Ghost is, crucially, the ghost of Hamlet's dead father. This gives to my analysis the abiding idea of spectrality being linked to patrilineal relations: fathers and sons are key, both in their specificity, but also as a way of emblematising the ways in which the historical present is built on and out of a past that it carries within itself. On a broader plane, we see that Shakespeare offers an origin of sorts for the father–son motif in literature. In *Hamlet* the father's spirit's story compels Hamlet to seek revenge for his father's murder; in *Playboy* Old Mahon is the focus of his son Christy's ire; in 'Hades' Rudy and Virág condition their father's/son's response to life; and in *Ghosts* Freddie's relationship with his son provides the turning-point in Freddie's attitude towards ghosts and his own existence in the world. In other words, *Hamlet* acts like the ghostly father haunting later Irish literature. It haunts, lingers, and accompanies the later texts; it is difficult to shed, but also worthwhile to appropriate. 'Remember me', says the Ghost to Hamlet, and much like the son who is compelled to follow his father's injunction, so does Irish literature remember *Hamlet*'s Ghost, especially when its authors are attempting to shore up their own literature. Referring to Marx,[5] but stating an idea equally applicable here, Derrida refers to the 'the shadow of a filial memory, [through which] Shakespeare will have often inspired' (Derrida, 1994: 3).

However, in asserting the historical genealogy of literature through time from Shakespeare to Synge, to Joyce, to Banville, I come up against the innate problem of ghostliness. Peter Buse and Andrew Stott point out what is at stake:

Ghosts are a problem for historicism precisely because they disrupt our sense of a linear teleology in which the consecutive movement of history passes untroubled through the generations. Again we return to the question of anachronism because ghosts are anachronism *par excellence*, the appearance of something in a time in which they clearly do not belong. But ghosts do not just represent reminders of the past – in their fictional representation they very often demand something of the future. The ghost in Hamlet is a well-known example of this. Old Hamlet arrives from the past in order to make a demand on his son's future actions. He, like many of the ghosts of later gothic and modern fictions, serves to destabilize any neat compartmentalization of the past as a secure and fixed entity, or the future as uncharted territory. (Buse and Stott, 1999: 14)

Not only do Buse and Stott turn my attention again to the future, but they also raise the issue of ghostly anachronism. Gibbons's point that the 'persistence of the spectral in the modern world derives from a literal failure of memory' (Gibbons, 2015: 146) is limited in its applicability because of his reliance on post-Freudian psychic theories. Instead, that which Buse and Stott describe about ghostliness can also be said of memory itself: there is no demand that memories recur in the order in which their original *eikon* took place, or in the order in which they are narratively placed in memory. Remembering when I read *Hamlet* at school, I first recall my teacher's explanation of the word 'ecstasy' in the closet scene, even though that scene (III.iv) occurs over halfway through the play; but my first recollection of *Hamlet* is of my mother telling me when a child that it was the play she had watched most. Memories, like ghosts, are 'out of joint', sometimes temporally recurring as and when they will. Buse and Stott term this 'anachronism', and Derrida labels this behaviour 'hauntology'.

It would seem foolhardy, therefore, to outline a simple and straightforward linear genealogy in my connection between ghosts, memory, *Hamlet*, and Irish literature.[6] It needs to be more fluid, and needs to take account of the disruptions that ghosts represent and instigate. As Nicholas Royle points out, a more fruitful way of thinking this through is via 'phantom texts', which are 'textual phantoms which do not necessarily have the solidity or objectivity of a quotation, an intertext or explicit, acknowledged presence and which do not in fact come to rest anywhere. Phantom texts are fleeting, continually moving on, leading us away, like Hamlet's Ghost, to some other scene' (Royle, 2003: 280). Not only does this account for my linear genealogy – Irish literature remembers *Hamlet* and its Ghost – but also the possibility that remembering of other texts takes place, too. Joyce's writing remembers Synge's; Banville's remembers Joyce's; they each remember Shakespeare. Moreover, remembering, like ghostly irruptions, can take place without the explicit signifiers of *anamnesis*: 'I remember', 'I recall', 'A memory stirs', etc. Uninvited, lingering, sometimes barely recognisable: these words equally describe memory and the ghost taking place and taking shape in literature. In this regard, Lachmann's three memorial categories of (1) the quoted intertext, (2) the 'troping' process of rejection and of turning away, and (3) the satirical or parodic 'transformation', all seem inadequate. It is my own trope of 'dismemory' that can adequately and sustainably account for this new category in its description of disruptive memories that corrupt linear genealogy, all the while deriving power from historical linearity.

In the following I will assert a historicised linear genealogy from Shakespeare to Banville, but I will also explore how the ghostly memories allow for that patriarchy to be overturned: sons dominate fathers; dead sons teach fathers how to live; fathers cede life to their younger charges as they dominate death instead. This is to say that ghosts, like memories, take control, and are taken control of; at the very moment the linear father–son genealogy is recognisable, it is also destabilised. If as Patrick Crotty argues that 'A son's attitude to his father need not be emblematic of his relationship with his inherited culture … but in Irish literature it usually is' (Crotty, 1992: 17), then these chapters reply that ghostly memories provide one way for Irish writers to write their history another way, even if they start as the son to the Shakespearean father.

Notes

1 This intergenerational memory store will below become a focus of my interest when I look at Yeats more closely in Chapter 6.
2 See esp. the 'Introduction' in Yeats (1986).
3 There is a perverse irony in the omitting – nay, *forgetting* – of this speech in the so-called 'bad quarto' of 1603 (see Shakespeare, 2006b: 5.86). By contrast, the passage in which Hamlet bids the Player to recite

a speech 'I chiefly loved' (II.ii.383) is written nearly identically to the later 'good' editions (q.v. Shakespeare, 2006b: 7.336 ff.). One difference merits noting: Hamlet says that there was 'a speech in it I chiefly *remember*' (7.336; my emphasis). It is no accident, I am sure, given that Q1 was long considered a 'memorial reconstruction' by fellow actors (see Zachary Lesser, 2015: passim) of an early performance of the play, that the actors were able to remember lines referring directly to dramatic text, but struggled to remember lines that referred to scrubbing memory clean and writing down the Ghost's diktat instead.

4 Adrian Turnèbe, a contemporary adversary of Ramus, offered the following ironical jest on the topic: 'Method – no word is more popular in our lectures these days, none more often heard, none gives off a more delightful ring than that term. Everything else, if you use it often enough, will end by nauseating your readers. This is the only thing that never makes them sick. ... If you use it often, they will believe that anything you give them is the ambrosial and nectared food of the gods. ... I am aware that this subject has been thrashed out to the last grain and meticulously disputed by Peter Ramus' (qtd in Ong, 1958: 228–9).

5 The paper that became *Specters of Marx* was delivered at a conference entitled 'Whither Marxism?' – and Derrida (of course) played on the conference title pun.

6 Foucault points out the foolhardiness of this argument. See my discussion of Yeats in Chapter 6.

1

'Go on from this': J. M. Synge's *Playboy*

Spiritism, whether of folk-lore or the séance room ... will have it that
we may see at certain roads and in certain houses old murders acted
over again[.]

– from *Anima Mundi* by W. B. Yeats

Introduction

The Irish National Theatre, and its version that found a home at
the Abbey Theatre, 'often declared its mission ... to elevate the Irish
drama, to *banish* the stage Irishman from the theatre' (Kilroy, 1971:
19; my emphasis).[1] Its project can therefore be read as a process of
forgetting. This amnesiac effect was threatened, said contemporary
reviewers and audience members, by J. M. Synge's *Playboy of the
Western World*. Synge's drama – although 'the greatest play Yeats's
theatre produced' (Edwards, 1979: 211) – countered the Abbey's
mission to '"hold as 'twere up to Nature"', to banish the meretricious
stage, and give, for the first time, true pictures of Irish life' (Kilroy,
1971: 20). Here quoting Hamlet (III.ii.21–2), the *Journal* reviewer
remembers Hamlet's instruction to the Players. This unthinking
promotion of Hamlet's troubled metatheatrical ideas indicates
that, regardless of *Hamlet*'s true effect on mimetic theatre, the play
stands as a long-remembered beacon of idealised theatrical perfection, and that Hamlet 'is not simply a paradigmatic actor; he is the
impersonation of theatre, insofar as theatre is a space for working out the complex relations between remembering and forgetting'
(Rayner, 2006: 51–2). *Playboy* stands at the avant-garde of the Irish
theatre that intends to rid the stage of stereotypes propagated by
English theatre – but is supposed to do it following the arch-English

text's ideas. I think this is achieved, though not in the ways that contemporary theatre critics thought. The ways in which Hamlet confirms the veracity of the Ghost establishes an inverted temporality
of memory – it is only considered a truthful spirit because Hamlet
decides to pursue vengeance, and therefore historical action gives
life to (and precedes) the memory – which is deployed in *Playboy*
when Christy seeks to consign his father to memory by attempting
to murder him twice. In doing so, Christy establishes the possible
ground for the overthrow of his father's authority, analogising the
seemingly imminent Irish revolution.

Anthony Roche has recently remarked on the most obvious
Synge–Shakespeare connection, writing that 'The most relevant
Shakespeare play, and the one explicitly referenced within Synge's
Playboy of the Western World, is *Hamlet*' (Roche, 2015: 20). And
yet, as Roche also notes, there has been scant critical attention paid
to Synge's engagement with Shakespeare. This is despite the evidence unearthed by Nicholas Grene (1971) in the Trinity College
archives that Synge attended Edward Dowden's Shakespeare lectures while a student and 'Synge records only two visits to the theatre in his 1890s diaries, one in September 1892 to see Beerbohm
Tree's *Hamlet* in Dublin' (Hewitt, 2021: 110).[2] Roche attempts to
counter this critical omission, citing several intertextual memories
in Synge's oeuvre, from *King Lear* in *The Well of the Saints* (1905),[3]
from *The Merchant of Venice* in a letter to the *Irish Times* (Qtd in
Roche, 2015: 19), and from *Hamlet*. For Roche, Synge borrows
Shakespeare's 'linguistic richness' (Roche, 2015: 22) as he joins the
bard as a 'realist' playwright 'reaching out to a land of the fancy'
(Roche, 2015: 17).

Roche's article borrows the title of Christopher Murray's mono-
graph on Irish drama: *Twentieth-Century Irish Drama: Mirror up
to Nation* (1997). In its title's deliberate intertextual memory of
Hamlet's instruction to the players, Murray's book is clearly interested in the ways in which Shakespeare's and modern Ireland's
drama share a relation between the staged and real dramas of a
nation, albeit with differences: '[I]n Irish drama the mirror does
not give back the real; it gives back *images* of a perceived reality.
The play as mirror up to *nation*, rather than to nature in Hamlet's
sense, results in a dynamic process; you have to stop it in freeze-
frame to distinguish what happened (history) from what yet might

happen (politics)' (Murray, 1997: 9; emphasis original). The spectre arrests time to allow for the freeze-frame, and opens the window on to the future. Whilst Murray inexplicably does not explore the Synge–Shakespeare connection, he nonetheless draws attention to its possibility. This is especially true considering the Abbey's afore-mentioned avowed intention to stage drama – with Synge as its foremost dramatist – in the Hamletic style.

However, Synge apparently rejected Hamlet's instructions, and a journalist (erroneously) noted that 'That was going in direct oppo-sition to the first rule laid down by the foremost playwright [i.e. Shakespeare]' (Kilroy, 1971: 23).[4] As I will show, though Synge rejects early modern ideas of theatrical mimesis, his drama is still haunted by the ghostly memory of *Hamlet*, particularly in the way that Old Mahon haunts Christy Mahon, threatening severally to return to the stage when it seems as though he has been dismissed absolutely and finally. To this end, *Playboy* provoked riots among the 'metrocolonial'[5] Dublin populace because of the way it depicts a western Ireland that has not progressed, but has instead seen the recurrence of the past and the lingering authority of those thought dead. In staging a dialectical contest between the 'old' – Old Mahon, cottiers like Shawn Keogh, dowries constituted of heifers – and the 'new' – Christy trying to kill his father and celebrating his infamy, winning all the sports – *Playboy* replays Hamlet's own avenging remembrance, but Synge recognises that the revolution must take place offstage, and in the play's aftermath – in Ireland's implied future.

Gregory Dobbins has also argued that *Playboy* is essentially con-cerned with conjoining the present with the past:

> By representing [in *Playboy*] this version of the west in prose and on stage in the more metropolitan context of the Dublin-based Revival, Synge offered a seemingly alternative conception of the present that did not appear remarkably different from the past but was very dis-tinct from the processes of modernisation identified with both capi-talism and colonialism which prevailed within more developed parts of Ireland. (Dobbins, 2009: 134)

Dobbins's Synge wrestles with twin versions of history. There is modernity, represented in the audience and in Christy, and 'tradi-tion', the elements of society rejected by modernity and represented in the play's Mayo shebeen and Old Mahon. Whilst Christy Mahon represents the 'distinct ... processes of modernisation', Synge's text questions whether the depicted rural and 'backward' west maintains its relevance for the modernity of east-coast Ireland. In his 1907 'Preface' to the play, Synge remarks that 'In Ireland ... we have a popular imagination that is fiery and magnificent and tender; so that those of us who wish to write start with a chance that is not given to writers in places where the springtime of the local life has been forgotten, and the harvest is a memory only' (Synge, 1995: 97). *Playboy* is thus theatrically playing with memory by refusing the slide of present practices *only* into memory, and by suggesting that the Mayoites' behaviour is still current, and a viable model for modern Ireland. Synge thereby questions the legitimacy of the revolution in advance of its taking place through the push-and-pull of (wilful) social amnesia and memory.

In this schema, Old Mahon is, by name and nature, symbolic of 'old' Ireland and is the play's lingering ghost. However, Old Mahon is not the first revenant talked about. Rather, just prior to Old Mahon's entry, Jimmy and Philly wonder what would happen if Old Mahon's split-skull was ever found unearthed in the field:

> PHILLY Supposing a man's digging spuds in that field with a long
> spade, and supposing he flings up the two halves of that skull,
> what'll be said then in the papers and the courts of law?
> JIMMY They'd say it was an old Dane, maybe, was drowned in the
> flood. [*Old Mahon comes in and sits down near door listening.*]
> Did you never hear tell of the skulls they have in the city of
> Dublin, ranged out like blue jugs in a cabin of Connaught?
> (Synge, 1995: 130)

Talking about the emergence of Old Mahon's body from the earth just pre-empts Old Mahon's surprise revival and arrival onstage. Ghosts come to life at the right time. Moreover, in what is clearly 'a loaded and recognizable reference to *Hamlet*' (Roche, 2015: 20), Philly's and Jimmy's conversation seems to be about Danish skulls – the very same things that obsess Hamlet in the Graveyard Scene (V.i). In *Hamlet* there is a connection between Hamlet's obsession with the unearthed skulls and his haunting by the Ghost: in both instances, people and things are unusually unearthed. The same is true in *Playboy*, with Christy Mahon surprised by the return of his father whom he had thought he had committed to memory. How he confronts his revived father explains the play's attitude to memory and is redolent of early modern attitudes to ghosts. In both *Hamlet* and *Playboy*, the heroes act on (and confirm the veracity of) ghostly memories, but also become offstage, spectral legacies themselves. For Hamlet, this resulted in tragedy; for Christy Mahon, the possibility of a modern Irish revolution becomes possible.

Early modern spectrality

Barnabe Rich (c. 1540–1617), writing at the turn of the seventeenth century, explains what the Irish should do when confronted with a ghost – and it is a lesson that Christy Mahon appears to have learnt when he is continually confronted by his father. Rich instructs that the Irish should recognise the ghost and reveal it as spectral, belonging not to this world: 'Take heede you bee not deceiued by any of these spirits, which shall seeke to abuse you, by pretence of reuelation, by visions, by dreames, by shew of holinesse: such spirits are walking and daily conuersant amongst vs in *Ireland*' (Rich, 1609: 53; emphasis in original). Spectrality in these circumstances is twofold. First that ghosts are 'daily coneuersant amongst vs', and second that one should 'take heede' to avoid being 'deceiued': the ghost must be discovered and its spectral falseness proven. For Rich, the devilish spirits are embodied in Catholic priests and his advice is therefore salient to Reformation England and to an examination of contemporary literature. Nathan Johnstone corroborates this Protestant relation to devils and demons (and their physical manifestations), pointing out that rather than practising Catholic exorcism and *post hoc* rituals to cleanse the individual of demonic or satanic possession, 'Protestants instead advocated a personal engagement with the demonic within the conscience, and they stressed that every individual was ultimately responsible for resisting Satan's influence' (Johnstone, 2006: 2). There are similarities between Rich's position and that of Calvinist Richard Baxter (1615–91), who also blames papist priests for the ongoing visitation of ghosts, although 'Catholic chicanery does not explain everything'. Nevertheless, 'Sorting real from fake ghosts, apparitions, and other manifestations of the spirit world presents enormous and serious epistemological problems because everything about the aerial world is "unknown to us here"' (Laqueur, 2015: 73). Ultimately, the Protestant strategy against the devil was prophylactic – preparing the mind in advance of satanic attack via temptation. It also focused on the individual mind, and at that level is consonant with the growth of individual self-consciousness, commonly considered a sign of modern individualism.

Moreover, a discourse ought to be created between the individual tempted and the satanic manifestation. This could equally be ascribed to the rise of the soliloquy on the early modern stage as to the rise of the modern individual. The Renaissance self-fashioning as considered by Stephen Greenblatt implies 'a distinctive personality, a characteristic address to the world, a consistent mode of perceiving and behaving' (Greenblatt, 1984: 2). A theory of diabology such as the one described by Johnstone is culturally significant not least because culture produces individuals, and culture is also a set of control mechanisms that, in the words of Clifford Geertz, 'govern behavior' (qtd in Greenblatt, 1984: 3). As one of the cultural forces at play, diabology is important because it is one of the Renaissance 'control mechanisms, [constituting] the cultural system of meanings that creates specific individuals by governing the passage from abstract potential to concrete historical embodiment' (Greenblatt, 1984: 3–4). And so diabology is borne out in behaviour, and allows watchers of *Hamlet, Macbeth, Julius Caesar* and *Richard III* whether to judge as normative or transgressive the reactions of Hamlet, Macbeth, Brutus, and Richard III to the ghosts who haunt them onstage. Marcellus, for example, shirks his Protestant responsibility, telling Horatio 'Thou art a scholar – speak to it' (I.i.41). Speaking and direct addresses thus become a critical manifestation of diabology in and through self-fashioning, for which reason Hamlet's discourse with the Ghost and direct addresses to the ghosts offstage – viz., the audience – are worth considering as part of this diabology. Greenblatt's brief description of the 'soliloquies of *Hamlet*, [as] words that claim not access to the inner life but existence as the inner life' (Greenblatt, 1984: 87), proves the relation I am adumbrating between fully fledged modern interiority and diabology – a diabology that also generated 'valuable theatrical capital' (Greenblatt, 2013: 157). After all, 'self-fashioning occurs at the point of encounter between an authority and an alien' (Greenblatt, 1984: 9): Hamlet becomes Hamlet by virtue of meeting the absolute other – the Ghost, his father's spirit.

Diabology encourages dialogue between the two figures, rather than an absolute cleansing or expurgation. Just as 'modernity' created 'tradition', so too did the individual need the devil to prove their reformation:

> The post-Reformation Devil was a powerful figure not because the reformers neglected to clip his wings, but because they were adamant he should remain so. When set in its religious, social and political contexts, early modern diabology appears not simply as an uncritical inheritance from the medieval world, but as a powerful and reflective belief, subtly but importantly different from its predecessor, and one that, in both its continuities and changes, expressed what was a profound experiential reality for its adherents. (Johnstone, 2006: 12)

Diabology is central to the experience of reformed Protestantism in England.[6] 'The question of whether the Ghost will speak', notes Garber, 'is a central preoccupation of the whole first Act of *Hamlet*, and has a great deal to do with the way it is described and addressed' (Garber, 2010: 193). It is interesting therefore when Horatio is urged to talk to it by Marcellus, especially since Horatio is called to action because of his learning, student as he is (like Hamlet) in the Protestant Wittenberg: '[H]e might be able to resolve the crucial question that hung … over all apparitions' (Greenblatt, 2013: 209). He will be well versed in Protestant practices of discoursing with the devil and, because of his scholarship, will 'better understand how to establish the necessary distance or how to find the appropriate words for observing, better yet, for apostrophizing the ghost, which is to say also for speaking the language of kings or of the dead' (Derrida, 1994: 12).

Much like ghosts, theatres were similarly vilified in early modern England. For example, in his *Refutation of the Apology of Actors* (1615) – responding explicitly to Thomas Heywood's *Apology for Actors* (1612) – John Greene offers an extended litany of immorality to be found in only one place:

> [I]f you will learn falsehood; if you will learn cozenage; if you will learn to deceive; if you will learn to play the hypocrite, to cog, to lie and falsify; if you will learn to jest, laugh and fleer, to grin, to nod and

mow; if you will learn to play the Vice, to swear, tear and blaspheme both heaven and earth; if you will learn to become a bawd, unclean, and to devirginate maids, to deflower honest wives; if you will learn to murder, flay, kill, pick, steal, rob and rove, if you will learn to rebel against princes, to commit treasons, to consume treasures, to practise idleness, to sing and talk of bawdy love and venery; if you will learn to deride, scoff, mock and flout, to flatter and smooth; if you will learn to play the whoremaster, the glutton, drunkard, or incestuous person; if you will learn to become proud, haughty and arrogant; and finally, if you will learn to contemn God and all His laws, to care neither for Heaven nor Hell, and to commit all kind of sin and mischief, you need to go to no other school, for all these good examples may you see painted before your eyes in interludes and plays. (qtd in Pollard, 2004: 268)

This hyperbole testifies to the strength of opinion of those enraged by the theatre's popularity, even if these invectives 'are more literary than doctrinal' (Greenblatt, 2013: 153). Written in 1615, Greene's *Refutation* witnesses the feeling against the *established* cultural mode. These feelings, however, were also present at the theatre's outset. Writing in 1577, the year after the opening of The Theatre and the first Blackfriars theatre, and the year that saw the opening of the Curtain Theatre, John Northbrooke rages against the English-language public theatre. In his dialogue between Youth and Age in *A Treatise Against Dicing, Dancing, Plays, and Interludes, with Other Idle Pastimes*, Age wilily asserts that

Chrysostome sayeth the devil found out stage plays first, and they were invented by his craft and policy; that they contain the wicked acts and whoredoms of the gods, whereby the consciences of goodly men are grievously wounded, and wicked lusts are many ways stirred up. And therefore the devil built stages in cities. (qtd in Pollard, 2004: 12)

Much like the plague that closed their doors severally in this period, the theatres must be avoided. The plays represent a particular kind of devilry that exploits temptation, especially since 'Many can tarry at a vain play two or three hours, when they will not abide scarce one hour at a sermon. They will run to every play but scarce will come to a preached sermon' (Pollard, 2004: 8). It could be argued that the theatre's perception as devilry incarnate constituted a major element of early modern Protestantism. Moreover, it is now just to say that the ghostly devil and the theatrical devil are of a piece in certain strands of early modern society: to be avoided, protected from, and vilified at all costs. It is not insignificant that Seán Hewitt describes, independent of any early modern diabology, Synge's characters engaging in just such a diabolical strategy in *The Well of the Saints* (1904): '[T]he Douls can no longer trust whether the Saint is benevolent or otherwise, and so cannot decide whether a curse or a prayer would protect them against him. The ironic thrust of Synge's work has led to a position from which the distinction between the "good works" of the Church and the evildoing of the devil has become impossible to determine' (Hewitt, 2021: 134). Here we spy the memory of early modern diabology in Synge's modern Irish drama.

The Ghost in *Hamlet* is related to both diabology and the antitheatrical discourse. First because Hamlet is compelled to speak to the Ghost, and second because Hamlet takes the Ghost's injunction as an opportunity to instruct players to elicit his uncle Claudius's guilt. Looking at the former of these, Horatio raises the topical issue of whether the Ghost will '*tempt* you toward the flood' (I.iv.69; my emphasis), showing the fear that the men have of the Ghost. Hamlet nonetheless continues and demands of the Ghost, 'Whither wilt thou lead me? Speak! I'll go no further' (I.v.1). Hamlet, like Horatio, is keen to start a conversation with the Ghost. Critically, Hamlet questions the Ghost's motives. This is also part of Rich's spectrality, through which the conversant must question and interrogate the spirit's motivations. These ideas appear, albeit differently, in other Shakespeare plays such as *Julius Caesar* and *Macbeth*. In the former, when Brutus sees the ghost of Julius Caesar he questions the 'monstrous apparition' primarily about what it is, not its motivation: '[A]rt thou anything? / Art thou some god, some angel, or some devil / That mak'st my blood cold and my hair to stare? / Speak to me what thou art!' (IV.iii.276–9). Brutus's concern that the ghost is malevolent is proven true, with Brutus himself exclaiming, 'O Julius Caesar, thou art mighty yet! / Thy spirit walks abroad and turns our swords / In our own proper entrails' (V.iii.94–6). Brutus lays his loss of the civil war squarely at Caesar's ghost's feet, but all that Caesar did was tell Brutus that he would meet him again at Philippi. Macbeth, meanwhile, tries to find out who is mocking him when Banquo's ghost first appears, asking 'Which of you have done this?' (III.iv.48). Macbeth later commands the ghost to leave when he accuses it of falseness. Seeing it then go: 'Hence horrible shadow, / Unreal mockery hence! – Why so; – being gone / I am a man again' (III.iv.106–7).

Rich's forewarned spectrality is salient here. In one instance Brutus follows Rich's argument but is still undone by the ghost; in another, Macbeth realises his power by admonishing and dismissing the ghost. However, this also proves short-lived as Banquo's ghost reappears along with the future kings of Scotland, threatening Macbeth further. The connection, however, between Caesar's and Banquo's ghosts is their intimidation, and their inability to take full control of the action onstage. Banquo scares Macbeth, and Caesar unsettles Brutus, but in neither case is the ghost the cause of what follows onstage. Though both Brutus and Macbeth follow Rich's ideas, the results are fruitless: they may as well have ignored the ghosts, for the results would have been the same. A contrasting example appears in Thomas Kyd's earlier drama *The Spanish Tragedy* (?1582), when one ghost is the narrative guide, and another is guided. The narrative guide also guides the audience: Dante and Virgil are transposed. However, the Ghost of Andrea and Revenge converse only with themselves onstage; similarly, neither appears onstage to instruct or scare any of the living characters. *The Spanish Tragedy* presents central ghosts who are not offered up for spectral roles. Between Kyd's play and *Julius Caesar* and *Macbeth* there are different versions of ghosts, but none truly rises to the level of threat or interest suggested by Rich's warning.

Hamlet offers a more exact version of Rich's spectrality. The Ghost in *Hamlet* connotes offstage power made clear in Rich's implication that the spirits are the devil's doing. Spirits are threatening, that is, because the source of their power is not of this world. Their power derives from hell, a place not visible on earth except through these spiritual visitors. These ideas are also evident in *Hamlet*, such as when Horatio and the guards assess whence the Ghost comes and why. Horatio says that the Ghost 'harrows me with fear and wonder' (I.i.43) and that its appearance 'bodes some strange eruption to our state' (I.i.73); it is clearly an 'extravagant and erring spirit', which means that it is 'wandering beyond its proper bounds' (I.i.153 and note). Spectrality in this vein is also to locate one's power not in presence, but in absence. Spectrality is thus both the task to reveal the spirit's true nature – to uncover its deception, to make truth out of myth, to authenticate, to demythologise – and to have a power located offstage, or to be defined positively by absent presence. The latter is often glossed as 'representation', the power of which is double: both the substitutive 'representation' (or *Vertreten*) visible in art, from which symbols and metaphor derive; and 're-presentation' (or *Darstellen*) visible in politics, from which delegation and metonymy derive. Both these forms can also be understood as 'remembering'. The Ghost remembers Hamlet's father in his spectral body but might equally re-member the devil and his tendency to tempt mortal man. Only Hamlet is able to test the Ghost's memory.

Hamlet's testing the Ghost results in his own elevation, as might be expected of someone who is combating early modern demonism. In the Ghost's absent presence, Hamlet both 'remembers' the Ghost and proves that the Ghost is no demon through the same act: revenging his father's murder. In this way, Hamlet's demythologising act in the mode advised by Rich reinforces the Ghost's stability, making the Ghost an authenticated and infallible memory of his father. This authentication and infallibility are cemented by the Ghost's absence for much of the play. As I have shown elsewhere,[7] the absent or offstage sovereign is critical to Shakespeare's writing. Once offstage, the Ghost is metaphorically above or outside the law that he has prescribed. Linking this with Giorgio Agamben's ideas of the sovereign lawmaker who stands outside the law they create, it is important to note the power generated by an invisible sovereign. The Ghost of King Hamlet is just such a sovereign, and it is Hamlet's remembering of the Ghost that validates the Ghost's own embodied memory of the King. Ultimately, though Hamlet does check to see whether the Ghost is demonic in the vein of Rich's spectrality, this check results in validating and not disproving the Ghost's actions.

Key here is that acting on a memory confirms the memory's truthfulness. The action *makes it true* and, in that sense, writes time backwards according to Ricoeur's chronology: history – action and consequence – precedes, presupposes, and gives form to memory. In this argument, Hamlet perversely becomes a definitive, historical actor – '[I]t is plausible to say that Hamlet constructs his own Ghost' (Garber, 2010: 196) – and his father and the Ghost become merely secondary memories, both in rank order and chronology. Rayner describes the action of the play as taking place in 'the syncopation between the past moment and the future moment, which are both moments of nonbeing' (Rayner, 2006: xxxi) but makes no mention of the play's inverted temporality that is central to understanding the work of memory in *Hamlet*. Like Old Mahon's entering after his skull has been unearthed in Philly and Jimmy's conversation, the 'time is out of joint' (I.v.186): disruptive memory – dismemory – begins to take shape and take hold.

Playboy's spectrality

Like Hamlet, Christy derives his onstage power from a dead father offstage, albeit in adapted circumstances. Rather than his father being murdered and asking Christy to avenge his murder onstage, Christy is the man who killed his father; from his father's absence, Christy is revered as a hero. Christy's inheritance, much as Hamlet's, is perverse: Christy inherits authority from his recently killed father. Rather than the memory of his father granting Christy authority, it is the recounted memory of the murder of Old Mahon that elevates Christy to the status of hero. By telling his story – by making public the memory of killing his father – Christy seeks to make true his own legacy of detachment. Christy explains how 'it was a bitter life [Old Mahon, my father] led me till I did up a Tuesday and halve his skull' (Synge, 1995: 110). Christy proceeds to explain to Widow Quin what triggered his murderous action:

> [T]here I was, digging and digging, and 'You squinting idiot', says he, 'let you walk down now and tell the priest you'll wed the Widow Casey in a score of days'. ... [She was a] walking terror from beyond the hills, and she two score and five years, and two hundred-weights and five pounds in the weighing scales, with a limping leg on her, and a blinded eye, and she a woman of noted misbehaviour with the old and young. ... 'I won't wed her', says I, 'when all know she did suckle me for six weeks when I came into the world, and she a hag this day with a tongue on her has the crows and seabirds scattered, the way they wouldn't cast a shadow on her garden with the dread of her curse'. (Synge, 1995: 118)

Old Mahon is killed for two reasons: for controlling Christy's destiny, and for being obsessed with preserving the land. Old Mahon as a sovereign figure tries to control desire, refusing to grant Christy full modern, self-fashioned status of being in control of his own future. In so doing, Old Mahon urged a quasi-incestuous relationship between Christy and the Widow Casey who nursed him: Old Mahon advocates a relation of atavistic circularity that prevents novelty and modernity. It is possible to see in Old Mahon a version of Claudius: Claudius kills King Hamlet to control Elsinore's polity. Christy, like Hamlet, must kill Old Mahon – commit him to memory – in order to become a modern individual himself: the past must be overthrown in order for the present to thrive. In *Hamlet* this is legitimised through the Ghost's demand that Hamlet 'Remember me' and that that remembrance should come through his 'reveng[ing] [your father's] most foul and unnatural murder'; in *Playboy* Christy's murder of Old Mahon is legitimised by the shebeen community that confirms Old Mahon's existence as immanent memory. Christy's power derives from offstage, memorial spectrality.

The second reason for Mahon's murder is encoded within references to Widow Casey's being a 'walking terror from beyond the hills', and Old Mahon's role in making Christy dig the land. These characters are connected to the land, which I equate with an old, pre-industrial Ireland; but this is no Revivalist pre-industrial, idealised Ireland. Instead, this is a negative spin on that latter version of Irish history, one which has at its heart the problem of Old Mahon: he seeks to replicate and continue these ideas. By casting these ideas as negative, Synge dismisses Old Mahon's sovereignty because of its roots in the land, cleaving to Hewitt's reading of the play as promoting the law*breaker* over the law*maker* (Hewitt, 2021: 192–5). The same is true for Shawn Keogh who offers a 'drift of heifers' and a 'blue sneem' as a dowry for his marriage to Pegeen Mike (Synge, 1995: 139–40); he, too, is dismissed as pre-industrial and undesirable, and it is Christy's arrival onstage that undermines Shawn's favour. Like Old Mahon, Shawn is 'the embodiment of an oppressive and backward heritage' (Crawford, 2008: 487). In the first act, when the two are still betrothed, Pegeen Mike and Shawn discuss their forthcoming marriage:

SHAWN [W]hen we're wedded in a short while ....
PEGEEN You're making mighty certain, Shaneen, that I'll wed you now.

SHAWN Aren't we after making a good bargain, the way we're only
waiting these days on Father Reilly's dispensation from the bish-
ops, or the Court of Rome. (Synge, 1995: 100)

The wedding's process is in full flow at the play's beginning, though
it seems to be far from a joyous affair since 'She is writing a mundane list of provisions that serves to associate prospective marriages
with eternal tedium, with a kind of living death' (Crawford, 2008:
487). By the end of the first act, after Widow Quin refers to Pegeen's
and Shawn's upcoming marriage, Christy is concerned:

CHRISTY What's that she's [Widow Quin] after saying?
PEGEEN Lies and blather, you've no call to mind. ...
CHRISTY And you're not wedding him at all?
PEGEEN I wouldn't wed him if a bishop came walking for to join us
here. (Synge, 1995: 113)

Pegeen's denial condemns Shawn, thereby ending their betrothal.
By stopping Shawn and Pegeen from marrying, the patricidal ideas
that Christy brought on to stage are translated into social terms.
The present must be murdered and committed to memory in order
to progress into the future.

If Synge is advocating a break from tradition through the figure
of Christy, then the play also manages to problematise that break,
first by having Old Mahon return to the stage from offstage memory, and second by having Christy leave the stage with Old Mahon
at the end of the play. In the first instance, Christy's power, located
offstage in his father's murder, deflates with Old Mahon's reappear-
ance onstage. The return of memory, much as in Freud's trauma
theory, weighs heavily on Christy's power. Pegeen consequently tells
Old Mahon to 'Take [Christy] on from this, for I think bad the
world should see me raging for a Munster liar, and the fool of men'.
The Crowd jeer accusingly, 'There's the playboy! There's the lad
thought he'd rule the roost in Mayo! Slate him now, mister!' The
way that Pegeen phrases it a few moments later is telling. She realises, as she tells Christy, that 'there's a great gap between a gallous
story and a dirty deed' (Synge, 1995: 144). Pegeen now appears to
take heed of Rich's advice from centuries earlier: she uncovers the
truth of the ghost, the one whose power lies offstage. The ghost

of Old Mahon is revealed as living, undead, non-mythological: it returns the onstage and offstage audiences to truth, to the demands of being and to the real. Christy's authority is undermined and disabused and sovereignty in *Playboy* returns to those whose relation to the land is their principal characteristic, for whom the land testifies as the only memory they need of the past. A land, that is, seamlessly, genealogically transferred from generation to generation.

Christy is forced to leave the community. Not long after, Old Mahon's second return to life heralds his and Christy's removal from the stage. But their departure is on Christy's terms, as he explains to Old Mahon: 'Go with you, is it? I will then, like a gallant captain with his heathen slave. Go on now and I'll see you from this day stewing my oatmeal and washing my spuds, for I'm master of all fights from now. Go on, I'm saying. ... Not a word out of you. Go on from this' (Synge, 1995: 146). Old Mahon and Christy leave the stage for a space in which Christy overturns the relationship with his father and is now in control. Another way of thinking of this relation and the shift in the power dynamics is through Hegel's notion of the dialectic: thesis, antithesis, synthesis.[8] The father (thesis), the son (antithesis), and then their synthesis result in the new relation of the son leading the father. Whilst Crawford (2008: 493–4) contests the reading of this power structure, he ignores the spectral structure that conditions the new relation between Christy and his father. Rather than Crawford's reading of the 'message' of the play as the idea that only 'an act of imagination' can 'subvert' Old Mahon's 'inexorable authority' (Crawford, 2008: 483), it is precisely the temporal reversal – manifested in Christy's attempt at an enforced memorisation of his father – that outlasts the play. That temporal reversal is inherited from *Hamlet*'s temporal reversal.

With Christy and Old Mahon located offstage by the play's end, Pegeen has not merely lost the 'only Playboy of the Western World' (Synge, 1995: 146), but the father and son have synthesised into a new, offstage law in an unseen (viz., offstage) future. This Ghost offers a modern sovereignty, once again located offstage. Pegeen's lament is not only that she cannot have Christy to sate her desire. As is implied in Valente's term 'metrocolonial', there is always a space forgotten by modernity and Pegeen now realises that her shebeen and its community will be forgotten and omitted from modernity. While the dialectic between father and son is resolved, 'Instead of closing with one another in a dancing dialectic', the Mayoites and Christy 'move farther apart, leaving society unredeemed and apparently unredeemable. A revolution occurs, but it is happening offstage' (Kiberd, 1996: 170).

Nelson O'Ceallaigh Ritschel attributes the crowd's rejection of Christy's second murder of Old Mahon, and therefore the resistance against the prospect of revolution, to the crowd's implied complicity that comprises personal, rather than systemic violence. 'The second murder is rejected not because it is too close', writes Ritschel, 'but because it is attempted for personal reasons – violating the dominant theme of the pre-1916 Irish theatre of public duty to Ireland over private concerns' (O'Ceallaigh Ritschel, 2002: 47). Whilst Ritschel's argument is helpful in drawing together the play and its historico-political context, the second murder also alludes to the issue of sovereignty: *Playboy*'s society cannot take part in the overthrow of an old regime. By doing so they would advocate the modern break with the past and assume the old society's sovereign mantle, and also undermine the old system still in place; that is, they would be supporting revolutionary politics onstage, the origin and power of which could not be deferred offstage, nor proven to be false as in spectrality. Roche sees this also as a result of Synge's decision to engage with the full complexity of Shakespeare's drama, by choosing to script a play whose genre vacillates between tragedy and comedy. 'The failure of the play to end with the marriage of Pegeen and Christy – the traditional end of Shakespeare's romantic comedies', writes Roche, 'means that the social order of the Ireland represented by Synge remains untransformed and unrenewed and hence subject to continuing critique' (Roche, 2015: 21). No memory means no modernity.

Shaun Richards reads the play more positively and has noted that through this modernist play 'Synge demonstrates that the corollary of the overthrow of the past is its necessary reintegration into the future', to which I add the acute focus on the idea of a spectral sovereign. And, as explained above, that spectrality is marked by its offstage-ness; or, the 'radical alternative occupies an ungraspable off-stage infinity' (Richards, 2009: 39). This ties in with my previous comment that Synge problematises the status quo by leaving it onstage, and by allowing a spectral, memorial presence from offstage, and Dobbins glosses this by writing that 'Synge's plays emphasise the centrality of a recalcitrance which serves as an obstacle to progress' (Richards, 2009: 140). Memory plays with that recalcitrance because it signifies the exit of the living into the past, becoming a *tupos* in personal or social records. To that extent, memory signifies the *end* of the obstacle. And yet, memory also signifies the impossibility of absolute nonbeing, with the *eikon* remaining persistently present, albeit 'offstage', as it were. Old Mahon represents that Janus-faced recalcitrance, because he represents a past set of ethics that insists on being relevant 'today', the 'play negotiat[ing] the power of the past by insisting upon the present, even as that present is weighed upon by the past, and even as the future is implicit in every incipient moment' (Crawford, 2008: 491). Christy Mahon attempts, twice, to kill his father – to commit him to memory – and leave him lying in the earth where he belongs so that Christy can supersede his authority. But while there is community, memory may be restored to, or maintained in, life – just as Synge argued in *Playboy*'s Preface. After all, as Pegeen's father, Michael, explains to Christy, 'Go on to the foreshore [a transformation of the Ghost's 'tempt[ing] Hamlet] to the flood' (I.iv.69)] if it's fighting you want, where the rising tide will wash all traces from the memory of man' (Synge, 1995: 139) – only the deep can offer true oblivion. Christy is thus a new kind of Hamlet because instead of proving the Ghost truthful by acting on his memory of the father, he instead wants to kill the father, to commit Old Mahon to memory, and in that way prove himself as the new truth. Spectrality is important for Christy because it gives him something to reject, on which to base his own living authority. Rather than remembering the past in the present, Christy is consigning what he considers outdated to memory.

Remembering forward

That is not to say that Christy is not involved in some kind of backwards-facing anamnesis, as well. Rather, following Kiberd, I argue that Christy is *remembering forward*[9] by becoming an offstage memory himself. Christy's parricide remembers the spectre of the father at the very moment that he commits it to memory. It is in this sense that Christy is remembering at all, recalling the older law to mind. At the same time, Christy is also made in the mould of the

Mayoites invested in the land, and as such is imprinted with their memories that he also manages to reject. In both cases, remembering gives him the opportunity to reject the past. This is the power of dismemory. As Kiberd writes, 'In [Synge's] hands, the meaning of Gaelic tradition changed from something museumized to something modifiable, endlessly open. ... [H]is deepest desire was to demonstrate the continuing power of the radical Gaelic past to *disrupt* the revivalist present' (Kiberd, 1996: 187; my emphasis). In this way, Christy becomes a dismemory himself, able to last beyond the 1907 productions, showing the way to rid the present of the past. Christy becomes a version of the devilry that the theatre and ghost represented 300 years earlier – and that Synge had already evoked in his earlier drama – tempting the audience to overthrow the *status quo*. Without the past, there is of course only one way to look, and here we see Christy as an emblem of remembering forward. Christy's is a future in which the father is subordinated beneath the son, and which stands 'endlessly open' as the possibility for future action: by being offstage and spectral, Christy himself becomes the ghost that disruptively haunts modern Ireland.

It is precisely like the Hamlet of Act Five Scene One. When confronted with the skulls that are thrown out of the ground by the Clown, Hamlet is able at last to get to grips with what happens next in life. For Hamlet death is no longer a pure idea but has material traction in the bones that structure bodies. 'If it be, 'tis not to come. If it be not to come, it will be now. If it be not now, yet it will come', says Hamlet. 'The readiness is all, since no man of aught he leaves knows what is't to leave betimes. Let be' (V.ii.198–201). The skulls act as memories for Hamlet, but they also are future versions of himself: in thinking backwards, Hamlet *remembers forwards*. He perceives himself living in a temporality that is not locked within mortal limits, but that he may also leave a legacy – and one that is less pernicious and demanding than his father's ghostly memory. Thereafter, of course, Hamlet is proactive, becoming the man of dynamic history rather than meditative contemplation. Thinking himself into the future, Hamlet fulfils his role as dutiful son; at the same time, he confirms the Ghost's truthfulness.

Both Christy and Hamlet are burdened by their fathers. They are also bedevilled by the memory that their fathers leave. For Hamlet, his father's memory in the form of the Ghost turns Hamlet's narrative from one of inheritance to revenge; Hamlet's death is the only plausible ending. Similarly, the unstable memory of Christy's father imperils Christy's own independence as a young man willing to separate himself from tradition, and eager to create a new future according to his own rules. And yet both Hamlet and Christy find themselves driven by the logic of spectrality: of concretising and making certain a memory through action. Christy's action is to leave with his father in tow; Hamlet's to avenge his father's death. In both instances, the characters become disruptive memories – dismemories – themselves, remembering themselves forward, Hamlet by recognising his own material form after death, Christy by becoming spectrally absent. He becomes a mythic ghost, the 'only playboy of the western world', and alongside 'Synge himself … becomes the emblem of revitalization, a symbol of an alternative and postcolonial modernity' (Hewitt, 2021: 202).

The transmission of the Danish skulls from *Hamlet* to *Playboy* definitively links these plays and allows for Synge to make 'modernist play with the literary ghost of Shakespeare's *Hamlet*' (Roche, 2015: 20). Philly and Jimmy's conversation at the beginning of Act Three about the Danish skulls shows *Playboy* remembering *Hamlet*; moreover, it shows *Playboy* remembering Hamlet's *remembering forward*. These skulls, talked about in passing, are the ghostly remnants of *Hamlet* on Synge's stage.[10] Hewitt has noted how a draft of *Playboy* included references to yet more skulls and other skeletons. 'The interest shown by the shebeeners in the heroic past' as symbolised by these bones, writes Hewitt, 'establishes Synge's Mayo as a place seeking its own regeneration, either by turning towards a more vital past or by overthrowing a stifling present' (Hewitt, 2021: 197). The skulls become the symbol of Ireland's hauntological future and they remind the Mayoites of the power of remembering offstage and underpin the links between Shakespeare's premiere play and modern Ireland's preeminent drama.

Notes

1 This Kilroy volume collates excerpts from contemporary newspapers reporting on the *Playboy* riots. This and the next excerpt are taken from 'The People and the Parricide', *Freeman's Journal*, 29 January 1907, 6.

2 The other, of general salience to my discussion in this section, was 'to see Ibsen's *Ghosts* at Paris's Théâtre Antoine'.

3 See Synge (1995: 72).

4 This excerpt taken from the Dublin *Evening Mail*, 29 January 1907, 2.

5 Joseph Valente glosses the metrocolonial as 'interval or remainder, a border zone both joining and dividing an imperialist and an irredentist culture under the always contestable titles of "West Britain" and the capital of Ireland, respectively' (Valente, 2011: 194).

6 I have elsewhere considered lingering post-Reformation Catholic practices. See Nicholas Taylor-Collins (2020b: 88n.)

7 See Nicholas Collins (2015).

8 Hewitt has demonstrated Synge's familiarity with Hegel (Hewitt, 2021: 114–17).

9 A term I borrow from Carol Chillington Rutter.

10 Remembering, of course, that this *memento mori* – or *memento Hamletis* – had already been employed in Thomas Middleton's *The Revenger's Tragedy* (1606).

2

'Remember me': *Hamlet*, memory, and Leopold Bloom's *poiesis*

There's a touch of the artist about old Bloom.
– Lenehan in 'Wandering Rocks' from *Ulysses*

As true as I'm drinking this porter if [Bloom] was at his last gasp he'd try to downface you that dying was living.
– Narrator in 'Cyclops' from *Ulysses*

Introduction

There is no shortage of criticism exploring the Joyce–Shakespeare connection, though little if any has focused on *Ulysses*'s sixth episode 'Hades'. Instead, most criticism either examines the comparison between Stephen and Hamlet, or examines *Ulysses*'s ninth episode, 'Scylla and Charybdis', during which Stephen Dedalus explains his Shakespeare theory to the other visitors to the National Library of Ireland on Kildare Street. There are also explicit references to Shakespeare in 'Circe', the novel's fifteenth episode. Regarding the former, Kiberd remarks that 'Like Stephen, Hamlet appears in mourning clothes at the start', and adds that Stephen 'knows that Hamlet was too shrewd ever to play a part himself, contenting himself merely with writing or directing them. Hamlet is in fact an early warning system for Stephen that the intellectual may be one who can play every part except his own' (Kiberd, 2009: 332–3). In this framework, Hamlet is the model for Stephen, connected as they are by their youth and their shared interest in 'interior monologue' (Kiberd, 2009: 334).

With regard to criticism on the 'Scylla and Charybdis' chapter, Justin Beplate has usefully described Stephen as 'repeatedly draw[ing] on the imaginative possibilities of ghosts and ghostliness to fuel his own artistic ambitions' in his presentation of *'Hamlet* as a kind of ghost story' (Beplate, 2014: 166). Elsewhere, Adam Putz's exploration quite deftly thinks through the Joyce–Shakespeare connection. 'For Stephen', writes Putz, 'the Shakespearean text necessarily reflects the life of its author' (Putz, 2013: 154). Stephen's biographical reading lends his Shakespeare theory a market value. However, he refuses to publish this theory and in so doing 'avoids making a spectacle of himself by selling out. He retains his own authenticity by denying his theory and setting a price for the privilege of seeing it in print' (Putz, 2013: 170). Whilst Putz's reading is neatly woven, it retains the dominant focus on the Stephen–Hamlet connection as with Kiberd and Beplate, and also on the question of authenticity that has long been prominent in criticism of Hamlet. 'Scylla and Charybdis' would also seem the natural text to transition from Synge to Joyce since 'Synge is the ghost who haunts the library scene in *Ulysses* through absence' (Roche, 2015: 11).

However, I depart from the dominant critical mode to focus instead on the spectrally rich 'Hades'. The sixth episode 'Hades' charts Bloom's journey from the centre of Dublin to Prospect Cemetery in the city's northwest quadrant. He attends the funeral of Paddy Dignam, and the journey, the service, and the burial all prompt memories, both voluntary and involuntary, of people and events to flood Bloom's consciousness. Whilst there is no specific memorial lexicon in the chapter – 'memory', 'remember', and related words appear only seven times here out of over 150 in the novel – 'Hades' is one of the novel's memorially rich chapters. I will show how Bloom's engagement with two of the technological apparatuses of memory – the phonograph record and the photograph – recalls the same technical prostheses of *Hamlet*'s Ghost. This parallel, underpinned by Derrida's reading of *Hamlet*, will show how Bloom is 'hauntologised' – brought to full self-recognition and self-determination through the haunting by ghosts from his past – not through his dead father, but rather by remembering his dead son, Rudy, who gives him the strength to continue living as a marginal character in Dublin's metropolis. Bloom, like Hamlet, is able both *to be* and *not to be*, by virtue of his empowering connection to ghosts.

One memorial aspect that critics have drawn attention to in 'Hades' is the national *milieux de mémoire* that the funeral cortège passes, namely statues of heroes of Irish independence (Cheng, 2014:

12; Jones, 2014: 131). And, of course, there are also memories of other epic poems in 'Hades'. Bloom travels in a carriage with three other Dubliners – Martin Cunningham, Jack Power, and Simon Dedalus – from Sandymount to Glasnevin. In the process, the carriage crosses the four waterways in Dublin – the River Dodder, the Grand Canal, the River Liffey, and the Royal Canal – thereby mimicking the epic trope of the νέκυια, the *nekuya* or descent into hell.[1] Odysseus's descent into hell in *The Odyssey*, as with Aeneas in *The Aeneid*, requires him to cross the four waterways of Hades, the underworld. Maurice Halbwachs argues that 'The "Nekuya" … provides a background against which we can more clearly discern both Olympus with its misty lights and a society of men who are above all lovers of life' (Halbwachs, 1992: 85). As with Odysseus, Bloom's journey to the cemetery exposes him as a 'lover of life', though 'no external wisdom guides him' (Kenner, 1952: 98). By placing 'Hades' as a direct descendant of these previous *nekuyata*, the text remembers *The Odyssey* and *The Aeneid* even as Bloom's narrative departs from theirs. In Lachmann's terms, *Ulysses* 'tropes' the classical epics. The text invites its readers to remember both Odysseus – as does the novel as a whole – and Aeneas – the founder of a new civilisation – in Bloom. Aeneas is an outsider who carries relics – remembrances, that is – of the old gods from Troy to Italy in order to lay the foundations for the next great civilisation of men. The implication is that Bloom is these heroes' descendant, carrying their legacy in Dublin.

Hamlet's hauntology

I have already described *Hamlet* as a play of memory and I develop those ideas here. I will now summarise elements of Derrida's reading of hauntology in the play before examining hauntology in relation to Bloom in 'Hades'. I then establish that Bloom, like Hamlet, is vitally enhanced by the ghost of a dead loved one; however, in place of Hamlet's father's spirit, Bloom is compelled to life by the future-memorial ghost of his late son, Rudy. I finally show that Bloom begins to appreciate the presence of the dead in his life, imagining scenarios in which they can be brought back to quasi-life through the use of technology. This disruptive technological memory is a kind of dismemory. My conclusion is that Bloom's more positive outlook on life, following his encounters with the dead, endows him with a mind that 'remembers poetically' – though not writing poetry, Bloom is conditioned by ποίησις (*poiesis*), a sensibility that privileges liminality and potentiality. This in-betweenness advocates a national cause that relies less on Revivalist integrations of the past with the present, when 'a glorious past functioned as compensation for a degraded present' (Pine, 2011: 6), and more on a modern Ireland that constantly discourses with its past in order to move on to the future. In this, the hauntological aspect of memory, as found and advocated in *Ulysses*, gives rise to an Ireland that is energised by the presence of ghosts, and does not seek to set them at ease by absorbing them into ideological narratives that seek to frame Ireland in the present. The task, in other words, is *not* to wake up from the nightmare of history,[2] but to think of new ways of remembering that past.

In *Specters of Marx* Derrida offers his reading of the Ghost's relationship with Hamlet. Under the category 'hauntology', Derrida likewise considers the connection between Hamlet and the Ghost as integral to the drama. In Garber's idiom, hauntology is 'a manifestation of the haunting presentness of the past' (Garber, 2010: 210) and is a particular aspect of the play *Hamlet* as well as its own haunting Ghost. The absolute singularity of the coming of the Ghost – the inexplicability of the Ghost's presence suggests it is a singular event, therefore happening both for the first and last time[3] – leads Derrida to label it 'Staging for the end of history':[4]

> Let us call it a *hauntology*. This logic of haunting would not be merely larger and more powerful than an ontology or a thinking of Being (of the 'to be', assuming that it is a matter of Being in the 'to be or not to be', but nothing is less certain). It would harbor within itself, but like circumscribed places or particular effects, eschatology and teleology themselves. It would *comprehend* them, but incomprehensibly. How to *comprehend* in fact the discourse of the end or the discourse about the end? Can the extremity of the extreme ever be comprehended? And the opposition between 'to be' and 'not to be'? *Hamlet* already began with the expected return of the dead King. After the end of history, the spirit comes by *coming back* [*revenant*]. It figures *both* a dead man who comes back and a ghost whose expected return repeats itself, again and again. (Derrida, 1994: 10)

Hauntology is greater than ontology, and refers to the singularity of the encounter with the spectral Ghost, despite the Ghost's prior appearance: the paradoxical repetition of the singularity. Hauntology also refers to the question 'To be, or not to be?' (III.i.55), and therefore also to the Ghost's being or non-being. Moreover, for my purposes hauntology is constituted by three ideas emerging from the actual encounters with the Ghost. These are (1) the 'visor effect' that includes a 'spectral asymmetry'; (2) the 'anachrony' that 'makes the law'; and (3) the work of mourning that would seem to act as a counter to the first two, though actually reinforces the work that the Ghost can achieve (Derrida, 1994: 6, 6–7, 9).

The 'visor effect' derives from a simple concept: the observer(s) of the spectre – Marcellus, Barnardo, Horatio, or Hamlet – cannot see the spectre looking back at them. This is owing to the armed Ghost, whose visor is semi-permeable to sight:

> The armor lets one see nothing of the spectral body, but at the level of the head and beneath the visor, it permits the so-called father to see and to speak. Some slits are cut into it and adjusted so as to permit him to see without being seen, but to speak in order to be heard. The *helmet*, like the visor, did not merely offer protection: it topped off the coat of arms and indicated the chief's authority, like the blazon of his nobility. (Derrida, 1994: 7)

Authority is visible onstage, so the Ghost's clothing denotes someone of a high, if not the highest, rank. Furthermore, the authority is what allows the Ghost to restrict this visibility or 'ocularity': the visor does not let the observers see that the Ghost is looking at them. Here is the spectral asymmetry of which Derrida writes.

The ability to identify the Ghost is central to Hamlet. He asks Horatio with successive, stichomythic questions: 'Armed, say you? ... From top to toe? ... What looked he, frowningly? ... Pale, or red? ... And fixed his eyes upon you?' (I.ii.225–33). The energetic questions climax with Hamlet's final inquiry in this sequence asking whether the Ghost looked at Horatio. The question of identity is resolved on the premise that the Ghost did look at Horatio, and that look confirmed the Ghost's appearance. Hamlet's next comment that 'I would I had been there' (I.ii.34) reveals that he is satisfied as to the Ghost's identity.

HAMLET Then you saw not his face.
HORATIO O yes, my lord, he wore his beaver up. (I.ii.227–8)

Despite this obvious proof that the Ghost was able to avoid the semi-permeable problem of the visor and its slits, Derrida persists in focusing on the 'visor effect'. To counter this complaint, he adds that

> Even when [the visor] is raised, *in fact*, its possibility continues to signify that someone, beneath the armor, can safely see without being seen or without being identified. Even when it is raised, the visor remains, an available resource and structure, solid and stable as armor … The helmet effect is not suspended when the visor is raised. Its power, namely its possibility, is in that case recalled merely in a more intensely dramatic fashion.[5] (Derrida, 1994: 8; emphasis original)

The visor effect and its subsequent spectral asymmetry – of ocularity and of power – is all the more effective because of its *potentiality*: even when it is not in play, it threatens to reassert itself. This threat renders the spectral chief, the authoritative Ghost, always ready to 'see and to speak', and therefore the Ghost's interlocutor must always be ready to listen to it without interruption. (This is proved in the Closet Scene when the Ghost does, in fact, force Hamlet to see himself and to speak with it.) In effect, the visor effect turns the spectre into a living authority possessing a living voice able to bend others to its will. The envoy from the dead can control the stage.

This is also visible in the second hauntological idea, that of ghostly 'anachrony' making the law. When the Ghost speaks and gives his authority some vocal force, he then gives the law. The law, coming from a spectre, 'thy father's spirit' (I.v.9), is given by a representative of *time before the play*. The play's time, which I have already shown is confused owing to the repeated singularity of the Ghost's visit (and is termed 'syncopat[ed]' (Rayner, 2006: xxxi)) is again shown to be riven with anachronisms. Or, as Hamlet says to Horatio and the others, 'The time is out of joint' (I.v.86). The idea of anachrony is compounded by another element of the Ghost's giving the law: the fact that it is the Ghost of Hamlet's father. Not only is the lawgiver's spirit dead, but there is a generational separation between the lawgiver and the legal prosecutor: the father instructs the son what to do. The twin injunctions to 'Revenge'

and 'remember me' become inherited laws that must be executed
by someone who was not the victim of their initiating act (King
Hamlet's murder). In this, then, *Hamlet* is actually the Ghost's play,
and not the prince's.

The element of *Hamlet* that appears to counter hauntology is the
central idea of mourning. Hamlet, of all characters, mourns most
obviously in the play, evident from the moment he is seen onstage in
his mourning weeds. It is also clear, argues Derrida, in Act Five Scene
One when Hamlet is taking account of and addressing the skulls
of dead people. Derrida asserts that mourning 'consists always in
attempting to ontologize remains, to make them present, in the first
place by identifying the bodily remains and by localizing the dead'
(Derrida, 1994: 9). In the graveyard, Hamlet 'demands to know to
whom the grave belongs .... Nothing could be worse, for the work
of mourning, than confusion or doubt: one *has to know* who is
buried where – and it is *necessary* (to know – to make certain) that,
in what remains of him, *he remain there*. Let him stay there and
move no more!' (Derrida, 1994: 9). This work of mourning is characterised by giving name to, or 'ontologizing' the remains of the
dead, and also of locating them geo-temporally – in their grave and
in their right temporality of death, and not life – and because the
'sepulcher as the material place thus becomes the enduring mark of
mourning, the memory-aid of the act of sepulcher' (Ricoeur, 2006:
366). Mourning leads into memory because knowing of the dead
allows Hamlet to detach his living self from their physical remains,
condemning or burying them in memory.

However, the work of mourning is interrupted by the arrival of
the spectre. Through the visor effect, the spectre seeks to destabilise
the ability of the observer to localise or ontologise the dead – to
mourn. The Ghost instead 'freez[es the] young blood' (I.v.16) of
Hamlet. After the Ghost's threat through spectral asymmetry,
Hamlet learns that the living cannot control the dead, but that the
dead in fact control the living. Moreover, Hamlet's legal framework,
which had previously been prescribed by 'the Everlasting' and his
'canon' (I.ii.131–2), is now upset by the Ghost's injunctions to
revenge and remember. Hauntology gives mourning a hiatus and
denies it its full course.

Conversely, mourning contests hauntology: the power of those
living to establish their distance and difference from the dead denies

hauntology its full force. In this vein, Hamlet's mourning serves to exemplify the power of suffering

> the whips and scorns of time,
> Th'oppressor's wrong, the proud man's contumely,
> The pangs of despised love, the law's delay,
> The insolence of office and the spurns
> That patient merit of th'unworthy takes[.] (III.i.69–73)

However, it must be borne in mind that hauntology casts a shadow over mourning that reveals the full living force of grief: mourning contests hauntology, and its power is redoubled through that contest. Without the shadow of death, and the threat of the returning dead to command the living, the force of mourning is weakened. Thus, hauntology is a necessary part of a successful and powerful process of mourning. And since revenging and remembering constitute a cornerstone of hauntology in *Hamlet*, then mourning must also be considered both *ante* and *post hoc* to those twin acts. Mourning remembers just at the moment when it seeks to detach the living from the dead.[6]

Hauntology, therefore, is a powerful force for the living, though it comes at a cost. It removes Hamlet's agency from the stage – the law is not his own and he was not the victim of the murder that instigated the laws to revenge and remember. And it relies on an asymmetry that manifests itself in ocularity as Hamlet must learn to trust in not seeing, in not always being able to identify the originator of the law. And yet, conversely, hauntology reinforces the importance and power of mourning, of ontologising remains and localising and fixing them in the grave. Hauntology both interrupts and expedites mourning.

Bloom's mourning

Not unsurprisingly, 'Hades', situated in a quasi-mythological underworld and site of the afterlife, is a chapter coloured by death. R. M. Adams describes how Bloom is 'haunted throughout the chapter by an amazing assortment of ghosts, spooks, and hobgoblin doppelgängers' (Adams, 1974: 99), fearing even stories of ghosts returning after death: 'I will appear to you after death. You will see my ghost after death. My ghost will haunt you after death' (Joyce, 1986: 6.1000–1). Memory in the order of spectrality, as in *Hamlet*, is conditioned by the encounter of the living with ghosts and the anachronistic return of those who do not belong with the living. As Bloom's journey to and through Glasnevin Cemetery progresses, Bloom encounters more ghostly memories of his dead loved ones. This leads to Shari Benstock commenting that 'Bloom is haunted by the ghost of his dead loved ones, is obsessed with his own dead past, is discovering on this day that the "spirit" world is very much a part of his everyday life' (Benstock, 1975: 409). As I will show, Bloom learns to appreciate this community of the dead.

One of the first 'ghosts' to visit Bloom takes the form of an involuntary memory⁷ while they are still *en route* to the cemetery. It is the memory of his father, Virág's, death.

> That afternoon of the inquest. The redlabelled bottle on the table. The room in the hotel with hunting pictures. Stuffy it was. Sunlight through the slats of the Venetian blind. The coroner's sunlit ears, big and hairy. Boots giving evidence. Thought he was asleep first. Then saw like yellow streaks on his face. Had slipped down to the foot of the bed. Verdict: overdose. Death by misadventure. The letter. For my son Leopold.
>
> No more pain. Wake no more. Nobody owns. (6.359–65)

This is hauntology in the mode of *Hamlet* with the father appearing to the son. For example, as in Derrida's description of mourning in *Hamlet*, Bloom also uses the memory as an archaeological dig for ascertaining knowledge. Bloom first locates the memory geotemporally, not only in the deictic 'that' indicating elsewhere from the carriage, but also in the 'afternoon'. The text then describes the coroner's room through the vignetted 'redlabelled bottle', the 'hunting pictures' and the 'Sunlight' illuminating the coroner's 'ears, big and hairy'. Then the porter, 'Boots', is brokenly recalled 'giving evidence' of finding Virág dead. Aside from the 'Stuffy' coroner's room, all descriptions are images irrupting into Bloom's mind. Like a zoetrope, Bloom's memory of the inquest consists of a series of disparate images strung together consecutively in a disruptive fashion that never fully erases the joins between the images. The static sequence, with only an imperfect hint towards dynamic movement, offers a version of the asymmetrical ocularity originating in *Hamlet*.

However, this father–son encounter circumvents hauntology and fails to hauntologise Bloom, despite the similarities. As such, the element of authoritative control evident in *Hamlet* does not continue in *Ulysses*. Here, Bloom alone is able to see the revenant memory, and any authoritative speech is markedly missing. Even Boots's evidence is related indirectly without any kind of speech marker. In light of this reading, Bloom's mourning for his father is incomplete because, paradoxically, the memory is not strong enough to act as catalyst to hasten the end of mourning. Without Virág's hauntology, Bloom will never have full control over his mourning for his father.

There is the potential vessel for Virág's authoritative instruction to the son here in the form of the letter. Earlier in 'Hades', Bloom alludes to the letter, noting its most significant feature: 'Be good to [my dog] Athos, Leopold, is my last wish' (6.125–6). Though this is an odd injunction to pass from father to son, it nonetheless qualifies as inheritance. However, its bathos undermines the authority that Virág attempts to impart, thereby undermining Virág's ability to control his son. As if to correct this failure, in 'Circe', *Ulysses*'s fifteenth episode, Virág talks to his son while dressed in his own, traditional outfit (much as the Ghost did): 'the long caftan of an elder in Zion and a smokingcap with magenta tassels' (6.248–9). In this exchange between Bloom and the ghost of his father, Virág condemns the past behaviour of Bloom. Virág complains that 'One night they bring you home drunk as dog after spend your good money'. Bloom's reply that it happened 'Only that once' fails to console Virág, who continues: 'Once! Mud head to foot. Cut your hand open. Lockjaw. They make you kaput, Leopoldleben.' Virág finally finishes '(*with contempt*) Goim nachez!' (15.266–79) In her edition of the novel, Jeri Johnson translates this Yiddish phrase as a contemptible 'The proud pleasure of the gentiles!' (Joyce, 1998: 417, 12n.). The whole effect of the exchange is to show that the ghost of Bloom's father is not so concerned with Bloom's future actions – there are neither injunctions nor commandments – but purely with Bloom's past acts. In this sense, Virág does not act authoritatively and he does not deny his son the ability to see him speaking and watching him; in spite of the homological similarities between Ghost–Hamlet and Virág–Bloom, Virág does not hauntologise Bloom in the way that the Ghost hauntologises Hamlet.

Bloom also mourns the death of his son, Rudy. The chief element of his mourning centres on the idea that a son provides someone to whom Bloom can pass on his inheritance. The memory starts with, 'If little Rudy had lived.' This phrase implies a conditional future tense in which a whole counterfactual world becomes possible. However, this future is denied both to Bloom and Rudy and as such, so is the power of Bloom as memory *eikon*: he will not become a memory for his son to draw on. Memory fails with the failure of the son to survive the father.

However, it becomes clear that this counterfactual, ghostly, dismemorial Rudy is able to hauntologise Bloom: 'See him grow up. Hear his voice in the house. Walking beside Molly in an Eton suit. My son. Me in his eyes' (6.74–6). It is easy to draw analogies between *Hamlet*'s Ghost and Bloom: both figures seek anachronic futurity in their sons; both are connected to the ocular or spectral blindness, as Bloom here sees not Rudy's eyes, but his own eyes in Rudy's (which also connects to anachrony). Both figures are also, in their connections with their sons, in a relationship with death or non-being: the Ghost is the return of a dead figure, whilst Bloom imagines the restoration of his own dead son. But in this last idea, the homological connection between the Ghost, Bloom, and Hamlet breaks down, for Bloom is never able to give the law to his son. However, if I reverse the anachrony, then hauntology reappears with Rudy hauntologising Bloom according to the three features of hauntology I enumerated above. For instance, as with Virág, Rudy also appears to Bloom in 'Circe'. Unlike his grandfather, this younger 'Rudolph Bloom' does not speak. Instead, Bloom watches him. The ghost's/memory's clothes are again important, but so are his eyes:

> RUDY (... *Against the dark wall a figure appears slowly, a fairy boy of eleven, a changeling, kidnapped, dressed in an Eton suit with glass shoes and little bronze helmet, holding a book in his hand. He reads from right to left inaudibly, smiling, kissing the page.*)
> BLOOM (*wonderstruck, calls inaudibly*) Rudy!
> RUDY (*gazes, unseeing, into Bloom's eyes and goes on reading, kissing, smiling. He has a delicate mauve face. On his suit he has diamond and ruby buttons. In his free left hand he holds a slim ivory cane with a violet bowknot. A white lambkin peeps out of his waistcoat pocket.*) (15.4956–67)

Two things merit specific attention in this passage. The first is Rudy's reading backwards, it appears, from right to left. The second is Rudy's unseeing gaze that continues while he carries on reading. This is in part a result of Rudy wearing a *little bronze helmet* that is not in keeping with his Eton suit, but reminiscent of the Ghost's armour. Both the backwards-reading and unseeing gaze draw attention to the importance of ocularity and the notion of inheritance. The former is easily comparable with the Ghost's relation to Hamlet. The unseeing gaze is as it is seen by Bloom, and therefore it is unclear whether the ghost of Rudy sees Bloom or not. And yet, Rudy is also using his eyes to read; he is in ocular control. He reads, I argue, an authoritative Jewish text for which reason he scans the Hebraic text from right to left. Though Rudy's kissing the page is a Joycean interpolation that does not quite reflect Judaic practice,[8] the implication is clear: Rudy's practice indicates the reinstitution of the authoritative Judaic word that Bloom has been ignoring.

The hauntological process appears to be complete: Rudy is anachronically haunting Bloom from the position of a younger generation that is now past; he is also denying Bloom the satisfaction of knowing whether or not he is looking at Bloom, and it appears that Rudy is giving the (Jewish) law back to Bloom. Neil Davison sees in moments such as this an opportunity for Bloom to reinvigorate his role as 'Jewish father' (Davison, 1996: 228) – something he performs in looking after Stephen Dedalus, ironically in 'orthodox Samaritan fashion' (16.3). Whilst Catherine Hezser contests Davison's idea that Bloom re-commits to Judaism, particularly given that in 'the following chapters, … [Bloom] repeatedly renounces his Jewishness' (Hezser, 2005: 179),[9] Hezser's position ignores the nuance of Davison's argument that to identify as Jewish for Bloom is to identify positively as an outsider, rather than passively accept the objectification from characters such as the Citizen in 'Cyclops'.[10] Rudy's hauntological appearance at the end of the fifteenth episode, 'Circe', precedes Bloom's charitable fatherliness towards Stephen, narrated in the sixteenth episode, 'Eumaeus'. In this sense, Rudy brings Bloom back to life when reminding him of his mortality.

And so, on two separate occasions, ghosts appear to Bloom in 'Circe' who originally spring to mind in 'Hades'. Moreover, there are clear connections between their appearances in these scenes:

Virág's yellow-streaked face and Rudy's dressing in an Eton suit. I stress this to show the specific connections that these moments have, rather than the myriad other references in *Ulysses* to Virág and Rudy. However, as I have shown, Virág's appearance, although homologically closer to the Ghost–Hamlet relationship than Rudy–Bloom, is less hauntological than the latter. This reveals one of the memorial, troping adjustments that Joyce's text makes to Shakespeare's tragedy: a generational change that enacts an anachronic shift from the power of the dead father to the power of the dead son. This argument finds strength in another of *Ulysses*'s own, this time from Stephen Dedalus in 'Scylla and Charybdis': '[S]o through the ghost of the unquiet father the image of the unliving son looks forth' (9.380–1, 867–70). Far from this *Hamlet* theory being devised by Stephen, my argument shows that Bloom is the first to adjust the generational politics at work in modern Ireland.

Bloom's revival

Neither of the memories of Bloom's relatives emerges from moments of mournfulness, even if they are themselves sad. For example, Bloom's memory of Rudy is inspired not by thoughts of death or childhood mortality, but rather by a moment of respect for Simon Dedalus in the latter's concern for his son:

> – I won't have her bastard of a nephew ruin my son. A counterjumper's son. Selling tapes in my cousin, Peter Paul M'Swiney's. Not likely.
> He ceased. Mr Bloom glanced from his angry moustache to Mr Power's mild face and Martin Cunningham's eyes and beard, gravely shaking. Noisy selfwilled man. Full of his son. He is right. Something to hand on. (6.70–4)

This grudging respect for Simon and his demanding behaviour for his son compels Bloom to think about the future that might have been for Rudy. Inheritance is central in this interaction.

Bloom's memories about his father in 'Hades' are also triggered by one of the Dubliners in the carriage with him. Rather than Simon Dedalus, the focus is now on Martin Cunningham: 'Mr Bloom, about to speak, closed his lips again. Martin Cunningham's large eyes. Looking away now. Sympathetic human man he is. Intelligent. Like Shakespeare's face. Always a good word to say' (6.343–5).

Martin Cunningham is subtly alluded to as a friend of Bloom's who knows more than the others in the carriage about Bloom's personal history (a point stressed at 6.526 ff.).[11] Moreover, whilst both memories are triggered by moments of inspiration inside the carriage, the future-memory of Rudy inspires a yet more positive outlook from Bloom, since he starts recalling how and when Rudy was conceived: 'Must have been that morning in Raymond terrace she was at the window watching the two dogs at it by the wall of the cease to do evil. And the sergeant grinning up. She had that cream gown on with the rip she never stitched. Give us a touch, Poldy. God. I'm dying for it. How life begins' (6.77–81). Behind the ghost of the dead Rudy stands the memory of Rudy's beginning. This shows that Bloom's journey through Hades may be contaminated by a host of ghosts and goblins, but can always return to life and living given the right circumstances. That the memory of his father does not return Bloom to thoughts of life shows the greater potency of Rudy's memory over Virág's: Rudy is not only the hauntologising, but also the disruptive (or *dismemorial*) ghost from whom Bloom inherits. Gibbons writes:

> Joyce maintains the openness to external promptings found in Proust's involuntary memory, but there is also a sense in which they come from *within*: not from within the self, as in Freud, but from the unrequited pasts *of a culture*. Hidden pasts may lie outside the realm of the self, but this is only to say they lie in other selves, in the intersubjectivity of shared pasts and cultural memory. (2015: 75; emphasis in original)

Gibbons's unacknowledged reference to Halbwachs is applicable to Bloom. Not only are his memories conditioned by others' presence – Boots, coroner, Rudy, and Molly – but the memories are summoned to presence by collective, social triggers. The first of these communities is that of the 'spirit world', as Benstock noted above. On his journey, Bloom encounters his own memories, but also comes across a series of others' memories of loved ones and late friends. Additionally, even those in the carriage, let alone those at the graveyard, make mention of memories, or trigger Bloom's memories of Rudy and Virag.

A case in point is Martin Cunningham whose amiable, Shakespearean face twice prompts Bloom to open up to his grief.

On the first occasion, as I have quoted, Bloom can only examine Simon Dedalus's moustache and Jack Power's 'mild face'; however, when he turns to Martin, he is able to connect with his eyes. On the second occasion, Bloom pinpoints Martin Cunningham's 'large eyes' before they look away. These ocular moments remind the reader of the importance of the visual connection and show that all Bloom is after is to look someone in the eyes. This is a motif throughout *Ulysses*, with Gibbons arguing that there is a special intimacy accorded to those who can converse by looking in one another's eyes (Gibbons, 2015: 46–7).[12] However, in neither of the memories does Bloom achieve this, though he comes close with Rudy: 'Me in his eyes'. In this, notwithstanding Bloom's desire to imagine how Rudy would look, Bloom fails to hauntologise Rudy. He gets further in Rudy's ghostly appearance in 'Circe' when Rudy 'gazes unseeing' – on this occasion, however, the subjective ocularity is Rudy's obligation as he hauntologises Bloom.

These ideas confirm that, though mourning for his son and father, Bloom chases the living gaze to help him return to life. They additionally show that although Bloom is made to feel unwelcome at certain points in 'Hades' – such as when John Henry Menton curtly thanks Bloom for pointing out the dint in his hat (6.1026) – his fellow Dubliners do see him as a member of their community, albeit on the fringe. Just as they collectively trigger his memories, he becomes constitutive of theirs, merely by being a part of the social ritual that constitutes the funeral. Bloom equally becomes part of the community of dead in whose presence he now stands.[13] Walking round the cemetery causes Bloom to pause and wonder: 'How many! ... Besides how could you remember everybody?' (6.960–2). In response, as he heads through the cemetery, Bloom seeks evermore outlandish strategies for remembering. These strategies recreate the dismemorial effect that has energised Bloom and restore his agency that hauntology would remove.

Technological strategies

Derrida labels *Hamlet*'s Ghost's armour a 'technical prosthesis, a body foreign to the spectral body that it dresses, dissimulates, and protects, masking even its identity' (Derrida, 1994: 7). The supplementary aspect of the armour adds a layer to the spirit and adds to the Ghost's general dissimulation. But the armour also grants the Ghost material form (q.v. Laqueur, 2015: 64). In this way, the armour is both suspicious, but a necessary element of the Ghost's hauntology. It also signals to Hamlet that the Ghost is *between* the spiritual and profane worlds. As I will show, Bloom himself considers technical prostheses to help maintain the living with the dead, whilst never fully restoring them to life. He does this in order to reproduce artificially the process of dismemorial hauntology that so energises him.

It is first important to note the subtle suspicion of old technology in 'Hades'. Commenting on the pointsmen who work the tramlines, Bloom wonders: 'Couldn't they invent something automatic so that the wheel itself much handier?' He answers his own enquiry: 'Well, but that fellow would lose his job then? Well but then another fellow would get a job making the new invention?' (6.175–9). Later in the chapter, Bloom additionally complains about hearts and their fallibility: 'A pump after all, pumping thousands of gallons of blood every day. One fine day it gets bunged up: and there you are. Lots of them lying around here: lungs hearts, livers. Old rusty pumps: damn the thing else' (6.674–6). In the former passage, Bloom is an economic industrialist, seeing in new technology the possibility of new economies and therefore new employment – hence his veneration. In the latter passage, by contrast, older technology is considered second-rate and frail as its failure leads directly to death.

If Bloom is to be considered a latter-day Hamlet, then the technical prostheses he seeks in Glasnevin to counter the 'rusty pumps' must maintain the liminality of being; or, in Gibbons's terms, they must 'play with the persistence of the ghost under modernity' (Gibbons, 2015: 7). Bloom's first idea focuses on the voice – that medium of authority that the Ghost uses to command Hamlet.

> Well, the voice, yes: gramophone. Have a gramophone in every grave or keep it in the house. After dinner on a Sunday. Put on poor old greatgrandfather. Kraahraark! Hellohellohello amawfullyglad kraark awfullygladaseeagain hellohello amawf krpthsth. (6.962–6)

This comical moment considers a technology that would allow the dead to appear after their death via their voice, and is thus, in Benjamin's terms, 'meet[ing] the beholder halfway'

(Benjamin, 1999: 214); or, in Gibbons's phrasing that is more useful here, is 'linked ... to spectral memory beyond the grave' (Gibbons, 2014: 196).[14] Confusingly, Bloom imagines that the speaking voice would illogically say that it is 'awfullygladaseeagain' (my emphasis): it would imply that it can *see* those to whom it is talking, despite that obvious impossibility. Once more, the ocular is joined with the spectral voice, thereby intensifying its hauntological power.

Moreover, Bloom's suggested use of the gramophone record is identical to some of the earliest analogies of memorial storage. Plato's Socrates instructs in *Theaetetus* to envisage the mind as 'wax' on which memory is imprinted 'as if we were making impressions from signet rings; whatever is imprinted on the block, we remember and know for as long as its image is in the wax' (Plato, 2015: 191c–e).[15] This imprint is the *tupos* of memory. Just as the wax block is a representation of the space for memory, so the waxen record is a technological storage space; the difference lies in the personal accessibility of the former and the communal accessibility of the latter, and perfectly analogises Halbwach's argument about the impossibility of individual memory – all memory is collective. Though Fritz Senn criticises Bloom's choice of gramophone,[16] the deficiencies Senn highlights are central to the hauntological experience that Bloom recreates. Technically, the voice presents an absence to the collective, rendering the dead person indeterminate between life and death, 'ontologiz[ing] remains, to make them present' (Derrida, 1994: 9).

Bloom proceeds to think carefully about the visibility of those brought back to life by technical prostheses. He continues: 'Remind you of the voice like the photograph reminds you of the face. Otherwise you couldn't remember the face after fifteen years, say'[17] (6.966–8). At the heart of Bloom's strategy is the bid to avoid forgetting other people – to avoid oblivion. It is as if he, as well as Hamlet, has received the injunction from the Ghost. As with the record, the photograph is a mediated form of memory that is both distinct from that which or whom it memorialises – it is only a 'remind[er]' of the dead person's face – and yet its mediation renders it immemorial because it relies on no living being in order to exist. Highlighting the deathly aspect of the photograph, Maud Ellmann writes that 'Through the photographic image we survive the grave but also die before our death, disenfleshed before our hearts have ceased to beat' (2004: 83). Roland Barthes's (1980) meditation on photography corroborates this idea of the photograph's intimate relation to death. Not only in the photograph 'taken of me' does Barthes reveal that 'Death is the *eidos*' but also any photograph that acts as replacement for the monument has as its *punctum* – 'A photograph's *punctum* is that accident which pricks me (but also bruises me, is poignant to me)' (Barthes, 2000: 15, 27) – the idea that '*he is going to die*. I read at the same time: *This will be* and *this has been*; I observe with horror an anterior future of which death is the stake. ... Whether or not the subject is already dead, every photograph is this catastrophe' (Barthes, 2000: 96; emphasis in original). With this indeterminate temporality and liminal occupation between life and death, Bloom's ideas approach a man-inspired hauntology.[18] Gibbons writes that in revolutionary Ireland, 'Holding on to the now and then in one frame, the capacity of the photograph to suspend the flow of time opens up the present to unrequited pasts, re-connecting with other narratives' (Gibbons, 2016: 15) – that is, with other futures. Ellen Carol Jones corroborates this idea when she argues that 'Joyce's texts examine how public "memory" is created by projecting a future not yet realized – a projection that is, paradoxically, also a "retrospective arrangement"' (Jones, 2010: 4). Here, also, is dismemory. The spectres raised in the record and photograph are both temporally and spatially liminal and out of joint, and it is at this juncture that the individual memory transfers into a collectively accessible consciousness.[19] This archive, as it were, would enable the dead to hauntologise everyone in Dublin, offering an alternative to the statues of the nationalist figures that were erected by the establishment (often British, colonial) authorities that the funeral cortège passed at the beginning of 'Hades'. This hauntologising archive also validates my theory of the memorial intertext – *Hamlet* in this case – hauntologising *Ulysses*. Ellmann's conclusion to all of this is salient here for a number of reasons: 'To be or not to be is no longer the question' (Ellmann, 2004: 83).

Conclusion: Bloom's 'eternal validity'

I argue that the question has transformed in Bloom's mind into a definitive statement: 'To be, *and* not to be.' The shift from 'or' to 'and' mirrors Bloom's fascination with the technological prostheses that render the memorial ghosts both dead *and* living at once. This eases his mourning, apparently, and though Bloom leaves the cemetery still separate from his fellow Dubliners (6.1027–8), he does so with renewed vitality: 'The gates glimmered in front: still open. Back to the world again. ... How grand we are this morning!' (6.995–1033). Whereas Hamlet's relationship with the Ghost led to his reduced agency, Bloom's consideration of technological prostheses restores his agency in spite of the imbalanced hauntology. The opportunity to access more readily and create collective memory puts a spring in Bloom's step.

Søren Kierkegaard theorises this shift from questionable 'or' to liminal 'and' in his 1843 essay 'Either/Or'. Kierkegaard's 'A' analogises it through agricultural cultivation, claiming that when the land's potential for growth and harvest is considered, 'every particular change still falls under the universal rule of the relation between *recollecting* and *forgetting*' (Kierkegaard, 2000: 56; emphasis in original). It is important to ask whether it is possible to choose both recollecting and forgetting: whether in forgetting the liveliness of people, they can still be re-membered back into the world. In answer to this question, Kierkegaard writes: 'But what is it, then, that I choose – is it this or that? No, for I choose absolutely, and I choose absolutely precisely by having chosen not to choose this or that. I choose the absolute, and what is the absolute? It is myself in my eternal validity' (Kierkegaard, 2000: 79). In Bloom's choice to have the dead nearly living, and therefore both dead and alive at the same time, he maintains his own potential for being in his 'eternal validity'. Bloom's predilection for liminality in 'Hades' maintains his own *potentiality*, his *own liminality*, though with the stress on his inability to die absolutely, rather than the ability to be brought back to life.[20] He, like the ghosts he revives, becomes liminal in his remembering: he partially joins the community of the dead, just as they are summoned to meet him. This is the process of the *nekuya*, such as when Odysseus meets Achilleus, or Aeneas meets Dido: it is modernised with Bloom (via *Hamlet*) in 'Hades'.

Kierkegaard further describes a position such as Bloom's as 'remember[ing] poetically' (Kierkegaard, 2000: 79), a process that prevents nostalgia – the painful return of memories. Since mourning is a process in which memories return painfully, it is possible to equate 'remembering poetically' with completing the work of mourning. Here hauntology is seen to expedite mourning. Critically, remembering poetically is *not* the same as writing poetry. Rather, it needs to be considered as closer to an ethic of *poiesis*. In Plato's *Symposium* Diotima schools Socrates in *Eros* and the love of absolute beauty. An analogy for erotic love is *poiesis*, through which Diotima explains: 'There is poetry, which, as you know, is complex and manifold. All creation or passage of non-being into being is poetry or making, and the processes of all art are creative; and the masters of arts are all poets or makers' (Plato, 1978: 205b–c).[21] A commitment to *poiesis* is a commitment to perpetual becoming, to thriving in liminality between being and non-being, life and death, the past servicing the future – a commitment to 'eternal validity'. *Poiesis*, though similar to the classical idea of *tekhnè* – an art or skill more concerned with end product than process[22] – differs in the idea of mediation. John Frow sees in τέχνη (*tekhnè*) and technological forms of memory a mediation that implies 'institutional conditions of existence' (Frow, 1997: 230). To suggest that the photograph and record are 'Monuments of unageing intellect', to quote Yeats's 'Sailing to Byzantium' (Yeats, 1997b: l. 8), renders them static, ignoring their potential for maintaining potential (just as with the Ghost's visor): their *poiesis*. 'This is no longer or, rather, not yet action (*praxis*)', writes Hannah Arendt (1998: 195) of Socratic political discourse, though relevant to Bloom here, 'but making (*poiesis*), which they prefer because of its greater reliability'. Bloom is thus the reliable, master craftsman of *Ulysses*'s Dublin.

And so, to suggest that Bloom is remembering poetically changes the common perception of him. Bloom is nominally considered the Everyman in *Ulysses*, to Stephen's poet-hero; Stephen is often compared to Hamlet. However, in this chapter, I have shown that Bloom is Hamletic through his *poietic* mourning which in 'Hades' is overcome by more, not less death; but death that, in being brought back to life, hauntologises Bloom. The technological prostheses of the record and the photograph represent versions of remembering poetically that allow the representation of those long dead to those who still live. This hauntology is exemplified in 'Hades', but is valid throughout the novel, and is even cemented by the appearance of the ghosts of Bloom's father and son in 'Circe'. Memory, understood in this way both as intertext and impetus for personal life, is present in 'Hades' in spite of its explicit absences. In fact, 'Hades' gives the model of memory for *Ulysses* as a whole and shows that the dead – be they dead texts or dead characters – still constitute an irrepressible dismemory and necessary part of *Ulysses*.

As I have shown, anachrony and 'time [being] out of joint' are characteristic of all of the aforementioned analyses: a dead past is giving the law to the living present. It is important also to pay attention to the role of the anachronic future in hauntology. Importantly, through the *poietic* technology, Bloom would create an 'eternal validity' – the revenant dead would survive *ad infinitum*. Just as Rudy and Virág appear again in 'Circe', as if thrown forward in the text from 'Hades', so too would Bloom's communally accessible archive of memory be available in the future; this recalls the endless openness of Synge's treatment of Celtic myth, as instantiated in Christy's offstage futurity. Rudy's hauntology of Bloom allows the latter to consider a method of surviving into the future without the more natural opportunities that patrilineal inheritance affords. In this final sense, memory in 'Hades' is not just about reviving the past or summoning up ghosts of the dead, but also about remembering faultlessly into the future – via a liminal, eternal existence. The Ireland that proceeds from this is not Revivalist, but *hauntological*, taking its past along with it as it becomes a Free State in 1922. Whereas the Revivalist technique was to infuse the present with an idealised past – an idea critiqued in Synge's *Playboy*, as I described above – Bloom's Ireland is a nation in which the past lives alongside its citizens, readily accessible at any point along the journey. This disproves Pine's argument that 'The haunting of the present also suggests that the cultural obsession with the past is damaging' (Pine, 2011: 27). Rather than 'reviving' the past – and thereby signalling the distance the past maintains from the present – by positing the past in a dismemorial, hauntological relationship with the present, the modern Irish nation-state is coeval with, and haunted by, its past *eidola* which are ever ready to be remembered.

Notes

1 The term καταβασις, *katabasis*, more exactly describes the visit to the underworld, but *nekuya* is used as a generic term for summoning and conversing with the dead.

2 As Stephen advocates at 2.377.

3 Though the Ghost's singularity is repeated, as is obvious in the text and is accounted for in Derrida's argument. See Derrida (1994: 10).

4 Also as a corrective to Francis Fukuyama's slightly earlier *The End of History and the Last Man* (1992).

5 On this clear misreading, Royle asks: 'Why does [Derrida] put so much emphasis on something that runs counter to the words that actually appear in Shakespeare's text? Is it possible (such would be the feeling I have, and one of the possibilities I am interested in excavating here) that his concern with the visor-effect is traced, spectralized, "supervised" by a certain mole? Isn't that above all what the figure of the mole evokes, at least in the West, namely an uncanniness around the question of seeing, an uncertainty about whether the mole sees or not, or, if it sees, how it does? Might this in turn throw another light or another sense on the logic according to which Hamlet addresses the figure with the visor-effect as a mole?' (Royle, 2003: 248).

6 Consider Hamlet's 'Must I remember?' (I.ii.143) when he is explaining the power of his mourning and its relation to his mother's hasty remarriage.

7 See Marcel Proust in Steinberg: '[A] fragment of life in unsullied preservation ... which asked only that it should be set free, that it should come and augment my wealth of life and poetry' (Steinberg, 1979: 87).

8 It is common to kiss the prayer book if it has been dropped on the floor, and when closing the book at the end of a prayer service. It is also customary to use the fringes of the prayer shawl to touch the Torah parchment prior to kissing the fringes upon reading the Torah during communal services.

9 For example, See 16.1082–5, 16.1119–20, and 17.530–1.

10 See 12.1131–2, 1156–9, 1430, and 1491.

11 See Luca Crispi (2012: 22).

12 Gibbons also analogises this with the reader's relation to the text she reads: she must look for Dublin's and *Ulysses*'s returned gaze – i.e. get to know its character by reading it.
     See also, Emmanuel Levinas's lecture 'Dying for...':

> Or, on the contrary, would not *to be*, that verb, signify – in *being-there* – non-indifference, obsession by the *other*, a search and a vow of peace? Of a peace that would be, not the silence of non-interference in which the freedom of the artistic act takes pleasure, and in which the beautiful creates silence, maintains silence, and protects it, but rather a peace in which the eyes of the other are sought, in which his look awakens responsibility? A peace that Western man has wished for, and in which he has sought fulfillment just as much

as in independence or the artistic act. Does not the memory of ethical values – perhaps grown dim in the 'Scriptures', which are proclaimed 'obsolete' – solicit humanity even in modern times, in the
form of literature, which is inspired by this memory and widely
disseminated? (Levinas, 2006: 179–80; emphasis in original)

13 It is therefore reminiscent of Gabriel Conroy's awkward welcome into
the community of spirits in Joyce's story, 'The Dead': '[I]n the partial
darkness he imagined he saw the form of a young man standing under
a dripping tree. Other forms were near. His soul had approached that
region where dwell the vast hosts of the dead. He was conscious of, but
could not apprehend, their wayward and flickering existence. His own
identity was fading out into a grey impalpable world: the solid world
itself which these dead had one time reared and lived in, was dissolving
and dwindling' (Joyce, 2008a: 176).

14 In this sense, Gibbons elsewhere cites Steven Connor's argument that
since the gramophone voice 'is not *live* … Bloom's imagining of a conversation from the grave is closer to a telephone than a gramophone'
(Gibbons, 2015: 8; emphasis in original). This correction emphasises
the asymmetry of the encounter in 'Hades'.

15 Cf. Cicero (2001: 219), who also uses the wax impression analogy.

16 'The inconsistencies are grotesque. Also, the greatgranfather [*sic*] could
neither have hoped to see his listeners nor take any pleasure from this
communication, since he was already dead' (Senn, 1992: 233–4).

17 Gibbons additionally goes so far as to argue that Rudy's appearance
in 'Circe' links to contemporary interest in 'spirit photography'. See
Gibbons (2015: 159–64).

18 This strategy also circumvents the dangers of the failure of involuntary
memory, when 'we cannot give a name to the sensation, or call on it,
and it does not come alive' (Proust in Steinberg, 1979: 87).

19 It is also worth emphasising that Virág's and Rudy's appearances in 'Circe'
adhere to this temporal displacement by appearing in the same accoutrements much later in the novel than their reference point in 'Hades'.

20 There are twin liminal positions: the dead are made liminal when being
brought back to near-life through technology; the living are made liminal when absolute death (i.e. oblivion) is denied to them.

21 I use this edition of Plato here for its clearer enunciation of *poiesis*'s
intimate relation to non-being and being. Diotima does immediately
after this quotation specifically say that poetry – 'music and metre' – is
necessary in order to be a poet. Nevertheless, my point is that Bloom
adopts a poetic sensibility, in which continued generation and liminality
are privileged.

22 See Aristotle (2011: 305).

3

'Someone wholly other':
John Banville's *Ghosts*

Henceforth, he was bound to death by a surreptitious friendship.
— from *The Instant of My Death*
by Maurice Blanchot

Introduction

In the previous chapters, I explored the power of memory to alter the present through the logic of the ghost. In *Playboy*, Christy became a memory himself, and therefore dispelled the power of his own father to control him. Politically, however, Christy could not survive onstage as this revolutionary ghost, and so took his politics away with him. He became a ghostly dismemory offstage and, in the mould of *Hamlet*'s Ghost, all the more powerful for it. Christy's behaviour reveals a macropolitics of revolution, becoming as powerful as *Hamlet*'s Ghost. By contrast, Bloom's is a micropolitics that endows him with greater assuredness on leaving Glasnevin Cemetery. Compelled by the imagined dismemorial future of his son, this father imagines better prospects for himself; how apt that he achieves this in Prospect Cemetery. This attitude allows Bloom to exist *poietically*, by focusing on regeneration and potentiality, rather than being put down by the negative attitudes of certain members of the Dublin community. His ripostes to the Citizen in the 'Cyclops' episode perhaps emblematise the Bloom who manoeuvres through Dublin society so deftly. From memory, Bloom is *hauntologised*, just like, after his confrontation with the memorial Ghost, Hamlet spends some time trying to 'find himself'.

In this chapter, I continue to examine the importance of ghosts, the dead, and their relation to memory. However, by exploring the postmodern *Ghosts* (1993), I show the preference for memory is no longer to accept its dismissal, as in *Playboy*, nor to be revived by it, as in 'Hades', but to live it fully in a continuous present. To disremember thus becomes a mode of being. Ricoeur (2006: 8) points out (with Aristotle behind him) that memory tacitly points to a past event, but in *Ghosts* the temporal moment of memory is constantly being reforged in the present. A parallel, present reality is the space from which Freddie, the narrator of *Ghosts*, has escaped. In this way, Freddie lives as if in the realm of spectrality throughout. Moreover, when Freddie declares the death of his son during the course of the novel, it shows how he would rather live in the fantasy world of memory and imagination than engage with the real. His model in this regard is the Ghost, rather than Hamlet: the father, rather than the son, becomes the hero. In doing so, Freddie becomes master over death, thus giving him the ability to write.

Ghosts begins with castaways arriving at an island and is strongly reminiscent of *The Tempest*. While Mark O'Connell (2013: 84) and Hedda Friberg-Harnesk (2018: 154) argue that the narrator is of a Prospero-type, Elke D'Hoker figures Freddie as 'a very unconvincing Caliban' and 'clearly a Prospero' (D'Hoker, 2018: 230, 235), following Hedwig Schwall (1997: passim) who sees Freddie as a combination of Prospero, Ariel, Ferdinand, and Caliban. However, that connection ignores the series of 'Lists' on the first page, which both serve to describe the listing boat, but also recalls *Hamlet*'s Ghost's 'List, list, O list' (I.v.22), leading me to argue that Freddie remembers the Ghost from *Hamlet*. Freddie is a former convict whose murder of a housemaid (as documented in the 'prequel' *The Book of Evidence* (1989)) sent him to prison. By the time of the *Ghosts* narrative, Freddie has been released and runs out his parole on a sparsely populated island off the coast of Ireland. He lives in a big house with two other occupants: Professor Kreutznaer, an art historian, and Licht, a local lad whose shadowy presence unsettles the others in the house. On the island are a motley crew of stranded mainlanders, among their number a nanny, Flora, and her two charges,[1] and also someone spectrally emerging from Freddie's pre-murderous past, someone whom Freddie is forced to confront: Felix. In that confrontation with this memorial emissary, Freddie explains his own becoming a ghost.

'Worlds within worlds'

While Synge's Christy will thrive offstage, and Joyce's Bloom is inspired by and enjoys the idea of perpetual non-being, Freddie also likes the idea of other worlds. His island retreat is just such an other world. O'Connell claims the island 'is both a place of self-imposed isolation from the world and a new territory in which Freddie can reinvent himself' (O'Connell, 2011: 334). The island represents a liminal space that welcomes natives (such as Licht), self-exiles (such as Professor Kreutznaer), and those shipwrecked. Freddie's interest in these liminal, other worlds extends when he considers the mirror:

> Worlds within worlds. They bleed into each other. I am at once here and there, then and now, as if by magic. I think of the stillness that lives in the depths of mirrors. It is not our world that is reflected there. It is another place entirely, another universe, cunningly made to mimic ours. Anything is possible there; even the dead may come back to life. Flaws develop in the glass, patches of silvering fall away and reveal the inhabitants of that parallel, inverted world going about their lives all unawares. And sometimes the glass turns to air and they step through it without a sound and walk into *my* world. (Banville, 1998b: 55)

For Freddie, this mirrored world intermingles with his world: mutually visitable and mutable. This is not merely spatial, but temporally conditioned too, 'For is it not possible that somewhere in this crystalline multiplicity of worlds, in this infinite, mirrored regression, there is a place where the dead have not died, and I am innocent?' (Banville, 1998b: 173). In other words, Freddie wishes to alter the past; failing that, all he can do is change the memory of the past. Time therefore becomes unstable and no longer identical with itself, and the past becomes something that is both central to the narrator's current being and also that which cannot be relied on: Freddie's time is out of joint. This line from *Hamlet* forms a critical part of Derrida's criticism of the play since Hamlet's railing against the Ghost's injunction is directed against time, not the Ghost. Hamlet also laments that it is a 'cursèd spite / That ever I was born to set it right' (I.v.186–7). Not only is time out of joint, but Hamlet's existence rests on his task to stabilise time, or events in time. This 'cursèd spite' derives from the Ghost: spectral time is unstable time, rocking the real and living present. Spectral temporality, in other words, allows a life to be lived differently from the now: re-imagined worlds can become real.

This is explicitly exemplified near the end of *Ghosts* when Felix, one of those shipwrecked on the island, is heading with Freddie to embark on the boat that will take Felix and the other passengers back to the mainland; Freddie is to stay on the island. In this scene, the mirror is breached, creating a new space of potential existence: 'It was as if all along we had been walking side by side, with something between us, some barrier, thin and smooth and deceptive as a mirror, that now was broken, and I had stepped into his world, or he into mine, or we had both entered some third place that belonged to neither of us' (Banville, 1998b: 241). Joseph McMinn signals that for Banville's narrators 'Imagination and memory are their only escape routes' (McMinn, 1988: 23).[2] Imagination and memory become a third space of spectrality, and return us to the twin poles of Socratic philosophy of memory: the Platonic embedding of memory within imagination, or Aristotelian enclosing of imagination within memory. 'These are the two versions of the aporia of imagination and memory', writes Ricoeur, 'from which we can never completely extricate ourselves' (Ricoeur, 2006: 7). Freddie refuses to attempt that extrication, instead finding a way to live, dismemorially, within the third place's paradoxes, and within a 'curious ontological position' (Murphy, 2020: 113).

This third place shows that ontology in *Ghosts* can be and is governed by something that ghosts the narrative and haunts the narrator. The third space is also a space of no time, when things are no longer out of joint; it is a space of resolution. In order to be a space of resolved time, it can be said to collapse the time of imagination – prospection – and memory – retrospection. The dynamic between Freddie and Felix is separate from the main strand of the novel: Felix threatens to bring Freddie's secrets into the open. As such, Felix nearly disrupts Freddie's existence on the island; however, the 'third space' into which Felix and Freddie enter is not new to Freddie, but Freddie has instead supported and resided in a third space of memory throughout his stay on the island, co-inhabiting with the art expert Professor Kreutznaer. My argument corroborates O'Connell's idea that 'for much of the novel [Freddie] is a kind of spectral, omniscient god presence' (O'Connell, 2011: 335). Only when Felix threatens Freddie is Freddie's potency temporarily destabilised. In the preceding passage, however, Freddie's equipoise is re-established and he is able, at the end of the novel, to continue living in the third space of memory in which he continues to re-imagine himself. Freddie's appeal is to *Hamlet*'s Ghost, the directorial, modern sovereign who nevertheless remains offstage. In this, Banville's text advocates a private, personal modernity contingent upon a modern space that permits spectrality, but which nevertheless privileges the individual citizen. In that privileging, memory is at stake as Freddie detaches it from the past, instead seeing memory and imagination as interchangeable – a 'double imbroglio' (Ricoeur, 2006: 50) – and thus undoing centuries of nuanced and delicate metaphysics (q.v. Ricoeur, 2006: 44 ff.). This is to disremember. Rather than the aphoristic, 'having a great future behind me', Freddie has great memories ahead of him.

Perhaps the first is the most important of these memorial third worlds. Freddie enters while preparing to leave the mainland and to go to the island. While narrating how he turned up on the island, Freddie tells the story of his release from prison, and the journey he takes with a fellow convict, 'Billy the butcher' (Banville, 1998b: 157). Billy takes Freddie via his childhood home, Coolgrange, in which Freddie's estranged wife and son now live. Freddie returns to his past. Entering Coolgrange, Freddie is confused, recognising his own absence as an uncomfortable presence, as though he sees himself as a ghost in a space to which he does not truly belong. He senses that even his memory has been excised from this place. He implores someone in reality to help him, starting: 'And now as I stood in the midst of my own absence, in the birthplace that had rid itself of me utterly, I murmured a little prayer, and said, O, if you are really there, bright brother, in your more real reality, think of me, turn all your stern attentions on me, even for an instant, and make *me* real, too' (Banville, 1998b: 181; emphasis original). Freddie's prayers are answered in the arrival of his son, Van, that forces Freddie to live two moments simultaneously. The man and his double exist in these moments, when Freddie either does or does not embrace Van:

> In my imagination I got up out of myself, like a swimmer clambering out of water, and took a staggering step towards him, my arms outstretched, and pressed him to my breast and sobbed. ... In reality I am still sitting on the window-sill, with my hands with their whitened

knuckles clamped on my knees, looking up at him and inanely, help-
lessly smiling; I never was one for embraces. (Banville, 1998b: 84)

Freddie's 'swimmer clambering out of water' is reminiscent of his
mirror analogy: the site for another world that resembles our own
but differs in its reality. This shows Freddie metaphysically entering
the third space of the spectre.

The subsequent scene is significant. When Freddie returns to
Billy, they talk about Freddie's son. Freddie responds tersely to
Billy's questioning: '"I told you", I said, "I have no family. I had a
son once, but he died"' (Banville, 1998b: 197). Freddie metaphysically kills his own son. Much like in *Playboy* and 'Hades', Freddie's
son is dismissed from the narrative permitted onstage and centre
stage – but the space that Van enters is not the spectral world of
the Ghost and Rudy. Instead, Van is dismissed from the narrative
of *Ghosts* on to the centre stage of reality; Freddie is left to play
protagonist in his own story characterised by the very things reality
leaves behind: Christy Mahon, Rudy Bloom, *Hamlet*'s Ghost. In this
space is represented the unrepresentable, the undecidable that conditioned *Hamlet*'s narrative. In Agamben's terms, we are presented
with the 'nonrelational', 'the principle of every juridical localisa-
tion' (Agamben, 1998: 19). In short, Freddie is the protagonist of
memory, that thing that is only representable in history or fiction:
instead of representing it, however, Freddie plays with it, turning it
into dismemory. By murdering his son, Freddie changes how his life
is remembered to others: to the characters who populate his 'real'
life, Freddie is now only a memory: death has taken him.

Productive death

Murder is productive for Freddie here, much as for Claudius in
Hamlet: 'A bloody deed – almost as bad, good mother, / As kill a
king and marry with his brother' (III.iv.37–8). In a Heideggerian
vein, Maurice Blanchot also writes about the productive death and
its relation to art and artists, dually applicable here to *Hamlet* and
to *Ghosts*:

> Oui, il faut mourir dans le mourant, la vérité l'exige, mais il faut
> être capable de se satisfaire de la mort, de trouver dans la suprême

insatisfaction la suprême satisfaction et de maintenir, à l'instant de
mourir, la clarté de regard qui vient d'un tel équilibre. (Blanchot,
1968: 108)

(Yes, you have to die during dying, truth demands it; but you have
to be capable of being satisfied by death, of finding, in the supreme
dissatisfaction, a supreme satisfaction and being capable of maintaining, in the exact instant of dying, a clarity of look which comes
from such an equipoise.)[3]

Here Freddie assumes the equipoise of one who has rendered death
possible, assuming sovereignty over death and benefiting from what
ensues. Blanchot's explanation pertains to writers and, as we shall
see, Freddie becomes a writer of sorts.

Hamlet, too, decides that he must also commit to oncoming death
to configure it as freedom, and not imprisonment. 'If it be, 'tis not
to come. If it be not to come, it will be now. If it be not now, yet it
will come', says Hamlet. 'The readiness is all, since no man of aught
he leaves knows what is't to leave betimes. Let be' (V.ii.198–201).
Rather than the death towards which Hamlet's father did not know
he was heading, Hamlet now makes of death a liberty and a possibility – specifically through words. 'In "Let be"', writes Carol Rutter,
'Hamlet achieves the knowledge he needs to live—then exits to the
duel' (Rutter, 2001: 144). Hamlet is thus satisfied by a death in which
memory is set free. So too is Freddie thrilled by living a life in which
fixed links between living, dying, and memory are contested and
renegotiated. However, Freddie appears to improve Hamlet's ideas:
Hamlet sees in death a freedom from worrying about memory –
especially after he commits to remembering the Ghost's injunction –
where Freddie sees in Van's death the opportunity to free himself
from the living and instead become a dismemory (a future, disruptive memory) to his family. Freddie sees in becoming dismemory a
freedom from living. In this regard, the crossover between Hamlet
and Freddie is figured as an exchange between death and memory.
For Freddie, the opposite of living is memory – just as it is for
Hamlet's Ghost. Freddie as a ghost is the true birth-child of memory
and death that Yeats had described in *Anima Mundi*.

In his (non-)encounter at Coolgrange, Freddie not only engages
with Van but also tacitly remembers the past father–son relationships that are operative in Irish literature such as those between

Christy and Mahon and Rudy and Bloom. Christy saves his father but only to overthrow and tame him in offstage, spectral space, and Bloom derives his future happiness from his late son's mortality. And at this juncture in *Ghosts* Freddie considers the possibility 'of being saved through [Van], as if the son by his mere existence might absorb and absolve the sins of the father' (Banville, 1998b: 185). *Ghosts* is itself ghosted by these earlier literary ghosts and their father–son relationships; *Ghosts* remembers that linear progression from *Hamlet* through to *Playboy* and *Ulysses*, even if it destabilises that genealogy.[4] *Ghosts* remembers from these texts the notion of the son as a means to establish the ground for innovation. Through remembering, *Ghosts* innovates memory.

Refusing the possibility of embracing his son lets Freddie enter the spectral space in which imagined memory becomes his reality. However, Freddie's negotiation of that world also requires a full acceptance of the doubles that he experiences. When I consider doubles, I am also thinking about the double-death outlined by Blanchot:

> Cela revient à penser qu'il y a comme une double mort, dont l'une circule dans les mots de possibilité, de liberté, qui a comme extrême horizon la liberté de mourir et le pouvoir de se risquer mortellement – et dont l'autre est l'insaisissable, ce que je ne puis saisir, qui n'est liée à *moi* par aucune relation d'aucune sorte, qui ne vient jamais, vers laquelle je ne me dirige pas.[5] (Blanchot, 1968: 126; emphasis in original)

> (The one death circulates in the words of possibility, of liberty, and that has at its extreme horizon the freedom of death and the power to risk fatality; the other death is elusive, that which I do not know how to grasp, which is not linked to *me* by a single relation of any sort, which never arrives, towards which I never direct myself.)

For Blanchot, these double-deaths are linked intimately to art and the artist. Donald G. Marshall, writing about Blanchot's *L'éspace littéraire*, might as well be describing Banville's Freddie when he explains that the 'impersonal death' forged in the process of writing 'is also the source of imagination's transforming movement in the work of writing (*l'oeuvre*)' (Marshall, 1985: 234). This sense of the double-death – one of assailable freedom, the other of elusiveness – conditions Freddie's relation to society. The question of doubles is also visible in *Hamlet*. The Ghost confirms to Hamlet that 'I am thy father's spirit, / Doomed for a certain term to walk the night' (I.v.9–10). As I have already outlined, this is not Hamlet's father but rather his spirit – a representative, an emissary. Hamlet's decision to believe the Ghost or not is not only conditioned by Derrida's argument of asymmetry; it is also conditioned by the idea that the Ghost is separate from King Hamlet. King Hamlet is doubled, in short.[6] Hamlet's decision to believe the Ghost leaves the play underpinned throughout by a perpetual uncertainty: *Hamlet*, the most modern of early modern plays, hinges and is built on an undecidability. Kiberd explains how it is the Ghost – the spectral sovereign – who governs the play's plot, but Freddie gives another version of this: 'Hamlet's father made what I cannot but think were excessive calls on filial piety. Yet, for myself, I know I would be grateful for any intercourse with the dead, no matter how baleful their stares or unavoidable their pale, pointing fingers' (Banville, 1998b: 83). Freddie's slippage between father and Ghost reveals his view that the Ghost can indeed be a living and not a dead figure. His desire to 'intercourse with the dead' suggests that Freddie's belief is in living spirits, and that it is dead people who walk the earth, and not their emissaries or ghosts. Hamlet's father, in Freddie's reading, controls Hamlet and makes the stage his own. The play is called *Hamlet* but it is the father's 'excessive calls on filial piety' that give rise to Hamlet's revenge story and as such the father is the director of the onstage action. Freddie sees in the Ghost the possibility of being in charge – but of being in charge without relying on the son to execute his will. In this sense, *Ghosts* offers a father–son narrative that improves on *Hamlet*.

Freddie does not wish to die himself, keeping mortality at arm's length; and yet his existence is premised on a death that gives him life. This death is his son's verbalised murder that does not happen in 'reality' but 'circulates in the words of possibility, of liberty'. But the double that first assails Freddie is one he is unable to control. In *The Book of Evidence* (1989), the narrative of which ghosts and precedes *Ghosts*, Freddie calls himself 'bifurcate' (Banville, 1998a: 95). Though Freddie initially claims that his Other is an 'invented … grotesque version' of himself (Banville, 1998b: 176), he later concedes that he houses an Other within himself named Bunter. Whilst O'Connell (2013) and Schwall (1997) touch on Freddie's

bifurcation, they both skip over Bunter as this Other, instead focusing on Felix as Freddie's Other, or split self. My priorities are different, for this internalised other governs Freddie, most notably when
Freddie commits the murder of Josie Bell in *The Book of Evidence*.
Freddie wonders:

> Perhaps that is the essence of my crime, of my culpability, that I let
> things get to that stage, that I had not been vigilant enough, had not
> been enough of a dissembler, that I left Bunter to his own devices,
> and thus allowed him, fatally, to understand that he was free, that
> the cage door was open, that nothing was forbidden, that everything
> was possible. (Banville, 1998a: 143)

Bunter is evidence of Freddie's dual personality and is Freddie's psyche let loose, an equivalent of Freud's *id* controlling the *ego*. Schwall
corroborates that Banville's protagonists 'are utterly dividual, their
split is their essence' (Schwall, 2006: 120), while O'Connell comments usefully on the detached, third-person narration of Freddie's
murderous act in *Ghosts* (Banville, 1998b: 83–4) (which formed
the main narrative of *The Book of Evidence*). 'In this way', argues
O'Connell, Freddie 'places himself at a double remove from his
actions, from the intractable reality of himself: not only were these
crimes not really committed, it was not him who committed them'
(O'Connell, 2013: 99). In a critical parallel, Geoffrey Hartman
describes Blanchot's 'ghostly Other [as] the fictional double to the
point of passing from a state of negative to that of real transcendence, as the writer is tempted to pass from the first person (*Je*) to the
third person (*Il*) form, and thus into full estrangement' (Hartman,
1961: 12). Hartman perfectly describes Bunter as Freddie's doubled,
ghostly Other who inheres in Freddie, rather than existing outside
him.

Since Bunter governs Freddie, Bunter threatens because he
removes from Freddie his sovereignty over himself – his ability to
control his own actions. If Freddie is to be a god, then Freddie must
somehow tame Bunter in order to become a modern citizen in full
self-control – the ability to conceive of and fashion himself fully
as an individual is one of Hamlet's chief, modern characteristics,
after all. Bunter destabilises Freddie's ability to control himself
and, therefore, Freddie's existence in the modern world. 'Perhaps',
Freddie wonders, 'this is how I shall go mad in the end, perhaps

I shall just fly apart like this finally and be lost to myself forever' (Banville, 1998b: 177). The internal ghost, in other words, is lawless according to the law of the conscious; however, it gives its own law and decides to kill Josie Bell. By the time of *Ghosts*, Bunter is no longer simply the *id* driving the *ego*; instead, Bunter is the *memory* of Freddie's past actions.

As outlined above, Freddie learns to control Bunter – to control memory – by entering into the third space of the liminal island. Early in *Ghosts*, Freddie notes how he had changed since spending time in prison (another liminal space):

> I was not at all the same person that I had been a decade before (is the oldster in his dotage the same that he was when he was an infant swaddled in his truckle bed?). A slow sea-change had taken place. I believe that over those ten years of incarceration – life, that is, minus time off for good, for exemplary behaviour – I had evolved into an infinitely more complex organism. (Banville, 1998b: 21–2)

That complexity as I see it creates a being who is contemporary with his own memory, whose present is in constant battle with his past – a being who actively disremembers. Freddie has realised that he has other options open to him. Seeing his freedom from prison as an 'objectless liberty' and a 'burden', he wishes to 'forget the past, … give up all hope of retrieving my lost selves … And then be something new' (Banville, 1998b: 195). Freddie indeed does become something new in the third space, and the new Freddie is characterised by his ability to control the doubled Other. By manipulating memory in the present, by disremembering, Freddie is able to target and direct himself towards Blanchot's death that exists in words of possibility and liberty; equally, through words of possibility and liberty, Freddie controls memory in the present. This immanence, aligning closely with a Judeo-Christian religiosity that inheres in God and the Messiah alone, offers another connection between *Ghosts* and Synge's *Playboy*, where a sense of Hamlet's martyrdom and the abuse of the trope of the Second Coming is repeated (the Ghost in *Hamlet*; Old Mahon in *Playboy*). In *Ghosts*, Freddie both abuses the messianic return and casts another (his son) as a sacrificial victim in his pursuit of survival and authority. Though apparently successful, Freddie's approach is also daunting in its hubris.

Freddie's doubles

Bunter is the first of three doubles. Professor Kreutznaer is an art expert for whom Freddie ghostwrites and Jean Vaublin is the painter on whom the Professor is an expert and who has painted the contested painting *Le monde d'or*. In *Ghosts* Freddie depicts his own (doubled) version of *Le monde d'or*, thereby becoming ghostpainter, and inserting himself into the history of the painting itself. Both Kreutznaer and Vaublin have masteries over the past: Kreutznaer as the authenticator of art and Vaublin as artistic creator, endowing something from nothing. Vaublin is the Dutch master who, in his later years, feared that someone was following him around the city, haunting him and badly impersonating his paintings, exaggerating his flaws and inadequacies in technique. This impostor becomes Vaublin's double:

> All the experts, Professor Kreutznaer included, agree that it was all a delusion, a phantasm spawned by fever and exhaustion in that last, desperate summer of the painter's brief life. ... I seem to hear mock laughter, he wrote, and someone is always standing in the corner behind me, yet when I turn there is no one there. (Banville, 1998b: 128)

In the figure of the painter-as-sovereign we must hold the notion of the doubled painter in our minds, his being haunted by something outside himself that is also a version of himself; Vaublin is alleged to be ghosted by his own double, not unlike Freddie. Moreover, given Vaublin's mastery over art, *Le monde d'or* represents art's greatest achievement. And yet *Le monde d'or* is the painting under scrutiny in *Ghosts* for its inauthenticity since *Le monde d'or* might be the product of Vaublin's double. Freddie conjectures that it might even have been painted by the Professor, the Vaublinian expert. Having said that, we might pin the true Vaublinian expert as the novel's painter – Freddie himself. Given the short third part of the novel in which the visitors to the island are described in terms of figures in *Le monde d'or*, the novel *Ghosts* charts Freddie's ghostpainting *Le monde d'or* himself. As Schwall corroborates, '"Le Monde d'Or" functions as a "mise en abyme" of the whole story' (Schwall, 1997: 296; and q.v. Murphy, 2020: 116).

In her article 'Ghostwriting', Spivak responds to Derrida's *Specters of Marx* but prefers to consider the spectral relation as a 'ghost dance', an idea she derived from James Mooney's book on the Sioux. The Sioux 'wanted to be haunted by the ancestors rather than treat them as objects of ritual worship'. According to Spivak 'the ghost dance is an attempt to establish the ethical relation with history as such, ancestors real or imagined'. Further, 'It is not ... a past that was necessarily once present that is sought', but instead involves seeking 'other pasts' (Spivak, 1995: 70). This represents the collision of imagination and memory, acting almost as a corrective to Ricoeur's argument that 'A phenomenology of memory cannot fail to recognize what we ... called the pitfall of the imaginary, inasmuch as this putting-into-images, bordering on the hallucinatory function of imagination, constitutes a sort of weakness, a discredit, a loss of reliability for memory' (Ricoeur, 2006: 54). This memory-imagination is a kind of dismemory, and is perhaps best glossed by Ricoeur's reading of, first, Jean-Paul Sartre, and then Henri Bergson:

> Hauntedness is to collective memory what hallucination is to private memory, a pathological modality of the incrustation of the past at the heart of the present, which acts as a counterweight to the innocent habit-memory, which also inhabits the present, but in order to 'act it' as Bergson says, not to haunt it or torment it.[7] (Ricoeur, 2006: 54)

Ricoeur's reversion to the language of haunting here is significant in returning Banville's construction to a question of ghosts. Moreover, Spivak turns this ghostliness to the future, declaring that 'a ghost dance cannot succeed' unless it is 'supplemented by inspired scholarship and a feeling for the limits of "identity". ... Thus the "end" of the ghost dance ... is to make the past a future'. Several salient thoughts emerge from Spivak: first, that the Sioux wanted to turn objectivity into subjectivity; second, that the quest for 'other pasts' also bifurcates the present being seeking the past; third, that the 'ghost dance' will only succeed when there is a full appreciation for identity and its limits; finally, that the dance disrupted chronology in making the haunting past a version of the future. Each of these ideas applies to Freddie. They also apply to Hamlet and, as Garber points out, when Hamlet writes down the Ghost's commandment on his 'tables', Hamlet's writing becomes 'a copy, a substitution, a revision of an original that does not show its face in the text. ... Hamlet's writing is always ... ghostwriting' (Garber, 2010: 205). To engage with ghosts in the manner of Hamlet and of Freddie is therefore to engage with memory; to ghostwrite (or ghost*paint* in Freddie's case) is a version of disremembering and makes memory the work of the future, and not a mere object of the past.

Added to this, in the idea that Freddie ghostpainted *Le monde d'or*, it is important to remember the characteristics of a painter in relation to their painting. Given the novel's fascination with doubles and liminality, the painter is also spectral because, as Freddie notes, 'The painter is always outside his subjects ...; he holds himself remote from these figures, unable to do anything for them except bear witness to their plight' (Banville, 1998b: 35). This description, in addition to reminding us of *Hamlet*'s Ghost, also overlaps with the painter's paratextuality: neither inseparable nor definitively related to the text he paints. The painter is reminiscent of Derrida's *parergon*, situated neither fully inside nor outside the work of art, which the painter nonetheless frames: 'There is always a form on a ground, but the *parergon* is a form which has as its traditional determination not that it stands out but that it disappears, buries itself, effaces itself, melts away at the moment it deploys its greatest energy' (Derrida, 1987: 65). From the inside, the painter looks like an external constriction, marking where the painting ends and reality begins; from the outside, the painter seems an internal figure, his name inscribed on the painting itself. The painter, in short, disappears into the third space. In this description, the parergon-painter is not dissimilar to memory: the moment when it is created is also the moment when it disappears, receding from presence to absence, from the now to the past. Freddie, assuming the role of doubled painter, firmly cements his place in the third space and enters into the memory of the painting, haunting the original painter, and ghosting the painting itself.

In connection with Freddie's relation to the Professor, Schwall has already gone some way to making this connection, noting that in *Ghosts* 'The frames do not hold, the anarchy of possible worlds is loosed upon this tale' (Schwall, 1997: 310). It is possible to analogise and further concretise the painter–parergon relation via the following: 'My name will not appear on the title page; I would not want that. A brief acknowledgement will do; I look forward to penning it myself, savouring in advance the reflexive thrill of writing down my own name and being, even if only for a moment, someone wholly other' (Banville, 1998b: 33). Freddie has found the 'good

way of signing' by 'writ[ing] things that, finally, are things, worthy
of going without [his] signature', perfecting the strategy of making
the signature 'remain and disappear at the same time, remain in
order to disappear, or disappear in order to remain' (Derrida, 1984:
34, 56).[8] The latter could also stand as a definition of the relation
between *eikon* and *tupos* in memory, the one disappearing into the
other's remainder.

This sums up Freddie's happiness at being the Professor's amanuensis. After all, 'The name is double, the double is already in the
name' (Royle, 2003: 191). As Hartman writes in another context,
for Freddie 'a "book" is a portable and condensed experience
… [that] involves the questioning of the idea that portable and
condensed experiences are possible: the *oeuvre* of an artist is the
path he takes to realize his *désoeuvrement*' (Hartman, 1961: 7).
Freddie writes not 'to set the darkness echoing' as Heaney does
in 'Personal Helicon', but to set himself in silhouette against the
world he writes about. In contrast with another of Banville's novels, Freddie's book counters the failure of Max Morden's book
in *The Sea* (2005), which arises from its 'aborted attempt … to
construct on paper a portable site of memory for the purpose of
immortalizing his own life and self-constructed identity' (Friberg,
2007: 252), whereas Freddie's ghostwritten book exactly produces
a portable site of Freddie's memory even as (or *because*) it hides
Freddie's name in its leaves. Just like the painter whom he doubles,
Freddie looks forward to ghostwriting the Professor's books and
refusing most of the recognition he arguably deserves: he rejects
the real. Like the parergon Freddie both frames the work and is
the framed work. If the ghost remains in the spectral space outside living daylight, then Freddie – as the ghostwriter hidden as
a remembered acknowledgement – also ought to be considered
ghostly. Blanchot's claim that writing only emerges when you have
sovereignty over death is no clearer for Freddie than when he is the
Professor's amanuensis.

Conclusion: mastery over death

There are three authorities now. Freddie's messianic mastery of
death makes him sovereign over his life, replacing Bunter:

La mort, dans l'horizon humain, n'est pas ce qui est donné, elle est ce qui est à faire: une tâche, ce dont nous nous emparons activement, ce qui devient la source de notre activité et de notre maîtrise. L'homme meurt, cela n'est rien, mais l'homme *est* à partir de sa mort, il se lie fortement à sa mort, par un lien dont il est juge[.] (Blanchot, 1968: 115; emphasis in original)

(Death, in the human horizon, is not that which is given to man, but that which it is to do: a task that we actively grab hold, a task that becomes the source of our activity and of our mastery. Man dies – that is nothing – but man emerges from his death, and he is strongly linked to his death by a tether over which he is judge[.])

Freddie thus tames his own death by living in the spectral space of dismemory and 'kills' his son, dismissing Van's life to the real, leaving himself purely a memory for those living a real life. The result is Freddie's mastery over death, yes, but Freddie is also made mortal: '[I]l fait sa mort, il se fait mortel et, par là, se donne le pouvoir de faire et donne à ce qu'il fait son sens et sa vérité' (Blanchot, 1968: 115) ('He is made mortal and, through this making, he is given the power to create and to give to the creation its meaning and its truth'). Freddie's creationism, strongly reminiscent of Bloom's *poiesis*, manifests in his haunting of the painter – Vaublin – and the author-authenticator – the Professor. The writer and the painter are both ghosts of memory, and both bear a relation to death since 'la mort, la mort contente, est la sallaire de l'art, elle est la visée et la justification de l'écriture' (Blanchot, 1968: 110) ('[D]eath, the happy death, is the cost of art, it is writing's *telos* [*visée*] and justification'). Freddie doubles their hidden authority, in being a doubled double: 'Il ne lui suffit pas d'être mortel, il comprend qu'il doit le devenir, qu'il doit être deux fois mortel, souverainement, extrêmement mortel' (Blanchot, 1968: 115) ('It is not enough to be mortal, man understands that he must become mortal, that he has to be mortal twice over, sovereignly, extremely mortal'). Man's chief sovereignty, in other words, is over the law that governs human mortality, and in *Ghosts* access to that law is provided by spectral memory. Here Freddie finds his vocation and tames his own internalised double by becoming his own living dismemory.

As Royle pointed out in reference to phantom texts, *Hamlet*'s Ghost leads people offstage: the Ghost is alluring, desirable, seductive. Seducing offstage, the Ghost invites flight from the living world of culture – the living world of the self-fashioning behaviour as described by Greenblatt. Seduction and flight are two of the characteristics that Thomas Docherty (1990: 15–33) identifies in the postmodern. In *Ghosts* these are two crucial characteristics not only of Freddie's journey from *The Book of Evidence* to the third novel in the trilogy, *Athena* (1995), but also in his narrative in the novel itself: he flees the living world, residing instead in a third world of spectral memory. He becomes a dismemorial ghost. Attending that ghostliness is a temporal out-of-jointedness: anachronicity, an a-chronicity in which temporality is not interested in linear flow. Memories are rewritten in the now, opening up the future to an increasingly unstable past.

It is worth recalling Buse and Stott's remark from the introduction to this part, when they asserted that 'The ghost in Hamlet is a well-known example' of 'anachronism … the appearance of something in a time in which they clearly do not belong'. When I introduced their term, I also glossed it as my idea of dismemory. This might be called ghost-time, and it is the lasting mark of *Ghosts*; but it is a mark that can only be defined by temporariness. This deracination (another chief characteristic for Docherty of the postmodern) from lasting, concretised time allows the visual, material painting in *Ghosts* to come to life: the monadic picture is freed from its temporal, as from its material, frames. An analogue for this freeing of time from its presentism is when the Ghost relates his murder at the hands of Claudius, his brother. When the Ghost hastens his tale because 'I scent the morning air' (I.v.58), he urges Hamlet to be quiet: 'Brief let me be' (I.v.59). And yet this recourse to timeliness, to the sense of an ending, only precipitates the Ghost's *disregard* of time. For another thirty lines and more he recounts the story of his murder to Hamlet. Moreover, the tale the Ghost tells is the second version of the story, with the first coming in the Ghost's previous speech. Not only is the time out of joint for Hamlet, whose 'cursèd spite' is to 'set it right', but so is it for the Ghost: he comes from the dead past to disrupt the present and loosen it from its temporal bounds, forever altering the future not only of the play but of Hamlet's life. Hamlet's life henceforth is haunted by a memory that is not his own. Dismemorial ghost-time is a time of *living memory*, anachronistically shaping the present of the play. Freddie, entering the world where ordinary temporality is no longer in effect, not only plays with his memories in the present, thereby shaping the future, but does it as a postmodern ghost, remembering the tale-telling of *Hamlet*'s Ghost all the while. 'List' is read on the opening page, and Freddie is hearing *Hamlet*'s Ghost spirit throughout, channelling his commanding spectrality as the disappearing, memorial narrator.

*

By way of conclusion to Part I, I should point out that despite my best efforts to deny the prominence of chronology and teleology, I have nonetheless sketched out a picture of spectrality in Irish writing that develops through time. In each case remembering Shakespeare's *Hamlet*, the spectrality has developed in relation to one another, but equally in relation to the demands of historical context. The developments have centred on time and its renovation and therefore on memory itself. Their interest in ghosts also confirms their interest in the disruptive work of memory.

In *Playboy* Christy overturned the prominence of fathers – the future being privileged over the burdensome past where land and legacy are memorialised. However, the political climate of pre-revolutionary Ireland forced this diabology offstage, showing the inherent, devilish threat contained in Abbey Theatre drama. *Playboy* time was borne out offstage with Christy and Old Mahon wandering Mayo and with the metrocolonial Dubliners protesting the dramatic conceit that threatened to overturn time. The Dubliners, in short, were protesting against the violence done to temporality and memory originating in *Hamlet* that had been remembered in Synge's drama.

In 'Hades', Bloom remembered the Ghost's relation with Hamlet that hastened mourning and, for Bloom, led to a return to life. As with Christy, the son is the more prominent of the two males, with Rudy hauntologising Bloom, returning him to the *poietic* possibilities of memory. However, unlike Christy, Bloom's story is told from the perspective of the father. It is a story, in other words, that follows the marginalised through society, wherever the wanderer wends – this time a wandering Jew, and not a Mayo farmer. Life lessons emerge from death, but they also emerge from the young Rudy and not the wise grownup. Time, again, is overturned, even at the moment of memory – tacitly pointing to the past – and its efficacy is proved.

Finally in *Ghosts* Freddie is a father whose perspective is given to the reader. But in a final permutation of the father–son organisation, this living father is also the Ghost. This time living and shaping the memory in the present, Freddie is released from the temporal bounds and binds of living, instead enjoying an impersonal death in the realm of words and potentiality. Freddie's is a postmodern deracination from time, writing his story on the hoof. Far from the 'excessive calls on filial piety', for which he condemns the Ghost, Freddie instead adopts a strategy wherein he frees his son by dismissing him to reality. This reality remembers the memorial drama of *Hamlet* when the son has to deal with a missing father; however, that is not the story that Freddie tells. Freddie's story, instead, is the Ghost's transposed to modern Ireland, fully exploring the possibility of a life in the impressionable wax of memory, rather than the world of cause and effect.

In remembering *Hamlet*, these texts adopt different levels of recognition and various approaches. However, in my project to show how Irish literature becomes modern all the while intertextually remembering the colonial mother country through its archetypical cultural touchstone, ghosts provide an apt starting point and begin to characterise my chosen term: dismemory. Dismemory is the disruptive memory of Christy Mahon, that can only succeed offstage. Dismemory is the impossible future memory of his son that re-energises Bloom. And disremembering is Freddie's living in the material world as a messianic ghost. Each of these dismemories represents a textual engagement with Shakespeare's *Hamlet*. The ultimate message of this part is that ghosts persist in memory and find myriad ways of disrupting the world. Whether haunting or keeping company, ghosts are origins of sorts, providing either the Other against whom the drama of history has to contend, or the space in which *a future can be shaped through memory*. In remembering the Ghost, that is, memory not only haunts the present, but shapes it favourably for the future.

Notes

1 Characters not too dissimilar from those written into Banville's *The Sea* (2005), itself derivative of Henry James's 'Turn of the Screw' (1898), a pre-eminent ghost story.

2 Cf., also, Schwall's final line in her essay on *Ghosts*'s parallels with *The Tempest*: 'Rather, the "third world" it is set in is that of the imagination' (Schwall, 1997: 311).

3 This, and other translations, mine.

4 J. Hillis Miller would no doubt argue that *Ghosts* plays parasite to these earlier 'hosts' (a cognate of 'ghost'); he would equally argue, I imagine, that the earlier texts also cannibalise *Ghosts* as host to their inheritance.

5 Derrida, in his reading of Blanchot's *The Instant of My Death*, notes the fractured subject of one who experiences death and the other who relates the experience of death: 'There are two deaths, and the two die as much as they make or let die. Just as there are two subjects – two "I's", an "I" that speaks of a young man, an "I" that is divided by what happened there – so there are two, concurrent deaths. One ahead of the other, in countertime, one making an advance to the other, an advance that it demands be returned by returning itself. They run toward one another, into one another, one running to encounter the other. ... What remains for him of existence, more than this race to death, is this race of death in view of death *in order* not to see death coming' (Derrida, 2000: 95; emphasis in original).

6 Think also of Laertes and Fortinbras as doubles of Hamlet; Claudius is a double of King Hamlet; Fortinbras is also a double of his father, King Fortinbras. Garber writes: 'Every critical observation on doubling in the play, from the psychoanalytic ... to the rhetorical ... is an implicit commentary on the compulsion to repeat. Moreover, *Hamlet* is a play that enacts the repetition compulsion even as it describes it' (Garber, 2010: 173).

7 For my own argument charting Banville's growing interest and investment in Bergson's philosophies, see Taylor-Collins (2020a).

8 In *Signsponge*, Derrida also gives an unintended reading of Banville's literature more generally. In the following I think especially of Banville's habit of rewriting characters' names or his own name as a character's name in his fiction: 'The rebus signature, the metonymic or anagrammatic signature, these are the condition of possibility and impossibility. The double bind of a signature event' (Derrida, 1984: 64). In *Ghosts*, 'Vaublin' is a near-anagram of 'Banville'.

Part II

Bodies

Hard-handed men that work in Athens here,
Which never labour'd in their minds till now,
And now have toil'd their unbreathed memories
With this same play, against your nuptial.
                    – Philostrate in *A Midsummer Night's Dream*

Introduction

Addressing the ongoing debate between the primacy given to memory over the body in matters of personal identity, D. E. Cooper comes firmly down on the side of the body:

> I conclude, then, that faced by the choice between the memory criterion and the bodily continuity criterion of personal identity, the latter is the wiser to opt for. For the intuitions, in strange cases, which tempt us to hypothesize changes of bodies, emerge from the less privileged perspective. (Cooper, 1974: 263)

His 'imaginary experiment' to prove his theory considers a fantastic example of two people whose neural patterns are switched absolutely, such that person A exists in body B and *vice versa*. By virtue of the idea that A's neural patterns are completely new, the only remaining point of contact A has with the world is through his body. Thus the body is privileged. However, Cooper also offers the alternative argument that is set by John Locke's 'prince/pauper example, in which … the ability to remember experiences of a person having a different body guarantees, nevertheless, that one is that person – and hence that the memory criterion is dominant over the bodily identity one' (Cooper, 1974: 255). This experiment falls into the philosophical trap of extremes that Henri Bergson lamented – Cartesian dualism on one hand, on another Berkeleian idealism – while Bergson wished instead to leave the question of matter – here, the body – between the extremes 'where it is seen by common sense' as an 'aggregate of images' (Bergson, 1991: 11, 9). These discussions, and these thought experiments, establish the terms of the discussion in the following two chapters: is there Irish identity without body? Is there Irish identity without bodily memory? In response, I will show how the combination of these twin origins of identity can provide a way into understanding the production of the modern Irish nation and modern Irish identity. Moreover, this combination is illuminated by looking at Shakespeare and how his drama's bodily memory is remembered. To show this, I will be looking at two trilogies: Samuel Beckett's *Three Novels* (1951–53) and Edna O'Brien's *Country Girls Trilogy* (1960–86).

One way into this discussion is through the body's relation to power. Agamben's concept of modern sovereignty, and its biopolitical element, is essentially tethered to the body of the citizen. Quoting Foucault, Agamben states:

> [A] society's 'threshold of biological modernity' is situated at the point at which the species and the individual as a simple living body become what is at stake in a society's political strategies. ... In particular, the development and triumph of capitalism would not have been possible, from this perspective, without the disciplinary control achieved by the new bio-power, which, through a series of appropriate technologies, so to speak created the 'docile bodies' that it needed. (Agamben, 1998: 10)

These docile bodies become, in modernity, the bare life that makes up the biopolitical. The living body is docile at first, yes, but becomes the bearer of modern sovereignty purely by living life. Agamben's sketch of the transfer of power from political life – βιος, *bios* – to bare life – ζωή, *zōe* – relies wholly on the material body. Biopolitics, in turn, relies on a type of oblivion: the individual forgets and forgoes their personal identity and needs when interpellated into a state-dominated social space. Biopolitics therefore relies on a kind of personal amnesia.

The second consequence – the importance of imagination and creation to the body–world relation – was partially in evidence in the previous chapters, perhaps especially so for Bloom's *poiesis* and Freddie's ghostpainting. There is an earlier conception of this creation–body nexus in *A Midsummer Night's Dream* when Theseus considers the sleeping lovers in Act Five. His monologue begins by considering the 'lunatic, the lover and the poet', stressing how the three are 'of imagination all compact' (V.i.7–8). Theseus proceeds to think through the implications of imaginative creation:

And as imagination bodies forth
The forms of things unknown, the poet's pen
Turns them to shapes, and gives to airy nothing
A local habitation and a name. (V.i.14–17)

Theseus asserts that imagination converts unknown forms – 'potential' – and actualises them through poetry. The result is temporo-spatial specificity. Critically for my argument, moreover, the transition from (im)potentiality to material production is metaphorically invoked through the body. Imagination makes ideas material through the body; the body is the entry point for creative imagination into the world. Agamben's modern, biopolitical citizenship thus requires amnesia of the self or autonomous agent; but the body responds by being imaginatively creative.

As Ricoeur explored, imagination and memory have long been closely related, and their distinction is at the heart of understanding the veracity of memory. In fact, in the anamnestic process, Ricoeur distinguishes between 'retention' and 'reproduction' of memories, the latter inviting an imaginative corollary, leading to the 'formidable question … that of knowing under what conditions "reproduction" is reproduction of the past. The difference between imagination and recollection depends on the answer to this question' (Ricoeur, 2006: 35). There exists a continuum therefore between memory and imagination, particularly in the process of recollection. As Banville explains in *Time Pieces: A Dublin Memoir* (Banville, 2016: 2), 'Certain moments in certain places … imprint themselves on the memory with improbably vividness and clarity – improbable because, so clear and so vivid are they, that suspicion arises that one's fancy must have made them up: that one must, in a word, have imagined them'. For Ricoeur, as well as Theseus, these ideas lead inevitably to a question of identity, and within that, of bodies. 'I am speaking of the polarity between *reflexivity* and *worldliness*', writes Ricoeur (emphasis in original), continuing:

> One does not simply remember oneself, seeing, experiencing, learning; rather one recalls the situations in the world in which one has seen, experienced, learned. These situations imply one's own body and the bodies of others, lived space, and, finally, the horizon of the world and worlds, within which something has occurred. (Ricoeur, 2006: 36)

This constitutes Ricoeur's version of Halbwachs's collective memory, though crucially adding the fact of the material body to the experience. As I will show over the next chapters, this is important not only in the twentieth, but also the sixteenth and seventeenth centuries.

Throughout my argument, the body is a material object that discloses itself to itself and to others in the world. Writing about other human beings, Maurice Merleau-Ponty (1948) writes that 'I only know them through their glances, their gestures, their speech – in other words, through their bodies'. There are a 'host of possibilities contained within this body when it appears before us'. What the body discloses is not just possibility, but a combination of its materiality along with its being. Merleau-Ponty's is 'the idea that rather than a mind *and* a body, man is a mind *with* a body, a being who can only get to the truth of things because its body is, as it were, embedded in those things' (Merleau-Ponty, 2008: 62, 43). This material body is coincident with its being and with the world, and is wholly typical of early modern thinking as well as applicable to modern thought. Michael Schoenfeldt summarised that for Renaissance writers, 'the Galenic regime of the humoral self that supplies these writers with much of their vocabulary of inwardness demanded the invasion of social and psychological realms by biological and environmental processes' (Schoenfeldt, 1999: 8). In 'The Extasie' John Donne explained this idea in relation to consciousness, asking,

> Our bodies why doe wee forbeare?
> They are ours, though not wee, Wee are
> The intelligences, they the spheares.
> We owe them thankes, because they thus,
> Did us, to us, at first convay
> Yeelded their senses force to us,
> Nor are drosse to us, but allay.[1] (Donne, 1991: ll. 49–55)

The persona proceeds to explain that when heaven dispenses souls, they must 'to body first repaire'. The 'extasie' – which Donne described in a letter as 'a departing, and secession, and suspension of the soul' (Donne, 1991: l. 7 and p. 100n29) – is the reducibility of living consciousness to the body. Or, the body and '[t]he intelligences' (i.e. consciousness) are inextricable; without the body to house the consciousness, and without the consciousness to think of and look at others' bodies, there is no love. This pre-Dualistic unity of consciousness with body provides the basic corpus of my investigation – even in the twentieth-century texts – but central to my concern is the idea that the body is made a primary referent and datum of selfhood in the literary texts under investigation; or, the self *is* 'the mundane inwardness of living inhabited bodies' (Schoenfeldt, 1999: 38). I will eventually show how Beckett's characters, whose egoistic testimonials are front and centre of their respective novels, and O'Brien's protagonist, Caithleen Brady, are all conditioned by the concentration of their selves with their bodies. This is not a uniformly positive phenomenon. Nevertheless, through these novelists' interactions with Shakespeare's characters for whom the self–body nexus is a similar *fait accompli*, I will show how Malone invents his own memories to obviate the forgetfulness he experiences as a quasi-audience member; how the Unnamable commits to a kind of theatricality in which his body satirises society; and how Caithleen Brady comes to terms with her body at the moment she de-materialises it through an elective hysterectomy. It allows her to become the kind of Mother Ireland who stops a patronising and paternalistic Irish nationalism from taking hold. In all cases, the body–self overlap is the site and origin of these political interventions.

To explore best how memory and bodies overlap and interrelate, I will employ a range of theoretical material that emerges from engagements with different historical bodies: Holger Syme's take on early modern theatricality, Jean-Paul Sartre's mid-twentieth-century existentialism and Elaine Scarry's late twentieth-century ideas on bodies in pain.

Syme's early modern theatricality

Syme persuasively argues for a reconsideration of theatricality in early modern politics, suggesting that the period did not suffer a crisis of representation, as many have argued, but instead a crisis of primary presence (Syme, 2012: 2n2). Syme argues that in the realms of politics and law, for example, theatricality – or mediated re-presentation – was the *modus operandi*. An initial example is the manner in which Elizabeth's speech to her second parliament was actually pronounced 'by Lord Keeper Nicholas Bacon, with

Elizabeth present by his side': 'The Lords and Commons thus witnessed a complex orchestration of presences and representations:
seeing both the monarch and her officer, hearing his voice speaking
her words, grammatically adopting her person as his own persona'
(Syme, 2012: 3). When this trope is replicated throughout England
in different arenas, there is then a 'very precise' logic of 'theatricality', the form of the period's predominant literary representation
in the theatre. 'There, too', writes Syme, 'the *script* was the source
and *locus* of authority, at least state authority: the playtext, not its
enactment, was "seen and allowed" by the Master of the Revels'
(Syme, 2012: 5). The extended implication of Syme's argument is
that early modern theatre's preeminence was no historical accident, but accorded with the dynamics and authority of the polity.
Finally, in Syme's understanding of the authoritative script's centrality, I recall my argument above that memory was of critical importance to early modern theatre precisely because of the presence of
a script. The script becomes the nexus of these arguments: memory
and bodily theatricality join forces in the pre-eminent cultural force
of early modern England. In Philostrate's terms, the script is the
origin of the 'unbreathed memories' (V.i.74) of actors, whose bodies then exhale the lines for others to inhale and remember in the
theatre. Even accepting the argument that the script can be and was
departed from by the actors – see, for instance, Hamlet's insistence
that the Players 'Speak the speech [...] as I pronounced it to you'
(III.ii.1–2), which acknowledges that actors were liable *not* to stick
to the script – we must also then accept that the actors departed
from something. That something – the script – is thus reinscribed a
second time with authority.

   Consequently, it is necessary to pay as much political attention to
the theatrical literature (both literature *qua* theatrical, and the theatrical in the literature), as to the politics; the two, via the medium
of the body, are inextricable: 'In the theatre, the body bears the
brunt of performance; it is the material Shakespeare's text works
on, works through. No body in the theatre is exempt' (Rutter,
2001: xii). Within this framework, the operability of theatricality
to promote self-knowledge and identity must be considered. Nancy
Selleck argues that selfhood in early modernity was concerned with
the perception of the self by others – what I gloss as theatricality –
in order to grasp self-knowledge:

Renaissance usage characteristically defines selfhood as the experience of an *other*. For instance, when Shakespeare's Henry IV tells his lords, 'I will from henceforth rather be my Selfe, / Mighty, and to be fear'd', the 'Selfe' he speaks of is constituted not in his own inward experience but in his outward manifestation – in *their* experience of him. The fact that Henry posits this as something that *he* controls, that he can choose to be or not to be, certainly makes his own will part of the picture, but it also ties that will to the other's perception. (Selleck, 2008: 8; emphasis in original)

In linking this point with Syme's, my conclusion is that theatricality is both a feature of our perception of others and, through this same structure, our perception of ourselves through the theatricalisation of ourselves for others; or, 'how the Self performed what it thought about the Self' (Rutter, 2001: 149). As I will show in relation to Sartre's philosophy shortly, all bodies, through theatricalisation, are alienated from the audience (i.e. parliament, or the Globe's patrons) who 'appropriate' the bodies to themselves as objects of their intentional consciousness; but this 'alienation' is a governing principle of Renaissance bodies. Additionally, since bodies were the principal site of early modern signification – whether in the theatre or in parliament – then bodies provide and produce the world; bodies are everywhere. Moreover, bodies are everywhere implicated in time and in space.

Sartre's phenomenological existentialism

Another profitable way of thinking of this relation is through Sartre's philosophy in *Being and Nothingness* (1943) – a text that has also proven especially relevant for reading Beckett.[2] Sartre explains that 'Being-for-itself must be wholly body and it must be wholly consciousness; it can not be *united* with a body. Similarly being-for-others is wholly body … There is nothing *behind* the body' (Sartre, 2003: 329; emphasis in original). Sartre considers the body in two modes, either in the being of agency, the For-itself, or in the contested being, the For-others. In both cases, however, being and the body are inseparable, just as when Sartre describes the waiter who, through his body – stepping quickly, bending obsequiously to the customers, walking like an automaton – 'is playing *at being* a waiter in a café' in a kind of '"representation" for others and for myself'

(Sartre, 2003: 82–3; emphasis in original): here, again, is the pre-dominant model of theatricality, in which the body–self relation re-presents a fictional, though necessary and useful, unity.

Simultaneously, for Sartre the body is the contingent relation with the world: just as there is no world without consciousness, there is no world without 'consciousness (of) the body':

> Thus to say that I have entered into the world, 'come to the world', or that there is a world, or that I have a body is one and the same thing. In this sense my body is everywhere-in the world ... My body is co-extensive with the world, spread across all things, and at the same time it is condensed into this single point which all things indicate and which I am without being able to know it. (Sartre, 2003: 342)

The body is central to our being-in-the-world at all, contends Sartre. But troublingly, my body is 'inapprehensible' to me, the being coinci-dent with the body. So the body is both the world and the 'center of reference' of objects in the world – everything eventually refers back to the body, is given to the body and the body is 'my very adapta-tion to tools, the adaptation which I am' – and yet the body is never visible except as object for consciousness (Sartre, 2003: 348). The body presupposes its being-for-others and its 'theatricality'.

The body For-others has several ramifications in Sartre's philoso-phy, which are important when I think of my own body-for-others, and of the Other's body for me. Both these bodies are not only sites, but intentional objects of consciousness, and they are each a 'body-which-points-beyond-itself; it is at once in space (it is the situation) and in time (it is freedom-as-object). The body For-others is the magic object *par excellence*' (Sartre, 2003: 374). But, in assuming a role as object of intentional consciousness, and in entering time and space, the risk of one's own body For-others is that the conscious-ness of that body becomes alienated – this is even more troubling than its refusal to be apprehended by self-consciousness:

> My body as alienated escapes me toward a being-a-tool-among-tools, toward a being-a-sense-organ-apprehended-by-sense-organs, and this is accompanied by an alienating destruction and a concrete collapse of *my* world which flows toward the Other and which the Other will reapprehend in *his* world. ... My body is designated as alienated. (Sartre, 2003: 376; emphasis in original)

Here are two, obverse sides to the being-for-others coincident with body, resulting from its 'theatricality': its existence in time and space, and its betrayal of the consciousness (of) the body. Consciousness, for Sartre, is left to know its own body purely as a 'quasi-object' perceivable only through the Other's body. To exist temporo-spatially, the body and its consciousness must admit its own aliena-tion: '[T]he perception of my body is placed chronologically after the perception of the body of the Other' (Sartre, 2003: 382). A perceptual circle is conceived in which to know one's own body – which gives rise to and is given to by consciousness[3] – is to think of it theatrically, as observer. Body consciousness and passive per-ception are necessities of existence; alienation is a necessary evil attendant on freedom.

Sartre's comprehensive philosophy offers a reading of time and memory that twins with that of the body. Thus 'we can speak of the evanescent value of the past. Hence arises the fact that memory presents to us the being which we were, accompanied by a pleni-tude of being which confers on it a sort of poetry' (Sartre, 2003: 142). Much like the experience of the present body, the past is only known in and through the present. Furthermore, Sartre addresses part of the question of identity through memory, suggesting that when Pierre, in his example, explains the meaning of his own life, he repeatedly roots himself in the present, 'temporalizing himself'. However, when Pierre is dead, 'only *the memory of the* Other can prevent Pierre's life from shriveling up in its plenitude in-itself by cutting all its moorings with the present' (Sartre, 2003: 562; empha-sis in original). This is to say that the sustenance of any being after death requires a scission from the present, which not only enters that life and its identity into memory, but also concomitantly pre-cludes that being's exit from self-identity. In this way, and explored more fully below in relation to Beckett's prose, Sartre's existential phenomenology also sees in the overlap between theatrical bodies and memory a path to enduring self-identity.

But it is with Sartre's idea of protention – projecting into the future – that my reading of Beckett's prose will most controversially engage. Sartre writes that whilst the self is founded, inevitably, on the past, he also argues that 'we continually preserve the possibility of changing the *meaning* of the past in so far as this is an ex-present *which has had a future*' (Sartre, 2003: 139; emphasis in original). For Malone in *Malone Dies*, the ability to 'live and invent' is pre-cisely the shaping of the ex-present as a new future: imagination and memory are thus confounded, and Sartre's argument that 'We

must abandon ... the idea that the future exists as *representation*'
(Sartre, 2003: 147; emphasis in original) is placed in jeopardy.

Scarry's painful bodies

In *Body in Pain: The Making and Unmaking of the World* (1987),
Scarry broadly argues that pain has a dual role in the world, but it
always manifests in the body: in terms of war and torture the body
serves to unmake or deconstruct the world in which the body is
painfully situated:

> [T]hat torture and war are acts of destruction (and hence somehow
> the opposite of creation), that they entail the suspension of civiliza-
> tion (and are somehow the opposite of that civilization), are things
> we have always known ...; the only thing that could not have been
> anticipated from a distance but that is forced upon us as self-evident
> once we enter the interior of these two events is that they are, in the
> most literal and concrete way possible, an appropriation, an aping,
> and reversing of the action of creating itself. (Scarry, 1987: 21)

Against these ideas, Scarry explains that there remains, through the
body in pain, the possible remaking or creation of the world. This
is done through imagination and creation. Crucially, this not only
appears in art for art's sake, but is also a political concern:

> Because the deconstruction of creation takes a specifically politi-
> cal form (torture, war), it might seem most appropriate to trace the
> outlines of the opposite event again in a specifically political form,
> such as the moment when a new country is being conceived and con-
> structed (made-up, made-real), or when an already existing country,
> having been partially destroyed, is being re-imagined and re-con-
> structed (remade-up). (Scarry, 1987: 177)

When Scarry writes in these terms the pertinence of her argument to
the modern Irish case is self-evident: forming the nation of Ireland
takes place through the body and its pain. A summary of Scarry's
argument is offered by turning Theseus's comment about imagination on its head: Scarry argues that the body imagines forth the
form of things unknown.

As with Ricoeur's confusion between imagination and memory,
so is there an implicit complex between the imaginative creation of
the world and memory in Scarry. Her central tenet about memory

also coincides with the body in her refrain, 'What is remembered in the body is well remembered' (Scarry, 1987: 109, 110, 112–13, 152). Citing initially the proof of never forgetting how to ride a bike, Scarry adds the 'body's self-immunizing antibody system' as hæmatological evidence of how memory is constitutive of the corporal experience. This too is bound up with identity: the girl who rides a bike can declare the *savoir faire* of bike-riding; the antibodies, too, offer self-evident proof of immunity. Further, Scarry highlights the possibility of reading a national self-identity in and on a body: 'The political identity of the body is usually learned unconsciously, effortlessly, and very early – it is said that within a few months of life British infants have learned to hold their eyebrows in a raised position' (Scarry, 1987: 109). This body produces British-ness by virtue of remembering a British corporal-idiom. Thus the body's memory is crucially intertwined with the production and creation of a (political) world, proving the salience of Scarry's ideas.

Taken together, these three theories provide a vocabulary for me to write about bodies and memory in Beckett's and O'Brien's trilogies. Syme and Sartre will be most useful for reading bodies of memory in Beckett; Scarry will be most relevant for O'Brien's bodies of memory. As will become clear in the next chapters, both male and female bodies bear a particular relation to memory that links especially with the present and the future. As such, memories of Shakespeare provide liberation in the now and tomorrow that allow the creativity of Scarry's painful bodies to take hold. For the male bodies of Beckett's trilogy – Molloy, Moran, Malone, and the Unnamable – their inevitable theatricality keys into the Renaissance theatrical understanding of selfhood as observed by others, but imagined memories provide an avenue of escape from the body's limits. For O'Brien's female bodies in Kate and Baba, their socially enforced temporality turned towards the future – their wombs as vessels for tomorrow's children – is undone by Kate's elective hysterectomy that recodes Mother Ireland while instantiating her own radical (though fatal) social agenda.

Why Beckett and O'Brien?

The connection between Beckett and O'Brien is little mentioned, but is underpinned by both body and memory. To adumbrate, I will first turn to the trilogies' respective storytelling *modes*, before considering the pre-existing substantive connections between Beckett and O'Brien. The two considerations are connected. I begin, then, by exploring Beckett's testimonial storytelling in comparison with O'Brien's memoir-like approach, both of which will invite me to investigate what it means 'to be subject to desubjectification[.] How can a subject give an account of its own ruin?' (Agamben, 2002: 142).

Two elements underpinning testimony need stating. The first is its temporal structure, in which a voice – subject, speaking-I – is diachronically fractured, speaking *now* about a *before*. The second is testimony's intimate connection to *witness*, and thus to observation becoming evidence (*OED*). For Ricoeur, the issue of the witness and testimony is elemental to a discussion of memory (Ricoeur, 2006: 388), while Docherty has written that the testimonial text 'is said not for the first time, even if it attests to something happening for the first time. … [I]t is an encounter between an event that happens for the first time and … the second time of its happening for the first time.' It is therefore not only that a testimony recalls past events, but that the recollection affects the one who is recalling the events: the speaking-I 'must be marked by an internal fracture or difference' (Docherty, 2013: 143), analogous to theatrical re-presentation. The speaking-I is thus both *now-now* and *now-then*.

Regarding the latter, there is a testamentary structure that not only employs the full 'chain of operations that begin at the level of the perception of an experienced scene, continuing on to that of the retention of its memory, to come to focus in the declarative and narrative phase of the restitution of the features of the event' (Ricoeur, 2006: 162), but there is also the ontological event that transforms the agent of the witnessed event, to the observer who, herself, becomes a reenactor of the primary event. The witness, in short, becomes an actor, theatrically testifying to what happened. We can elaborate this by virtue of the connections between law and theatre in early modern England that are well sketched. For instance, two (re)presentations of vengeance were available to an early modern audience:

> Public vengeance at that time could mean two very different things. On the one hand the legal system as a civic institution made

punishments increasingly public affairs .... Understood in another way, public vengeance was being made available in the playhouses of London and beyond for the price of admission. (Dunne, 2016: 16)

As with Syme's arguments about theatricality, the contemporary expectations about testimony were closely aligned to the drama of early modern England – and therefore perhaps most closely associated with the soliloquy. Whilst a broad conception of 'testimony' is fundamentally non-literary and linking instead to 'documentary proof' and steering us away from 'declared memory' (Ricoeur, 2006: 161), in a twentieth-century literary mode the inheritor of the soliloquy was first-person narrative, in all its guises, such as those practised by Beckett and O'Brien.

Ricoeur announces the 'crucial question' regarding testimony: '[T]o what point is testimony trustworthy?' (Ricoeur, 2006: 162). This is also the question implied in Lorna Hutson's (2008) account of mimesis in early modern England when she explains the role of jurors to inquire into and doubt witnesses' testimonies in court;[4] no audience, by contrast, doubts the veracity of the soliloquiser onstage, whether Hamlet's vacillations or Richard III's machinations – even if the speaker's limited knowledge restricts the usefulness of their confession. Therefore, whilst Ricoeur's question of trustworthiness is relevant when referring to the archive and the use of testimony solely in a juridical context, in a literary mode different questions become useful. For Docherty, for instance, the question of the witness-speaker's ontological status within the question of trustworthiness becomes central. Thus, describing how 'the Augustine who signs' his *Confessions* 'is not the Augustine who lived the story that he tells as the story of his life', Docherty returns the question of witness to the diachronic observer-witness: the *now-now* versus the *now-then* of the speaking-I. For Docherty, this is not merely a matter of temporal fracture, but also of ontological conversion and transformation (Docherty, 2013: 154).

Inasmuch as Beckett's *Three Novels* include at least four first-person narrators – Molloy, Moran, Malone, and the Unnamable, all of whom make extensive use of the word 'I', and who tell stories of the past – and inasmuch as at least two of them make explicit reference to writing down the stories that are then relayed in the texts we read – Moran at either end of his testimony, and Malone throughout his – it seems straightforward to cast the *Three Novels* as testimonies of all stripes. However, in other ways the Beckettian testimony defies the qualities ascribed to testimonies described above. First, 'Beckett performs language's inability to represent a coherent subject alongside figural reminders of human life that has lost all subjectivity' (McNaughton, 2010: 129): Beckett's narrators' 'I's are not just temporally fractured, but also incoherent and ineloquent. It is possible to see this as a failure of postwar Irish masculinity to express a coherent sense of self – a failed masculinity that was depicted equally successfully, though fundamentally differently, by John McGahern.[5] Second, the ontological transformation as outlined by Docherty does not seem to apply to Beckett's heroes in the same way as they do to, say, Augustine in his *Confessions* (Docherty's example); after all, Moran ends his journey where he began it and his 'knee is no better. It is no worse either' (Beckett, 2009: 169). Docherty's economy of testimony, in which the testifier ontologically develops between the *now-now* and the *now-then* by virtue of a conversion 'as such' presupposes a coherent and eloquent speaking-I. However, far from suggesting that the incoherence and ineloquence forestall testimonies proper to that name, in the *Three Novels* new kinds of testimony emerge: whilst the theatrical, embodied actor is present, and the speaking-I is present, nevertheless incoherence and ineloquence ally to the way that Beckett's narrators – and especially in the supine Molloy and largely disembodied Unnamable – appear to be unchanged through their fictional testimonies, making the question one of 'the empty place of the subject' (Agamben, 2002: 145) rather than of the fidelity of the speaker. When I write about Beckett's testimony in Chapter 4, it is to this I refer. This question of subjecthood and testimonial authenticity also intervenes in the question of Beckett's characters' nationality and the state of the modern Irish nation. I will think through how a scripted text – i.e. an enforced language – represents both the colonial British legacy that the Unnamable is forced to regurgitate and also the Irish Republic's increasingly conservative political majority; I will also explore how the theatrical bodies of Beckett's *Three Novels* also lament the British colonial legacy.

In contrast to Beckett's testimonies is O'Brien's mode of memoir. Memoir, self-evidently, is a literary form concretely linked to memory. Where I have argued that Beckett's testimonies do not allow for the historical development of the protagonist speaking-I as might be expected of the novel form, the use of memoir (and of quasi- or near-memoir literary forms) is premised on the idea, however valid, that the memoirist has lived a life worthy of commemoration, containing scenes, moments, or narratives of development. O'Brien's memoir *Country Girl* (2012) is one such memoir, positing that O'Brien herself has undergone a radical change from the west of Ireland country girl – living on an increasingly dilapidated farm, whose wasting is symptomatic of her father's 'heedless alcoholi[sm]' (Kiberd, 2017: 61) as an '"archetypal" Irishman' (O'Brien in Kersnowski, 2018: 31) – into the cosmopolitan Londoner writing bestsellers that enter the Irish literary canon. In the case of this memoir, 'O'Brien' as the speaking-I is the author–hero character who has developed.

More tellingly, O'Brien's first novel, later becoming a trilogy under the name of the first, is called *The Country Girls* (1960). The trilogy as a whole, and the epilogue published in 1986, tells the story of two west of Ireland girls, Caithleen 'Kate' Brady[6] and Baba Brennan, whose friendship leads to a typical, if controversial, life for these two grown women. *The Country Girls* was succeeded by *The Lonely Girl* (1962) and *Girls in Their Married Bliss* (1964), with an Epilogue added later in 1986. The implication, however complicated its consequences, is that Caithleen is *a version of* O'Brien (or, vice versa) and that, therefore, it is possible to read *The Country Girls Trilogy* as a near-memoir.

However, there are differences between the novel and memoir. Whilst both may use the first-person narrative perspective, at stake between the two is the process of creation. In the novel, where fiction is supposedly primary (however framed), the narrative impulse precedes transcription. The story may unfold in the process of writing it, or it may be planned to the last full stop, but the creative *poiesis* provides the impetus. By contrast, with memoir, the imaginative source – memory – pre-exists the writing of the text. However, the process of writing gives shape to those sources, fashioning some sense of narrative trajectory to what are otherwise fragmented and discrete memories. A different type of creativity is called for, one which Plato records in *Timaeus*. This kind of creativity does not alter the thing itself (read: memory), so much as help an object (read: memoir) 'come to be' (Plato, 2013: 50d). Rather than a process, Timaeus describes a third kind of being[7] in which becoming takes place. Timaeus gives two artistically creative examples of how this becoming begins:

> [J]ust as in the manufacture of fragrant ointments the artist first contrives the same initial advantage; he makes the fluids which are to receive his perfumes as scentless as he can. So, too, those who essay to model figures in some soft vehicle permit no figure whatsoever to be already visible there, but first level the surface and make it as smooth as they may. (Plato, 2013: 50e–51a)

The point here is that the process of becoming does not blemish the form being given shape. This is crucial to the process of memoir-writing, in the purest form of which the memory is supposed to be translated truthfully into the literary text – with apparent 'truthfulness' at the cornerstone of 'memoir ethics' (Martin, 2016: 1, 5) – such that 'the auto-ethnographical author is *created by a text* and not the other way around' (Freeman, 2015: 60; my emphasis). Mike Martin uses the example of Beryl Markham who asks how it is possible to 'bring order out of memory' (quoted in Martin, 2016: 85), and Martin explains that the 'order' does not have to be chronological, but seeks a 'pattern in the warp and woof of her experience, some coherence' (Martin, 2016: 85). This coherence does not require beginning–middle–end narrative, however. Martin expects Markham's coherence to be framed 'round the achievement that brought her fame … [as] the first woman to fly solo across the Atlantic Ocean'. But Markham surprises Martin, instead 'structur[ing] the memoir as a set of interlocking vignettes, each a magnet attracting additional memories' (Martin, 2016: 85–6). It allows Markham sometimes to recount chronologically, and at other times to 'combine' memories 'as in the lengthy opening vignette' (Martin, 2016: 87). Either way, the point is that the memoir is a kind of placeholder, in which memories are transformed into a literary narrative – but that narrative can take place in a variety of shapes. In summary,

> narrative meaning is the meaning of a memoir and the story it tells about a life. … To write a memoir is to fashion a text using memory and discovery, reflection and artistry. There are countless decisions about narrative elements such as plot (sequencing of actions and events), chronology and perspective, tone and diction, explanation and justification of key decisions. (Martin, 2016: 149–50)

As I understand it, this 'fashioning' takes place *in* the memoir as a vessel for narrativisation. For Timaeus this kind of process takes place vaguely in 'Something of this kind: ... the receptacle [ὑποδοχή; *hypdoche*], the foster-mother as I might say, of all becoming' (Plato, 2013: 49b). The terms 'receptacle' – 'the most insistent determination' (Derrida, 1995b: 117) – and 'foster-mother' are metaphors, as is the idea that it is a 'natural matrix [ἐκμαγεῖον; *ekmageion*]' that, in John Sallis's explanation, 'is called a matrix ... in the sense of a mass of wax or other soft material on which the imprint of a seal can be made' (Sallis, 1999: 108), even using the same word (*ekmageion*) as in Socrates's description of memory imprinting a block of wax from *Theaetetus* (Plato, 2015: 191c–d). All 'the translations remain caught in networks of interpretation' (Derrida, 1995b: 93), thus adding another layer of complexity to understanding what this 'receptacle' is; belatedly, it is called the name that now gathers all its discursive commentaries and interventions: χώρα, *khôra*.

No translation can do *khôra* full justice, though Taylor designates it as '*space*[8] which never perishes but provides an emplacement for all that is born; it is itself apprehended without sensation, by a sort of bastard inference, and so hard to believe in' (Plato, 2013: 52a–b; emphasis in original). And when Timaeus gives another of his explanations – 'but if we say it is a somewhat invisible and formless, all-receptive and partaking of the intelligible in a manner most puzzling and hard to grasp, *we shall not be wrong*' (Plato, 2013: 50a–b; my emphasis), Derrida asks: 'The prudence of this negative formulation gives reason to ponder. Not lying, not saying what is false: is this necessarily telling the truth? And, in this respect, what about testimony, bearing witness [*témoignage*]?' (Derrida, 1995b: 90). Where Derrida asks about *testimony* – albeit the juridical form, rather than Beckettian that I have just elaborated – I instead wonder about *memoir*: how this kind of receptacle that carries marks of the memorial thing turns the memorial thing into an object called memoir.

If, as I have suggested, memoir gives form and narrative (but not content) to the memories, then memories either transition through my chosen metaphor of the *khôra*, or the *khôra* 'harbors, shelters, nurtures' the memories 'like a nurse', and also 'bears, gives birth to, them (and so to all that arises from them): it is the mother' (Sallis, 1999: 113–14). The objects are the same and remain unblemished, but are just contained within a new shape that, like Lacan's vase, also shapes their meaning: memories are 're-made' (Freeman, 2015: 22). Derrida establishes the idea of *khôra* as both more thorough in *Timaeus*, and more relevant to my argument. When he describes how *Timaeus* itself resembles 'that place which *receives* everything' (Derrida, 1995b: 115) – i.e. the *khôra* – he does so through an exploration of the development of memory as writing underpinning memory in *Timaeus* (Plato, 2013: 22e–23a). Thus when it can be discerned at all, the *khôra* looks like a thing that stores memories: 'The discourse on *khôra* thus plays for philosophy a role analogous to the role which *khôra* "herself" plays for that which philosophy speaks of, namely, the cosmos [read: memoir] formed or given form [read: narrative] according to the paradigm [read: memory]' (Derrida, 1995b: 126). In Kristeva's reading, the *khôra* is an 'extremely provisional articulation' of a 'semiotic motility' that is 'generated in order to attain [a] signifying position'. If it is a place, then the 'semiotic *chora* is no more than the place where the subject is both generated and negated', a place that I see working in the *'passage from one sign-system or another'* (Kristeva, 1986: 93, 95, 111; emphasis in original) – in my terms, this describes the trajectory from the memory into memoir, as also from the memory into the novel.[9] Both require the suppression (the negation of the subject) and selection (the generation of the subject) of narrative events.

The novel form, by contrast, is *poietically* creative and, through *tekhnè*, gives shape to the poetry. The memoir and novel can mix, and Beckett's testimonial novels represent one extreme of the mélange. Another way of imagining that mix is through *The Country Girls Trilogy* as a memoir-like novel, one that breaks down in the third part (*Girls in Their Married Bliss*) – when Caithleen's third-person supersedes her first-person narrative – and absolutely fails by the time of the Epilogue. As I explore more in Chapter 5, the idea that the *khôra* is a woman or womb-like generative receptacle is not coincidental to this breakdown in form, and is wholly concerned with the woman's body, both in modern Ireland and early modern England, where a self-disciplined body results in a woman who is womb-less and all surface: compliant but apparently independent.

The argument begins with an examination of how O'Brien's *Trilogy* ties in closely with O'Brien's much more recently published memoir *Country Girl*. Where in *Country Girl*, there is a way of seeing O'Brien's narrative as feeding into a *Künstlerroman* form and genre – the novel charting the development of an artist – no such success or artistic liberation is granted to Caithleen or Baba. By the end of the trilogy, Caithleen decides to have 'herself sterilised' (O'Brien, 1987: 507), a violent attack on her body that brings Caithleen's corporeal existence in line with Beckett's Unnamable, and becomes a point of focus in my examination of *The Country Girls* in Chapter 5. O'Brien, by contrast, never recollects any such experience in her memoir. Nevertheless, there are similarities in the narrative events of the two texts – Caithleen's/O'Brien's elopement from Ireland to Britain – and the cast of characters – the farmhand, the alcoholic father, an exotic, continental gentleman who woos the young Caithleen/O'Brien, and another continental figure with whom Caithleen/O'Brien elopes.

   I also want here to make concrete the otherwise under-explored connection between Beckett and O'Brien. Significantly, it is not only recorded in the memoir *Country Girl* – in which a thematics of lethargy and corporal illness is deployed – but also developed in O'Brien's 'brilliant performance' *Night* (1972). The novel is told from the perspective of Mary Hooligan in her bed over the course of one night, recounting memories that come to her, bidden and unbidden, in both 'Elizabethan turn[s] of phrase' and through 'a hundred Jacobean parries'. It is a novel, reports Andrew O'Hagan that 'has a superabundance of the great, gasping utterance, the basic splutter of verb and noun, such as made Samuel Beckett a master' (O'Hagan, 2014: paras 2–3). O'Hagan's salient reference to the 'gasping utterance', returns me again to the question of separation between testimony and memoir in relation to the *Three Novels* and the *Trilogy*, as charted by Agamben's reading of Foucault, in which the question of the enunciated 'statement' shifts attention from the speaker to the spoken (Agamben, 2002: 139–41, 145), much like the distinction between memoir (O'Brien's speaker) and testimony (Beckett's spoken).

   Aside from the way *Night* evokes Beckett's *Three Novels*'s corporality – compare, for instance, Molloy's crude reference's to the 'hole between [Lousse's] legs, oh not the bunghole I had always imagined, but a slit' (Beckett, 2009: 51) with Mary's own crude explorations when discussing her birth: 'the slit of absurdity into which we chose to pass' (O'Brien, 2001: 10–11) – is the supine posture of Mary in her bed. Much like Malone and the Unnamable, this position puts Mary's ability to remember in jeopardy ('I try, I try so hard to recollect – not that recollection is of any use' (O'Brien, 2001: 8)), but also anticipates the substantive meeting between O'Brien and Beckett described in *Country Girl*. It takes place when O'Brien narrates her LSD trip with R. D. Laing, the consequences of which include long-lasting hallucinations. Escaping to Paris to try to evade the hallucinations, O'Brien falls ill and is bedbound in her hotel. A third unexpected visitor – after Marguerite Duras and Peter Brook – is Beckett who seats himself next to O'Brien's bed, drinking whiskey from the minibar (O'Brien, 2013: 193). Here, after taking LSD in May 1970 – and therefore prior to the publication of *Night* – O'Brien encounters, while bedbound, Beckett, the master of narratives (born out) of paralysis. The thoughts that spring to O'Brien's mind are telling, focusing on Beckett's self-exile from Ireland, and yet the lingering Irishness in his body: 'Yet there remained so much of Ireland in him, in his voice, his walk, his stick, and in his writings .... Not even Synge had captured Ireland with such feeling' (O'Brien, 2013: 195). In this constellation of connections – the bedbound body, memory, the mode of remembering – O'Brien's Beckett is cast in the mould of his own characters from the *Three Novels*, whether the walk (the narrative centrepiece of *Molloy* is Molloy and Moran's walking journeys), the stick (one of the proprietary objects over which Malone claims ownership), and his writings (likewise, the work that Malone undertakes from his bed). And, moreover, these are all characteristic features of Beckett's Irishness that I read as implied in his characters' bodies.

O'Brien's connection to Ireland is amply sketched out in her early writing, not only in the *Country Girls Trilogy* but also in *Mother Ireland* (1978) in which she charts the typology – both cultural and juridical – of Irish women. Irish women become brides and mothers to Irish children, the framing of which I elaborate in Chapter 5: Kate appears to be a typecast Irish woman, with all the attendant disappointment and betrayal. However, less easy to detect and pin down is Beckett's Irishness among his literary lands of indistinct and unspecified waste. Nevertheless, in the turn-of-the-century resurgence of historicism in Beckett studies, such as Seán Kennedy's *Beckett and Ireland* (2010) and Kennedy's and Katherine Weiss's *Samuel Beckett: History, Memory, Archive* (2009), there has been an upsurge of contemporary desire to resituate Beckett historically and geographically, arguments that I will develop. For example, in spite of the long tradition of asserting Beckett's ahistorical and apolitical nature, Kennedy argues that 'it has long been noted that traces of history–memory appear throughout Beckett's *oeuvre*' (Kennedy, 2009: 2) and that it is time to find the signifieds to which these signifiers point. Indeed, in Beckett's writing 'the question of testimony becomes significant, and it is a vexed one, in that Beckett's status as "witness" or "survivor" cannot simply be assumed. What exactly did Beckett witness, and what survive?' (Kennedy, 2009: 5). After Eoin O'Brien's photograph essay *The Beckett Country* (1986), 'many scholars admitted surprise at the extent to which Beckett's texts were rooted around the specific area of Dublin in which he was born' (Kennedy, 2009: 11) even if there is not 'direct evocation or historical representation' (Gibson, 2010: 122). Moreover, for Kennedy, even Beckett's post-war writing 'is, at times not so much a work of mourning as a refusal to mourn, a haunting, or failing to forget' (Kennedy, 2009: 15). In other words, Beckett's post-war writing, while he was resident in France, is conditioned by memories of Ireland, however 'oblique' the references: 'The obliquity is crucial, as is the sporadic and unreliable Irishness of the characters, in holding the historical material at a remove. But the point par excellence ... is that history in the *Trilogy* exists as rubble, as debris strewn across its pages' (Gibson, 2010: 122). Beckett's failure to forget Ireland, as set out by Kennedy and O'Brien, provides reason to think that Beckett's writing produces (dis)memories and ideas relating to the shape and force of modern Ireland. It is to Beckett's bodies as dismemories in the *Three Novels* to which I now turn.

Notes

1 The alchemical references in 'drosse' and 'allay' also point us towards Ben Jonson, whose relevance to this part is outlined below in relation to Beckett's novels.
2 See, for example, Steven Connor (2009: 56):

'Beckett and Sartre' was at one time as reliable a double-act as Marks and Spencer or Abbot and Costello. For 20 years or so, it was almost impossible to make any sense of Beckett outside the paradigm of existentialist phenomenology, with its bifurcated emphasis on the themes of anguish, arbitrariness and absurdity on the one hand, and of choice, freedom and transcendence on the other. Above all, it was the figure of Sartre and the arguments he developed in *Being and Nothingness* which were the source of these principles.

3 In phenomenology, consciousness is always consciousness of something, the intentional act of which gives being to consciousness. In this instance, the body gives rise to consciousness. Conversely, there is no world without the Being-for-itself directing its consciousness outward and surpassing itself: consciousness gives rise to the world.

4 See esp. chs 2 and 3.

5 See Kiberd (2017: 332) where he explicitly links McGahern's Moran in *Amongst Women* (1990) to Beckett's Moran from *Molloy*.

6 For reasons that will become apparent, I prefer to call the main character 'Caithleen'.

7 Following the original and insensible paradigm, and then its mimetic form.

8 Sallis adds:

> If, following Cornford and A. E. Taylor, one proposed to translate χώρα as *space*, then one would have to set about immediately withdrawing from the word much that we cannot but hear in it. For clearly the χώρα is not the isotropic space of post-Cartesian physics. Nor is it even empty space, the void, as discussed in Greek atomism; for this is called τό κενόν and is in fact discussed as such later in the *Timaeus* (58b). It would hardly be otherwise if one were to translate χώρα as place, following Thomas Taylor, who in effect translated Chalcidius' translation of χώρα as *locus*; for one would then have conflated the difference between χώρα and τόπος and would risk assimilating Plato's chorology to the topology of Aristotle's *Physics*. (Sallis, 1999: 115)

9 For Kristeva, this transposition between sign-systems also provides the basis for intertextuality (Kristeva, 1986: 111).

4

'[M]y genius for forgetting': Samuel Beckett's theatrical bodies

Introduction: the self-knowing body

There are clear and obvious connections between Shakespeare and Beckett's drama, some of which have already been described and unpicked. David Wheatley has rounded up the references to Shakespeare in Beckett's work. Plays referenced include *Hamlet*, *Love's Labour's Lost*, *A Winter's Tale*, *The Taming of the Shrew*, *Romeo and Juliet*, *Twelfth Night*, and, importantly for Wheatley, *King Lear* (Wheatley, 2010: 166–7). Wheatley himself follows Jan Kott's example in comparing *Endgame* with *Lear* (Wheatley, 2010: 176). Graley Herren extends Beckett's 'striking affinities' for Shakespeare to reading *Hamlet*'s influence in *Eh Joe* (2012: 61), though van der Ziel more recently takes a different approach. He notes that in *Waiting for Godot*, Vladimir and Estragon do not merely cite or allude to Shakespeare, but also 'transmut[e] the abstracted theological argument of the original into an absolute material reality' (van der Ziel, 2019: 41). This is particularly the case when van der Ziel spies *Hamlet*'s influence over Beckett's drama, but van der Ziel also spots references to *Love's Labour's Lost*, *King Lear*, *A Midsummer Night's Dream*, *Henry V*, and *The Tempest*. With regard to the latter, van der Ziel argues that Lucky 'is Hamlet and Caliban rolled into one' (van der Ziel, 2019: 45) and situates *Godot* in contemporary postcolonial discourses, even if it in part rejects standard postcolonial resistance.

One key strand of van der Ziel's argument, though not foregrounded, is the theatrical nature of Beckett's intertextual memories in *Godot*. I will take this theatricality seriously, exploring how it works in Beckett's prose writing of the 1950s, before his turn to drama. Referring to 'Lucky's great feat of "thinking" in Act 1', van der Ziel claims that it 'probably contains the highest concentration of Shakespearean allusions of any passage in the play' and this confirms that it 'is also one of Godot's most overtly and self-consciously theatrical passages' (van der Ziel, 2019: 41). This parodic, absurdist version of the soliloquy firmly establishes the metatheatrical connection between Shakespeare and Beckett. Similarly, invoking *Midsummer* as well as *The Tempest*, van der Ziel concludes that

> The late romance of Prospero and Caliban's island may also have suggested a theatrical idea that would allow characters like Vladimir and Estragon to transcend the traumas of their age by conceiving that it may just be possible that their lives are only a dream – the mere 'impression' of existence conjured, magician-like, out of thin air of which they speak early in Act 2[.] (van der Ziel, 2019: 51)

In this instance the sense of bodily theatricality that is obviously included in Beckett's drama links directly to the discourses of sleep and lethargy. By firming up that connection, van der Ziel's argument invites an exploration of Beckett's drama of sleep with the early modern (anti)theatrical concern with sleep and amnesia – whether the 'Extraordinary … tricks that memory plays' (Beckett, 2006: 71) or the dozens of occasions when sleep and fatigue overtake Estragon and Vladimir. These memorial tricks are manifold in Beckett's drama and merit particular scrutiny along the lines of the influence of Shakespeare's theatrical body.

Clearly, as I have outlined here, this has already been undertaken in relation to Beckett's drama; however, I now undertake it in relation to the 1950s' prose *Three Novels* that also exhibit an interest in the theatrical body, in amnesia as a positive constructor of character, and in early modern drama. I am offering a corrective to what Paul Sheehan lamented in the fallacious 'notion that the appearance of the live actor onstage automatically furnishes a performance with an immediate and unambiguous presence' when I focus on 'the intensely corporeal character, the often over-assertive physical being, of the actor's body' (Sheehan, 2009: 158) in Beckett's evidently immaterial prose bodies. Moreover, since Tatyana Hramova has sketched the possible overlaps between *As You Like It* and *Molloy* and has therefore opened the critical door to reading beyond the explicit intertext, she has implicitly encouraged others to examine other kinds of textual memory such as Lachmann's amnesiac troping and satirical transformation. In what follows, I first chart the importance of self-knowing 'coenæsthesia' – a word that Beckett's Molloy gives us – in both that novel and in Coriolanus, before more concretely examining the theatrical body in the Malone Dies and The Unnamable as it crosses over from Shakespeare's Coriolanus, and Jonson's Volpone, which is about theatrical lying – that is, acting.

With a focus on the fraught bodies of those onstage – such as Coriolanus – as well as those playgoers in the theatre, as configured negatively by antitheatricalists, I explore how the amnesiac lethargy that afflicts Molloy opens up an opportunity for him to invent memories that sustain him. When it comes to the Unnamable, Volpone demonstrates how the lying body – that of the actor – provides a way of persisting corporally in spite of social mores that demand something called 'authenticity'. The result is that early modern theatricality – privileging the re-presentable body – provides Beckett's antiheroes with a way of thinking through the body–nation relationship, and contesting the lingering colonial attitudes in modern Ireland, as also the near-puritan Irish Republic.

There is a parallel interest in Shakespeare and Beckett in the self-knowing body. It is no surprise that Shakespeare's drama deals widely with the correlation between the body and self-identity. Indeed, Greenblatt explains in Renaissance Self-Fashioning on the macro level how Queen Elizabeth I's 'visible being was a hieroglyphic of the timeless corporate being with its absolute perfection' (Greenblatt, 1984: 167). Invoking the mediaeval idea of the 'King's Two Bodies' first fully explicated by Ernst Kantorowicz (1957), in which the bodies natural and political elide their difference and instead unite in the monarch's physical body, Greenblatt discusses both the temporal and immortal body of the monarch. Elizabeth's is clearly a special case, however, and Greenblatt also describes how the growing secularity in early modern England made use of the mortal body of the commoner. Citing the example of 1531 Protestant heretic Thomas Rainham and his treatment at the hands of Sir Thomas More, Greenblatt notes that 'secular power is essentially the ability to perform certain operations upon the body: to remove it from one place to another, to confine it, to cause it

extreme pain, to reduce it to ashes' (Greenblatt, 1984: 80). The fact
that the body becomes the focus of secular power demonstrates the
growing understanding that the person – the individual – is located
in that body in advance of Descartes's revolutionary Dualistic ideas
in the seventeenth century. This proto-Dualism is distrusted, for
example, in the poetry of Thomas Wyatt for whom 'This centrality
of the body, a given of modern consciousness, is seen as unbearable,
at once vulnerable to mutability and presumptuously independent'
(Greenblatt, 1984: 123). Thus the body becomes one of the contested sites of the modern, self-fashioning individual in Renaissance
and early modern England.

The unbearable body is explicitly discussed in relation to memory in *Coriolanus* in which the hero complains about the plebeians
discussing his wounds that 'smart / To hear themselves remembered'
(I.ix.28–9). For Coriolanus the issue is not that his wounds are
signifiers of his character, but because they have become, to borrow Greenblatt's idiom, 'presumptuously independent' of his own
self-identity. Indeed, Coriolanus is comfortable with this modern
individuality being tied ever closer to the body. He displays no discomfort when he is wounded at Corioles, declaring that the wounds
are more 'physical / Than dangerous to me' (I.v.18–19), and he
commits to appear in front of his enemy, Aufidius, thus wounded.
Referring to these lines of Coriolanus, in *The Body Embarrassed*
Gail Kern Paster writes that Coriolanus makes a 'hyperbolic assertion of personal control in a therapeutic idiom', thereby claiming
'self-control' (Paster, 1993: 98, 97) through the bloodletting.

Garret Sullivan makes the case for the memory and forgetting
discourses in Renaissance thinking being located in the body. 'Each
of these forms' of memory 'is best understood as fully embodied'
(Sullivan, 2005: 7). Moreover, in focusing on dramatic texts Sullivan
identifies the controversy over embodied memory and forgetting in
the theatre, and in tracts in which 'antitheatricalist writers routinely
construed the theatre as a catalyst for forgetting and the somatic
states with which forgetting was associated' (Sullivan, 2005: 40),
with sleep and lethargy the prime sites for attack. However, unlike
the antitheatricalists, Sullivan conceives of early modern dramatists
making positive use of forgetfulness, thereby 'making forgetfulness
and lethargy the signs under which subjectivity emerges' (Sullivan,
2005: 25). As with other corporeal discourses, for Sullivan memory

and forgetfulness also corporealise the individual subject, and subjectivise the individual body.

Whilst not discussed by Sullivan, *Coriolanus* clearly engages with these discourses. After the battle in Corioles the newly named Coriolanus asks Cominius to spare a citizen who used to house Martius when he stayed there (I.ix.81–6). Lartius then asks Martius for his name but, in the immediate aftermath of the battle, Martius is stumped. His weary body leads to forgetfulness:

> CORIOLANUS By Jupiter, forgot!
> I am weary; yea, my memory is tired.
> Have we no wine here? (I. ix. 89–91)

This typifies Sullivan's examples of the somatic conception of memory and forgetfulness. On one hand, Sullivan shows how memory as both 'recorder and guardian' is a physical 'repository' in the body, its function dependent on the balance of the four humours. On another, whilst 'forgetting is *placeless* ... it is recognizable as a *somatic process*, one that manifests itself in diseases, bodily dispositions and humoral excesses' and is the 'conceptual ground for memory' (Sullivan, 2005: 27; emphasis in original). Thus, Coriolanus's lethargic weariness – his improper bodily disposition – causes his forgetfulness. This bodily memory is underpinned by the productive forgetfulness that Sullivan describes, including the erasure of Martius's cognomen in the final scene, thus returning Martius to himself (quite literally). Aufidius's deliberate forgetfulness of 'Coriolanus' (V.iii.91) is corroborated finally by the stage direction that not only confirms the body's indelibility (as if that were in doubt), but also the productive nature of forgetfulness in *Coriolanus*:

> Exeunt bearing the body of Martius. (V.vi.156 SD)

Two critical ideas merit memorialising from this brief discussion. First, a framework of early modern memory provides a productive way of analysing and thinking through *Coriolanus*, and amnesia is as powerful as the processes of remembering in the play. Second, this memory is embodied, therefore tying the manifold discussions of corporeality in *Coriolanus* into discussions of memory and forgetting.

Like Coriolanus, Beckett's characters also derive a foundational understanding of themselves through their bodies, specifically through the idea of coenæsthesia. This term first appears on its own before it is implicitly tethered to memorial self-identity. First, coenæsthesia is especially relevant in *Molloy*, when thinking about both Molloy and Moran. Molloy explains that 'coenæsthetically speaking of course, I felt more or less the same as usual, that is to say, if I may give myself away, so terror-stricken that I was virtually bereft of feeling, not to say of consciousness, and drowned in a deep and merciful torpor shot with brief abominable gleams' (Beckett, 2009: 49). Molloy's coenæsthesia encourages consideration of the textual body as a true testimony of Molloy and, conversely, that his body also speaks truly of himself. It is important to foreground the so-called testimonial truthfulness of the material body. For Molloy that material body is disabled and is one of the reasons why he falters on his journey to his mother. He mentions early on that he uses crutches, followed shortly by his announcement that 'crippled though I was, I was no mean cyclist, at that period'. His disabled body is restricted, but not something to dismiss. Later, Molloy aptly labels his body a 'nuisance' (Beckett, 2009: 12, 71). For Sartre coenæsthesia comprises 'some privileged experiences in which [affective qualities] can be apprehended in [their] purity, in particular what we call "physical" pain'. Feeling pain, 'the translucent matter of consciousness, its *being-there*, its attachment to the world' (emphasis in original), is the point at which 'we come close[st] to touching that nihilation of the In-itself [i.e., the world and the Other] by the For-itself [i.e., consciousness] and that reapprehension of the For-itself by the In-itself which nourishes the very nihilation'. 'Pain-consciousness' 'constitutes the very consciousness which surpasses it' (Sartre, 2003: 355; 357): interiorised pain-consciousness emerges from a world of pain and gives that pain to the world.

Pain, writes Scarry, is an exceptional 'psychic, somatic, and perceptual state … by having no object in the external world. … [I]t is also its objectlessness that may give rise to imagining'. And, in her description of imagination, Scarry is also (albeit unintentionally) describing memory in the state of confusion that memory–imagination engenders: '[T]he only evidence that one is "imagining" is that imaginary objects appear in the mind' (Scarry, 1987: 162). As

I have already discussed, the image that presents itself in the process of remembering and of imagining are often interchangeable, confounding Bergson's truism that 'To *picture* is not to *remember*' (Bergson, 1991: 135). Scarry and Sartre thus set out the ways that selfhood (under the banner of coenæsthesia), pain and memory are interconnected, and this seems to be a shared concern for both Coriolanus and Molloy; nevertheless, it is important to maintain that in Beckett's *Three Novels* 'Bodily experience is continually submerged in the problematic of voice, in apparent negation of Elaine Scarry's analysis of physical pain' (Jones, 2012: 135): the nature of the novels' testimony must also be considered.

There are moments in the *Three Novels* when the coenæsthetic relationship between the narrative subject and his body is strained, specifically in memorial terms. When in the police cell, for example, Molloy is unsure whether he wishes to sit down, 'remembering what I had learnt in that connexion, namely that the sitting posture was not for me any more, because of my short stiff leg' (Beckett, 2009: 18). This is succeeded by the bathetic epiphany in which Molloy recalls his name: 'And suddenly I remembered my name, Molloy. My name is Molloy, I cried, all of a sudden, now I remember.' The sequence of events is telling: Molloy turns away from the police sergeant and feels the 'bland' sun and sky shine on his face, which triggers his memory of his discomfort when sitting down. Immediately, another memory of his name is triggered involuntarily. The world and the body interweave, resulting in anamnesis and recollected memory. The link between the world, self-knowledge of the body and memory is thus central to *Molloy* as it is to *Coriolanus*. We might go far as to assert that these characters can be pieced together – re-membered – solely through their pain: their pain gives rise to their body and self.

Just as in the latter, coenæsthesia is not always a positive phenomenon in the former. Whilst Molloy benefits from understanding the functioning of his body, Moran suffers. Moran's knee problems that begin as he prepares to leave to track down Molloy recur on the journey itself: 'One night, having finally succeeded in falling asleep beside my son as usual, I woke with a start, feeling as if I had just been dealt a violent blow.' This blow is a 'fulgurating pain … through my knee'. Moran concludes hopefully that 'It's a touch of neuralgia brought on by all the tramping and trudging

and the chill damp nights' (Beckett, 2009: 132–3), and it is possible
to read that pain as correlating with Moran's employment by an
authoritarian-style business that can be connected to the question
of Irish governance. As Moran's narrative develops, coenæsthetic
knowledge adopts a memorial language – both in terms of anamnesis and amnesia. Later in his testimony the tense and mood of
Moran's narration shift:

> I seemed to see myself ageing as swiftly as a day-fly. But the idea of
> ageing was not exactly the one which offered itself to me. And what
> I saw was more like a crumbling, a frenzied collapsing of all that
> had always protected me from all I was always condemned to be.
> (Beckett, 2009: 142–3)

Here Moran is reluctant to accept the facts of his failing body,
instead conditioning his existence as something that 'I was always
condemned to be': acceptance of his present body confronts
him – the future moment to which his body has inevitably carried
him – and Moran resists. As death closes in, Moran fears the annihi-
lation of the future possibilities his present once had (Sartre, 2003:
150–1). Moran's body's accelerated ageing is emphasised through
the blind and amnesiac moment of its excesses. Moran loses control
and coenæsthetic knowledge of his body and, just as Molloy was
accosted on his travels (Beckett, 2009: 78–9), so too is Moran:

> What is your business here? he said. Are you on night patrol? I said.
> … I do not know what happened then. But a little later, perhaps a
> long time later, I found him stretched on the ground, his head in a
> pulp. I am sorry I cannot indicate more clearly how this result was
> obtained[.] (Beckett, 2009: 145)

Moran's murderous fight, far from being remembered in minute
detail as was Molloy's corresponding fight, escapes memory through
euphemistic police-speak. The amnesiac process seems to empty
Moran's self-consciousness of stability and structure, signalled by
the vacuous and incongruous phrasing, 'I am sorry I cannot indicate
more clearly how this result was obtained.' Moran later – almost
consequentially – admits to not recognising his own face, noting
that the 'face my hands felt was not my face any more, and the
hands my face felt were my hands no longer' (Beckett, 2009: 164).
This signifies Moran's absolute amnesiac alienation from his body,

accompanied by his surprise at the objectification of his body parts
to his consciousness and recalls the hollow face that Moran imagines earlier in his narrative. It comes just after Moran has 'tried to
remember what I was to do with Molloy, once I had found him'
before he pivots 'on [to] myself … on me so changed from what I
was'. He sees

> A little globe swaying up slowly from the depths, through the quiet
> water, smooth at first, and scarcely paler than its escorting ripples,
> then little by little a face, with holes for the eyes and mouth and other
> wounds and nothing to show if it was a man's face or a woman's
> face, a young face or an old face, or if its calm too was not an effect
> of the water trembling between it and the light. … Similarly the miss-
> ing instructions concerning Molloy, when I felt them stirring in the
> depths of my memory, I turned from them in haste towards other
> unknowns. (Beckett, 2009: 143)

Alyssia Garrison considers this moment presenting 'the terrifying
consciousness of [Moran's] formlessness: the zero point of the dwindling bodily form' (Beckett, 2009: 96). It is in this sense absolutely
present, but a presence that differs from prior iterations of Moran's
consciousness. Moreover, moments of (attempted) remembering
frame the appearance of the hollow face. Both before and after,
Moran seeks in the depths of his memory for the 'missing instructions' for what to do with Molloy when he eventually finds him. For
Moran, the act of remembering Molloy compels instant consideration of his own body. It is not merely that Molloy's remembered
presence turns Moran inwards, but that the process of anamnesis
turns Moran towards images of corporal dissolution and recognition of his own degradation. For Moran, the memory of others
triggers the degradation of his own subjectivity, whereas Molloy's
concern with (and forgetting of) himself, returns his subjectivity to
him.

Though both the early modern and Beckett texts offer a conception of the individual self that rests wholly or in part on the
remembered body, in the later writing this self-knowing corporeality emerges in a language that touches on memory and forgetfulness. The body and memory thus interweave. In the next section, I
develop these ideas more thoroughly in terms of how theatrical bodies are bound up with memory and amnesia, in both early modern

drama and Beckett's *Three Novels*. I first examine the audience's body in *Malone Dies* and *Coriolanus* via early modern antitheatrical invective, concluding that Malone's becomes the inventive *locus* of memories in the mode of an infected audience member. I then explore how the Unnamable becomes a bad actor who deliberately forgets his lines, signifying a broken body, in the mode of Jonson's satires. When viewed with these ideas in mind, Beckett's theatrical prose bodies even more closely remember their early modern forebears.

Malone Dies: the audience's theatrical body

Early modern antitheatricalists railed against the damage done to the public theatre's audiences. In 1599 John Rainolds warned of the dangers of watching a play, and invoked memorial language in the process:

> [W]hen at midsummer, in very hottweather [*sic*], ... manie brought home a burning ague from the theater: about the seventh day folowing, they were ridde thereof, some by much bleeding, some by sweating, but all, as soone as they were abroade out of their beddes, did fall into a strange distemper and passion of a light phrensie. The which exciting them to say & cry aloude such things as were sticking freshly in their memorie, and had affected most of their minde, they grewe all to Tragedie-playing, and full lustily they sounded out *Iambicall speeches*[.] (Rainolds, 1599: 118; emphasis in original)

Rainolds's invective places the faculty of memory firmly within the discussion of antitheatricality, especially from the perspective of the audience. Following a physical illness – placing the body at the centre of theatrical transmission – and because of a fully functioning memorial faculty, the audience is at risk of impersonation and theatricality.

These reasons compel Eve Sanders to compare Rainolds's treatise with *Coriolanus*. In light of Coriolanus's experience as a member of a two-man audience who witnesses the rhetorical power of Volumnia, his mother, Sanders notes that Rainolds's text 'puts in relief Shakespeare's engagement with current ideas and conflicts about the actor's subjective experience of acting' (Sanders, 2006:

389). The moment when Coriolanus is made to feel a 'dull actor' who has 'forgot [his] part' (V.iii.40–1) is the carnivalesque moment when he temporarily changes his mind about theatricality. The arguments by Volumnia

> force Coriolanus to reexamine his views about theater and the body and bring him to new conclusions: that his mind may be made subordinate to the body without loss of dignity; that outward signs of identity are variable rather than fixed; that his actions are performative, as well as instrumental; and that agency may be enhanced, not diminished, by the breaching of social categories. (Sanders, 2006: 391)

I began this chapter outlining the important tether between body, self, and memory in early modern England, and Sanders pinpoints the moment of Coriolanus's becoming-audience as a reason for his 'about-face' (Sanders, 2006: 391) in terms of how his body and self correlate. For Sanders 'Coriolanus's rote iteration of the standard arguments of antitheatrical pamphleteers, almost as if he had prepared his oration with talking points cribbed from them, steers the play away from Roman history and anachronistically into the thick of early modern antitheatrical politics' (Sanders, 2006: 399). But in that argument, Sanders overlooks (or forgets) the importance that corporeal *memory* has in this play. Sanders's focus is exclusively about the self–body relation. For example, when Coriolanus tries to stand to leave his mother's audience and he announces that 'I have sat too long' (V.iii.131), the women then kneel in front of him and he responds by holding his mother's hand (V.iii.182 SD). For Sanders, this merely shows that once Coriolanus-as-audience watches his mother's theatrical body 'in the worn clothing of a victim of war' (Sanders, 2006: 406), he is compelled to respond corporeally: '[H]is body's action teaches Coriolanus's mind' (Sanders, 2006: 407).

Sanders's overlooking of the corporo-memorial elements of *Coriolanus* is not unusual. Kent Lehnhof similarly argues that 'Almost as soon as Coriolanus learns the power of theatricality, he becomes its victim' (2000: 40), and more recently contends that by holding his mother's hand, Coriolanus acknowledges that he 'cannot sustain his posture of self-sufficiency' (Lehnhof, 2013: 364). But Robert Ormsby points out that 'In the entire First Folio, this is the only stage direction that specifically demands a total stop to both speech and action' (Ormsby, 2008: 52). That suspension is brought about through Coriolanus's audience-body, modelling how the Globe's audience should respond to the scene unfolding before them onstage. Significantly, Coriolanus re-members (that is, pieces together physically) his mother holding *his* son's hand lines earlier (V.iii.23–4) by holding her hand in response. This shows how the onstage audience experiences and does indeed repeat a corporal theatrical memory, as Rainolds alleged.

Thus the structure of memory endemic to the theatrical audience, derided by antitheatricalists such as Rainolds, is that the watching body – the body that is, at least notionally, passive – in fact becomes endowed with agency. The same logic applies to the Mousetrap of *Hamlet*. It is staged because Hamlet has

> heard
> That guilty creatures sitting at a play
> Have by the very cunning of the scene
> Been struck so to the soul that presently
> They have proclaimed their malefactions. (II.ii.523–7)

Hamlet and Horatio – in what must have been Rainolds's worst nightmare in terms of theatrical contagion – watch Horatio and Hamlet 'observe' Claudius (III.ii.76), and watch Claudius in the onstage audience watching the players in the Murder of Gonzago (ll. 128 ff.). The Globe's audience watch Hamlet, Horatio, Claudius, *and* the players, and witness Claudius's physical response to the Mousetrap: he 'rises' (l. 258) and storms out. Whilst in *Coriolanus* the hero re-enacts his mother's physical performance, Claudius remembers his own actions when he is a member of the audience and responds guiltily. Or, at least, Hamlet and Horatio 'perceive' (l. 279) Claudius's actions *as though* he guiltily remembered his own actions, and themselves become an audience endowed with agency, willing to 'take the Ghost's word for a thousand pound' (ll. 278–9). In these instances, Shakespeare's audience's bodies are expected to respond in the way that Hamlet and Horatio do, and the way they think Claudius does – but not just through metaphor. Memory characterises the audience's corporal relationship with the action onstage.

These antitheatrical ideas are central to my reading of *Malone Dies*, in particular in the ways in which forging memory – as undertaken through Malone's imagination – helps to establish the character's corporal subjectivity. Just as in the structure outlined above, through which the audience remembering what they see onstage leads them to respond corporeally, so too does Malone respond corporeally to the stories he remembers. What is more interesting and specific to the case of Malone is that he imaginatively creates these memories afresh, in a bid to 'stave off the yawning abyss of *ennui*' (Pedretti, 2013: 589). These memories are both effectively corporal, and they (continue to) endow Malone with a subjectivity that threatens to disappear otherwise. In this structure – allied to the memories of Shakespeare and early modern antitheatricality – Malone is, like Coriolanus, empowered by being a member of the audience.

In addition to the explicit mention of Punch and Judy (Beckett, 2009: 272) – the importance of which I elaborate in the following – there are also several intertextual memories of Shakespeare in *Malone Dies*. For instance, when Moll talks to Macmann – a (Gaelic) version of 'son of man', and thus another version of the Irish messiah, remembering Synge's Christy Mahon – while he is convalescing, she tells him to 'Consider moreover that the flesh is not the end-all and the be-all' (Beckett, 2009: 254), transforming (in Lachmann's terminology) Macbeth's doubting soliloquy when he hopes that the assassination of Duncan 'Might be the be-all and the end-all here, / But here, upon this bank and shoal of time' (I.vii.5–6). Where Macbeth longs for the inconsequential – a future outside Christological structures of morality – Moll parodically says that the body can be overlooked 'especially at our age, and name me lovers who can do with their eyes what we can do with ours' (Beckett, 2009: 254). Moll's and Macmann's bodies are as impotent as Duncan's shortly will be.

Another transformative intertextual memory appears when Malone laments that he is 'Weary with my weariness, white last moon, sole regret, not even. To be dead, *before her, on her, with her*, and turn, dead on dead, about poor mankind, and never to die any more, from among the living' (Beckett, 2009: 257; emphasis mine). This passage recalls Iago's provocative comments to Othello that Michael Cassio is 'with' Desdemona:

OTHELLO With her?
IAGO With her, on her; what you will.
OTHELLO Lie with her! lie on her! We say lie on her, when they belie
    her. (IV.i.34–6)

Iago feeds Othello's jealous mind with the merest morsels of information, and Othello takes the bait. In contrast, Malone's belle is the
'white last moon' with whom he longs to live in death. Othello fears
the exchange of physical fluids between his wife and his lieutenant,
where Malone longs to accelerate his own death to meet his celes-
tial love. Like the *Macbeth* intertext above, this allusion parodically
transforms its predecessor, showcasing Malone's narrative imagination and, crucially, intensifies the probability that Malone and
Moll – the narrator and the narrated – share intertextual memories and vocabularies. The stories that Malone narrates, in short,
may not be real, but merely stories and invented memories that help
Malone to fill the time between now and death.

   If Moll is part, or an extension, of Malone, then other questions
relating to memory emerge, such as the question of propriety and
memory. On the one hand, it is possible to consider it in the discussion
surrounding communal or collective memory, such as in Halbwachs
and Nora. In this argument the focus on *lieux de mémoire*, such as
war memorials, suggests that no one individual can lay singular claim
over a memory that is publicly shared with a community; Ricoeur
asserts that this emptying of the possibility of individual memory is
an inevitable consequence of the critical emergence of 'sociology at
the turn of the twentieth century, … [when] individual memory, as a
purportedly original agency, becomes problematic' (Ricoeur, 2006:
95). Marianne Hirsch's postmemory equally troubles the notion of
memorial propriety when she charts the authenticity of the children
of Shoah survivors who, though not alive during the Second World
War, 'remember' the camps. 'Postmemory', proposes Hirsch, 'is a
powerful and very particular form of memory precisely because its
connection to its object or source is mediated not through recollection but through an imaginative investment and creation' on the
part of those who 'grow up dominated by narratives that preceded
their birth' (Hirsch, 1997: 22): post-memories are memories that
do not properly belong. Sullivan also sees the discussion of early
modern memory relating to property and identity:

In an account of the interconnections between property ownership and identity, James Turner asserts that '"Land" and "place" are equivalent to "propriety" – meaning in seventeenth-century English both property and knowing one's place'. 'Propriety', then, requires 'knowing one's place', a process connected to ownership of property; it entails the physical and social placement of the individual. To forget oneself by violating propriety – by no longer performing the actions inherent in occupying a specific place in a (largely land-based) social order – is to become dislodged from such a network, disengaged from that which determines your identity.

This disengagement helps bring into focus interrelations of property, propriety and memory. (Sullivan, 2005: 15)

Sullivan's argument locates the origin of the nexus of propriety, memory, and identity in the seventeenth century and the problem that 'self-forgetting' or amnesia entails for the subject. Given that 'Shakespeare frequently dramatizes self-forgetting' (Sullivan, 2005: 16), the question of memorial propriety is equally important to that drama.

When Coriolanus says that his wounds 'smart / To hear themselves remembered' (I.ix.28–9), he contests their existence in the public sphere. That is, he lays claim to them as *his* and not belonging to the people. This argument intensifies with Coriolanus's refusal to show his wounds to the plebeians in the marketplace when they offer to support his bid to be consul – if only he should show them his wounds. Comparing him with the physiological and artistic wound-man, Cynthia Marshall argues that 'In their instability as "appropriable … signifiers"', the wounds can be the historical markers of Coriolanus's heroism, the emblems that give him access to the consulship, or even the symbol of Volumnia's pride. Their appropriability violates the individuality that should be afforded to a citizen and his body, as Coriolanus is forced 'to grasp impropriety itself' when he 'finds himself, on the one hand, irremissibly consigned to his body and, on the other, just as inexorably incapable of assuming it' properly (Agamben, 2015: 84). Coriolanus conveniently 'forgets' to show his wounds to the plebeians and quickly changes back into his own clothes so as to 'know myself again' (II.iii.145) and escape the risk of bad faith,[1] while yet relying on the plebeian-audience's acceptance of his body's theatricality. For Sanders, in the scene in the marketplace, Coriolanus is involved in 'an explicitly theatrical exhibit of shame' that comprises 'sound track and gesture ...[,] emotion and narrative ... and, in short, [Coriolanus] tak[ing] on the role of an actor' (Sanders, 2006: 387). Coriolanus: actor; plebeians: audience. Coriolanus gambles on this premise and his ability to convince his audience to remember his realistic acting, the logic of which argument underpins antitheatricalist rhetoric. This is a strategy designed to rebut antitheatricalism by paying greater attention to 'intellectual claims of theater's opponents' through which Coriolanus 'finds, in his own body and in the theatrical arena of the marketplace, possibilities and constraints that contradict his initial conception of performance as inherently debasing' (Sanders, 2006: 388).

More successfully for Malone, Moll, and Macmann – those who remember *Othello* and *Macbeth* respectively – are the living 'memories' that extend from, and belong to, Malone's imagination. Best known of these, perhaps, is Malone's inventory of items that grows and shrinks along with the confidence in his own narrative. As part of this inventory, Malone concludes at one point that 'In the meantime nothing is mine any more, according to my definition, if I remember rightly, except my exercise-book, my lead and the French pencil, assuming it really exists' (Beckett, 2009: 248). Here overlap the discourses of propriety, memory, and imagination for Malone. In respect of Malone's inventory, Gilles Deleuze wrote in *Fold* that

> It is not easy to know what we own, and for what length of time. ... The great inventory of Beckett's Malone is consummate proof. Malone is a naked monad, or almost naked, scatterbrained, degenerate, whose zone of clarity is always shrinking, and whose body folds upon itself, its requisites always escaping him. It's hard for him to tell what remains in his possession, that is, 'according to his definition', what belongs to him only partially, and for what duration of time. Is he a thing or an animalcule? If he does not have belongings, then to whom does he belong? That is a metaphysical question. He needs a special hook, a sort of *vinculum* on which he can hang and sort through his different things, but he has even lost this hook. (Deleuze, 1993: 109)

Deleuze's discussion of propriety leads on to subjectivity ('Is he a thing[?]') and also on to the body – the vinculum is a kind of tendon that joins soft tissue to bone. Or, as Dowd writes, 'The vinculum is

... the fold which at once separates and conjoins the soul and the body' (Dowd, 2007: 141) – it is the corporalised junction through which character is embodied, through which self is tethered to the body. The *vinculum* is necessary for Malone in order to sustain the self's memorial underpinning and to avoid self-forgetting, particularly in relation to the inventory: 'Among these objects and stories is the image of the body' (McFeaters, 2010: 63). Further, Dowd (ventriloquising Leibniz) also points out the inherent danger of Malone trying to lay claim to his inventory as a means of remembering himself, arguing that Malone 'possesses virtually the [inventoried] series expressed in its clear zone, while the series reverses the possession by claiming [Malone] as part of its prolongation' (Dowd, 2007: 141). In the same soliloquy cited above, Macbeth fears the identical reversal of consequence for himself as Dowd does for Malone:

> MACBETH   [T]hat but this blow
> Might be the be-all and the end-all here,
> But here, upon this bank and shoal of time,
> We'd jump the life to come. But in these cases,
> We still have judgment here, that we but teach
> Bloody instructions, which, being taught, return
> To plague th'*inventor*. This even-handed justice
> Commends th'ingredience of our poisoned chalice
> To our own lips. (I.vii.4–12; my emphasis)

Where Macbeth's fear (ultimately proven true) is that he will suffer the justice he metes out to Duncan, the danger for Malone is that he will forget himself in the process of inventorying – not only the objects, but also the characters Macmann, Sapo, Moll, etc. – and of imaginatively constructing memories. If so, the memories will come to claim him as proper to them, and he will be forgotten. This places agency firmly in the phenomenological category of memory, underlining the possibility that Beckett's characters are embodied – re-membered into being – prior to assuming an internally monologuing consciousness. This kind of ontology could also accurately describe Coriolanus.

Agamben takes the argument of propriety a step further, claiming that 'the originary character as "mine" of the donation of a body never stops giving rise to aporias and difficulties'

(Agamben, 2015: 82), thereby troubling the idea that even one's body can be guaranteed. He draws on Edith Stein's conception of empathy to point out that, in relation to one's own body, 'however much one affirms the originary character of the "propriety" of the body and of lived experience, the intrusiveness of an "impropriety" shows itself to be all the more originary and strong in it, as if the body proper always cast[s] a shadow' (Agamben, 2015: 83). The point is that the experience and knowledge of one's own body may in fact emerge from the experience of another's in a 'non-originarily living an originality' (Agamben, 2015: 83). This logic – that the other body's experience is appropriated into and on to the body of the self *after* the other has experienced it, but *as if* it were the first experience – also describes the antitheatrical theories of drama's work on the audience's bodies.[2] In these theories, the ways in which Rainolds's audience remembers the '*iambicall speeches*' means that they, too, experience the actor's bodies in a 'non-originarily living an originality', also re-membering the character's experiences. In Coriolanus's practice, this extends beyond speech to corporal mimesis and holding his mother's hand that has recently held his son's hand:

> Even as she is staking her claim on her son, however, Volumnia is holding her grandson by the hand, using the boy to both establish and assert the maternal attachment of which she speaks. And Coriolanus appears to get the message. ... Moving over to his mother, he places his hand in hers and stands silently at her side – just like young Martius. (Lehnhof, 2013: 364)

Coriolanus is returned to himself by virtue of re-membering the other's body.

For Malone, this 'non-originarily living an originality' appeals as he focuses on memorialising his inventory and constructing memories of others. After all, he says that 'I have pinned my faith to appearances, believing them to be vain' (Beckett, 2009: 204). Malone acknowledges this strategy early on, claiming that 'I do not remember how I got here', and that 'All that belongs to the past. Now it is the present I must establish' (Beckett, 2009: 177). As part of the process of 'establish[ing]' the present, he tells stories of others – but when he stops, Malone worries about himself: 'There I am forgetting myself again' (Beckett, 2009: 189). Malone articulates this fear in the language of early modern theatricality through which, as Sullivan shows, 'self-forgetting entails the staging of subjectivity' (Sullivan, 2005: 18). Malone stages his subjectivity – '*I … myself*' – through the physical act of his self-writing, in the first instance, and then extends his memories to Sapo: 'And yet *I* write about *myself* with the same pencil and in the same exercisebook as about him. It is because it is no longer *I, I* must have said so long ago, but another whose life is just beginning. It is right that he should have his little chronicle, his memories' (Beckett, 2009: 201; my emphases). This passage proves the nature of Malone's written memories – both others' and his – that they are the source of subjectivity. The '"I" is positioning a "he" which is positioning the "I"', argues Andrew McFeaters, 'each determining a testimony in support of each other's "historical – and therefore subjective – existence"' (McFeaters, 2010: 64). Rather than a marked difference between Malone's *now-then* and his *now-now*, McFeaters urges us to think of Malone's testimony as theatrical witnessing by the *I* of the *he*, and vice versa. This is a theatrical, rather than a juridical, testimony.

Later, Malone confirms that the physical act of writing and memorialising the others is entirely selfish. 'A few lines', he starts, 'to remind me that I too subsist. He has not come back. How long ago is it now? I don't know. Long. And I? Indubitably going, that's all that matters' (Beckett, 2009: 276). There is a clear, comforting self-assurance in Malone's narrative memories that help him to remember himself, added to by the near-final description of the 'absurd light, the stars, the beacons, the buoys, the lights of earth and in the hills the faint fires of the blazing gorse. Macmann, my last, my possessions, I remember, he is there too, perhaps he sleeps' (Beckett, 2009: 280). The intrusion of Macmann into Malone's own world confirms that they indeed share an original inventive *locus*: Malone's mind. Moreover, the comment that Macmann might be sleeping is consistent with Malone's own experience throughout the novel when afflicted by his tendency to fall asleep, a corporal lethargy that also threatens his ability to write since 'In vain I grope, I cannot find my exercise-book. But I still have the pencil in my hand' (Beckett, 2009: 202). Lethargy, as in both early modern antitheatrical ideas and mid-twentieth-century phenomenology (Merleau-Ponty, 1988: 115–16), leads to forgetfulness of the body and therefore threatens the self, too. To reiterate, Sullivan details how 'antitheatricalist writers routinely construed the theatre as a catalyst for forgetting and the somatic states with which forgetting was associated' (Sullivan, 2005: 40). Without his ability to establish these memories in the present, therefore, Malone is unable to stage his subjectivity.

Malone describes the ability to establish the stories – the memories, the inventory – with two key terms: 'Live and invent. I have tried. I must have tried. Invent. It is not the word. Neither is live. No matter. I have tried' (Beckett, 2009: 189). This confession confirms the fictive nature of his stories: the inventory develops from his invention. A few lines later Malone confirms what kind of invention he preferred as

> all alone, well hidden, [I] played the clown, all alone, hour after hour, motionless, often standing, spellbound, groaning. That's right, groan. I couldn't play. I turned till I was dizzy, clapped my hands, ran, shouted, saw myself winning, saw myself losing, rejoicing, lamenting. Then suddenly I threw myself on the playthings, if there were any, or on a child, to change his joy to howling, or I fled to hiding. ... There I am forgetting myself again. (Beckett, 2009: 189)

The reference to the clown returns the argument again to the Punch and Judy that, for Malone, was a memory forged in Moll's mind that she narrated to Macmann: 'Macmann remembered those words' (Beckett, 2009: 272). On this occasion, though, Malone becomes the Punch figure, the dramatic clown whose own excessive corporality leads to dizziness and slapstick behaviour, falling on to the toys and the children. The audience's antitheatrical infection, and the way Malone invents and inventories as a means to live and to be remembered, are all about establishing memories in the present so that Malone can become a legacy – as McFeaters corroborates, 'The stories, whether recalled or invented, act like ... memories' (McFeaters, 2010: 70) – and not a clown who 'groans' and corpses onstage. Malone thus rejects the antitheatrical bias against mimetic behaviours, instead using the inventor's prerogative to create, and to have his subjectivity endowed by those theatrical creations. Or, 'The very experience of imagining being able to project physically, even under circumstances where it is impossible, is itself a kind of Sartrean project, a surpassing of the condition of helplessness' because 'Its projections beyond the body are always bodily projections and therefore as much bracing as scattering' (Connor, 2009: 59): Malone's inventories are corporeal projections. With this, the danger of sleep – the antitheatrical fear of lethargic bodies – also threatens Malone because when he sleeps he cannot invent and live. Invention *is* living for Malone, because for Malone inventing is projecting bodily memories in the present in order to sustain Malone into the future: Malone's theatricality is conditioned by future dismemories.

The Unnamable: the actor's forgetful body

In addition to *Malone Dies*, in several places in *The Unnamable* the narrator makes overt mention of a theatrical show:

> Referring to his planter-box dwelling as 'my Punch and Judy box' [Beckett, 2009: 333], the Unnamable suggests that he is putting on a performance for the amusement of others, the 'college of tyrants' who 'want to be entertained' [Beckett, 2009: 304, 365]. The narrator performs 'so that they might be pleased with me' [Beckett, 2009: 328] but his Punch and Judy analogy suggests that 'my tormentors' are also behind the scenes acting as puppeteers, 'ramming a set of words down your gullet' [Beckett, 2009: 341, 292].
> (Pedretti, 2013: 588)

This description of a slapstick performance ('Punch and Judy') aligns the Unnamable's conception of theatre with the antitheatricalists of Shakespeare's England. The first Punch shows in England became popular after the restoration of the monarchy and the reopening of the theatres in 1660. However, they had descended in England from the popular early modern puppet theatre that had lasted through the Puritan closure of the theatres in the 1640s, becoming one of the rare forms of entertainment that escaped Puritan censure (Speaight, 1970: 38). In his history of the Punch and Judy shows, George Speaight notes that the English version of Punch was influenced by the changing shape of the mediaeval Vice figure who transformed into the early modern onstage clowns and fools. Falstaff's tomfoolery, Lear's Fool's dour witticisms, and even Richard III's hunchback (Weimann, 1978: 160) provide the blueprint for the English Punch in their later manifestations. Just as those Shakespearean types assumed the *platea*[3] space on the early modern stage partly to talk back to, mock, and parody the moral and societal strictures in place both inside and outside the theatre, so too does Punch and Judy parade its theatricality before the audience, inviting censure and claims of immorality. The Punch and Judy show is an antitheatricalist's perfected vision of the chronic failings of theatre and its immoralities – and this is the style of theatre in which the Unnamable conceives of himself being forced to act. The Unnamable's 'performance', as it were, is an affront to lovers of theatre and is an attempt to confound the 'college of tyrants'.

Early modern antitheatricalists made several claims about the theatre, including the accusation that theatrical entertainment threatened to supplant church services that had their own type of theatricality, what Barish describes as the church's 'potent competitor for men's imaginations, the secular stage' (Barish, 1985: 89). Whilst certain writers explicitly defended the theatre from these accusations – Thomas Heywood's *Apology for Actors* (1612) perhaps chief among them – the Unnamable here appears to side with the idea that theatrical entertainment torments the actor's body, especially in and through the process of learning lines. As an actor, 'learning' becomes a euphemism, with the Unnamable using a violent corporeal metaphor to describe his transformation into a thespian. Already in the opening pages, the Unnamable states that he understands that 'The fact would seem to be ... not only that I shall have to speak of things of which I cannot speak, but also (which is even more interesting) that I shall have to, I forget, no matter' (Beckett, 2009: 286). The words that, later, are described as being 'ramm[ed]' (Beckett, 2009: 341) down the Unnamable's throat, are also part of an obligation on his part to tell his story. Elsewhere in his narrative, the Unnamable records that he has been 'crammed ... full' so that his puppeteers may 'prevent me from saying who I am, where I am' (Beckett, 2009: 318). That is, as an actor, he is prevented from being himself, perhaps even by an implied prescribing and proscribing colonial or new-fangled Irish administration. And yet, even at the beginning of his acting on behalf of the 'tyrants' and 'puppeteers', he lapses into amnesia: 'I forget'. The link between the theatrical body and amnesia, discussed above in relation to *Molloy*, is also evident here in *The Unnamable*.

Ben Jonson's *Volpone* is apposite to this discussion because it cites and satirises the accepted belief and understanding of the actor's theatrical body in early modern drama. The plot depicts Volpone tricking several others into thinking that they are to inherit his fortune, thereby playing the 'rascal ... engaged in various games of pretense' (Barish, 1985: 145). He does this through feigning illness and using his parasite, Mosca, to discourse with the potential inheritors, and also by disguising himself onstage, such as when he acts as a mountebank selling his wares. *Volpone* thus tells a story about the dissimulating body, acting, and the economy. The acrostic prefacing the play summarises its story:

V OLPONE, childless, rich, feigns sick, despairs,
O ffers his state to hopes of several heirs,
L ies languishing; his parasite receives
P resents of all, assures, deludes; then weaves
O ther cross plots, which ope themselves, are told.
N ew tricks for safety are sought; they thrive, when, bold,
E ach tempts th' other again, and all are sold. (Jonson, 1966: 39)

The acrostic serves as a mnemonic, offering itself as a comic prelude to the play about to be read,[4] but also as a takeaway idea that can be stored in the memory of the readers once their experience of the play is over. *Volpone* thus establishes itself in its opening as a play partial to commitment to memory. Moreover, the acrostic–mnemonic describes the economical 'tricks' that Volpone plays on his heirs, using a specifically economical way of transmitting information. That this acrostic is written in the present tense is but one signal that this is a play about the present, the *now* in which Volpone draws together his plans for the *future*, especially in terms of his legacy and inheritance. The now, as with Malone, is all about its future (dis)memories.

Volpone's acting forms the centre-piece of the play with him convincing three others that they might individually inherit his wealth; his failing health (through his dissembling body) encourages their belief in the likelihood of their inheritance: 'Now, my feigned cough, my phthisic, and my gout, / ... Help, with your forcèd functions ... / Wherein this three year I have milked their hopes' (I.ii.124–7). This theatricality, which relies in particular on corporal manipulation

of his own body, also bleeds into puppetry as he 'milk[s]' others
and manipulates them. Alexander Leggatt writes that Volpone 'sees
life as a play, and himself as an actor-playwright improvising and
manipulating the scenario for his own amusement. His real out-
rage against nature is not that of treating money as a god, but that
of treating people as puppets' (Leggatt, 1969: 22–3). This cultured
theatricality shows that, through Volpone's commitment to trickery,
he manages to wield power over time: when he feigns his death,
Volpone's actions allow him to continue living *during his afterlife*.
This present becomes an antitheatrical dismemory in a played-out
future.

A large part of the comedy derives from seeing the three potential
inheritors – Voltore, Corbaccio, and Corvino – attempt to influence Volpone and Mosca. Their attempts take the form of making sure that they are remembered by Volpone in his will (I.iii.10).
That enforced remembrance takes place, for example, through economical exchange, such as when Corvino comes to visit the ailing
Volpone:

> MOSCA Signior Corvino! come most wish'd for! O,
>   How happy were you, if you knew it, now!
> CORVINO Why? what? wherein?
> MOSCA The tardy hour is come, sir.
> CORVINO He is not dead?
> MOSCA Not dead, sir, but as good;
>   He knows no man.
> CORVINO How shall I do then?
> MOSCA Why, sir?
> CORVINO I have brought him here a pearl.
> MOSCA Perhaps he has
>   So much remembrance left, as to know you, sir:
>   He still calls on you; nothing but your name
>   Is in his mouth: Is your pearl orient, sir?
> CORVINO Venice was never owner of the like.
> VOLPONE Signior Corvino.
> MOSCA He calls you; step and give it him. He's here, sir,
>   And he has brought you a rich pearl.
> CORVINO How do you, sir?
>   Tell him, it doubles the twelfth caract.
> MOSCA Sir,

He cannot understand, his hearing's gone;
And yet it comforts him to see you –
CORVINO Say,
I have a diamond for him, too.
MOSCA Best show 't, sir;
Put it into his hand; 'tis only there
He apprehends: he has his feeling, yet.
See how he grasps it! (I.v.1–19)

Mosca's clear *volte face* when Corvino offers a pearl to Volpone drives the comedy in this exchange, and it is underpinned by memory ('Perhaps he has / So much remembrance left'). Corvino presses his claims further by highlighting the quality of the pearl ('Venice was never owner of the like. / ... it doubles the twelfth caract') and by interrupting Mosca to offer something even more valuable to Volpone ('Say, / I have a diamond for him, too'). Tellingly, Volpone only 'apprehends' the diamond once it is placed in his hand: the corporal verification *now* is necessary as part of his theatrical body in order to secure Corvino's remembrance *in the future*. Amnesia thus threatens the future of the economy, and corporal memory can set it right. This acting appears to mock the antitheatricalists' concerned connection between the treacherous body and memory.

This corporal, theatrical trickery is exactly the sort of thing that piqued the antitheatricalists such as John Rainolds, whom I quoted earlier, and William Prynne, the 'megalomaniac' (Barish, 1985: 84) who wrote the 1633 antitheatrical diatribe *Histriomatrix*. Sanders interrogates one particular turn of phrase of Rainolds, namely when he derides the manner in which acting 'breedeth, principally to the actors, in whom the earnest care of liuely representing the lewde demeanour of bad persons doeth worke a great impression of waxing like vnto them' (Rainolds, 1599: 108). Sanders comments that

> The choice of 'wax' to mean 'grow', in conjunction with the word 'impression', registers the perceived passivity of the behavior being described; the actor busying mind and body with action is conceived as merely on the receiving end of that activity, like wax imprinted involuntarily, by the forms of thought and motion he mimics. (Sanders, 2006: 393)

Sanders highlights the intimate connection between the terms 'wax' and 'impression', without going so far as to argue that these terms

are connected by a classical formulation for memory, as I have outlined above. In Rainolds's criticism of acting and actors, he implicitly
targets the role of memory in the acting process. In his ambiguous
relationship with the theatre, Jonson does likewise in the opening
of his masque *Hymenaie* (1606): 'And, though *bodies* ofttimes have
the ill luck to be sensually preferred, they find afterwards, the good
fortune, when *soules* live, to be utterly forgotten' (Jonson, 1970:
47; my emphasis). In combination with Sullivan's arguments about
the somatic abilities that are threatened by forgetfulness – evident
in the *Volpone* passages I quoted above, in which the body's forgetfulness threatens Corvino's future inheritance – *Volpone*, like *The
Unnamable*, is ably advancing the antitheatricalists' arguments.
In particular, if theatrical bodies are used to the wrong end, they
threaten to produce dismemories.

The antitheatrical body therefore connects *Volpone* (and early
modern drama) with *The Unnamable*. There are other possible
connections between these writers, such as in the staging of a puppet show in Act Five of Jonson's *Bartholomew Fair* (1614), an
entertainment antecedent of Punch and Judy. Like the later show,
Leatherhead's 'motion' includes crude humour ('kiss my hole here
and smell' (V.iv.129)), slapstick performance (V.iv.301 SD), and it
provokes Busy's antitheatrical invective, calling it 'profane' and
'idol' (V.iv.60). This antitheatricalism is comically put down when
Busy is bathetically turned in favour of the play:

> BUSY Yes, and my main argument against you is that you are an
> abomination; for the male among you putteth on the apparel of
> the female, and the female of the male.
> PUPPET DIONYSIUS You lie, you lie, you lie abominably. ... It is your
> old stale argument against the players, but it will not hold against
> the puppets; for we have neither male nor female amongst us. And
> that thou may'st see if thou wilt, like a malicious purblind zeal as
> thou art.
> *The puppet takes up his garment. ...*
> BUSY I am confuted; the Cause hath failed me. ... Let it go on. For I
> am changed, and will become a beholder with you! (V.v.90–110)

Here Busy rehearses typical antitheatrical arguments, such as
Rainolds's condemnation of actors for wearing 'wemens apparel'
(Rainolds, 1599: 97–8, 101–2). Viewed in the same light, *The
Unnamable*'s puppet theatre becomes a way to respond to

antitheatricalism, suggesting that the Unnamable is being controlled by puppeteers – allegories for Free State and Republican puritans – who want paradoxically to parade the body's free ability to perform, while the Unnamable himself wants to keep his body strictly to himself. In Coriolanus's terms, the Unnamable wants to 'play / The man I am' (III.ii.15–16), thereby countering antitheatrical discourses.

I am not the first to draw a comparison between Jonson and Beckett, with Barish writing that

> Jonson himself would not have countenanced the suggestion that he was attacking the theater in its essence. He would have claimed to be reforming it, scouring off its excrescencies, restoring it to nature and truth after its long bondage to false conventions. … Samuel Beckett has pioneered an analogous reform in our own day, trying to revive an art that has rotted in its own pomp by stripping away all theatrical tinsel, so as to get back to the bedrock of reality[.] (Barish, 1985: 135–6)

Barish clearly refers to Beckett's drama, but the tramps and clowns that populate Beckett's stage are rehearsed in his prose characters, from Mercier and Camier to the Unnamable – his final prose work before *Waiting for Godot*. In both the Jonson and Beckett texts, the eponymous character is the ambassador for the antitheatrical narrative. The Unnamable develops this seam of thought by the very presentism of his testimony, during which he confesses to his reader that 'My inability to absorb, my genius for forgetting, are more than [the puppeteers] reckoned with'. Indeed, owing to this proclivity to forget his lines, the Unnamable foresees a promising future: 'I'll be myself at last. … On their own ground, with their own arms, I'll scatter them, and their miscreated puppets. Perhaps I'll find traces of myself by the same occasion' (Beckett, 2009: 318–19). The connection between the actor's enforced and scripted role and his ability to forget in order to 'find … myself' or to 'be[come] myself' is an idea that predominates in early modern drama in which 'forgetting generates a subject who is defined in terms of desire, or lethargy, or the willful rejection of what she or he knows. … [F]orgetting is more than the antithesis to memory; it is both a condition of being and a pattern of behaviour' (Sullivan, 2005: 15).

In the case of the Unnamable, he establishes a temporal paradox through his testimony when he forgets the script given to him, one that parallels Coriolanus's 'Like a dull actor now, / I have forgot my part and I am out, / Even to a full disgrace' (V.iii.40–2). In *Coriolanus*, this is the moment that begins Coriolanus's refusal to sack Rome alongside his sometime enemy, and his return to his Roman and familial roots. Coriolanus finds and re-founds himself, as it were. For the Unnamable, alongside his self-discovery the effect of the present is keenly felt, given that he is able to narrate his forgetfulness in the narrative present, explaining that when he is able to speak for himself, rather than speaking lines he is given, he will in the future be able to find himself. However, the paradox is that he is already able, in a testimony taking place in the present, to speak his mind, thus demonstrating the lack of historical development in the *Three Novels*, and instead a theatrical kind of testimony. The Unnamable is trying to gain the fruits of his fraudulent legacy for the present time of the play, acting as a dismemory in the now, therefore testifying to the future existing now, just as with Volpone.

The corporal element of the Unnamable's testimony should not be forgotten. As Garrison points out, *The Unnamable* is an example of 'embodied "testimonial art"' (Garrison, 2009: 91). Senses are in evidence, but often fragmentary. When considering the visual sense, for example, it is important also to consider the impossibility of not seeing, especially for someone whose eyelids are unable to blink. There is instead an inevitability and unavoidability in seeing what is put directly in front of the Unnamable, thereby confirming Bergson's argument that whilst 'Images themselves cannot create images' they 'indicate at each moment ... the position of a certain given image, my body, in relation to the surrounding images'. Through these indications, the images 'foreshadow at each successive moment [my body's] virtual acts' (Bergson, 1991: 23). The Unnamable admits that 'In a sense I would be better off at the circumference, since my eyes are always fixed in a certain direction', but is nonetheless aware that he is not at the circumference because he is not able to see that which does not pass in front of him, and being in the centre means that much passes outside his line of sight. The Unnamable's corporeal sight is negatively confirmed: he knows he sees because things happen to pass in front of his eyes. By extension, he knows that he lives because his eyes function: 'I, of whom I know nothing, I know my eyes are open, because of the tears that pour from them unceasingly.' The Unnamable later confirms the interlinking of his sight with his mortality when announcing that 'ceasing to be, I ceased to see' (Beckett, 2009: 289, 298, 334). The logic of this seems to confirm the structure of the theatrical body as described by early modern scholars and as exploited by Volpone to undo his suitors: to be seen is to be. Citing the Unnamable's commitment to 'another present, even though it be not yet mine' (Beckett, 2009: 300), Garrison argues that the Unnamable's 'tears are a *translucent* trace, the remnant not of presence but of absence, of something to come' (Beckett, 2009: 98; emphasis in original) in the future. Here, the present and future are united in the testimony of the Unnamable's body – a testimony that the Unnamable labels a 'distant testimony ... which I have not yet been able to quash' (Beckett, 2009: 299). The Unnamable's body speaks irrepressibly in an over-determined present conditioned by the future (Garrison's 'something to come'), thereby becoming a dismemory.[5]

The theatrical in *The Unnamable* continues until its end when the Unnamable announces 'I can't go on, I'll go on' (Beckett, 2009: 407). Evoking the clichéd lines of the theatre – 'The show must go on!' – the Unnamable knows that he has been 'carried ... to the threshold of my story, before the door that opens on my story' (Beckett, 2009: 407). These comments can be read as describing an actor's vocation, for whom the other side of the door is the stage that demands speech and performance – the very thing the Unnamable has sought to reject in this 'Punch and Judy' show he seems to be putting on. But the empty stage is also a space of silence, and of those kinds of spaces the Unnamable says that 'I speak of the silence before going into it, ... I emerge from it to speak of it, if it's I who speak, and it's not, I *act* as if it were, sometimes I *act* as if it were' (Beckett, 2009: 400; my emphasis). The Unnamable is evoking the actor's vocation and process of representation when he describes his being at all. But the Unnamable, unlike the actor or puppet, is more or less bodiless, despite his corporeality. Though he is headless (404–6), he is also the thinnest, most invisible part of the inner ear:

> [P]erhaps that's what I am, the thing that divides the world in two, on the one side the outside, on the other the inside, that can be as thin as foil, I'm neither one side nor the other, I'm in the middle, I'm the partition, I've two surfaces and no thickness, perhaps that's what I feel, myself vibrating, I'm the tympanum, on the one hand the mind, on the other the world, I don't belong to either. (Beckett, 2009: 376)

Dowd explains how this self-description proves that the Unnamable – in his form as Worm – is a monadic body without organs, in the Deleuzo-Guattarian vocabulary. He feels vibrations, but is unable to speak outwardly to the world. The Unnamable is mocking the actor's art, even if he is 'cramm[ed]' with words like actors and puppets are. In Dowd's reading, this means that 'A further requirement is that the monad in question possess an "archival" capacity' (Dowd, 2007: 154) – the ability, that is, to remember. Without that ability to remember the past, the tympanic-Worm is locked firmly in the present and bears out the lethargic and amnesiac qualities that typified Rainolds's actor. But the tympanum also places him firmly in the present, vibrating at the same moment of the reception of sound, just prior to the vibration's insignificance in the future. This tympanum is also Garrison's 'remnant trace' of 'something to come' – and it is also antitheatrical, refusing the barest duties of the actor to remember, even as he is coerced into the actor's position, and becomes memory-less in the process.

In the Unnamable's evocation of early modern antitheatrical discourses, *The Unnamable* recalls the early modern drama that also interrogates and responds to antitheatrical discourses. This includes *Coriolanus* and *Volpone*. Given that these latter texts also engage with the corporeal question of theatricality and memory – in particular, forgetfulness – it is becoming more clearly apparent that Beckett's novel, when viewed through the lens of the actor's body, remembers and restages the antitheatricalist arguments from the early modern period. In terms of the memorial intertextuality characterised by Lachmann, this approach comes closest to her third category of transformation. In both cases – the early modern and the modernist Irish – dismemory characterises the type of corporeal, theatrical memory that plays out.

Conclusion

The theatrical body is both that of the actors and of the watching audience. Both sets of bodies are afflicted by lethargy – that is, a loss of memory – and threatened by repeating memorialised behaviours. The theatre, in short, is a dangerous place to visit if you want to keep your body safe. In *Coriolanus*, the actor's body is threatened with a loss of self-identity, while in *Volpone*, the actor's is the malevolent body. Nevertheless, as Coriolanus proves, watching a performance may return the audience to themselves, thereby helping them to develop their self-identity through memory. The theatre enables and disables bodies.

In Beckett's drama, this is equally prominent; however, this is true also in his prose *Three Novels*. Moreover, for Molloy, Moran, Malone, and the Unnamable, their bodies are at the centre of their self-knowledge. Failed memory threatens that knowledge, a threat hastened through amnesiac behaviours such as falling asleep. However, Malone and the Unnamable survive the threats of lethargy by either performing the roles assigned to them, or by using the inventor's prerogative of creating memories. In these cases, the characters perform and invent memories *in the present*, but for a future not yet come, thus collapsing Sartre's three temporal ekstases, and privileging the future. In doing so, whilst Sartre's Past is the temporal Being that 'I am without being able to live it' (Sartre, 2003: 142), in *Malone Dies* the Future becomes not that which, in Sartre's schema is *'possibilized'* (Sartre, 2003: 152; emphasis in original), but again an unavoidable and unshakable past because of the invented (and therefore future-oriented) memories: Malone establishes the future; the Unnamable 'can't go on' yet vows he '[wi]ll go on'. The Punch and Judy shows they put on, as puppets in another's play, become sources of strength as they enact the antitheatrical behaviours visibly questioned and critiqued in Shakespeare's and Jonson's early modern drama. This drama is explicitly remembered in a fleshy way, signifying the bodily inheritance Beckett's narrators take on. Their bodies are antitheatrical emblems of how the body is a powerful tool in establishing dismemorial literature.

Notes

1 See especially Sartre's comment that 'We can see the use which bad faith can make of these judgments which all aim at establishing that I am not what I am' (2003: 80), seemingly a counter to Coriolanus's desire to 'play / The man I am' (III.ii.15–16).

2 For Levinas, this ethical relation with the other is a foundational feature of the *I think*, also describing it in memorial terms in 'Diachrony and Sociality': 'A past that is articulated – or "thought" – without recourse to memory[.] ... This hearing of a commandment as already obedience' (Levinas, 2006: 148–9).

3 See Robert Weimann for the original development of a theory of the *platea*:

> In the Renaissance ... the incorporation of comic plebeian elements produced a characteristic two-level structure in which the descendants of the Vice gradually became the nonallegorical center of the comic subplot. ... But at the same time, this traditional perspective is no longer exclusively connected to the descendants of the Vice. Wherever the modern representative of evil (Gloucester, Iago, Edmund) tends to dominate the serious part itself, other figures, such as Brakenbury or the Scrivener or Richard III, or Poor Tom and the Fool in King Lear, are brought in to enunciate a complementary vision of the main theme. Their dramatic is not a farcical one, but involves that special relationship with the audience which results from a *platea*-like position and allows the statement of generalized truth in a choric mode. Theirs, indeed, are 'countervoices' – voices from outside the representative ideologies – ushering in a contrapuntal theme, some countervision which, even in a comic context, cannot be easily dismissed in its thematic implications for the main plot. (Weimann, 1978: 158–9)

4 Assuming, with some academic knowledge, that the Argument would not have been read onstage, and was kept for the printed edition. It was included in the 1607 quarto.

5 Garrison's 'something to come', written in English, cannot be confirmed as a version of Derrida's '*à-venir*', but its possibility should be considered. If the 'something to come' is in a Derridean vein, then my notion of dismemory takes on an ethico-political dimension:

> But for this very reason, [justice] has perhaps an *avenir* [future], precisely [*justement*], a 'to-come' [*à-venir*] that one will have to [*qu'il faudra*] rigorously distinguish from the future. The future loses the openness, the coming of the other (who comes), without which there is no justice; and the future can always reproduce the present, announce itself or present itself as a future present in the modified form of the present. Justice remains to come, it remains by coming [*la justice reste à venir*], it has to come [*elle a à venir*] it is to-come, the to-come [*elle est à-venir*], it deploys the very dimension of events irreducibly to come. It will always have it, this *à-venir*, and will always have had it. Perhaps this is why justice, insofar as it is not only a juridical or political concept, opens up to the *avenir* the transformation, the recasting or refounding [*la refondation*] of law and politics. (Derrida, 2002: 256–7)

5

'Kate had herself sterilized': Edna O'Brien's self-disciplining bodies

Introduction

Shakespeare's texts form an intimate, memorial hinterland in Edna O'Brien's writing; however, the connection has never fully been explored. In a collection of interviews ranging from 1967 to 2010, O'Brien exclaims in 1984 that 'Shakespeare is God. He knows everything and expresses it with such a density of poetry and humor and power that the mind boggles' (O'Brien in Kersnowski, 2018: 25), notes in 2002 that 'the greatest teacher … is Shakespeare' because 'Shakespeare knows when to be lyrical and he knows when to cut' the writing (O'Brien in Kersnowski, 2018: 65), and in 2009 that Shakespeare's speeches 'are extraordinary' (O'Brien in Kersnowski, 2018: 74). Indeed, even in the stultified environment of post-war Ireland, O'Brien recalled that she 'read and learned off by heart, spouting in fact, in the fields, around the home[,] the speeches of Shakespeare', while in 2010 she told an interviewer that 'It's like an athlete warming up – I read a scene or so of Shakespeare before I start work. It's so rich and complex' (O'Brien in Kersnowski, 2018: 80). Despite all these hints and expressions of admiration and of debt – and declaration of Shakespeare's emplacement in O'Brien's memory – no critic has yet undertaken an in-depth reading of Shakespeare's influence. Ellen McWilliams marks the critical limit in her acknowledgement of an 'echo' between O'Brien's (2006) *The Light of Evening* and 'Caliban's plot to steal Prospero's books in Shakespeare's *The Tempest*, [when] Eleanora finds freedom and escape, and her own expressive voice, through working her way through the contents of her husband's library' (McWilliams, 2013: 81). Declan Kiberd wishes away the fairy tale connection between *The Country Girls* and *The Winter's Tale* (Kiberd, 2017: 70). The Shakespearean intertexts that are veiled in the 1963 teleplay *The Wedding Dress*[1] and that become fully fledged citations in 2009's drama *Haunted* (based on the former) are yet to garner any critical attention.

By contrast, the exploration of bodies in O'Brien's writing is fulsome. As Sinéad Mooney summarises,

> Edna O'Brien's writing has always been interested in the ways in which female bodies are classified, disciplined, invaded, destroyed, altered, decorated, and pleasured. Her writing since 1960 systematically explores the condition of women as embodied subjects, specifically the ways in which western society disciplines women's bodies within a heterosexual economy, and the extent to which women may accept or contest this. (Mooney, 2006: 196)

I build on this kind of summary in reading O'Brien's *Country Girls Trilogy*, thinking through the very specific, gendered corporeality experienced by Caithleen and Baba, and the ways in which their experience as Irish women is conditioned by their lived experience in their bodies – bodies, moreover, that are specifically disciplined, in Mooney's Foucauldianism, because of their wombs.

The Irish woman's womb has been culturally nationalised through the symbol of Mother Ireland. After all, 'Ireland has always been a woman', writes Edna O'Brien in *Mother Ireland* (O'Brien, 1978: 11), 'a womb, a cave, a cow, a Rosaleen, a sow, a bride, a harlot, and, of course, the gaunt Hag of Beare'. Lady Gregory's and Yeats's *Cathleen ni Houlihan* (1902) featured one of these manifestations of the Mother Ireland trope in the Old Woman who metamorphoses into a beautiful 'young girl' with 'the walk of a queen' (Yeats, 2001b: 93). But critically, this Cathleen is dependent on a self-sacrificing masculinity. 'If anyone would give me help he must give me *him*self', says the Old Woman, '*he* must give me all' (Yeats, 2001b: 90; emphasis mine). She adds:

> They shall be remembered for ever,
> They shall be alive for ever,
> They shall be speaking for ever,
> The people shall hear them for ever. (Yeats, 2001b: 92)

This passage confirms that the masculine blood sacrifice provides an *eikon* to be remembered. This trope of de-feminisation of nationalism was also true for someone like the revolutionary Pádraig Pearse, with Joost Augusteijn explaining that he 'linked the Celtic and Gaelic vision, and made the feminised attributes of Celticism into a masculine ideal of pagan Irish civilisation' (Augusteijn, 2010: 171). Pearse's infatuation with masculinity thus even extended to the de-feminisation of Mother Ireland.

The Irish woman's womb has also been juridically nationalised. A brief examination of Article 41 of *Bunreacht na hEireann* – Éamon de Valera's 1937 Constitution of the Irish Republic – makes plain what is at stake for women biopolitically. In the first clause, the family is recognised as a 'natural primary and fundamental unit group of Society', before, in the second clause, 'by her life within the home, woman gives to the State a support without which the common good cannot be achieved'. The second clause then transforms, without pronouncement, 'woman' to 'mother' who 'shall not be obliged by economic necessity to engage in labour to the neglect of their duties in the home'.[2] Helen Thompson adds that we should also pay attention to Article 45 because in Ireland 'work is an inherently gendered activity, thus suggesting that Irish society has been structured according to a policy of "separate but equal" genders' (Thompson, 2010: 53). Mooney's focus on the discipline of women's bodies is no clearer than in this juridical example, making salient what Foucault condemns as the state's co-opting 'biopower': The 'supervision' of 'biological processes: propagation, births and mortality, the level of health, life expectancy and longevity, with all the conditions that can cause these to vary' (Foucault, 1990: 139). These can all be exploited advantageously by the modern Irish nation.

And yet it is clear the Irish nation owes a huge amount to women – both before 1916 and to this day, even if their contribution has not been fully recognised (Pelan, 1996: 49). Two women have held the position of President – Mary Robinson (1990–97) and Mary McAleese (1997–2011) – and other female figures in the last 100 years feature prominently in the memory of the Irish nation: Lady Gregory and Constance Markievicz constitute the original celebrities of modern Irish femininity, but others including Rosamond Jacob (1888–1960) and Alice Milligan (1866–1953) are finding a resurgent profile.[3] Nevertheless, real living women despairingly remain minority figures in the national Irish memory.⁴ Moreover, women's exclusion from the narrative of blood sacrifice further disbars them from re-entering the national memory. However, in the remainder of this chapter I will demonstrate that, by memorially accessing and imaginatively redeploying several of Shakespeare's heterosexual relationships – from *Macbeth*, *Othello*, and *The Taming of the Shrew* – and at least two 'hysterical' women – Thaisa from *Pericles* and Hermione from *The Winter's Tale* – O'Brien's *Country Girls Trilogy* gives us a way of seeing how Mother Ireland can still figure prominently, turned to the utopian future, but with the haunting body of Caithleen Brady attached to the symbol, replete with her antimaternal, future-denying associations: her dismemorial body.

Memory of men

I have already explored the epistemological differences between Beckett's testimonies and O'Brien's memoir (and memoir-like) writing. In the latter, the reader is given a greater sense of the speaking-I's historical development from the *now-then* to the *now-now* through the use of memory-becoming-narrative. This allows us to piece together the tapestry-like, complex interrelations between the wholly fictional *Country Girls Trilogy* and the self-proclaimed memoir *Country Girl*. This includes the ways in which the two casts of characters correspond. For instance, when O'Brien recounts meeting Sean McBride, son of revolutionaries Major John McBride and Maud Gonne, the speaker recalls that

> his accent [was] slightly French from having grown up in Normandy. He took me to lunch in Jammet's, Dublin's grandest restaurant, and afterwards he smoked a cigar and had a cognac, while I had a peppermint frappé, my first ever. ... McBride offered to drive me part of the way [home] ... I was too frightened to let him hold my hand on the journey. That rectitude, combined with my longing, was what made him the protagonist in my first novel, *The Country Girls*, the aloof and mysterious barrister, whom Kate would moon over and lose her heart to, in fiction. (O'Brien, 2013: 89)

Aside from this explicit correlation, the overlaps between Sean McBride in this vignette and Mr Gentleman across *The Country Girls* are manifold. Mr Gentleman is French, he takes Caithleen for lunch in Dublin where they drink wine, Mr Gentleman drives her home, and when Caithleen holds his hand – denied in the 'real life' encounter – the frisson leads to Caithleen's joyful pronouncement that 'My soul was alive; enchantment; something I had never known before. It was the happiest day of my whole life.' On another car journey Mr Gentleman kisses Caithleen, and 'It affected my entire body. My toes, though they were numb and pinched in the new shoes, responded to that kiss', much in the same way that, later, 'when he kissed me, my body became like rain. Soft, Flowing. Amenable' (O'Brien, 1987: 12, 55–6, 89–90, 157). In Lachmann's intertextual memory schema, the relation between the two texts could be characterised as 'transformation', dissimulating the one relationship within the other. Interestingly, the dissimulation foregrounds the corporal sensations that Caithleen feels: the memory becomes transformed and translated into a corporal language.

In another example, Eugene Gaillard from the *Trilogy* is a version of Ernest Gébler, O'Brien's husband. When he is introduced in the memoir, it is in the chapter entitled 'The Literary Bessie Bunter', a nickname that O'Brien had earned by virtue of 'spouting bits of poetry' (O'Brien, 2013: 110) – no doubt Shakespeare among the verses. Bessie, like her comic book brother, was known for her large size, and in *The Lonely Girl*, Caithleen and Baba's friend, Tod, points Caithleen out and tells Eugene that 'That's the literary fat girl I was telling you about' (O'Brien, 1987: 184). Again, the corporal hint in the memoir is a full-blown comment in the fictional text. The man's European ethnicity is emphasised in both texts by virtue of his body, whether the 'dark brown eyes and granite features' in the memoir, which remind O'Brien of 'a German actor' (O'Brien, 2013: 111), or Gaillard's 'long face' with its 'gray color', his 'Black, luxuriant hairs', or his complexion like a 'dark-faced God' (O'Brien, 1987: 185, 187, 197). There is another parallel in the respective plots of Caithleen with Eugene and O'Brien with Gébler when, in the former, Caithleen's family tries to repatriate Caithleen from Eugene's country home (O'Brien, 1987: 293–303); in the latter, O'Brien has gone to hide from her family with Gébler on the Isle of Wight when her father turns up with her brother and a priest to try to take O'Brien back home (O'Brien, 2013: 115–17). In both cases, the alluring and exotic married man with European features is in complete control of a young woman whose prospects back home with her family are less than appealing.

It is, of course, no surprise that fiction is born out of 'real life' experience. However, other correlations between characters in O'Brien's memoir and characters in Shakespeare's dramas also merit pointing out – in particular the male characters. For instance, in the 1960s Richard Burton is remembered when he recites some of Shakespeare's verse:

> Never on any stage have I been so mesmerised, so entranced, as I was that night, hearing Richard Burton recite Shakespeare, torrents of it. As a boy he had memorised those speeches and spoken them down in the Welsh valleys and vowed that all his life would be devoted to Shakespeare, a vow he reneged on and felt sorry about. ... [Burton was] a bard brother[.] (O'Brien, 2013: 185–6)

This 'bard brother', by the time of this meeting, had already played Hamlet (three times), Prince Hal in *1* and *2 Henry IV*, the king in *Henry V* (twice), Ferdinand in *The Tempest*, Coriolanus, Sir Toby in *Twelfth Night*, Sir Philip Cognac in *King John*, both Othello and Iago in the same production (on alternate nights), and Petruccio in *The Taming of the Shrew*. Famously he also played Mark Antony onscreen in *Cleopatra* (1963), another role that remembers Shakespeare's own drama, *Antony and Cleopatra*. With the exception of Sir Philip and Sir Toby, these are all characters whose masculine virulence is foregrounded. They are lovers, or fighters, or sometimes both. When O'Brien remembers Burton reciting Shakespeare, these associations are also remembered.

On the same page, O'Brien recalls 'Increasingly [meeting] people in the film world'. This includes 'Another bard' Marlon Brando, 'with an intelligence so quick and lethal, his whole being taut, like an animal, ready to spring'. Brando's masculine presence – whether in the Elia Kazan-directed *A Streetcar Named Desire* (1951), Mark Antony in Joseph Mankiewicz's *Julius Caesar*[5] (1953), or Vito Corleone in *The Godfather* (1972) – exerts itself here, much as it remains an indelible part of his legacy. After an unfulfilled night with O'Brien, Brando writes from the Connaught Hotel the next day: 'He took a long time puzzling over the words, in which he cast himself as Othello, and for good measure, gave me a spotted handkerchief, though it did not have the emblem of the strawberries'

(O'Brien, 2013: 186–7). Brando, whose identity is conditioned by masculine animality, casts himself as a character whose blackness is commonly associated in the play with his own masculinity – Iago's 'old black ram' (I.i.87).

As with the almost inevitable link between the life as lived and its fictionalisation, it can hardly be surprising that a well-read author uses literary characters as analogues for characters in their own writing. It is even less surprising that Shakespeare's characters become those analogues – especially for a writer like O'Brien who confesses her reversion to Shakespeare in the quotidian practice of her writing. However, I want to draw attention to three key things: the prominence of the male (and often (hyper)masculine) figures who are analogised with Shakespeare's characters; the (hyper)masculine Shakespeare characters who form the analogues; and the major absence (and therefore asymmetrical recollection) of female analogues with Shakespeare in *Country Girl*. With reference to the latter, just *As You Like It*'s Rosalind merits an explicit mention in the memoir – but only in a way to rebuke O'Brien. Thus Thornton Wilder 'admonish[ed] me for my yearning heroines, enjoining me to follow the pluck and dauntless humour of Rosalind' (O'Brien, 2013: 252). Wilder is implicitly condemning O'Brien for not being sufficiently Shakespearean in her imagination.

The memory–imagination asymmetry thus re-appears in my argument. Whilst O'Brien's literary memory is infused with Shakespeare, in specific relation to her female characters her imagination would appear to be wholly other. However, I want to frame this imbalance in light of O'Brien's 1984 claim in an interview that she is 'not the darling of the feminists' (O'Brien in Kersnowski, 2018: 27) because of her belief in the primacy of nature over nurture in the debate about gender equality:

> I believe that we are fundamentally, biologically, and therefore psychologically different. I am not like any man I have met, ever, and that divide is what both interests me and baffles me. A lot of things have been said by feminists about equality, about liberation, but not all of these things are gospel truth. They are opinions the way my books are opinions, nothing more. Of course I would like women to have a better time but I don't see it happening, and for a very simple and primal reason: people are pretty savage towards each other, be they men or women. (O'Brien in Kersnowski, 2018: 27)

From the position of an avowed female speaking-I – in both *The Country Girls Trilogy, Night*, and *Country Girl* – this intentional consciousness of 'interest' and 'baffle[ment]' manifests itself in the way that O'Brien imagines her male characters, and it little matters whether we as readers agree with her diagnosis about the nature–nurture debate. One way that she undertakes this imaginative exercise, evident in her memoir, is by drawing on her *memory* of Shakespeare's male heroes to sketch her own male characters, their actions, their psychology.

I am arguing, further, that female characters are not passive receptors of, for instance, Burton's recitations, or Brando's letter-writing. They are themselves cast by the heterosexual structures in which they are inextricably caught up. Thus, when O'Brien remembers a male Shakespeare hero, she is also remembering a female Shakespeare hero: Brando's 'Othello' writes his letter and sends his handkerchief to O'Brien who, willingly or not, is cast as 'Desdemona'. When we realise that the male Shakespeare character-as-analogue is not restricted to the memoir, but also breaks through into *The Country Girls Trilogy*, it becomes clear why it is worth exploring how Shakespeare's male characters become memorial archetypes for Mr Gentleman and Eugene as Othello, and later Eugene specifically as Petruccio, and therefore that Caithleen undergoes a transformation from remembering Desdemona to Katherina in her body. In the next section, I turn to examining these heterosexual structures in both Shakespeare's and O'Brien's texts.

The heterosexualised female body: Desdemona

On more than one occasion in the first of *The Country Girls* novels, Caithleen becomes a version of Othello's Desdemona. As I sketched above, this happens not through any specific behaviour or characteristic on Caithleen's part, but rather on the part of Mr Gentleman. The clearest example of this is the repeated reference to the gift of a handkerchief, much as the anecdote of Marlon Brando gifting O'Brien his handkerchief in her memoir. In *The Country Girls*, Caithleen explains that 'I had no handkerchief so [Mr Gentleman] loaned me his' (O'Brien, 1987: 90). This quotidian, banal, and seemingly innocent gift-giving contrasts with the symbolic weight – 'the

handkerchief is a "presentational image" which spans the entire
drama and connects within its fabric the motive forces of the play'
(Boose, 1975: 361) – sewn into the handkerchief that Othello gives
to his wife:

> That handkerchief
> Did an Egyptian to my mother give,
> She was a charmer and could almost read
> The thoughts of people. She told her, while she kept it
> 'Twould make her amiable and subdue my father
> Entirely to her love; but if she lost it
> Or made a gift of it, my father's eye
> Should hold her loathed and his spirits should hunt
> After new fancies. She, dying, gave it to me
> And bid me, when my fate would have me wive,
> To give it to her. I did so, and – take heed on't! –
> Make it a darling, like your precious eye! –
> To lose't or give't away were such perdition
> As nothing else could match.
> ...
> 'Tis true, there's magic in the web of it.
> A sibyl that had numbered in the world
> The sun to course two hundred compasses,
> In her prophetic fury sewed the work;
> The worms were hallowed that did breed the silk
> And it was dyed in mummy, which the skilful
> Conserved of maidens' hearts. (III.iv.57–77)

These two accounts, either side of an interjection from Desdemona,
establish the handkerchief as a quasi-hermetic object that conse-
crates the relationship between Othello and his mother, but also acts
as a pacifier between lovers when ''Twould make her amiable and
subdue my father / Entirely to her love'. This heterosexual economy
is the work that this object can achieve when Othello hands it on to
Desdemona, so that Desdemona – recipient of the gift – will 'subdue' Othello in turn.

The handkerchief not only catalyses, but also commemorates the
fact of Desdemona's and Othello's marriage: 'That the strawberries
could be emblematic of virgin blood is logical both visually and
metaphorically. ... [A]s an appropriately red fruit they picture forth
the desired dramatic idea' (Boose, 1975: 362). The handkerchief

as commemorative symbol of the consummation of their marriage extends further, to the 'double entendre referring to female genitalia' (Boose, 1975: 366) – 'your precious eye' (l. 68) – and to the 'spots dyed from the conserved blood of virgins' hearts' (Boose, 1975: 367) when Othello references the 'mummy' (l. 76). The strawberry-red of the handkerchief metonymically evokes the stained bedsheets that would have been displayed to stand as 'ocular proof' of the consummation of the lovers' relationship. The handkerchief carries the symbolic weight, not only of Othello's trust in Desdemona's fidelity, but of the entire play's instantiation as 'about a *marriage*, memorially the most ritualized and symbolized of all human acts' (Boose, 1975: 361; emphasis in original).

The gift of the handkerchief is also, therefore, the gift of consummation – O'Brien's description of Brando demonstrates an intimate understanding of this interchange – and we can again discern, as is clear throughout, Mr Gentleman's sexual intentions with Caithleen. Moreover, despite the contrasts between the banality of Mr Gentleman's loan of his handkerchief to Caithleen and the 'mythic elevation' (Boose, 1975: 367) of the handkerchief in *Othello*, it is valuable to read the symbolic weight as being transferred between the two texts. Indeed, Caithleen seems to fetishise the gift-giving – even if it is described as a 'loan' – compulsively repeating the gesture to herself. She does so in a way that explicitly cites the mid-century growth of consumer capitalism, and Caithleen's interest in it – this is where, in *The Country Girls*, 'The operation of the sexual exchange market' is initiated as a 'recurrent theme in O'Brien's work' (Greenwood, 2003: 26):

> Easter Saturday night, after I got paid, I went to confession and then came down to Miss Doyle's drapery and bought a pair of nylons, a brassiere, and a white lace handkerchief. The handkerchief was one I'd never use, never dare to; it was a spider's web in the sunlight, frail and exquisite. I looked forward to the summer when I would wear it stuck into Mama's silver bracelet, with the lace frill hanging down, temptingly, over the wrist. While I was out boating with Mr Gentleman, it would blow away, moving like a white lace bird across the surface of the blue water, and Mr Gentleman would pat my arm and say, 'We'll get another.' (O'Brien, 1987: 141)

The delicacy of this lace handkerchief directly echoes that of the magicked embroidery of Othello's handkerchief (compare the 'spider's web' with Othello's 'magic in the web'). The fact of Caithleen's religious cleanliness at this juncture – it is Easter, symbolic time for rebirth and new beginnings, and she has just cleansed her soul at confession – returns her morally to virginity, much like her body and the whiteness of the handkerchief. However, along with her intended temptation with the handkerchief tucked in under her bracelet, the other items on her drapery bill – nylons and a brassiere – demonstrate Caithleen's growth into a sexually interested young woman by virtue of the way she dresses her body. Not only is Caithleen turning into a young lover worthy of an older man's sexual attentions, but she does so via the handkerchief with all its symbolic weight. She is becoming a version of Desdemona to match Mr Gentleman's Othello.

The focus on magic in both these passages is important. In *Othello* this redoubles the belief that Desdemona has been ensorcelled by Othello's stories of cannibals, anthropophagi, and 'men whose heads / Do grow beneath their shoulders' (I.iii.143–6):

> My story being done
> She gave me for my pains a world of sighs,
> She swore in faith 'twas strange, 'twas passing strange
> 'Twas pitiful, 'twas wondrous pitiful;
> She wished she had not heard it, yet she wished
> That heaven had made her such a man. She thanked me
> And bade me, if I had a friend that loved her,
> I should but teach him how to tell my story
> And that would woo her.
> …
> This only is the witchcraft I have used. (I.iii.159–70)

These statements and their repeated amplifications ('strange … passing strange / … pitiful … wondrous pitiful') are also a feature of Othello's storytelling ('the tales *work*', records Rutter (2001: 154; emphasis in original)) and are part of what Brabantio condemns as 'witchcraft' (I.iii.65). The success of Othello's storytelling leads Desdemona to signal a 'divided duty' (I.iii.181) between remaining dutiful to her father and faithful to her husband, and Brabantio accuses Othello of theft and of 'enchant[ment]' (I.ii.62–3). This latter accusation invites comparison with *The Country Girls* when the Desdemona-like Caithleen twice configures her relationship with the exotic Mr Gentleman as enchantment. On the first occasion Caithleen haltingly announces (as I have already quoted), 'My soul was alive; enchantment; something I had never known before. It was the happiest day of my whole life' (O'Brien, 1987: 56). Later, much like Desdemona is convinced by Othello's words, so Caithleen finds Mr Gentleman's 'words sweet. Everything after that was touched with sweetness and enchantment' (O'Brien, 1987: 158). The heterosexual structure of the Mr Gentleman–Caithleen relationship remembers the enchanting relationship between Othello and Desdemona.

Brabantio's dismissal of his daughter's relationship with the Moor leads, ultimately, to his own death (V.ii.202). However, prior to that, his consternation with Desdemona and Othello carries echoes in the way that Caithleen is treated by her father when she elopes with Eugene in *The Lonely Girl*. When her father and his friends come to 'rescue' Caithleen, there are a series of exchanges that transform the discussions between Brabantio, Othello, and Desdemona. First, Brabantio's demand to know 'where hast thou stowed my daughter?' (I.i.62) anticipates Caithleen's father's 'Where is my only child?' (O'Brien, 1987: 297). Brabantio's accusations that Othello has 'Abused her delicate youth with drugs or minerals' (I.ii.74) is transformed in *The Lonely Girl* into Caithleen's father's accusation that Eugene 'got her with dope' (O'Brien, 1987: 296). There are of course differences, and in *The Lonely Girl*, the threatened arrest in *Othello* ('Lay hold upon him; if he do resist / Subdue him at his peril!' (I.ii.80–1)) turns into Eugene being beaten up: 'Andy and the Ferret were hitting and kicking him' (O'Brien, 1987: 300). There are parallels between Othello and (on this occasion) Eugene that again demonstrate structural parallels between *Othello* and heterosexual relationships in *The Country Girls Trilogy*.

The significant mainstay of the two relationships I have explored in *The Country Girls Trilogy* is, of course, Caithleen. And, as is plain, the narrative perspective in the first two novels is strictly Caithleen's: with a knowledge of Shakespeare, Caithleen is able to imagine her heterosexual relationships in Shakespearean forms. Invoking Desdemona also invokes the abuse that is visited upon Desdemona's body, abuse that fixates on Desdemona's virginity. Louise Noble has deftly figured Desdemona's dead body as the idealised and literal *fille vièrge*[6] – the chaste, eternally virgin body – that men in *Othello* repeatedly seek to consume. Othello describes this *fille vièrge* in its pharmacological context as being integral to the handkerchief when he says that 'it was dyed in mummy, which the skilful / *Conserved of maiden hearts*' (III.iv.76–7; emphasis mine). Mummy as a preservative is here the 'salvific' (Noble, 2004: *passim*) *fille vièrge* that, by its integral use in the handkerchief, becomes part of the handkerchief's enchantment, but also a paradoxical stay on the consummation that the handkerchief also represents: the presence of the *fille vièrge* is another example of culture's double-standards awaiting women in and through their body. Desdemona is condemned to fail as a woman because her body cannot remember its prelapsarian purity, nor can it prove her fidelity to Othello – unlike the handkerchief that testifies *both* to consummation (following Boose's argument) *and* to immanent virginity (following Noble's).

The same double standard is applied in *The Lonely Girl* when Eugene and Caithleen finally consummate their relationship, for the moment of absolute unity also marks the point when their relationship sours. Following the act, Eugene scathingly tells Caithleen that 'You're a ruined woman now' (O'Brien, 1987: 317). Not only does this obliterate any relationship Caithleen may have had with the idealised image of the Virgin Mary – especially since the Irish 'community encourages its women to emulate the example of the Blessed Virgin' (Thompson, 2010: 26) – but also the temporal zone 'now' is significant because it alerts us to a scission between the *past-Kate* – figured as the idealised Mother Ireland, in both the Irish Symbolic and juridical realms – and the *now-Kate* who is unchaste and irretrievably fallen. More troublingly for Kate, as she will learn through the domestic abuse and manipulation she proceeds to suffer at the hands of Eugene, this *now-Kate* becomes unchangeable, and is perhaps better described as a *now-and-future-Kate*. These terms are significant not least because they alert us to the troublingly paralysing force of Mother Ireland and those men who believe in her – much like the men in *Othello* idealise a woman who can become 'Suspended in the pristine moment of death' in the 'instant of corporeal purity' (Noble, 2004: 145) – but also because of the way that *The Country Girls Trilogy* relies on the logic of the memoir that, in Freeman's terms, remakes memories. If the past ends, and the present and future become historically mummified, then anamnesis and the creation of future memories become increasingly impossible. This is our first signal that memoir (albeit as quasi-memoir in the case of the fictional *Trilogy*) becomes impossible, and that signal emerges from Caithleen's body.

This is not just something visited upon Caithleen, but also something that Caithleen engages in – after all, she has imagined her role as Desdemona. Caithleen has achieved her desire, has been 'inspired' by the pain (O'Brien, 1987: 316), and her body has materially changed in losing her virginity. In the moments immediately after Eugene's comment about her ruination, Caithleen recalls memories of her mother that directly speak to her body's memories (confirming Scarry's point, to reiterate, that 'What is "remembered" in the body is well remembered'): 'I thought of Mama and of how she used to blow on hot soup before she gave it to me, and of the rubber bands she put inside the turndown of my ankle socks, to keep them from falling' (O'Brien, 1987: 317). The care of the mother is precisely established when she cools the soup to avoid the pain of burning, and keeps the socks up in order to avoid physical discomfort. Now these sensations are unleashed on the ruined *now-and-future Kate*, when the prospect of Eugene 'giv[ing] you babies' (O'Brien, 1987: 317) becomes a reality – when Mother Ireland looms into realistic view. By the beginning of the ironically titled *Girls in Their Married Bliss*, Eugene and Caithleen marry 'in the sacristy of a Catholic church. Question of having to', Baba tells us. She further explains, 'They wouldn't do it out front because he was divorced and she was heavily pregnant' (O'Brien, 1987: 381); or, as Grace Eckley described, 'The force that fixes [Caithleen] in [Eugene's] grasp is an unwanted pregnancy' (Eckley, 1974: 44). The realities of Mother Ireland are a far cry from *Cathleen ni Houlihan*'s four green fields.

The Catholic mores that underpin Mother Ireland's aspirational figure impelled Caithleen to seek romance; however, Catholic mores about women's sexuality then disbar her from polite society and from the nation. This paradox leads Greenwood to call *The Country Girls Trilogy* 'negative romance' (Greenwood, 2003: 23), because the novels 'examine the condition of women under the patriarchy by subverting "romance" while conforming superficially to the genre'. Kate's 'ruin' is thus also the instant of transition that seems to be formal only, but that signifies a substantive change from romance to negative romance, and from Catholic purity to perpetual damnation. The novel becomes anti-eschatological. Where the former in these pairs (romance; Catholicism) are locked into a Christological structure with the Second Coming as the ultimate destination, the *now-and-future Kate* whose historical development has been suspended is therefore locked into an anti-eschatological novel – visible in the latter of those pairs (negative romance; damnation) – where all hope of escape is neutered.

The heterosexualised female body: Katherina

The sense of this hopelessness is also evoked through an intertextual memory of another Shakespeare play. Where Mr Gentleman and Eugene were once Othellos, coercing and entrapping their would-be Desdemona through the consummate gift of a handkerchief, Eugene's tactics change as he becomes figured as a version of Petruccio from *The Taming of the Shrew*. We are invited to think of Eugene in such terms when, for instance, we compare the following passages. Here Petruccio and Eugene rename their respective future wives:

> PETRUCCIO Good morrow, Kate, for that's your name, I hear.
> KATHERINA Well have you heard, but something hard of hearing:
>   They call me Katherine that do talk of me.
> PETRUCCIO You lie, in faith, for you are called plain Kate,
>   And bonny Kate, and sometimes 'Kate the Curst';
>   But Kate, the prettiest Kate in Christendom,
>   Kate of Kate Hall, my super-dainty Kate –
>   For dainties are all cates, and therefore 'Kate'[.] (II.i.181–8)

> He called me Kate, as he said that Caithleen was too 'Kiltartan' for his liking – whatever that meant. (O'Brien, 1987: 202)

In the former, Petruccio's renaming of Katherina is the first stage in his strategy to 'tame' her through contrariness ('Say that she rail, why then I'll tell her plain / She sings as sweetly as a nightingale' (II.i.169–70)), and thus his use of the diminutive 'Kate' is part of his plan to diminish her independence. In the latter, Eugene's reference to 'Kiltartan' evokes Yeats,[7] and Lady Gregory's living in the Big House at Kiltartan Cross. Kiltartan, then, is derisively associated with a self-appointed Irish landowning class, whereas Eugene feels unwelcome in Ireland. In both, the renaming asserts control and denudes the future wife of self-mastery. Judith Butler, in a different context, explains how the practice of diminutive renaming is antifeminist – and how it connects to the very materiality of the body:

> Theorizing from the ruins of the Logos invites the following question: 'What about the materiality of the body?' Actually, in the recent past, the question was repeatedly formulated to me this way: 'What about the materiality of the body, *Judy*?' I took it that the addition of 'Judy' was an effort to dislodge me from the more formal 'Judith' and to recall me to a bodily life that could not be theorized away. There was a certain exasperation in the delivery of that final diminutive, a certain patronizing quality which (re) constituted me as an unruly child, one who needed to be brought to task, restored to that bodily being which is, after all, considered to be most real, most pressing, most undeniable. (Butler, 2011: viii–ix; emphasis in original)

In light of this statement, it is possible to read both Petruccio's and Eugene's diminution of Katherina's and Caithleen's respective names to 'Kate' not only as assertions of domestic power, but also as a way of disciplining their wives' wayward bodies.

There are other moments of visible connection between Petruccio and Eugene. For example, the prelude to their respective weddings when Petruccio ploughs ahead to buy the wedding ring in Venice by way of trampling over Katherina's resistance (II.i.27–8) is repeated by Eugene (O'Brien, 1987: 314) when he plays on Caithleen's devotion to conspicuous consumption. Nevertheless, when Eugene does so, Caithleen 'shiver[ed] and laughed', subtly signalling her unease. More troublingly, Petruccio and Eugene have a shared interest in animalising their wives. Petruccio, famously, is 'taming' a 'shrew', but also employs metaphors and imagery from the world of hawking. The following is from his soliloquy when he describes starving his wife:

PETRUCCIO Thus have I politicly begun my reign,
        And 'tis my hope to end successfully.
        My falcon now is sharp and passing empty,
        And till she stoop she must not be full-gorged,
        For then she never looks upon her lure.
        Another way I have to man my haggard,

To make her come and know her keeper's call,
That is, to watch her, as we watch these kites
That bate, and beat, and will not be obedient.
She ate no meat today, nor none shall eat;
Last night she slept not, nor to night she shall not. (IV.i.177–87)

Here the 'falcon' and 'haggard' are both tameable birds, in contrast
to the 'kites', and the former are tameable by being starved 'passing
empty'. There are a number of parallels in O'Brien's texts, such as
when Eugene has brought a couple of friends back to the house,
including an attractive American woman, Mary. Caithleen, sens-
ing Eugene's motivations with Mary, goes upstairs and leaves the
group to socialise without her. Eugene decides to summon her, and
in doing so treats her as a tamed animal: '"I'll just see if she's here",
I heard Eugene say downstairs. He called my name. "Kate, Kate,
Katie". And then he whistled. I did not answer' (O'Brien, 1987:
357). The whistling remembers Petruccio's assertion that Katherina
'know[s] her keeper's call', and Eugene's behaviour is in keeping
with his belief that Kate is 'wild' (O'Brien, 1987: 222, 365). On the
second of these occasions, Caithleen has left Eugene and returned to
Baba at her lodgings, and she 'pounded the brown linoleum' before
silently confessing that she is now wild after living with Eugene.
The response of Baba, along with landlords Joanna and Gustav, is
to 'lift me onto the bed, [give] me pills and whiskey, and more pills,
so that I would calm down' (O'Brien, 1987: 365). The response to
the domestic abuse and manipulation she has suffered is to continue the strategy of taming, and this time enact it more directly on
Caithleen's body.

There is one key confirmation that Caithleen is being cast as
Katherina in Eugene's *Shrew*ish drama and, as with her being cast
as Desdemona, Caithleen becomes Katherina-like by virtue of
other people's reading of her. A few days after Caithleen has been
'ruin[ed]' by Eugene, they go to the pub with Baba and their friend,
the Body:

> He [the Body] frowned, trying to puzzle out what it was about me
> that had changed, and I thought slyly, Being in bed and being made
> love to has altered my face, but in fact it was that I looked *tamer*
> because Eugene had asked me to make up more discreetly. He bought
> me paler powder and narrow black velvet ribbons for my hair and a

pair of flat, laced shoes which I saw Baba eyeing at that very minute. [Eugene] had showed me diagrams of ruined feet[.] (O'Brien, 1987: 322; emphasis mine)

Here the collision of Caithleen's outward-facing body – her made-up face, her hair, her feet in her shoes – with her taming is made explicit, even if she is not yet aware of the psychological damage that is being done to her.

When connecting the non-historical, anti-eschatological negative romance – with Caithleen cast as Desdemona – with the tamed body of Caithleen – when cast as Katherina – we are better able to make sense of the novels' most radical and troubling moment: Caithleen's elective hysterectomy. The baldness of the statement that announces Caithleen's decision redoubles the shock of that decision, especially because the narrative perspective – third-, rather than first-person – now denies us an intimate insight into Caithleen's conscience. Whereas in the first two novels 'The first-person narration … means that nothing will be hidden: the reader will know exactly how Caithleen processes everything, and also those things she hides from herself' (Kiberd, 2017: 62), these insights are now made opaque. Thus, on the penultimate page of *Girls in Their Married Bliss*, we are told:

After Christmas Kate had herself sterilized. The operation was done by a private doctor and it entailed a short confinement in an expensive clinic – money that might otherwise have been frittered on clothes or a summer holiday. …

'Well', Baba said after some time, meaning, 'What does it feel like?'

'Well', Kate said, 'at least I've eliminated the risk of making the same mistake again', and for some reason the words sent a chill through Baba's heart.

'You've eliminated something', Baba said. … It was odd for Baba to see Kate like that, all the expected responses were missing, the guilt and doubt and sadnesses, she was looking at someone of whom too much had been cut away, some important region that they both knew nothing about. (O'Brien, 1987: 507–8)

This is evidently a significant moment, not least because Caithleen deems it valid to violate her own body by way of punishing herself for the crimes of others – mainly Eugene. Her claim that she will not 'make the same mistake again' would seem to demonstrate her commitment to suspending her corporal future, symbolised in the child – almost as if she has anticipated the pleas of Lee Edelman's *No Future* (2004), and in accordance with Charlotte Nunes who argues that, 'Prey to a cultural paradox that puts proper motherhood against sexuality, [Kate] sees no option other than to surrender all potential for future maternity' (Nunes, 2007: 45). The logic of Caithleen's argument also anticipates Butler's understanding of performativity as iterability: '[R]epetition is what enables a subject and constitutes the temporal condition for the subject' (Butler, 2011: 60). By seeking to exit the performative cycle, Caithleen tries to reclaim her agency and, in Thompson's terms, to 'remov[e] from her body the last vestiges of her motherhood and her Dead mother' (Thompson, 2010: 46). But we need to go beyond Nunes's idea that Caithleen's 'decision to undergo a sterilization procedure shortly after being separated from her son comprises an effort to snuff out her own repeatedly disappointed desire' (Nunes, 2007: 44), because by exerting this emergency stop on the futurity implied by the potential of her womb, Caithleen is merely corporally confirming what Eugene's assertion of ruination already achieved: the suspension of her historical development and the forestalling of anything resembling memoir. Rather, like Katherina's ambiguous monologue at the end of *Shrew*, she is spreading the gospel of her (now-former) husband's superiority:

> KATHERINA Thy husband is thy lord, thy life, thy keeper,
> They head, thy sovereign; one that cares for thee
> And for thy maintenance; commits his body
> To painful labour both by sea and land[.]
> ...
> But now I see our lances are but straws,
> Our strength as weak, our weakness past compare,
> That seeming to be most which we indeed least are.
> Then vail your stomachs, for it is no boot,
> And place your hands below your husband's foot. (V.ii.152–83)

This speech quivers between obsequiousness and resistance, much like Caithleen's elective hysterectomy. In the latter case, I would argue that Caithleen may *feel* like she is reclaiming agency over

her body, but she is in fact weakening her corporal – and therefore socio-cultural – strength. Either way, Katherina's assertion that
her husband is 'lord' and 'sovereign' countenances her command to
Bianca and the Old Woman, to whom she is ostensibly speaking, to
'place your hands below your husband's foot'. However, the phrase
'vail your stomachs' merits closer inspection, especially in light of
the sly irony of the husband's 'labour' a few lines earlier. The Arden[3]
editor glosses 'vail your stomachs' as 'suppress your pride' (refer-
encing the *OED*'s *v.*[1]4a), the Norton (3rd edition) editors suggest
'lower your pride', while Dympna Callaghan in the Norton Critical
Edition glosses it as 'don't be so proud'. These sampled editions
all accept that the phrase is figurative, in keeping with the *OED*'s
repeated examples that cite 'vail your bonnet' as their primary reference in various contexts, literally to doff or remove one's bonnet,
and figuratively to show obeisance to someone superior. To 'vail
your stomachs' is thus also to *remove* your stomachs, whatever that
may mean;[8] in the context of women's corporality, however, there
remains suppressed in the figurative expression the violent association of female disfigurement.

   In her study, Scarry helpfully points out that what is at stake when
Caithleen elects to be 'sterilized' is nothing other than Caithleen
playing God. Scarry notes that, in the Torah, 'God's presence within
the story of human generation is exclusively verbal' (Scarry, 1987:
192), and that

> The ordinary alternation in the female body between the condi-
> tions of being sometimes 'not with child' and sometimes 'with child'
> becomes within these stories the intensified and absolute conditions
> of 'barrenness' and 'fertility': 'not with child' has become the much
> more extreme 'not with the capacity to conceive a child' and the
> capacity to conceive a child is now coterminous with (and exclusively
> reserved for) the phase of pregnancy. ... God closes, then opens, all
> the wombs of the house of Abimelech[.] (Scarry, 1987: 194)

In her fruitless attempts to retrieve and reassert control over her
own body, Caithleen attempts to restore some sense of the eschatological frame to her life by organising the removal of her womb.
We can also read it as an attempt to 'conceive of the body as "aliveness" or "awareness of aliveness" ... [in order to] reside at last
within the felt-experience of sentience' that is 'projected out onto

the object world' (Scarry, 1987: 285–6). By externalising her womb, Caithleen is trying to re-energise her body and restore sentience to her speaking-I – which, by the time of the third book in the trilogy, is effaced and substituted by third-person narrative – and by hoping to endow the now-external womb with the emotion of 'perceived-pain-wished-gone' (Scarry, 1987: 290). Shirley Peterson has described this similarly through the lens of sadomasochism, arguing that 'Kate's masochism seems oddly satisfying, even assertive' (Peterson, 2006: 165). In my own terms, however, as an irredeemably failed ('ruined') Mother Ireland figure, she recognises that, in Katherina's vocabulary, she must stop 'offer[ing] war' (V.ii.168), and yet 'the nation ... [is] registered in [her] limbs' – a registration that demands payment during war when the limbs become 'permanently loaned ... and amputated' (Scarry, 1987: 112). Caithleen's body cannot forget its Irishness, however she might try to excise the guilty organ.

That Caithleen attempts to restore her own femininity by targeting her womb indicates that, like the idealised and chaste body of the Virgin Mary, she is attempting to rewind time and return to a pure Desdemona-like corpse that 'is *"fille vièrge"*: ... the ideal remedy ... used to insinuate that the only truly chaste female body is a dead, embalmed one' (Noble, 2004: 139–40). Whilst it is not unambiguous that Caithleen has a death wish – to be discussed further with reference to the Epilogue, in the following – there are nonetheless intimations that she is seeking a corporal purity that emblems like the gifted handkerchief and enchanting husband already put into play. After all, Caithleen, like Desdemona, has 'so boldly [written] their will' into the text, and therefore she 'dictate[s] [her] punishment for such transgression; sexuality and punishment are irretrievably linked' (Peterson, 2010: 201). Moreover, the targeting of her womb leads to an investigation of Caithleen's self-diagnosis as a hysteric. This, in turn, invites us to consider the way that wombs and *hysterica passio* were figured in early modern culture – a culture that Caithleen is already remembering in her casting herself passively as Desdemona and Katherina. The consideration of the womb and wombless body will also take us to explore the significance of Hermione in *The Winter's Tale* and Thaisa in *Pericles*.

Early modern wombs

Where Kristeva has described the mother's body as that which 'becomes the ordering principle of the semiotic *chora*' (Kristeva, 1986: 95), Gail Kern Paster and Kaara Peterson have explored the relevance of the womb to early modern thought and drama. The following argument serves to join these two discourses. Paster charts the significance of the embarrassed body in early modern culture, and the way that an economy of shame was developed for women in respect of their own bodies. By examining medical treatises, Paster demonstrates how women were encouraged to feel alienated from their own bodies, in part through the use of medical illustrations that focused almost exclusively on exposing 'a female torso to an implied male gazer'. This 'construct[s] a discourse of knowledge alienating women from their own bodies and bodily self-experience, making them subject to those bodies and to those who can represent it' (Paster, 1993: 178n29). This womb – often glossed as 'the mother' or as the medical ailment *hysterica passio* (Peterson, 2010: 40) – becomes the original *locus* of almost all women's diseases. Indeed, the 'sixteenth- and seventeenth-century medical texts consistently emphasize women's special susceptibility to pathological conditions because of the unique accident of women's physiology and humoral complexion, going so far as to state the *inevitability* of uterine dysfunction' (Peterson, 2010: 31; emphasis in original). Given the emergence of both *hysterica passio* as a medical term from 1603, and interest in 'the mother' (in Latin, the *matrix*) from the 1580s (Peterson, 2010: 3), evidently the growing shamefulness of women's bodies aligns exactly with the growing medical interest in the womb as the origin of all women's maladies.

For example, women's wombs were considered unclean and that 'could not but contribute to the impurity of the milk' (Paster, 1993: 194), and the womb, as 'a body organ of such demonstrable material importance to society at large – in what was called its public action [read: in service to/as Mother Ireland] – [was] capable of the autonomous malevolence, the will to do harm, implied and authorized by a characterization of the womb as "breeder of poison"' (Paster, 1993: 175). After all, by virtue of its contiguity with the body's humours (including women's sperm), the womb is the source of 'a volatile "fluid ecology"' that becomes the 'central concern …

in most gynaecological and women's handbooks' (Peterson, 2010: 34), also signifying that the womb is a pollutant (Paster, 1993: 165), not only to the woman's particular body, but to general society also.

In terms of the social interest and investment in the womb, it is an exclusively patriarchal concern, as demonstrated by the volume of women's medical treatises written by men. Paster explains this patriarchal interest quite simply by explaining that, 'instead of containing merely its own humors and waste products', the womb 'housed and was accountable for the production of a baby in whom patriarchy claimed the presiding interest' (Paster, 1993: 182). Given the parallel juridical and cultural investment in Mother Ireland, it is easy to identify the stable cultural prejudices that join early modern culture with modern Ireland's. Beyond the patriarchy's interest in the products of the womb, the womb is also called into a moral economy, thus narrowing the general Renaissance attitude that 'Illness ... was perceived as a symptom of immorality' (Schoenfeldt, 1999: 7). Referring to Edward Jorden's significant *A Briefe Discourse of a Disease Called the Suffocation of the Mother* (1603), Paster writes that 'no stable semantic demarcation separated ethics and physiology' in medical treatises, and that 'ethical signifiers in Jorden's tragic narrative of corruption of seed make clear that conceptualization of bodily states was inseparable from moral judgement' (Paster, 1993: 169). This morality emerges, for example, in terms connecting the mother's behaviour to the infirmity of pregnancy, for she 'must submit herself quietly and submissively to her state' (Paster, 1993: 180). Ultimately, since the womb is the origin of women's disease, it becomes a site of discipline. 'Thus, [Nicholas] Culpeper instructs women who would conceive', writes Paster, 'how *"to preserve the Womb in a due Decorum"*' (Paster, 1993: 173; emphasis in original). This line of thought is significant because, in connecting with Mooney's reading of disciplined female bodies in O'Brien (cited above), it would seem straightforward to connect Culpeper's disciplining to a similar Foucauldianism. However, as Peterson points out, for Foucault the 'hysterization of women's bodies' wherein 'the feminine body was analyzed ... as being thoroughly saturated with sexuality' takes place 'in the eighteenth century' (Foucault, 1990: 103–4). However, Peterson and Laqueur both draw on evidence that this had already taken place earlier, with the latter describing how 'The seventeenth-century midwife Louise Bourgeois [...]

argues that [infertility] specifically in women is most frequently caused by wetness of the womb, that women would be as healthy in both body and spirit as men were it not for this organ' (1992: 108). Peterson likewise 'underscore[s] just how much *well before* the seventeenth century[,] female corporeality (and sexuality) was represented and perceived, apparently, as normatively licentious, pathological, and uncontrollable except through regular salutary sexual activity' (Peterson, 2010: 22; emphasis in original). This period of disciplining (and of shaming, in Paster's vocabulary) is early modern; and yet O'Brien remembers it in her Shakespearean hero, Caithleen Brady, several centuries later.

For both Paster and Peterson, Hermione in *The Winter's Tale* forms a significant literary example of women's hysterisation. On one basic level of correspondences, Paster demonstrates how Leontes's separation of Hermione from her children shows how he 'seems to collapse the never very stable distinction between two categories of pollution – the ineradicable stain of moral pollution and the temporary, if exigent, bodily pollution that still attached to parturience' (Paster, 1993: 273). Hermione typifies both the pollutant and immoral mother by virtue of her womb carrying another's child (as Leontes perceives). Likewise, Hermione's 'open' womb – as it loosely takes part in the fluid ecology of women's bodies – is characterised by Leontes's 'preoccupation with the signifiers of female grotesqueness …. Hermione is a sluiced pond, she is slippery, her womb is a thoroughfare' (Paster, 1993: 268–9). Another stable fact of the experience of women's bodies between early modern England and modern Ireland is the idea that the man's behaviour determines the woman's self-appraisal. Caithleen as Desdemona and Katherina relies on the idea that Mr Gentleman and Eugene are, first, Othello and Petruccio; her elective hysterectomy can also be seen as part of the men's 'preoccupation' with her body, such as Eugene's calling her 'ruined'. This abjection is also remembered from the earlier literature.

For Peterson, Hermione's 'revivification' is in keeping with a range of early modern instances of the revival of women thought dead.[9] These moribund women were thought to suffer from *hysterica passio* and, in particular, the 'suffocation' disorder, wherein the womb rises and presses on the lungs and oesophagus. Culpeper describes the symptoms as 'laziness, weakness of the legs, paleness, sad countenance' (quoted in Peterson, 2010: 161), and a 'sleepie extasie' (*passim*) 'very similar to hibernation, if not a fully fledged version of it' (Peterson, 2010: 144).[10] To summarise Peterson's reading of Hermione's revivification, 'Shakespeare's portrayal in *The Winter's Tale* of Hermione's tragic postpartum death, 16-year absence, and reanimation pointedly mirrors the hibernating hysteric and probably accounts for the title of the play' (Peterson, 2010: 145–6). With reference to the latter, for Peterson, the *hibernating* Hermione gives the play its *hibernal* title. In demonstrating the often-referenced revival of women suffering from *hysterica passio* – albeit through parody (157) and 'hyperbole' (149) on Shakespeare's part, and 'charade' (151) and 'pantomime' (152) on Hermione's and Paulina's – 'a reasonably accurate representation of how revivifications were believed to work, and a hysterical swooning and revivification is what Shakespeare aims to depict' (Peterson, 2010: 155). Ultimately, Peterson's Hermione is a realistic, if exaggerated portrayal, of the well-known sufferer from *hysterica passio* who faints under stress from all that assails her (III.ii.144), is presumed dead, and for whom the tests of liveliness are reserved (ll. 201 ff.) until her death can be confirmed (Leontes announces that 'Once a day I'll visit / The chapel' (ll. 235–6) where his wife and son lie). '[S]ince he specifies watching over his family's corpses', writes Peterson,

> 'nature's' allowance would seem to be the standard three days ... before female death could be determined and the bodies would be buried or placed in tombs. Of course, Shakespeare may extend the standard period it takes Hermione to revive for the romance plot and exaggerate the timeframe within which a normal revivification might occur[.] (Peterson, 2010: 148)

Peterson argues that Hermione is presently revived offstage by Paulina by virtue of her medical skills as a non-professional midwife, but then kept apart from Leontes until Perdita's return, thus confirming the prophecy of her return to Bohemia. Thus, there is a 'literalism operating behind the scene's representation of a hysterical revivification' (Peterson, 2010: 154) with 'the process of revelation' in the final scene 'merely the expression or elucidation of a distinct possibility, not a playwright's withholding information' (Peterson, 2010: 155).

Peterson's argument is persuasive and ably charts how literary representation can, like Paulina, work typical expansions, exaggerations, and artifice to an idea held common by society, if rare in practice. However, by adding Paster's argument to Peterson's, we can see how Hermione's revivification leads to hers becoming a well-remembered wombless body.[11] Significantly, it enables us to read statuesque Hermione as *both* a literalisation of revivification following *hysterica passio, and* as a symbol that tells us about women's relationship with her body in early modern England. According to Paster, once revived, Hermione 'as statue ... is all surface and no content, all opacity and no concavity (*read womb*), an object that can represent physical change without being so threateningly immersed in it' (Paster, 1993: 279; my emphasis). Comparing that description to Baba's of Caithleen on the final page of *Girls in Their Married Bliss* is instructive: 'It was odd for Baba to see Kate like that, all the expected responses were missing, the guilt and doubt and sadnesses, she was looking at someone of whom too much had been cut away, some important region they both knew nothing about' (O'Brien, 1987: 508). Both Hermione and Caithleen become a kind of 'formless femininity' (Butler, 2011: 25), by virtue of this depthless womblessness. Critically, where women in Paster's reading of early modern society suffer shame by virtue of the (patriarchal) social reading of their bodies – and a shame that necessarily derives from the mere existence of a womb that is the source of most (if not all) female ailments – Hermione differs. She is now 'mother in the full social sense ... without being subject any longer to the shame and the juridical disciplines that attended motherhood in the tragic action' (Paster, 1993: 279). Thus Hermione's generic prescription has now changed, from facing tragic fatality to romantic reconciliation. However, it comes at a cost, for whilst 'Hermione is visibly altered and diminished by her experience of patriarchal discipline ... as a living statue she is herself the subject of an evidently successful self-imposed discipline of shame.' Caithleen remembers this self-imposed discipline in and through her elective hysterectomy. This means that, ultimately, she is 'a perfect exemplar of the new bodily regimes of early modern selfhood' (Paster, 1993: 279). This memory seems to destabilise, rather than enable, the subject, contradicting Greenwood's diagnosis that 'woman' is merely a 'role which Caithleen adopts whilst recognizing its shallowness and being conscious of the extent to which she is "playing"' (Greenwood, 2003: 25). Hermione and Caithleen are alive, certainly, but on whose terms and in whose debt?

Epiloguing

To call these interconnections remembering, as I have done, needs some kind of correction. To remember, etymologically speaking, is productive, piecing something (back) together, making something materialise. What Caithleen undertakes, by contrast, might better be considered *de*materialisation, *pace* Butler, for whom 'materiality' is not merely a noun, but also a *process* of entelechy: '"Materiality" designates a certain effect of power or, rather, is power in its forma- tive or constituting effects'. The question that follows, argues Butler, is the extent to which 'materialization [is] governed by principles of intelligibility that require and institute a domain of radical *unin- telligibility* that resists materialization altogether or that remains radically dematerialized' (Butler, 2011: 9; emphasis in original). We should look for the dematerialised, for de-matter (all surface, perhaps, or de-wombed), to see how structures of power are con- structed and, consequently, whether they can be challenged.

For Butler, this challenge takes place in and through the figure of the *khôra* that, for Plato in *Timaeus* was the vessel through which forms were materialised. As I summarised above, it was fig- ured as a womb or a woman. I have already suggested that the form of memoir – giving shape, as it does, to memories so as to donate them a sense of narrative trajectory – differs from that of the novel. However, as a memoir-like set of novels, I read *The Country Girls Trilogy* as borrowing the idea of the *khôra*, but as has been clear, by *Girls in Their Married Bliss*, third-person substitutes for Caithleen's first-person narrative, suggesting that the *khôra*-like memoir is no longer applicable. The fact that the novel finally ends in the moments after Caithleen's elective hysterectomy – when she becomes, like Hermione, a self-disciplined woman of no depth and all surface – suggests a parallel or conjoining of the quasi-memoir with Caithleen's body.

In the Epilogue, Caithleen becomes merely body, much to Baba's chagrin. Her body, encased within its coffin, is reduced to an 'it'

(O'Brien, 1987: 523) in Baba's narrative. A week before, Baba has seen Caithleen and described her as 'all thin and trembly, like a lath' (527). Now wombless, Caithleen dies by drowning – whether by suicide or accident, it is never quite decided. Either way, her return to the water at this juncture suggests a return to the watery womb, almost as if attempting to incorporate the now-external womb. The fact that the watery death repeats her own mother's death decades earlier is significant, too: both these idealised women – 'Mrs Brady, the iconic suffering Mother Ireland' (Peterson, 2006: 154) and 'perfect mother' (Kiberd, 2017: 78) – have erred and died in nature's womb. Moreover, the evocations of Ophelia's death in *Hamlet* in the brook – a death, that like Caithleen's and her mother's, was 'doubtful' (V.i.216) – remember the absolute objectality of these women's bodies. Caithleen's is a dead weight in a coffin; Ophelia's is an unfeeling corpse in a grave.

But another Shakespeare memory stirs. In some ways the sister text to *The Winter's Tale*, *Pericles* (1607) has many parallels, mainly in the ways in which Thaisa and Hermione are (albeit for different reasons) separated from their husbands and daughters. After 'dying' giving birth onboard a ship, Thaisa's body is confined in a chest 'caulked and bitumed' (III.i.70–1; III.ii.59) and thrown overboard. It washes ashore in Ephesus, where the studied doctor, Cerimon, is invited to help revive Thaisa from the coffin that is 'wondrous heavy' (III.ii.53) – not unlike Baba's description of Caithleen's coffin (O'Brien, 1987: 523). However, Cerimon is not convinced of Thaisa's death because 'Death may usurp on nature many hours / And yet the fire of life kindle again / The o'erpressed spirits' (III.ii.81–3). Not long after, Cerimon, in the same way that Peterson's Paulina acts with Hermione, manages to revive the queen:

> Gentlemen, this queen will live. Nature awakes;
> A warm breathes out of her! She hath not been
> Entranced above five hours. See how she 'gins
> To blow into life's flower again.
> ...
> She is alive! (III.ii.91–6)

As with Paulina's midwifery and revivification of Hermione, Cerimon's work as a physician for Thaisa is in keeping with those outlandish though commonly known stories of women being revived after suffering *hysterica passio*. 'In all likelihood', writes Peterson, 'Thaisa's illness would have been perceived by the contemporary audience as a case of the morbid symptoms of *hysterica passio*; regardless of the exact nature of the illness, her affliction is represented as clearly hysterical and obstetrical in origin and causes the moribund syncope so commonly cited in *hysterica passio*' (Peterson, 2010: 88). Just like Cerimon and Paulina, Baba wishes to revive Caithleen at the last, this time in reference to the Christology that had long been denied to Caithleen: 'I'm even thinking of the Resurrection and the stone pushed away, I want to lift her up and see the life and the blood coming back into her cheeks, I want time to be put back, I want it to be yesterday, to undo the unwanted crime that has been done' (O'Brien, 1987: 531). But Caithleen's revival is not possible.

There are clear narrative reasons for this – Caithleen has died, verified by twentieth-century medicine – but there are also formal reasons. Returning to the idea of memoir as *khôra*, and in the idea that Caithleen is now wombless – statuesque, all surface – there is no longer a *khôra*; consequently, there is no longer memoir. The mere fact of the Epilogue demonstrates the end of the memoir because the end of memoir presupposes the end of memory-making: there are no more memories to record and form into narrative. The *Country Girls Trilogy*'s Epilogue thus confirms that the text is fully novel, and no longer even quasi-memoir. Like Caithleen's body, the textual body of the quasi-memoir is dematerialised. Caithleen's wombless body therefore disrupts the possibility of memory entirely, her dematerialised body now disremembering. *Khôra*-less, her body and its narrative now abort all kinds of creativity. She cannot be revived.

Signally – and finally – it is interesting that the last in-person interaction between Baba and Caithleen, as re-told by Baba, is at her husband, Frank's, birthday party. Caithleen and Frank had earlier argued about 'genealogy' and the notion of rightfully claimed Irishness. 'So you think I'm a phony?' Frank asks Caithleen when he has tried to 'prove that he went back to Brian Boru, on his mother's side' (O'Brien, 1987: 525). Caithleen mollifies him at that point in the evening, but then later (and accidentally) embarrasses him. He tells his friends that he has composed a poem called 'Corca Baiscinn' – a poem about the exiled Wild Geese from Clare that, in fact, is lifted from Emily Lawless's 'Fontenoy 1745' (1902). Entering halfway through the recitation, Caithleen 'took up the refrain' and thus proves his phoney Irishness. This image of Caithleen, reminiscent of Gregory's and Yeats's Old Woman who recites songs about her Four Green Fields, is entirely suggestive of Mother Ireland, the Kathleen ní Houlihan who can remember her country and its cultural calls to assembly without prompt. And yet, in fact what Caithleen is doing is *disrupting* the performance of memorial patriotism, as practised by Frank. Frank's creativity, phoney though it is, is aborted mid-flow, and the memories of Ireland in its own language ('Corca Baiscinn') are wholly undermined. Rather than this Mother Ireland figure who turns back to Ireland's mythic past in order to restore her to full glory, O'Brien's Caithleen disrupts discourses of exiled patriotism remembering an Edenic Ireland. Caithleen, by virtue of her womblessness, blemishes the Ireland that Frank is trying to produce.

*

The question of bodies that remember – or memories that embody self – has been amply answered. Whether through the pre-Cartesian texts of Shakespeare and Jonson, the theories of early modern theatricality (Syme) or self-disciplining body (Paster), or the modern theories of a phenomenological body (Sartre) or body-in-pain (Scarry), I have demonstrated the close association – if not coevality – of body with self. Buttressed by analyses of antitheatricality and *hysterica passio*, my arguments have shown how the early modern English and modern Irish bodies, as fictionally sketched and elaborated, bear sufficient similarities to confound the idea of cultural progression over several centuries. Rather, given the nature of intertextual memories of Shakespeare – both explicit, unacknowledged, or structural – it is clear that both Beckett and O'Brien have culturally shaped their characters in early modern fashion in order to advance their own cultural or political manifestos.

Those manifestos are, in part, about modern Ireland. For Beckett, whose Irishness by the time of the *Three Novels* appears suppressed, it is through the nature of testimony that Beckett's characters are trying to get beyond their past, searching for what Valente has called 'ethnostalgia, a homesickness for secure ethnicity that is also a longing to return to the ethnos as home'. It is signified by uncanny moments of 'not feeling' a communion with other sufferers of trauma, 'in not feeling it, to not feel Irish, to not *be* Irish, in the fullest measure' (Valente, 2014: 185). But, in order to sketch that process I have undertaken what David Lloyd called for: '[T]o read Beckett's work in relation to Ireland demands … a mode of cultural studies constantly capable of a shifting of frames, an Irish studies that would allow (for) its own perpetual displacement into other destabilizing contexts' (Lloyd, 2010: 51). This is the heterogeneous Irish cultural memory that Oona Frawley described (Frawley, 2011: xvii). Following this approach requires that we see what goes unmentioned (or unfelt), but silhouetted – visible almost in a photonegative – as central to the discussion. Thus, in my triangulation of memory, the body, and self, what is overlooked or omitted is the question of politics or of emplacement. This therefore becomes the question of *referrance*, to use Lloyd's term, in which 'the particular, the singular, does not seem to represent the totality of the culture but, happy in the gaps it happens to inhabit, refers one always onwards' (Lloyd, 2010: 51). The question of Moran's employment, only lightly referred to, is one such moment of *referrance*, where the colonial British or native Free State/ Republican administration may be called into representation. I have thus found – both 'discovered' and 'sought' – for Beckett's characters' respective homes, and they are alongside Coriolanus the playgoer and Volpone the antitheatricalist, for both of whom memory is shown, also, to be necessary to their bodies and selves.

For O'Brien, by contrast, geopolitical specificity is undeniable. O'Brien's mid-century Ireland, even as it is transported across the Irish Sea by Caithleen and Baba, is self-evident throughout, and the attendant figure of Mother Ireland comes packed in their suitcases wherever they go. In Caithleen's socially compelled attempt at embodying Mother Ireland, she takes on strategies[12] that Shakespeare's early modern characters also deployed. Where Thaisa's and Hermione's *hysterica passio* may have been part of a sociocultural dialogue with a knowing audience, by the time that Caithleen has remembered the impossible virgin purity of Desdemona and the gaslighting and manipulation suffered by Katherina, little but the self-disciplining version of Hermione's depthlessness is available. Nevertheless, as a dismemory in the Epilogue, we are still able to see how she can interrupt or abort a phony history of self-righteous Irish patriotism.

Molloy, through his sleepy amnesia, and the Unnamable, through his resistance to playing a prescribed role, both also become memories that disrupt futurity. If Irish futurity, as with Caithleen as a dematerialised Mother Ireland, then we see how the intertextual memories of Shakespeare continue to shape a mid-to-late-century sense of Irishness. This Irishness, however, now seems disfigured and paralytic: wombless, without a *khôra* to develop or produce it, and lacking historical development, as in Beckett's protagonists.

If my examination of remembering Shakespeare's ghosts suggested ways of reimagining Ireland through disruptively remembering the past, my examination of remembering Shakespeare's bodies would contrarily suggest that a certain fatality attends modern Ireland. One idea remains to be explored – the land – and I will show how when we see that remembered bodies either touch or dig into the land, then a sense of home emerges – and along with it, that missing version of positive Irishness.

Notes

1 Edna O'Brien, 'The Wedding Dress', *John McGrath Collection,* British Film Institute, London (1963), ITM-17689, Box 8, Item 1. Tara Harney-Mahajan (2015) does explore *Haunted,* but skips over the explicit Shakespeare references.
2 See www.irishstatutebook.ie/eli/cons/en/html [accessed 1 June 2020] for *Bunreacht* in full.
3 See Foster (2015: passim).
4 For example, see Eavan Boland's (1944–2019) conversation with Paula Meehan where the former raises this point exactly: 'It's still striking to me that the statues of male writers and orators in Dublin are official, named and legible. ... But the women statues are women out of a song ... or out of a place myth ... or anonymous' (Boland, 2016: 138).
5 Richard Burton had himself turned down this role.
6 Literally *the virgin daughter*, Noble describes *fille vièrge* as 'a drug produced from the embalmed corpses of virginal females, [which] is constructed as the superior form of mummy' (Noble, 2004: 135).
7 Q.v. 'An Irish Airman Foresees His Death', written about, and voiced from, the perspective of Lady Gregory's son:

> My country is Kiltartan Cross,
> My countrymen Kiltartan's poor[.] (Yeats, 1997b: ll. 5–6)

8 In the *OED*, meaning *n*.3 is given as: 'The part of the body containing the stomach, the belly, abdomen; sometimes (formerly often) applied to the chest'. This leaves open the possibility that the womb is included as part of the stomach. Schoenfeldt describes the stomach as 'the most literal site of human inwardness' (Schoenfeldt, 1999: 33), which helps to qualify what Katherina is asking, and also suggesting a connection with women's wombs that are also utterly integral to women's being.

9 See also Laqueur (1992: 1–3) who begins his study *Making Sex* with a story of a woman's revivification.

10 We should not forget that lethargy, similar to the 'sleepie extasie', is considered a threat to memory by antitheatricalists. I explore this, above, in relation to *Coriolanus* and Beckett's character Molloy.

11 Peterson reports that there are narratives of 'womb-less' women in the early modern medical treatises (Peterson, 2010: 78), such as in Jane Sharp's *The Midwives Book, or, the Whole Art of Midwifery Discovered* (1671):

> If one womb in a woman be the cause of so many strong and violent diseases, she may be thought a happy woman of our sex that was born without a womb: *Columbus* reports that he saw such a woman, and that her secrets were as the secrets of other women; and part of the neck out. (Y8[r]; emphasis in original)

12 I have elsewhere considered how Hermione's becoming a statue is a kind of proto-feminist strategy. See Taylor-Collins (2018).

Part III

Land

It is true that a country encapsulates our childhood and those lanes, byres, fields, flowers, insects, suns, moons and stars are forever re-occurring and tantalizing me with a possibility of a golden key which would lead beyond birth to the roots of one's lineage. Irish? In truth I would not want to be anything else. It is a state of mind as well as an actual country.

– from *Mother Ireland* by Edna O'Brien

Introduction

The land–memory nexus is commonplace in studies of identity – even if only at the level of metaphor. For example, the first chapter in Benedict Anderson's landmark *Imagined Communities* (1983) is entitled 'Cultural Roots'. Anderson's implied argument is that cultural identity, though characterised by separation across vast swathes of land, still has a *locus* of origin in the land. To this end, the 'imagined community' that joins individuals from different walks of life depends on a concrete referent in the land that gave rise to the name of this identity.

In relation to Ireland, the land–memory nexus has another key referent that cannot be avoided: the Famine. Terry Eagleton postulates that though 'It is not quite that the Famine strikes narrative cohesion out of Irish history ... It is rather that the Famine offers to reduce that history to what Walter Benjamin might have called the sheer empty homogeneous time of the body' (Eagleton, 1995: 13). Famine can be seen to threaten both national history and the way in which the nation continues to determine itself: '[T]he fundamental indeterminacy of the Famine should be understood as an exemplary instance of the epistemological elusiveness of the past itself, exacerbated in this instance by the nature of the event' (Morash, 1995: 3). It is possible to see memory as a way of rescuing the Famine from nihilism, since

> When we read a Famine poem or novel, we find ourselves faced not with a text whose pleasures (if the word 'pleasures' is justified in such a context) and interests can be attributed solely to the workings of an individual literary genius, but rather with a document whose 'social energies' are generated by 'memories' of the Famine. These 'memories' are, in turn, compounded of the collective beliefs, practices, and

modes of enunciation available for appropriation in nineteenth-century Ireland. (Morash, 1995: 6)

However, this recognition of memory in writing is undermined by the fact that, as Morash goes on to point out, there is a dearth of Famine memories – a clear logical consequence of the effects of the Famine on the population.[1] Corroborating this problem, Niall Ó Ciosáin's (2001: 95–100) brief historiographical survey of Famine memories is incidentally persuasive in proving Beiner's point that remembrance is the exception that proves the rule of amnesia. Alluding to Nora, Grace Neville likewise asserts that 'The Great Famine of the 1840s is often seen as a *lieu de mémoire*, or site of memory, but also as a *locus* of forgetting in Irish history' (Neville, 2012: 80). The Famine, and the land from which it derives, has become an unstable literary and cultural source, leading to 'a kind of *unimagined* community, whose members are bound together not by their synchronic mindfulness of the same immediate materials, such as the daily newspaper, but by their ongoing unmindfulness of the same distant events' (Valente, 2014: 186; emphasis in original). The Famine becomes a recurrently disruptive force: first, when it needlessly killed hundreds of thousands of Irishwomen and men; second, when it blockades anamnesis.

Part of the reason the Famine is a site of forgetting, or even a troubled site of memory, is because it derives from one of the chief memorial referents in Ireland: the land. In Patrick Kavanagh's 'The Great Hunger', for example, the persona tells the reader that 'We will wait and watch the tragedy to the last curtain' (i, l. 13), which includes spying the 'birds ... that were the birds of the years' (i, l. 37). These timeless birds are birds of memory, and yet they are scared away by farmer Patrick Maguire, the poem's protagonist, almost as if his role in the Famine is to arrest the past in its tracks through linear history. By the end of the poem, when the 'true tragedy' (XIII, l. 55) of the Famine has set in, Maguire nears his time for death and 'He will hardly remember that life happened to him (XIV, l. 49) as 'The hungry fiend / Screams the apocalypse of clay / In every corner of this land' (XIV, ll. 75–7). Linking the Famine with an eschatological time of Christian apocalypse, Kavanagh's poem also signifies that the land's story is the story of the farmer. Without the memories of the latter, the former is also lost to time. As I show in the following chapters, to varying degrees this is true in W. B. Yeats's and Seamus Heaney's poems. Linking the land with Irish identity, as Edna O'Brien does in the passage quoted in my epigraph, I show how these two Irish Nobel Prize winners claim an identity as national bards through restoration of heterogeneous landed memories, rather than Famine history. Importantly, these bardic strategies are not so interested in curing the 'syndrome' called 'Irishness' that Ó Ciosáin identifies in more recent narratives of 'the recovery of the suppressed memory' of the Famine 'and its narration' (Ó Ciosáin, 2001: 112). Rather, the bardic strategy emerges through poetically remembering the land (through counter-memory and counter-history), rather than its failure to provide.

After the Famine were the Land Wars, another touchstone of memory in literature. The Land Wars led, ultimately, to the Home Rule Bills in Westminster, leading to a ratified bill in 1914. The Home Rule Bill's passage into law, however, was stalled by the First World War; this false start cast Ireland's independent sovereignty adrift in the process. The subsequent Easter Rising, Anglo-Irish War, and Civil War moved from the realm of the sacred – from Easter and the idea of blood sacrifice – to that of the secular when the Irish citizen turned gun on neighbour. These wars hinged on the idea that Irish land should be Irish territory under the aegis of an Irish sovereignty.

Both Yeats and Heaney wrote poetry that engaged in different though important ways with the interaction of bodies and land. Yeats wrote before, during and after these wars, while Heaney's poetry contended with another kind of civil war, the Northern Irish Troubles, which also dealt with the question of territory. Critically, the land which Yeats and Heaney make modern is the same land on which Spenser had built his own laureateship in the late sixteenth century. Both Yeats and Heaney, having won a Nobel Prize, are considered national poets. Their writing venerates the land of Ireland; however, I will show that there is a resistance to territorialisation on the part of the poets. Instead, they create a protean, nomadic Ireland that finds home periodically in the poetry. The land is configured as Irish in their poetry, and through their poetry the land of Ireland dialectically gives rise to these two modern poets.

The land of Ireland is given a home through Yeats's veneration of dancing. This dancing reveals the importance of human impressions *on* the land, directing attention first to building and buildings in Yeats's poetry so that we can examine the prevalence of landed images across his oeuvre. I will show how Yeats's poetry looks to 'counter-memory' as a means of modernising the land of Ireland. For Heaney, the topic is not a body's impressions on the land, but the body's 'dithering, blathering' *in* the land, as if a root. This muddiness reduces the mythical land of Ireland to a site of disease and rot. Nevertheless, Heaney shows through this rotten land an Ireland that reaches far back into its undeniable, archaeological history in order to be modern now and in the future. It elevates Heaney from his 'dithering, blathering' to a poet laureate for the entire land. Heaney's strategy is that of a 'counter-historical' Historian, through which he excavates memories from Irish land, and re-archives them as memories in his poetry. Yeats and Heaney become not merely citizens of this land, but its authoritative autochthonic authors. Time and memory are functional concepts in these authorities.

To understand fully how the contestable land vacillates between territories – English, British, Irish – it is important to consider the tendency to historicise in early modern England. As I will show, the contest is ultimately between a memorial Irish land – unscripted and therefore considered as barbaric and in need of colonialism – and an English project of nation-statism that sought to impress itself in writing and therefore through historical narrative.

Early modern Irish land

Between Spenser's *Faerie Queene* (1590, 1596, 1609), *Colin Clouts Come Home Againe* (1595), and *A View of the Present State of Ireland* (written c. 1596, published 1633), Ireland was transposed from the writer's landscape, to part of the landscape of the epic, to the topic of debate and correction. Richard McCabe characterises the landscape in *The Faerie Queene*: 'Throughout the poem the landscape functions not just as a scenic backdrop but as a formidable agent which may, at any moment, assimilate person to place through some bizarre stroke of Ovidian metamorphosis ... thereby realizing the colonists' deepest fears' (McCabe, 2002: 57). Those fears were realised during this period in the Tyrone Rebellion (1594–1603), the result of a long history of deterritorialisation of Ireland at the hands of English governance. As early as 1541 King

Henry VIII had instituted Surrender and Regrant legislation that entailed Irish lords surrendering their clan lands to the king, and waiting in line to be re-granted lands that depended on the terms of their land-surrender and their relationship with the monarch. 'This', writes John O'Beirne Ranelagh, 'was a final body-blow to the Gaelic customs of Brehon Law and the common ownership of property. In return for surrendering their lands to the king and swearing fealty, Irish chiefs would have their lands regranted to them personally' (Ranelagh, 1983: 49). Brehon Law acted as a kind of testimony of fidelity to the land, with its practices decidedly non-historical in the sense that they were not established as written law. This Irish predilection for *memory* threatened the English pragmatism established through written *history*.

The grandson of one of the lords who surrendered was Hugh O'Neill, Earl of Tyrone who became the 'unexpected rebel' and 'renegade Elizabethan'. Hugh O'Neill had assumed the title of The O'Neill by the Gaelic ritual of standing on a 'pre-Christian stone at Tullahogue'. When Lord Mountjoy eventually put down the Rebellion in 1603, he was known to have smashed 'into pieces' the stone at Tullahogue, a symbolic abuse of the piece of Irish land that gave rise to its chieftain (Foster, 1989: 4–5). When the Earl of Essex fought Hugh O'Neill, he wrote to the Privy Council on 20 May 1599 about the desperate state of the land: '[T]he rebels fight in woods and bogs, where horse are utterly unserviceable; they use the advantage of lightness and swiftness in going off' (Her Majesty's Stationery Office, 1899: 36). Moreover, 'To the average Elizabethan, Ireland was a soggy, savage wilderness where no sensible person would willingly set foot' (Plowden, 1980: 141). 'Wood, bog, lake and mountain concealed and sustained resistance, and Elizabethan soldiers hated the terrain with vehemence' (Foster, 1989: 6). Anti-memorial famine was one tactic used to counter the rebels' knowledge of their own land (Ranelagh, 1983: 53). Not only is land important at the outset of the Tyrone Rebellion when Surrender and Regrant was instituted, but land is also crucial in determining the outcome of the Rebellion, either as a symbol (the stone at Tullahogue) or in actuality (Ireland's difficult terrain). Foster adds that 'local [Irish] realities can only be understood in terms of the Irish landscape' and that 'In traditional bardic culture, the terrain was studied, discussed and referenced: every place had its legend and its own identity' (Foster, 1989: 5). To the Irish the land was known, understood and exploited – it entered and lived in memory. To the English, the land was an obdurate obstacle and weapon used against them, halting their march into a narrative history of empire.

The Tyrone Rebellion's failure, coinciding with the end of Elizabeth's reign, nevertheless gave birth to the idea of the Janus-faced Irishman in Hugh O'Neill. Similarly Janus-faced, as will be shown in the following, is the land itself. For the English, it was a site in need of conquest, with planters instructed in 1609 to out-number natives.[2] Since this disenfranchised the Irish from their own land, the Irish were unable to maintain their mastery and owner-ship of the land, characterised by the '*tuath*, a tribal or kindred unit of land' within which 'chieftain, freemen and serfs sustained a mobile structure of client relationships' (Foster, 1989: 9). The land of conquest was predicated upon a land of contest between the two peoples, out of and against which emerged certain literature. It was a contest between lived memory and the march of history.

English poetic history

Spenser was writing during the Tyrone Rebellion and the Earl of Essex's armed response. The landscape plays a central role in Spenser's writing, as McCabe outlined above. McCabe's description emerges from reading Spenser, but would not sit out of place with the historical descriptions also discussed. In art as much as in reality, Irish land was central. This is visible in *Colin Clouts Come Home Againe*, in which Colin – Spenser's self-representation – explains that he returned to Faery Land (i.e. Elizabethan England) because he feared that he had been left to rot in the land where he now lives:

> When thus our pipes we both had wearied well,
> (Quoth he) and each an end of singing made,
> He gan to cast great lyking to my lore,
> And great disliking to my lucklesse lot:
> That banisht had my selfe, like wight forlore,
> Into that waste, where I was quite forgot. (Spenser, 1970: ll. 178–83)

A sort of wish fulfilment for Spenser, this passage explains Colin's travels back to England as a result of his piping (i.e. his poetry), but also 'that waste' breeding failed memory ('forgot'). This is indicative of what McCabe describes as the 'geographical distance from court [that] has bred a new political consciousness' (2002: 170). The 'waste' is the Ireland to which Spenser was sent on a diplomatic mission in 1580, resulting in his involvement in the Munster Plantation. His role as Elizabethan emissary is bound up in the question of English sovereignty, and Elizabeth's assertion of that sovereignty over Ireland in the latter half of the sixteenth century: history-making sovereignty. Out of Queen Elizabeth's sovereignty comes Spenser's 'authority'. Colin's labelling of that Irish land as 'waste' indicates the central importance of the land in his role in Ireland, but also figures it negatively. As opposed to the land of sheep that is England, tended by shepherds like Colin, Ireland is barren and overrun by wolves, for 'The shepheards there abroad [England] may safely lie / On hills and downes, withouten dread or daunger', whilst in Ireland 'rauenous wolues the good mans hope destroy, / … [and] outlawes fell affray the forest raunger' (ll. 316–19). Moreover, there is an additional, personal motivation in accusations in *A View* that the Irish practice of transhumance – '[A] form of pastoral farming which involves the seasonal movement of livestock and people between winter and summer pastures. Usually, the former is the main base of a community, with the latter located some distance away on less intensively used ground' (Costello, 2015: 47) – is repulsive, in part thanks to its nomadic ethic. 'I disliked the Irish manner of kepinge of Bollies in sommer vpon the mountaine', Irenius says, 'and lyvinge after that salvage sorte.' The savagery is particular to the distance between community and the Bollies or 'less intensively used ground'. Irenius continues: '[L]ett them make some townes nere to the mountaines syde where they maye dwell togeather with neigbors and bee conversant in the veiwe of the world' (Spenser, 1934: 203). Just as Colin laments his distance from Faery Land's civilised behaviours, so too does Spenser's persona criticise the Irish farmers' savagery by maintaining their pastoral control over the land away from their 'neighbors'. Transhumance, which otherwise might be praised for its more economical use of the land that encouraged seasonal regrowth of grazing pastures,[3] is summarily dismissed because it appears to be uncivilised. In other words, Spenser dismisses transhumance because it successfully enacts a nomadic ethic of periodic deterritorialisation and reterritorialisation counter to the historicising impulse of the English colonisers.

In Book 6 of *The Faerie Queene*, Spenser recalls the lupine, illegal behaviour of the Irish intruding on their neighbours when Serena ends up in 'wylde deserts' where 'dwelt a saluage nation':

> In these wylde deserts, where she [Serena] now abode,
> There dwelt a saluage nation, which did liue
> Of stealth and spoile, and making nightly rode
> Into their neighbours borders; ne did giue
> Them selues to any trade, as for to driue
> The painefull plough, or cattell for to breed,
> Or by aduentrous marchandize to thriue;
> But on the labours of poore men to feed,
> And serue their owne necessities with others need. (Spenser, 1987:
>   VI.viii.35)

The negative characterisation of the 'saluage' nation here is wholly consistent with other allegations made about the Irish, not only in *The Faerie Queene*, but also in *A View*. Savagery in this mode, according to McCabe (2002: 58), is not merely a description of Irish behaviour, but also a register of its remoteness on the map of the British Isles. The distance from the palaces of Westminster and Hampton Court indicates the Irishman's exteriority to the law. Irenius in Spenser's *A View* says that

> with Ireland yt is farr otherwise: For yt is a nacion ever acquainted
> with warrs though but amongst them selues, and in theire owne
> kynde of militarie discipline trained vpp even from theire youths
> which they haue never yet bene taught to laye aside, nor made to
> learne obedience vnto the lawe, scarselye to knowe the name of lawe,
> but insteade thereof haue always preserued and kepte theire owne
> lawe which is the *Brehon* lawe[.] (1934: 7)

Irenius here condemns the extra-judicial Irish existence as he explains to Eudoxus about Irish savagery.[4] This savagery is unruly because the Irish not only start outside the law, but they resist law's work and function as they cannot be made to 'learne obedience vnto the lawe'. Law constituted a key process of English modernisation in Ireland, and contributed to the emptying of memory from Ireland. It followed a renovated jurisprudence in England itself, across the fifteenth and sixteenth centuries. Richard Helgerson outlines how 'something of a *Corpus Juris* for England' was constructed particularly effectively by Edward Coke. 'Coke's very

insularity', writes Helgerson, 'his myopic insistence on the uninter-
rupted Englishness of English law, was the product of a constant
sense of legal and national difference, a persistent awareness of a
rival system of law against which English law had to defend and
define itself' (Helgerson, 1992: 70–1). And so,

> In law, as in other areas, national consolidation had a double face.
> It turned inward to find out and eliminate those practices and those
> institutions that failed to reflect back to its unitary image, and it
> turned outward to declare its defining difference – *and* to assure itself
> that such difference was not so different that it would be taken as a
> sign of backwardness or barbarity. (Helgerson, 1992: 71; emphasis
> in original)

I see in this legal project England's departure from the barbarism
characterised by Irish memory, and entry into a modernity in
which history can be written and national narratives scripted. Peter
Orr, comparing Spenser's *A View* with Sir John Davies's 1612 *A
Discovery,*[5] contends that whilst Spenser offered an 'ethnological
view of Irish society', characterising 'military and judicial violence'
as the civilising agent, Davies refines the colonising programme
by arguing that 'the common law itself was the regenerative agent
required to both civilize the native Irish'. The chief difference
between the two writers, argues Orr, is their 'competing *narrative*
models for writing the history of early modern Ireland' (Orr, 2003:
398; emphasis in original). In either case, the urgent focus on narrative, history, and law focuses on the civilising impulse.

   The remoteness from law shows Ireland to be barbarous, and,
more critically for my argument, the Irish are therefore rendered,
in two passages from *A View*, similar to the kind of savage nation
that terrorises Serena in *The Faerie Queene*. First, the Irish invade
neighbouring 'countries':

> [S]einge now theire [landes] so dispeopled and weakned, came
> downe into all the plaines adionyninge, and thence expellinge those
> fewe Englishe that remained, repossessed them againe, since which
> tyme they haue remayned in them and growing greater have brought
> vnder them manye of the English, which were before their Lordes.
> (Spenser, 1934: 11–12)

Second, Ireland is described as a wasteland and wild desert: 'Thus
was all that goodlie Countrie vtterlie waisted and lefte desolate,

and as yet remayneth to this daye which before had bene the cheif ornamente and bewtie of Ireland' (Spenser, 1934: 11–12). The relation for Irenius between lawlessness and a desolate landscape is inevitable in these two passages; similarly, the relation between this savage Ireland and the landscape of *The Faerie Queene* is clear. In its wildness and its giving rise to lawlessness, Ireland is irretrievably immoral and worthy only of colonising: it needs to conform to Court norms. The 'saluage nation' and 'saluage land' are interwoven. The Spenserian crossover between real Ireland and the 'darke conceit' of allegorical land gives force to the reading of land as something more than mere background or hinterland: land means and gives identity. Spenser's poetry enacts and consolidates a link between the so-called 'real' Ireland and its textual counterpart.

This overlap appears in one of the dedicatory sonnets to the first edition of *The Faerie Queene*. It was dedicated 'To the Right Honourable the Earle of Ormond and Ossory', indicating the politicisation of the author and the authorial space – Spenser thus intruding into the realm of sovereign authority:

> Receiue most noble Lord a simple taste
> Of the wilde fruit, which saluage soyl hath bred,
> Which being through long wars left almost waste,
> With brutish barabarisme is ouerspredd:
> And in so faire a land, as may be red,
> Not one *Parnassus*, nor one *Helicone*
> Left for sweete Muses to be harboured,
> But where thy selfe hast thy braue mansion;
> There in deede dwel faire Graces many one.
> And gentle Nymphes, delights of learned wits,
> And in thy person without Paragone
> All goodly bountie and true honour sits,
> Such therefore, as that wasted soyl doth yield,
> Receiue dear Lord in worth, the fruit of barren field. (Spenser, 1987: 28)

There is much bound up in this sonnet. The dedicatee merits first attention, because

Ormond was a member of the incumbent colonial group, the Old English, whose ancestors had come over with the Anglo-Normans in the twelfth century, so that his seemingly privileged relationship with the queen was much resented by the upwardly mobile New English who came to Ireland on the back of the renewed Crown interest under the Tudors. (Hadfield, 1997: 4–5)

This sonnet is therefore in intimate relation to the English sovereign's power abroad, though most specifically in Ireland. As with any dedication, the sonnet also bends the work which it prefaces to the authority of the dedication, whilst underscoring the writer's authority. *The Faerie Queene* is in part dedicated to, and thus partly stands as a representation of, Queen Elizabeth's sovereignty in Ireland, particularly in its centuries-old establishment: Spenser's poetry is a *via media* – sovereignty is established through *The Faerie Queene*.

In this, *The Faerie Queene* and its greatness are generated by the demand to civilise the land: the land's mistreatment at the hands of the Irish, merely alleged in *A View*, is tamed by Spenser's great poetics. And yet Ormond must be the recipient of the 'fruit of barren field' for it is his house in Tipperary that is the only equivalent of an Irish Parnassus or Helicone. In fact, it means that Ormond has tamed the land (and its inhabitants, those who live on the land), the same feat that Spenser has achieved in rooting his epic in Ireland and harvesting its fruit above the surface for Ormond to digest. As Hadfield explicates,

> the giving of culture, *The Faerie Queene*, to Ormond, is portrayed as dependent upon his success in spreading English civility, yet also as an independent creation of the poet's, the 'fruit' which must be harvested if the bad nature of Ireland is to be civilized. It suggests that *The Faerie Queene* serves an Orphic function [i.e., as poetic authority] in its ability to transform the wilderness left by the natives; that it is at once congruent with a political authority and simultaneously aware of a potential to undermine what it ostensibly relies upon. (Hadfield, 1997: 5)

This is therefore not merely about land as a site of genesis for the poetry, but also as poetry as genesis for the land.

I have established the following. First, *The Faerie Queene* is portrayed as the 'wilde fruit, which salvage soyle hath bred', a civilised text emerging from an uncivilised land. Second, *The Faerie Queene* tells stories of savage lands made civil – the virtue of Book 6 is 'courtesie' – and so it acts as an instance of the sovereign, colonial act. *The Faerie Queene* turns savage lands civil, and is the logical

product of civilised lands: it is a text that modernises and represents modernity through textual civility. Through and from the
land, Irish memory is successfully replaced by English poetic history. This means that the productive land, paradoxically, is the fruit
of Spenser's verse. The land is therefore rooted in the poetry, in a
dialectical anchoring that indicates the reliance of Spenser's English
epic on Irish land, and Irish land on English epic.

In the aforementioned, nomadism and the search for a new home
provide a common thread: Spenser and Colin Clout were re-housed
in Ireland, and Ireland became, in the Elizabethan early colonisation, a new home-space for England through the civilising practices
of law and historical narrativisation. In both of these analyses, and
those to follow, 'nomad' is a useful term to use instead of exile and
migrant. Whilst the term exile concerns 'an acute sense of foreign-
ness' and the term migrant denotes ideas of 'missing, nostalgia, and
blocked horizons', nomads contrastingly make their home wherever
they settle, opening up the space to hospitality through their perpetual travel (Braidotti, 1994: 24).[6] Nomadism creates Eden wherever
it goes, and is thus a motif of the secularising process of modernity
that is important in the remainder of this part. The other early modern nomads that concern me are Shakespeare's King Lear, Orlando,
Duke Senior, and Hamlet. Each of these characters searches for a
new home; for some, the same space as their previous home is on
offer, though it belongs to someone else: the nomadic process is,
among other things, a process of sovereign territorialisation.

The two Irish poets to whom I also turn are also on the look-
out for home. Yeats tries to find it in Revival Ireland, first, before
lamenting the land agitation and its effects on the Big Houses he
holds dear; Heaney is a nomad who moves from the north to the
south of Ireland, and is 'lost, unhappy and at home' when abroad
in Denmark. The former's consciousness of the ageing process and
his future legacy ties his story to King Lear's; the latter's concern
with the roots of and in a homeland links him to Hamlet. In these
cases, the characters and poets are national heroes because they
persistently address their homelessness through memory, rather
than through a nationalised narrative of history. Yeats's secularised
modernity manifests in the renovation of time and restoration of
memory as a nomadic Ireland periodically finds a home in poetry,
and Heaney's secularised modernity in an unruly, diseased land,

wherein he becomes an archaeological and an archiving poet. Yeats and Heaney both turn away from history, returning to Irish land in memory.

Nomadology also gives us a critical framework beyond the literal. It offers a theory of perpetual becoming, and Rosi Braidotti's configuration of this becoming also creates a specific nomadic memory. Opposing a Molar or Majoritarian politics, in which dominant subjectivities eclipse and subjugate minority interests, Braidotti offers 'Molecular or nomadic memories [that] are also, and more especially, a creative force that gives the "wretched of the earth" ... a head start toward the world-historical task of envisaging alternative world orders and more humane and sustainable social systems' (Braidotti, 2011: 32). In more specific terms,

Molecular, minoritarian, or nomadic memories are affirmative, destabilizing forces that propel subjects actively toward change. They are the kind of memories that are linked to ethical and political consciousness[.] ... Remembering nomadically amounts to reinventing a self as other – as the expression of a nomadic subject's structural ability to actualize selfhood as a process of transformation and transversality. Remembering is consequently not about being equal to yourself, but rather in differing as much as possible from all you had been before. ... It is not about being what I was like before (before what? and like whom?), in a relationship of spatiotemporal sameness between present and past self-representations, i.e., between me now and myself then. It is rather about differing from myself as much and as often as possible. ... Remembering is less about forgetting to forget than about retaking, as in refilming a sequence: it is about differing from oneself. (Braidotti, 2011: 32–3)

This approach to memory rejects the psychoanalytic fixation on lack and trauma, instead utilising difference as a positive phenomenon. Nomadic memory gives intimate access to difference and the process of becoming-different. Nomadic memory is close to the dismemories I have catalogued and described in this book. Braidotti's revolutionary sundering of nomadic memories from the past thus merits quoting:

Remembering in the nomadic mode ... is the active reinvention of a self that is joyfully discontinuous, as opposed to being mournfully consistent as programmed by phallogocentric culture. It destabilizes the sanctity of the past and the authority of experience. The tense

that best expresses the power of the imagination is the future perfect:
'I will have been free'. (Braidotti, 2011: 154)

This future perfect is the tense of dismemory, and astutely characterises the counter-memorial and counter-historical strategies I
describe in the following. Whether in Yeats's dancing or Heaney's
muddiness, there emerges a commitment to disrupting a past genealogy or a contaminated historical narrative. The 'Ovidian metamorphosis' of Irish land that threatened Spenser in the 1590s is
actualised in these modern poets' works. Moreover, in the framework and vocabulary of nomadology, the peripatetic ethic of transhumance is re-asserted, and the civilising practice of *corpus juris*
disrupted. In the following two chapters, these disruptions and anti-
historical narratives become my focus as I show how a molecular
nomadology can accurately describe the memorial practices of these
two poets which act to disrupt an English and British claim to Irish
land.

Notes

1 Foster examines the data in regard to the damage wrought by the
   Famine – though he caveats heavily that Famine deaths may be symptomatic of other macro-economic causes:

   The figures for Famine deaths are equally stunning, and equally
   they raise problems. At least 775,000 died, mostly through disease,
   including cholera in the latter stages of the catastrophe. Here again
   the authorities disagree. A recent sophisticated computation esti-
   mates excess deaths from 1846 to 1851 as between 1,000,000 and
   1,500,000, varying widely from county to county, as usual; after
   a careful critique of this, other statisticians arrive at a figure of
   1,000,000. The projection of decline in terms of 'excess' raises the
   question what rate the population would have gone on increasing
   at *without* the Famine, and whether it was still increasing when
   the Famine struck – which has become a contested question. But
   no amount of disagreement can conceal the devastating extent of
   depopulation or the horrific conditions in which lives were lost.
   (Foster, 1989: 324–5; emphasis in original)

2 Q.v. Ranelagh (1983: 5).
3 Q.v. Costello (2015: 64).

4 For my discussion on the power of excluded Ireland in the literary imagination see Nicholas Collins (2015) and also Stephen O'Neill (2018).
5 Full title: *A Discovery of the True Causes Why Ireland Was Never Entirely Subdued [and] Brought under Obedience of the Crown of England until His Majesty's Happy Reign.*
6 Above I showed secondarily why Spenser cannot be considered an exile, because Elizabeth is re-housed in his poetry of Ireland: Spenser moves England across the Irish Sea.

6

'[R]ights of memory': W. B. Yeats, surface, and counter-memory

For the Irish emigrant, the home place is elsewhere; it is 'imagined' in terms of both the past and the future – the past as a form of cultural memory and the future as a desire to return to the homeland.

– from *The Irish Dancing* by Barbara O'Connor

Introduction

In this chapter I examine Yeats's poetry as a recasting of the discourses of nomadism visible in *King Lear* and *As You Like It*. Yeats's strategy tacks against the logic of *Lear*, but figuratively recapitulates ideas from *As You Like It*'s pastoralism (along with *The Faerie Queene*) in poetry: Duke Senior is finally preferred to King Lear. The nomadic motif in Yeats's poetry contributes to creating a new Ireland out of an old one. As 'E. K.' writes in the epistle to Spenser's 'Shepheardes Calender' (1579), in adopting the chosen title, the author was 'applying an olde name to a new worke' (Spenser, 1970: 418). So too, I argue, does Yeats's motif of dancing seek to retrieve from the counter-memorial land a modern version of Ireland whose form is yet to be determined: it is what will have been. The texts create this renovated Ireland, moreover, within poetry, through Yeats's curation of images. From the destructed building via the scars on the surface of the land, we eventually arrive at the images of dancing and dancer. The former demonstrates how the surface of the land generates the opportunity to (re)territorialise, even when the detritus leaves rubble as its only marker. However, we eventually see how dance and nomadism, as in the final scenes of *As You Like It*, connect through the repetitive motions of leaping and landing, in which the dancer disconnects and reconnects with the land. In this repetition a leaping homelessness periodically finds a new home in landing. Dancing comes to represent forgetting and remembering, with the connection to the land the moment of memorial retrieval that is nonetheless predicted. In so doing, Yeats's poems become the memory that the inscrutable land is unable to signify fully. Yeats's texts construct a modern Ireland; the image of dancing and dancer is critical to this reading, prepared by the images of buildings, both whole and derelict. This new Ireland is modern in its establishment of an Irish space between the dancer and the land. What results is a kind of homelessness; however, in Yeats's poetry it appears as the nomadism linked with the land itself, periodically finding a home in the poetry. Another idea attends this: the renovation of time, which is secularised in its removal from a messianic Christian time to a modern Irish time – a renovation demanded by counter-memory that offers a 'transformation of history into a totally different form of time' (Foucault, 1980: 160) and that, as Braidotti updates, entails 'activat[ing] multiple ecologies of belonging' (Braidotti, 2011: 41) such that Oedipal structures of linearity (visible in *Lear*) are displaced and replaced by 'zigzagging' patterns (evident in *As You Like It*). The dance furnishes Yeats with just such a zigzagging pattern.

Nomadic homelessness is also central to *King Lear* and *As You Like It*. In both plays, there is a story of land that is deterritorialised, either by due process or usurpation, and then reterritorialised. Sovereignty links the two: in *Lear*, the king gives away his land to his daughters, relinquishing his claim to English territory so that he may 'Unburdened crawl toward death' (I.i.40), and in *As You Like It* Duke Senior is exiled to the Forest of Arden and 'lands and revenues enrich the new Duke' (I.i.102–3). Sovereignty in these plays is dependent on territorial possession. However, Lear and the Duke, to varying degrees of voluntarism, are divested of their land by others: Goneril and Regan, and Duke Frederick. Lear and Duke Senior (along with Orlando) become nomads, and their trajectories take them to find new homes. In this, and in Lear's and Duke Senior's sovereign control of the territories they call 'home', the drive to modernity – the transformation of land into territory – becomes evident. Not unlike Fortinbras's appearance at the end of *Hamlet*, when he arrives in court to declare that 'I have some rights of memory in this kingdom / Which now to claim my vantage doth invite me' (V.ii.373–4), land in *Lear* and *As You Like It* undergoes a reversion to its *right of memory* as opposed to its illegal reappropriation.

In Shakespeare's plays, Lear loses and Duke Senior wins back control over their respective lands. That both contain a version of civil strife is indicative of the modern struggle for sovereignty over land: quite often the enemy is within rather than without. To be sovereigns of their respective jurisdictions requires a return to their initial territorial spaces. Lear's land is ultimately owned by Edgar when Lear, aided by Cordelia, wins the war, but Duke Senior receives his own lands back from his brother Duke Frederick. Tragedy and comedy depart at this juncture: the tragedy ends with alien forces territorialising Britain, while the comedy ends when the rightful owners regain control over the courts. Nomadism in the comedy returns to its original site of departure. I will argue that the specific demands of nomadism do not disappear in this final reterritorialisation, but that nomadism characterises the new and modern relationship with the land for the sovereigns. A paradox emerges: to call their jurisdictions 'home', sovereigns must first have no home, either by choice or by violence.[1] This spatial nomadism has a memorial counterpart: '[N]omadic consciousness is akin to what Foucault called countermemory ... The nomadic tense is imperfect; it is active, continuous ... The nomad's relationship to the earth is one of transitory attachment and cyclical frequentation' (Braidotti, 1994: 25). I will think about these ideas in connection with homelessness and landlessness in modern Ireland, using this counter-memory as a version of my dismemory.

Yeats provides an important study given that he is one of those whose name often appears in the contents list of a book examining Shakespeare's connections with modern Ireland. In *Threshold of a Nation* (1979), Philip Edwards established a continuity between Shakespeare's early modern theatre and Yeats's establishment of a national Irish theatre in 1899. That continuity, however, was more surprising than is given credit since Yeats did so all the while rejecting popular poetry and praising elitism. Shakespeare's popularity escaped him at this point. As Edwards notes, 'It seems incredible that Yeats should speak of Shakespeare as one of his idols in an essay which contemptuously rejected popularity in favour of elitism.' Clearly the worship of the canonical father obscured the piercing gaze of ideology, which leads to Edwards's arguing that

Yeats's 'binary' praise of Richard II and dismissal of Henry V in 'At Stratford-on-Avon' 'is very clear[ly] … an Irish view'. Moreover, this 'Irish view' is in stark contrast to Edward Dowden's own. Dowden was Professor of English Literature at Trinity College and 'a determined Unionist, and his cultural views were as firmly cemented to *his* political views as Yeats's were to his'. This leads Edwards to finesse his argument that 'Yeats's Shakespeare is an honorary Celt' (Edwards, 1979: 202, 206, 207; emphasis in original).

To counter this, Adam Putz has more recently shown that in 'At Stratford-on-Avon', 'Yeats forwards Shakespeare … as an appropriative artist … and in this way the sort of artist to whom Yeats might appeal.' In so doing, this version of Yeats's Shakespeare is more like a son than a father, which makes Yeats all the more ready to appropriate Shakespeare as he positions himself as a son to writing more generally: 'Yeats saw … that Shakespeare's art works to affect identity through acts of appropriation' (Putz, 2013: 131, 133). Yeats thus envisions a specific type of Shakespeare – who acts like a son to other writers – on whom he models his own artistic practice. This practice then restores Shakespeare as a kind of father of sons. It is clear at least that Yeats exhibits an 'ambivalence towards Shakespeare's legacy' (van der Ziel, 2018: 361). Van der Ziel refines this ambivalence in his exploration of *Purgatory* (1938), one of Yeats's last plays and a 'Shakespearian tragedy in miniature' (Ure, 1963: 112). In it, a father shows his son a burntdown house in which the father used to live. The father recounts killing his father, tells of his mother's unsatisfactory death (hence her being in purgatory), and then kills his own son. After a lengthy exploration of this short, verse play, calling on Shakespeare's *King Lear* most prominently, but also *Timon of Athens*, *Coriolanus*, and *The Winter's Tale*, among others, van der Ziel concludes that Yeats's 'miniaturization' of Shakespeare is a 'tragic' 'refinement … because the attempt to improve Shakespeare of course constitutes an act of immense hubris. The attempt is always doomed to failure' (van der Ziel, 2018: 390).

None of this argument can be countered; however, it is perhaps surprising that van der Ziel does not focus on the clear structural and linguistic links between *Purgatory* and *Hamlet*, especially through the storytelling motif from father to son. As the Old Man tells the Boy of his job after he murdered his father, the Old Man says it was 'good enough / Because I am my father's son' (Yeats, 2001b: 540). The verbal echoes of 'I am my father's son' with *Hamlet*'s Ghost's 'I am thy father' (I.v.9), may be just that, but the Boy's earlier, 'There's nobody there' (Yeats, 2001b: 538) seems to answer Barnardo's opening 'Who's there?' (I.i.1) in *Hamlet*. The connection is particularly acute, given the presence of ghosts in *Purgatory*. The *Hamlet* connection is also audible in the catalogue of 'Great people [who] lived and died in this house' (Yeats, 2001b: 539), itself reminiscent of Hamlet's meditation on the skulls and skeletons that are surfaced during the graveyard scene (V.i.71 ff.).

However, there is also a concern with paternity and filiality. The Boy questions:

What if I killed you? You killed my grand-dad,
Because you were young and he was old;
Now I am young and you are old. (Yeats, 2001b: 339)

The result of this threat is that the father kills the son 'because he had grown up, / [And h]e would have struck a woman's fancy, / Begot, and passed pollution on' (Yeats, 2001b: 542). The Old Man's concern is specifically to do with inheritance and legacy. For the man who overcame his father, his wish is to forestall that murderous inheritance. The main reasons for this evasion are the sounds that haunt the Old Man. 'Listen to the hoof beats! Listen, listen!' (539) is not only reminiscent of *Hamlet*'s Ghost's 'List, list, O list' (I.v.22), but with 'Beat! Beat!' and 'Hoof beats! Dear God / How quickly it returns – beat – beat' (Yeats, 2001b: 541, 544) they collectively refer to the percussive sound of hooves on the surface of the earth. The ghost that haunts Yeats's Old Man is heard through the violent contact with the earth.

This earth and land are at the heart of many of Yeats's poems. Like the genealogy that brings Shakespeare down to Yeats, land is also conditioned by a linear inheritance signified by the word 'territory'. Territory is possessed land, and Ireland's land is a contested territory, particularly between the English/British and the Irish. In terms of the literary history that interests Yeats, Spenser is the earliest harbinger of contest in the late sixteenth century, though by the end of the nineteenth century, the Famine of the 1840s and the Land Wars of the 1880s (and beyond) are both critical markers in the land's genealogy. As I noted, the early modern English planters were urged to outnumber the Irish in order to seize control of the land, and make sure that insurrection and rebellion could be halted at the root: the planters deterritorialised the land and took it from the Irish, historicising it in the English imagination in the process. Though the English did not maintain their superiority of numbers in the following centuries, their descendants, in addition to the Ascendancy class, did maintain large swathes of control over the land as landlords. In this, landlordism in nineteenth-century Ireland modelled a classic hegemony: a control of a minority who held the power over the majority; the resultant Land War was so potent because of the numbers of people involved. Looking at the strategy of boycott in the 1870s and 1880s, Foster explains that 'Above all, rent was witheld [sic], evicted farms were kept empty, and landlords ostracized by the traditional weapon of excluding the transgressor from all transactions within the community' (Foster, 1989: 406). Clearly the boycotts were effective partly because of their popularity. Land was the political focus in this period of Irish nationalism, with even Yeats criticising his countrymen: 'A trumpery dispute about an acre of land can rouse our people to monstrous savagery' (Yeats, 1923: para. 2). The Irish, via the Land League and other like organisations, were starting to take back their land as their own territory, finding a foothold for modern Ireland: they became Fortinbras entering Elsinore, reclaiming forgotten rights. As at the start of Ireland's colonisation at the end of the sixteenth century, so with its removal from the British Empire at the beginning of the twentieth century: those who sovereignly control the land control the drive towards modernity. This more recent reterritorialisation is, as I explained above, a response to the emptying of history after the Famine.

To all these territorial dramas Yeats responded poetically. In *The Countess Cathleen* (1892, though much revised until 1919), Yeats explicitly addresses the Famine. Amid a countryfolk hounded by the blight, Countess Cathleen stands up to defend them – not just in the face of Famine, but in the face of Satan's emissaries, disguised as merchants, who have come to Ireland to buy the souls of those who despair in their starvation. In lieu of their souls, Cathleen offers the merchants her own soul:

CATHLEEN The people starve, therefore the people go
    Thronging to you. I hear a cry come from them
    And it is in my ears by night and day,
    And I would have five hundred thousand crowns
    That I may feed them till the dearth go by. (2001b: 49)

Cathleen's martyrdom confirms that this Famine can give rise to an Irish identity, as the *Mathair Éire* trope is brought into the narrative to cohere the disparate, individualised peasants around a single identity. As Adrian Frazier argued, in *The Countess Cathleen* 'What Yeats had done was to transvalue the greatest national experience of the Irish, turning a Protestant moral catastrophe into a miracle of benevolence' (Frazier, 1987: 461). In the play, Yeats is also concerned with a kind of failed paternity when Shemus and Teigue, father and son, are only too ready to be the first to sell their souls to the merchants – wife and mother, Mary, refuses and dies of starvation rather than sell her soul to the devil. Thus, father and son, paternity and filiation, fail the test of the Famine: their future history, in the form of a continued genealogy, is forestalled. It is not my aim here to deconstruct the play's politics or mores – nor its insufficiencies as a modern drama[2] – but suffice it to say that the play reveals an interest in the land and dance that stays with Yeats throughout his career.

    The favouritism he offers the landed gentry in *The Countess Cathleen* is repeated in 1910's poem 'Upon a House Shaken by the Land Agitation'. Referring to his friend Maud Gonne's house at Coole Park, the speaker laments about those who would see the house destroyed. 'How should the world be luckier if this house', asks the poem, 'became too ruinous / To breed the lidless eye that loves the sun?' (Yeats, 1997b: ll. 1–4). Yeats's emphasis on an Ascendancy territory that can breed – albeit breeding eagles in an image that is 'subtle, and relies on a complex net of allusion' (McCarthy, 2011: 38) – signals again a preoccupation with the future and inheritance. In a final example, in the 'Meditations in a Time of Civil War' (1928) sequence, the speaker moves from 'My House', where 'after me / My bodily heirs may find, / To exalt a lonely mind, / Befitting emblems of adversity' (Yeats, 1997b: ll. 27–30) to 'My Descendants' when the speaker hopes that he might 'leave a woman and a man behind / As vigorous of mind [as me]', but if he should fail, 'May this laborious stair and this stark tower / Become a roofless ruin' (Yeats, 1997b: ll. 3–4, 13–14). Within the generalised Yeats schema described by Richard Ellmann (1968: 7) as 'a concerted effort to bring ... contrasting elements ... into a single circle', these passages from 'Meditations' confirm that Yeats's focus on the land as a viable symbol for poetry is also connected to the passage of time.

Yeats's initial scepticism and development

The Land Wars were the period that marked the beginning of Yeats's career. If Yeats is a national poet, it could be expected that Yeats would approve of the movement towards sovereign independence and modernity. However, his Anglo-Irishness initially took precedence. Thus Yeats appears sceptical early in his career, but comes to understand that there is something useful to be found in the scars and traces of history on the land – the memorial residue that litters the land, 'the inscribed surface of events' (Foucault, 1980: 148).

The prime instances of this in Yeats's poetry are buildings and houses. In 'Upon a House', the mythical history of Coole Park is prioritised over the sovereign rights of the Irish tenants. The history of land agitation is important here. The Land League was founded in 1879, though that merely cemented the unification of those who were striving for an irredentist reterritorialisation of the Irish land from British landlords, Anglo-Irish landlords and, above all, absentee landlords. 'The more obvious outcome of the Land War', writes Foster, 'was Gladstone's Land Act of 1881' (Foster, 1989: 412). This was the first of a series of Acts and Bills passed in Westminster, indications that the *locus* of British power and its representatives were beginning to cede control to Ireland. The 1881 Act was followed by the 1887 Land Act, the 1885 Ashbourne Act and the 1903 Wyndham Act. These contributed, along with the land agitation, to the attempts to pass a Home Rule Bill for Ireland, with failed iterations in 1886 and 1893 before a Bill was passed in 1912. Amidst all this parliamentarianism, Foster records that 'the Land War created the Irish Parliamentary Party as accredited national leaders' (Foster, 1989: 415–16). The link between land agitation – certain attempts to reterritorialise Ireland as their home, and win it back from the

English – and parliamentary politics parallels that joining modernity with sovereignty. In this framework, it might be expected that
Yeats would support the work that the Land League accomplished
(not least because much of Yeats's writing was itself concerned with
the autonomous and sovereign Irish state). And yet Yeats was out-
spoken in 'Upon a House Shaken by the Land Agitation' in his condemnation of the havoc that the Land War was wreaking on the
landed gentry, specifically on his friend Lady Augusta Gregory:

> How should the world be luckier if this house,
> Where passion and precision have been one
> Time out of mind, became too ruinous
> To breed the lidless eye that loves the sun?
> And the sweet laughing eagle thoughts that grow
> Where wings have memory of wings, and all
> That comes of the best knit to the best? (Yeats, 1997b: ll. 1–7)

Collected in 1910's *The Green Helmet and Other Poems*, this keys
in to the War which had been raging since the 1870s. The clearly
conservative Yeats is stressing the immortality of Coole Park, the
site that generated much of his poetic creativity. The reference to the
timeless aspect of Coole Park indicates that at this juncture Yeats's
poetry is gesturing to an older, mythical Ireland that is remembered,
rather than concretely scripted. Yeats is opposing the narrativised
(and therefore historical, in the mode of the early modern English)
land war with a mythical time that approaches the mode of counter-
memory: regardless of his manifest politics, the turn to myth is an
abiding strategy for Yeats. However, Yeats's lauding of the house
at Coole Park has nothing to do with his politics; rather, something that sits on the land itself is what merits his praise, and he
laments its demise. Yeats's relation to the land is important precisely
because he is not concerned, as many were, with the agrarianism of
the land – how to cultivate it and produce food – but because he is
concerned with the physical impressions made on the land. In this
idea it becomes easier to see the metaphor of the memorial *tupos*
making itself apparent.

Whilst in 'Upon a House' the house on the land's surface merits Yeats's poetic attention, elsewhere it is the tower, the sídhe, or
dancers.[3] In 'Solomon and the Witch', for example, the witch is

compelled by the trace she and Solomon left on the grass. She tells
Solomon,

> 'The night has fallen; not a sound
> In the forbidden sacred grove
> Unless a petal hit the ground,
> Nor any human sight within it
> But the crushed grass where we have lain;
> And the moon is wilder every minute.
> O! Solomon! let us try it again.' (ll. 38–44)

The 'crushed grass' compels the witch to ask Solomon to re-enact
what they just completed: their impression on the grass, rather than
Solomon's impression in the witch's mind. In his concern with the surface of the earth, we see Yeats's drive towards territorialisation – the
long-term, sovereign ownership of the land's surface – but through
a mythopoetics.

It is possible to connect the concern in Yeats's poetry with privileging the land's surface to his mystical impulse. In his Nobel acceptance speech, Yeats praised his own, Lady Gregory's and Synge's
work for this reason: these writers brought 'the imagination and
speech of the country, all that poetical tradition descended from
the middle ages, to the people of the town' (Yeats, 1923: para. 11).
In lauding their focus on 'poetical tradition', Yeats reveals his own
'historical sense' (Foucault, 1980: 139–64) as someone interested in
genealogy.[4] Furthermore, Richard Ellmann usefully quotes Yeats's
thoughts on meeting Joyce for the first time: 'When the idea which
comes from individual life marries the image that is born from the
people, one gets great art, the art of Homer, and of Shakespeare'
(qtd in Ellmann, 1969: 88). As I described above, Yeats's own relationship with Shakespeare has been characterised as 'appropriation'. This attitude privileges vertical forms of inheritance: 'Yeats
saw himself as situated at the end of one era and the start of another
in history [which] qualified him as Shakespeare's heir, a poet well
placed for putting the pieces of fractured subjectivity back together'
(Putz, 2013: 96). Not only does this place Yeats as the receiver of
culture predating his own, but also as the medium and sender of the
culture before him. As King Lear would explain, ''tis our fast intent /
To shake all cares and business from our age, / Conferring them on

younger strengths' (I.i.3). Yeats and Lear, especially in their publicly visible ageing, and in their relation to their respective territories, share a trajectory: to pass on to later generations the land that they have made their own. The land, suffering a different trajectory to and outlasting those who possess it, embeds within it a series of heterogeneous and contradictory memories: counter-memory (cf. Foucault, 1980: 162).

Lear's relationship to territory is similarly inextricable from his valuation of tradition and inheritance. However, when violently breaking the so-called 'natural' transition of lands via inheritance, he can nonetheless be seen to continue his adherence to the style of a traditional historian. Foucault sketches this role critically: someone concerned with 'linear development' and 'monotonous finality' (Foucault, 1980: 139).[5] The corollary of Lear's attitude is that in giving away land, he also gives away his own time, allowing him to accelerate to his death. Lear explains to his daughters the transfer of his lands to them, on the condition that they declare the extent of their love for him:

> Tell me, my daughters –
> Since now we will divest us both of rule,
> Interest of territory, cares of state –
> Which of you shall we say doth love us most,
> That we our largest bounty may extend
> Where nature doth with merit challenge. (I.i.48–53)

Lear's divestment particularly involves losing his territory. Stuart Elden, commenting on Shakespeare's two plays that use the word 'territory', says that Lear's use here is about 'political control of and stake in' this land (Elden, 2013: 275). Divesting himself of political interest (and therefore also authority over homogeneous, unilateral temporality) in the land leaves King Lear a nomad on the land he previously commanded; Lear is hosted by his two daughters, Goneril and Regan, who benefit from his gift. They reduce his train and entourage as their tenant until he is left as 'houseless poverty' (III.iv.26) like Poor Tom: Lear becomes nomadic. In this way, Lear's giving away his territory and access to time – relinquishing thereby his claim to sovereignty over Britain – leads to his displacement, or deterritorialisation. And, as Braidotti noted, this also lends to him a temporality different to that of traditional kingship.

This happens at the same moment that Goneril and Regan reterritorialise England in their own image. The civil war that ensues, and its tragic outcome in the play, is in part a consequence of this territorial violence. The unnatural reassignment of territory (which is another way of saying the *modern* reassignment of territory, moving as it is away from inheritance and towards gift) is the cornerstone of tragedy in *Lear* and manifests itself in the civil war. Lear helps us to understand Yeats because of their shared interest in tradition and inheritance, and because of their roles as national icons. In both locales, however, civil war ensues because of this insistence on temporal succession with regard to land; even though Lear's Shakespearean story is fictional, a structural logic underpins this sequencing. The Irish Civil War took place as a reaction to the Anglo-Irish Treaty that secured most of Ulster as a British satellite state, resisting the radical break with Britain that the rest of Ireland was to enjoy. Yeats's promotion of maintaining what existed on the land 'Time out of mind', as in 'Upon This House', resembles certain opinions that part of Ireland must remain British in order to secure the rest of Ireland for the Irish; however, as his career evolved, Yeats changed his opinions on these topics – sometimes out of necessity and sometimes desire. This change also signalled a move away from territorialisation, just as Lear was forced away from thinking of the land as his territory, becoming instead nomadic, and adopting the 'transitory attachment' to land that Braidotti described, rather than the 'linear development[al]' attitude of Foucault's traditional historian. This will also lead Yeats away from Lear as a model.

One of Yeats's poetic evolutions revolves around the figure of the tower that gave its name to one of his later collections of poems. The following excerpt is from the title poem, 'The Tower':

> I pace upon the battlements and stare
> On the foundations of a house, or where
> Tree, like a sooty finger, starts from the earth;
> And send imagination forth
> Under the day's declining beam, and call
> Images and memories
> From ruin or from ancient trees,
> For I would ask a question of them all. (Yeats, 1997b: ll. 17–24)

In this excerpt the foundations – those that scar the landscape – are the poetic source of memory made equivalent to imagination. The speaker is searching for a way of expressing his imagination since 'Decrepit age ... has been tied to me' (l. 3), yet 'Never had I more / Excited, passionate, fantastical / Imagination' (ll. 4–6). The answer is to allow the remains of the building to enter and fire the imagination: memory comes to the rescue. Successively the persona remembers, from the perspective of standing among the tower's ruins, 'Beyond that ridge [where] lived Mrs French' (l. 25), how it was now only 'Some few [who] remembered still when I was young / A peasant girl commended by a song' (ll. 33–4), and his demand for 'Hanrahan,[6] / For I need all his mighty memories' (ll. 103–4). These memories are fleeting, heterogeneous, dispersed: they are signs of the persona's historical sense. They are joined by two other ideas worth mentioning.

First is the allusion to the 'certain men-at-arms ... / Whose images [were] in the Great Memory stored' (ll. 84–5). The Great Memory is an archive described by Yeats in *Anima Mundi*, in which ideas are passed on 'from generation to generation' (Yeats, 1994: 18). This universal storehouse is not dissimilar to the concept of memory espoused during the Renaissance and referenced during the period when there was an Art of Memory, as analysed by Frances Yates. Explored more in the following, for now it is sufficient to note that the Great Memory numbers among the resources that Yeats's persona desires to access in 'The Tower' owing to 'Yeats's anxiety about Irish memory' (Longley, 2001: 243). Second is the turn towards legacy when Yeats writes that 'It is time that I wrote my will; ... I declare / They shall inherit my pride' (Yeats, 1997b: ll. 121–7). As with Lear, Yeats's persona displays here a proclivity towards linear temporality and a belief in the concept of passing on appropriation through time. Set against the historical sense displayed in much of the poem, 'The Tower' becomes a transitional poem in Yeats's development towards a full-blown counter-memory.

In 'The Tower', however, it is key to recognise that it is not the tower itself but its remains that give the persona his creative space. Something similar is discernible in the sequence of poems 'Meditations in Time of Civil War' (this title indicates to us again the link between Yeats's evolving perspective and the civil war). In the poem 'My Descendants', already addressed in part above, the speaker asks:

And what if my descendants lose the flower
Through natural declension of the soul,
Through too much business with the passing hour,
Through too much play, or marriage with a fool?
May this laborious stair and this stark tower
Become a roofless ruin that the owl
May build in the cracked masonry and cry
Her desolation to the desolate sky. (Yeats, 1997b: ll. 9–16)

In this, the speaker understands the necessary pitfalls in relying on inheritance – that fraudulent historical idea – that may lead to a kind of homelessness and ensuing nomadism, and instead calls on the tower to become poetry itself, reminiscent of Spenser's own land-based poetics. Here signals another moment of Yeats's evolution. This tower is a strange kind of space, in which the scars are generative, rather than symptoms of an end. Indeed, writing about the next stanza that ends with 'These stones remain[ing] their monument and mine' (l. 24), Edna Longley suggests that ambiguously, either 'maximum or minimum traces will survive' – but traces nonetheless – and that '"monument" underlines the poem's own memorial function' (Longley, 2013: 133). In Braidotti's terms, Yeats is 'The Majority Subject [who] holds the keys to the central memory of the system' that, in this case, is the tower. For him and through his poetic persona, 'The line of becoming ... is consequently an anti-memory, which, instead of bringing back in a linear order specific memories (*les souvenirs*), functions as a deterritorializing agency that dislodges the subject from his/her sense of unified and consolidated identity' (Braidotti, 2011: 31). Yeats's poem is itself becoming the counter-memory, albeit from the majoritarian position (i.e. white, Anglo-Irish, educated). This suggests a productive confusion between the stones on the land's surface – the tower, that is – and the words on the page's surface – the poem: both subject and medium act as counter-memory and a different way to access the past through a building degrading on the land's surface. The poem/land space gathers signification to itself.

Yeats's poetry first laments the potential failing of a house upon the Irish land in a traditional historical mode; the poetry then allows the ruined building to become a space for imagination and poetic freedom in something approaching a counter-memorial sense. The new, renegotiated relationship with the land – which also brought Lear to madness before finding himself anew naked on the heath and in Poor Tom's hut – is something that Yeats's poetry finds apt for creating a modern Ireland. In the late poem 'An Acre of Grass' (1938), Yeats's persona asks for 'an old man's frenzy' because 'Myself must I remake / Till I am Timon and Lear'. These Shakespearean heroes 'Shake the dead in their shrouds, / Forgotten else by mankind' (Yeats, 1997b: ll. 13–23). Lear offers Yeats the ability to counter amnesia and to restore a joy to tragic loss because 'these heroes feel a joy which overcomes their fear' (Allison, 1997: 129). Where Lear becomes 'Unaccommodated' (III.iv.105), Yeats turns profitably towards heterogeneous 'desolation'. Nomadism, and its concomitant relationship with counter-memorial temporality, leads Yeats to decide ultimately that the land agitation is worth pursuing, even if civil war, along with its concomitant 'breach between public and private commemorative language' (Longley, 2001: 241), constitute the net result. This breach, in turn, demands a new, counter-memorial mode of commemoration.

This demand catalyses the change from 'Upon a House' (published in 1919) to 'Coole Park, 1929', a poem that considers 'form as legacy, legacy as form' (Longley, 2013: 206):

> Here, traveller, scholar, poet, take your stand
> When all those rooms and passages are gone,
> When nettles wave upon a shapeless mound
> And saplings root among the broken stone,
> And dedicate – eyes bent upon the ground,
> Back turned upon the brightness of the sun
> And all the sensuality of the shade –
> A moment's memory to that laurelled head. (Yeats, 1997b: ll. 25–32)

Yeats lifts the poem's neo-Romantic tone from Percy Bysshe Shelley's 'Ozymandias' in which a traveller is commanded to 'Look on my works, ye mighty, and despair' (Shelley, 2009: l. 11) – poetic sovereignty encapsulates a territorial, modern relation with land, even when only a memory of Ozymandias's life remains, abstracted from a linear history. In 'Coole Park', Yeats equally commends memorial storage. In the poetry the land becomes a space in which we can access modern Ireland. Longley explains that 'Although Gregory's actual house may end up as "a shapeless mound" (it did), her symbolic house has achieved permanent shape' (Longley, 2013: 195). The counter-memorial practice successfully restores Coole Park to life. But the *telos* of this trajectory in Yeats's poetry comes in 'Under Ben Bulben': 'Irish poets, learn your trade / ... Sing the lords and ladies gay / That were beaten into the clay / Through seven heroic centuries' (Yeats, 1997b: ll. 67, 78–80). Here, not only do the land and its impression provide the impetus for poetry, but the poetry becomes the land's impression: the land is impressed into the poetry itself, akin to a memorial *tupos*. The poem is the mode of thinking that turns the land into a more permanent space of dwelling, *pace* Heidegger. As the poem survives and continues to be read, Yeats maintains his position as poet of Ireland – not least because Ireland dwells in his poetry. By writing a counter-memorial history of secular Ireland – one that bears the scars of territorial battle – Yeats has made his Ireland modern, but through future perfect, nomadic, counter-memory, rather than historicisation.

To summarise, after the land's transference across generations and between nations, it should be thought of in terms of territory: ownership of the land turns it into territory. However, Yeats, in relation to Lear's historical, linear valuation of tradition, eventually sees the potential result of that inheritance: the land could well be lost or destroyed. The answer is to move away from territorialisation and instead render the land as memory in poetry. This suggests that as the poem is read and new poems are written, a new Ireland is perpetually created in the 'cyclical frequentation' of counter-memorial time as the land becomes Irish nomadically in poetry. A renewable Ireland emerges in the poetic space between poet and surface of the land. Time, therefore, is also implicated in this modernised and secularised Ireland. Improving on this – and on Lear's sense of time and inheritance – Yeats has one other counter-memorial strategy to play.

Maintaining nomadism

In negotiating a new treatment of the land, Yeats's poetry and Duke Senior in *As You Like It* share a deep cultural connection to their respective countries/terrains, establishing that modernity takes place in that renovated relationship. *As You Like It* is also a drama conditioned by failed inheritance, in which the legacy and memory of one character enshrined in law has been violently overturned. Charles the wrestler tells Oliver the news from the court of the Dukes:

> There's no news at the court sir, but the old news. That is, the old Duke is banished by his younger brother the new Duke, and three or four loving lords have put themselves into voluntary exile with him,[7] whose lands and revenues enrich the new Duke, therefore he gives them good leave to wander. (I.i.98–104)

The usurpation of Duke Senior by his younger brother, Duke Frederick, constitutes an act of defiant sovereignty. This act is intimately linked to the appropriation of the Duke Senior's lands – their reterritorialisation – and Frederick's assertion of his sovereignty over those lands. Similarly, as Orlando makes clear in the opening lines of the play, he is sad because his brother has denied him his dues: '[I]t was upon this fashion bequeathed me by will but poor a thousand crowns, and, as thou sayst, charged my brother on his blessing to breed me well' (I.i.1–4). The dual fraternal storylines in this way start from the same point at the play's beginning: what is due to one brother has been commandeered by another. This might be read as countering *King Lear* in which generational succession causes a problem. Here, instead, lateral appropriation of the land takes place, a different kind of land transfer: the 'rights of memory' encoded in the land are rankly abused. Duke Senior and Orlando, whose lands have been appropriated, become homeless nomads, both wandering in the Forest of Arden.

When, in the play's final throes, Duke Frederick confers on Duke Senior the lands that were his legally, and when Oliver marries Celia and gives Orlando what was his due, comedy rather than tragedy ensues: the nomads are restored to a fixed place, and time is set right. Their time of becoming has led back to land ownership, but with a difference. 'This repetition of the very terms one takes one's departure from, far from being the reiteration of a system of domination', argues Braidotti, 'constitutes the necessary anchoring point for the cartography of becoming' (Braidotti, 2011: 31). Most importantly for my argument, Duke Senior invites a dance to celebrate the return of the lands, and the stage resembles what Yeats would later describe as a scene typical of Celtic literature:

> Men who lived in a world where anything might flow and change, and become any other thing; and among great gods whose passions were in the flaming sunset, and in the thunder and the thunder-shower, had not our thoughts of weight and measure. They worshipped nature and the abundance of nature, and had always, as it seems, for a supreme ritual that *tumultuous dance* among the hills or *in the depths of the woods*, where unearthly ecstasy fell upon the dancers, until they seemed the gods or the godlike beasts, and felt their souls overtopping the moon; and, as some think, imagined for the first time in the world the blessed country of the gods and of the happy dead. They had imaginative passions because *they did not live within our own strait limits*, and were nearer to ancient chaos, every man's desire, and had *immortal models* about them. (Yeats, 1997a: 132; my emphasis)

Yeats appears to enjoy the idea of the dance as it demonstrates a freedom beyond 'our own strait limits' that are characterised by 'our thoughts of weight and measure'. The dance is also pagan; or, at least, non-Christian. The 'imaginative passions' he praises echo those espoused by Duke Senior in the forest in response to Jaques de Boys's news of Senior's brother, Duke Frederick's, religious conversion, at the end of *As You Like It*:

> Thou offer'st fairly to thy brothers' wedding;
> To one his lands withheld, and to the other
> A land itself at large, a potent dukedom.
> First, in this forest, let us do those ends
> That here were well begun and well begot;
> And after, every of this happy number
> That have endured shrewd days and nights with us
> Shall share the good of our returned fortune,
> According to the measure of their states.
> Meantime forget this new-fall'n dignity,
> And fall into our rustic revelry.
> Play, music! And you brides and bridegrooms all,
> With measure heaped in joy, to th' measures fall. (V.iv.165–77)

Senior's joyful 'measure' becomes a rhythmic 'measure' towards the end of the rhyming couplet, and both serve to counter Yeats's sense of a measured stricture. This passage serves two further functions. First, it makes secondary the issue of the land which was the main topic of Jaques de Boys's speech a few lines previously. Second, at the same time it embraces and surpasses ('forget') the 'new-fall'n' state, labelling it a state of 'dignity' – a secular state – rather than rejecting it or trying to convert it into a sacred space. Christological is supplanted by profane time. In this way, Orlando's helpmate Adam, whose old age and fatigue are renewed in the Forest – a symbolic and perverse (new) Eden – becomes the chief figure identifiable with this new treatment of the land. What was old becomes new, leading me to re-affirm that a nomad's contact with the land entails a cyclical time of becoming. That is, the counter-memories embedded in the land piece together ideas with the bodies that regularly make and break contact with the land. Remembering, in this light, is a recurrently available process that makes old memory new with each iteration, allowing the dancers to 'reinvent the self as other' and to 'empower creative alternatives' (Braidotti, 2011: 33). This remembering is staccato (now making, now breaking contact) and therefore potentially disruptive: disremembering. These ideas oppose Jaques's linear 'Seven ages of man' speech (II.vii. 139–66) – with its anticipation of Lear's 'crawl[ing] unburdened toward death', at once a babe and an old man – which perhaps partly explains why Jaques seeks out Duke Frederick, rather than staying with Duke Senior: a disremembered land without territory, though yet with a sovereign, is not something that Jaques can brook. The renovation is also the opposite of the treatment of land by Elizabethan and Jacobean courtiers, as Richard Wilson (1993) points out severally: enclosure preserved rather than renovated the land.

Dance

This counter-memorial modernity is bound up with time and its recirculation: whilst pre-modern ethics are locked into Christian time in which renovation is restricted to messianic Resurrection, nomadic modernity remembers and therefore reinvents. Likewise, in the work of the ageing Yeats there was also a secular modernity that sought temporal renovation of the land. In 'Coole Park' Yeats let Ireland dwell, such that it could be a new home to every new reader or reading. In the earlier Yeats an identical logic is discernible, but this time in the turn towards Irish myth – what would otherwise be considered Yeats's traditional imperative. As with the tower, the land's surface is key to this temporal regeneration. In Yeats's early *The Wanderings of Oisin*, Niamh takes Oisin to Tír na nÓg, where 'the days pass like a wayward tune / ... And the blushes of first love never have flown' (Yeats, 1997b: I, ll. 83–5). Eventually homesick after several journeys to other lands, 'the lure of earth persistently summons him home' (Kinahan, 1988: 114). When Oisin is permitted by Niamh to return on her horse Niamh stipulates that Oisin is not allowed to dismount from the horse and touch the ground: 'for if only your shoe / Brush lightly as haymouse earth's pebbles, you will come no more to my side' (Yeats, 1997b: III, ll. 127–8). However, when Oisin returns to the mainland and dismounts to help some passing men, time comes upon him like a curse, the counter-memory of the land infesting Oisin's mythic body and destroying it:

> [W]hen divided the girth,
> I fell on the path, and the horse went away like a summer fly;
> And my years three hundred fell on me, and I rose, and walked on
>   the earth,
> A creeping old man, full of sleep, with the spittle on his beard never
>   dry. (Yeats, 1997b: III, ll. 189–92)

Oisin's encounter with the surface of the earth is enough to bring him permanently back to the temporality of mortals, and the 300 years of his absence age him quickly, ultimately killing him. Oisin's original time, three centuries previously, becomes 'Sad to remember' because he is 'sick with years' (l. 5); after all, counter-memory constitutes 'a transformation of history into a totally different form of time'. Whilst the stresses on Oisin's contact with the earth in his story were not Yeats's creation, I understand Yeats appreciating that contact with the earth more broadly than in the poem itself, or even the poem's relation to nascent theosophical ideas that Frank Kinahan (1988: *passim*) points out.

I draw two inferences. First, Oisin's world (that is, our world) is of a mortal temporality that suggests its temporal restrictions and reluctance to achieve renovation or modernisation. Second, Oisin's world is not encountered by crossing its borders, but rather its rules apply when in contact with the earth's surface. This recalls 'the lords and ladies gay / That were beaten into the clay' in 'Under Ben Bulben'. It indicates that mortal temporality only takes effect when contact is made with the land. It also indicates that whilst Yeats is interested in Oisin's world – in which Yeats himself lives – he is attracted to a modernity that is not just about claiming territory, nor a land that changes who Irish citizens are at root (hence Oisin's death). Instead Yeats privileges the modernity of reinvigoration and eternal youth, a Tir na nÓg where both history and memory are unnecessary – 'the Ossianic Island of Forgetfulness ... where the point is not "remembering" forgotten beauty since its being forgotten constitutes its paradoxical charm' (Longley, 2001: 240) – but also admits Tir na nÓg's impossibility in the civilised world. In Oisin's retelling, Yeats also rejects the idea that permanent territorialisation by anyone is positive. Between these two positions Yeats's ideal modernity can be summarised: a secular land away from myth, giving rise to perpetual renovation or nomadic memory. The sovereign of this land will, by necessity, change, but the land will always dwell nomadically in poetry as counter-memory, and *vice versa*. *King Lear*'s Edgar[8] is this sovereign in the earlier period, privileging youth ('We that are young / Shall never see so much, nor live so long' (V.iii.324–5)) and changing form.

Yeats invents characters who fit the description of this sovereign. In *The Wanderings of Oisin*, the eponymous character recounts to St Patrick how his journey with Niamh into Tir na nÓg was taken over by a Druid who compels them to dance:

And in a wild and sudden dance
We mocked at Time and Fate and Chance
And swept out of the wattled hall
And came to where the dewdrops fall
Among the foamdrops of the sea,
And there we hushed the revelry;
And, gathering on our brows a frown,
Bent all our swaying bodies down,
And to the waves that glimmer by
That sloping green De Danaan sod
Sang[.] ...

We danced to where in the winding thicket
The damask roses, bloom on bloom,
Like crimson meteors hang in the gloom. (Yeats, 1997b: I, ll.
290–304)

This, much as Oisin's falling to the ground in our world, is the equivalent treatment of making an impression on the land.[9] In Tir na nÓg, where 'dancing is the chief pleasure of the "ever-living" ones' (Ellmann, 1968: 167), dancing and immortality are linked, just as in our world contact with the earth and mortality are connected. This is not merely incidental in Yeats's thinking, but also borne out in *Anima Mundi*, when Yeats writes that 'Hitherto shade [i.e. the dead] has communicated with shade in moments of common memory that recur like the figures of a dance in terror or in joy, but now they run together like to like, and their Covens and Fleets have rhythm and pattern' (Yeats, 1994: 25). Key terms of 'common memory', 'recur', 'rhythm and pattern' all point towards concordance with the transitory, nomadic remembering of land on body. This, by contrast to Oisin in our world, is the modern relation with the land that Yeats wants to promote.

Yeats was not only preoccupied with dance early in his career. In 'A General Introduction for My Work' (1937), he recalls as a young boy writing 'a poem upon dancing which had one good line' (Yeats, 1994: 214), and the symbol and figure of dancing and dancers maintain throughout Yeats's oeuvre. Richard Ellmann noted that, between the shifts in Yeats's early and late symbols, only 'the tree, the dance, and the sun and moon are seen to be the chief survivals'. According to Ellmann, dance 'united an abstract, stylized, and symbolic pattern with visible action'. This gave Yeats 'an impersonal element in his work' and often appears in poems with a 'resolved duality' (Ellmann, 1968: 170, 20, 168). In his own critical writing, in addition to the praise Yeats gives the autochthonic dance of the Celts in 1903's 'The Celtic Element in Literature' (Yeats, 1997a: 132), he also venerates dancing in Japanese Noh theatre in 1916's 'Certain Noble Plays of Japan' (Yeats, 1997a: 169), as well as dancers performing their Spanish national dance (Yeats, 1997a: 165). He acknowledges the beauty of Synge's writing in metaphorical terms, describing the latter's plays as making 'word and phrase dance to a very strange rhythm' (Yeats, 1997a: 217). Most entertainingly, in

'Discoveries' (1907), Yeats recalls taking drugs in Paris and going to a party. 'I grew very anxious to dance, but did not', he writes, 'as I could not remember any steps. I sat down and closed my eyes; but no, I had no visions, nothing but a sensation of some dark shadow which seemed to be telling me that some day I would go into a trance and so out of my body for a while, but not yet' (Yeats, 1997a: 205). Here there is an implicit connection between the act of dancing and memory ('I could not remember any steps'), as if the possibility of improvised dance does not exist, and that dance is always an act of anamnestic recall. To dance is to remember and, as I am showing, to dance is to be nomadic. Dancing is therefore intimately linked to a nomadic commitment to perpetual becoming, as evidenced by the inhabitants in Tir na nÓg for whom 'never on our graves / ... / Shall fall the damask leaves of roses. / For neither Death nor Change comes near us, / And all listless hours fear us' (Yeats, 1997b: I, ll. 311–15), confirming the counter-memorial transformation of time itself. Yeats's friend, Arthur Symons, remarked that dance represented 'possession and abandonment, the very pattern and symbol of earthly love. Here is nature (to be renounced, to be at least restrained), hurried violently, deliberately, to boiling point' (qtd in Ellmann), to which Ellmann himself added that 'This possibility of the symbol, that it might contain both self-expression and self-renunciation, attracted Yeats to it' (Ellmann, 1968: 167–8). This aptly describes the actualised possibility of the nomadically remembered Irish land as Yeats remembers it in his poetry of dance. These ideas are equally evident in the earlier period under study, notably in *As You Like It*, *The Faerie Queene*, and Sir John Davies's *Orchestra* in which dancing celebrates and constitutes freedom. This kind of dancing anticipates Yeats's modern Ireland characterised by the leaping and dancing that perpetually deterritorialises and reterritorialises[10] through nomadic disremembering, rather than the English colonial planting that set out to obtain, fix and make permanent English–Ireland.

In early modern literature, between the dancer and the land, a space emerges that also allows for a changed relation between land and dancer. Not only does the dancer restate her control over the land in the act of dancing, but the land also exerts some measure of control on the dancer. Thus emerges the idea that the dancer emerges from the land that the dancer herself has territorialised. The land nomadically remembers the dancer into being – the land actualises the dancer. This is apparent in Sir John Davies's[11] *Orchestra*:

> Sometimes [the Sea] his proud green waues in order set,
> One after other flow vnto the shore,
> Which when they haue with many kisses wet,
> They ebb away in order as before;
> And to make knowne his Courtly Loue the more,
> He oft doth lay aside his three-forkt Mace,
> And with his armes the timerous Earth embrace. (Davies, 1596:
> stanza 50)

Davies's Antinous establishes Love as conductor and composer of music that Antinous sees evident in all relations between two bodies; here it is the Sea on the Land. The Sea, having flowed on to the Land, is then compelled 'the timerous Earth [to] embrace'; Sea is turned to loving the Land. Dance links determinedly with Time, since 'if you judge them Twins, together got, / And Time first borne, your judgment erreth not'. Additionally, dance 'in lustie youth for euer flowers' and, like Time, is 'preserue[d] in his infancie' (stanza 23, ll. 6–7, stanza 24, ll. 2, 7). Reminiscent of Yeats's Great Memory, this is the eternal fullness of memory, not unlike the Daimon figure of Yeats's *A Vision*:

> In notes for *A Vision B* Yeats speculates about the *Daimon* in terms that partly unfold the implications of the phrase 'that age-long memoried self', seeing it as embodying a continuum of memory, yet pointing to the paradox that the *Daimon* is truly fullness rather than memory of the past, pre-existent archetype rather than remembered or lived experience. (Mann, 2012: 11)

The memorial archive for Yeats is not only counter-memory of the past, but also model for the future: it both preserves and shapes infancy, middle, and old age. It nomadically preserves the memory of a future that will have been lived.

Remembered sovereignty

The Irish land that Spenser delineates in his poetry becomes the basis of his poet laureateship. It is also an Ireland that Spenser sought to destroy by advancing a scorched-earth policy, a strategy that pursued eradication of autochthonic Irish history. Yeats seeks to retrieve his modern Ireland from Spenser's planted and scorched land in order to create himself as Irish poet laureate-designate: the land-as-counter-memory, rather than historicised-object, is his tool. I have already described the dancers Yeats creates, who 'waver' and 'wander' in *The Wanderings of Oisin*, and the 'in between' dancing of *A Vision*. But this strategy is also visible in Yeats's most famous drama, 'Cathleen ni Houlihan', in which the Old Woman introduces herself to Peter as someone who has been searching for someone or something for a while:

> PETER It's a pity indeed for any person to have no place of their own.
> OLD WOMAN That's true for you indeed, and it's long I'm on the roads since I first went wandering. (Yeats, 2001b: 88)

The Old Woman's indeterminacy is not aimless without reason. Instead, the wandering allows her to find Ireland's true hero to reclaim her 'Four beautiful green fields' (Yeats, 2001b: 88). She, like Fortinbras, has rights of memory over this land. Men have died for these fields and this woman, and she recalls the stories of 'yellow-haired Donough that was hanged in Galway' as she 'remember[s] him ploughing his field' (Yeats, 2001b: 89) – embedding his memory into the land – as well as the 'red man of the O'Donnells from the north, and a man of the O'Sullivans from the south, and there was one Brian that lost his life at Clontarf by the sea' (89) *inter alia*. Importantly, those who died 'shall be remembered for ever, / They shall be alive for ever, / They shall be speaking for ever, / The people shall hear them for ever' (Yeats, 2001b: 92). The Old Woman's rather prosaic song confirms that in the fight for the land's liberation, the Great Memory is accessible to those who die in the cause: eternal counter-memory awaits in and through the land.

These ideas are bookended in the play by two ideas of note. First is the pathetic connection between Delia Cahel – Michael's promised wife – and memory in the play. Prior to the Old Woman's arrival, Patrick asks, 'Will Delia remember … to bring the greyhound pup she promised me[?]' (Yeats, 2001b: 86). When set alongside what the Old Woman seeks to recall, Delia can only seem ridiculous.

Second is Michael's own forgetfulness once he is swayed by the vision and stories of the Old Woman: 'What wedding are you talking of? What clothes will be wearing to-morrow?' (Yeats, 2001b: 82). Michael remembers to take care – Dasein's utmost purpose, according to Heidegger – when he first forgets himself. Forgetting allows counter-memory to take hold, for which reason the Old Woman is remembered as a 'young girl' with 'the walk of a queen' (Yeats, 2001b: 93). This mode of becoming represents the paradigmatic version of Braidotti's nomadic becoming, for 'becoming-woman is a privileged position for the minority consciousness of all' and 'the becoming-woman is a fundamental step in the process of becoming for both and for all sexes' (Braidotti, 2011: 36). The Old Woman's becoming-young shows the value of a counter-memorial, nomadic memory, in which linear history is supplanted by perpetual becoming. The value of this becoming-woman is intensified in the understanding of the Old Woman-becoming-young as an allegory for Ireland itself: Ireland becomes-young, is renovated, and restored through a nomadic counter-memory.

Indeterminacy – wandering in 'Cathleen' and 'Oisin'; dancing above – is thus the task of sovereignty in modern Ireland, much like the nomadic wandering in the forest in *As You Like It* that serves to resolve all the play's muddles. Braidotti usefully explains the benefits of examining nomads and thinking nomadically, writing that 'It is the subversion of set conventions that defines the nomadic state' in which 'alternative forms of agency can be engendered' (Braidotti, 1994: 5, 7).[12] The latter in Yeats is the agency given through writing poetry. As such, perpetual nomadism is a central part of modernity as it opens up a new dwelling space in which modern Ireland can remember and be remembered, constantly questioning other stable, traditional history narratives of Ireland as given in Mother Ireland, the Catholic Church, and even *Bunreacht na hÉireann*.

Yeats gives us another form of dancing that first seems to work against the ideas established above. 'Nineteen Hundred and Nineteen', a poem bound up with the parliamentary politics associated with the beginning of the War of Independence as well as with artistic representation, does not just make 'the dance display the endless movement of life in miniature', as Ellmann (1968: 167) argued. The couplet, 'All men are dancers and their tread / Goes to the barbarous clangour of a gong' (Yeats, 1997b: ll. 57–8), connects

with Yeats's *A Vision* and the role of the cycle, with the 'gong' indicating a measure and rigorous tempo according to which everyone is
dancing. The idea suggests a tension between the limitless wavering
of the dancing and its restricted, if not predicted, form, according
to the gong. However, Yeats refutes such ideas; instead, he believes
that dancing is precisely the manoeuvring that allows man to exercise some agency or independence within the restrictive world of
the cones and gyres – and within a polity at war, but on the cusp
of independent nation-statism. Though humankind is restricted,
there remains hope.[13] In the poem 'The Double Vision of Michael
Robartes' – a character created by Yeats who features heavily in the
second version of *A Vision* (1936) – dancing becomes a transformative act, since 'little did they care who danced between, / And little
she by whom her dance was seen / So she had outdanced thought. /
Body perfection brought' (Yeats, 1997b: ll. 37–40). Ellmann argues
that the girl 'stands for a mid-point which participates in the qualities of both' the sphinx and Buddha, between whom she dances.
'Her dance is a solitary esthetic act', he adds, 'art so triumphant as
to lend an air of perpetuity, which is a kind of death, to movement'
(Ellmann, 1968: 168). Dancing transforms through the process
of perpetual remembering. In this, dancing allows the girl and the
sphinx and Buddha to have 'time overthrown' (l. 47). Far from being
restricted by the strict motion of the Phases of the Moon, the Great
Year, or the gyres and cones, dancing instead overthrows time, just
as Foucault describes the effect of counter-memory, and just as Oisin
narrates. Through dance, the indifferent flow of chronological time
is revealed to be sterile, while counter-memorial disremembering
is productive. For Yeats, memory is not purely about anamnesis –
memorial recall – but also about the productive mode of becoming that nomadic memory catalyses. Like the inhabitants of Tir na
nÓg, those who dance overthrow time and turn Ireland into a space
that constantly finds a new home at each renovation. This territorialisation is about the surface of the land: this sovereign territory is
made in Ireland by renovating it and having time overthrown and
restarted with every leaping and landing of the dancer on the land.

This secularisation of time is the becoming of a new, modern
nation. As Gilles Deleuze and Félix Guattari write:

> The constituents of the nation are a land and a people: the 'natal' ...
> The natal or the land, as we have seen elsewhere, implies a certain

deterritorialization of the territories … and the people, a decoding of the population. The nation is constituted on the basis of these flows and is inseparable from the modern State that gives consistency to the corresponding land and people. (Deleuze and Guattari, 2005: 456)

Against this there is one key example worth foregrounding in which a Yeatsian character does not approve of dancing and wandering. In *On Baile's Strand*, the Blind Man tells the fool what Conchubar thinks of the hero Cuchulain. Cuchulain 'ran too wild, and Conchubar is coming to-day to put an oath upon him that will stop his rambling and make him as biddable as a house-dog and keep him always at his hand' (Yeats, 2001b: 152). Conchubar then tells Cuchulain that a young man arrived in an act of war while Cuchulain was away: 'He [the young man] came to land / While you were somewhere out of sight and hearing, / Hunting or dancing with your wild companions' (Yeats, 2001b: 156). Conchubar's disdain for Cuchulain is clear, positing Conchubar in opposition to Cuchulain. Since Cuchulain is one of the heroes of Ireland, so Conchubar becomes Ireland's foe. Conchubar is a representative of British imperialism:

I am High King, my son shall be High King;
And you for all the wildness of your blood,
And though your father came out of the sun,
Are but a little king and weigh but light
In anything that touches government[.] (Yeats, 2001b: 157)

Conchubar's drive through linear inheritance to dominate Cuchulain and Ireland is akin to England's domination of Ireland; and at the heart of Conchubar's domination is his fear of Cuchulain's Celtic dancing – the act that constantly renovates the relationship between the land and the sovereign, opening up a new, secularised modern Ireland.

Conclusion

It is worth restating the journey that Yeats undergoes during his career. In his early poetry about the Land War, Yeats appears like *King Lear* to favour tradition and linear inheritance, albeit with a keen focus on the mythical. Whilst Lear averted the 'natural' law of

inheritance in giving his lands to his daughters prior to his death –
a chief factor, clearly, in his and Cordelia's tragic demises – Yeats
merely wanted to maintain the status quo. Coole Park needed to
remain the Big House in the landlord's hands. However, in 'The
Tower' Yeats's position began to change into a more counter-
memorial one. At the same time, I adumbrated the growing sense
of the creation of a metaphysical dwelling space between the land
and the poem: the land's metaphorical impression on the poetry, the
latter describing buildings' impressions on land.

Eventually, through the motif of dancing, Yeats's evolution is
seen to be complete, especially as it remembers the freedom it
encapsulates dramatised in a Celtically inflected *As You Like It*.
In that play the land's rightful return to those who have 'rights
of memory' over it is celebrated with a dance – a celebration
highlighting the nomadic relation with the land and its recircu-
lated time. Yeats's own scripted dances in *Oisin* and 'Michael
Robartes' also highlight the freedom that emanates in the per-
petuated rhythm of leaping and dancing that he praised in his
critical writing, leading me to conclude that 'rights of memory' in
Yeats's motifs become nomadic remembering: a re-engendering of
land and dancer that reveals the productive becoming of memory.
Anamnesis is no longer the destiny of memory, because it is locked
too firmly into the past. Instead, the future perfect tense comes to
dominate.

Finally, it is worth highlighting that *Oisin* is one of Yeats's early
poems, while *A Vision*,[14] in which 'Michael Robartes' was collected,
was not published until 1936. This fact casts into doubt my own
assertion of Yeats's linear development in his career. This serves to
strengthen my argument: Yeats's own thinking about dancing (and
by extension nomadic remembering), is best defined as recirculative,
counter-memorial, dismemorial – perhaps even archaeological. This
return to certain origins also compels my argument that Yeats is
also remembering – and remembered in and through – Shakespeare
in his own work. As Edwards compellingly argued:

> Yeats is a consequence of Shakespeare. His work to create an Irish
> national spirit, and a national literature and drama, could not have
> come into existence except as a counter to the results of the earlier
> English nationalism. Working at either end of a long historical epoch,

these two national opponents have a strange similarity. Each of them draws artistic strength from the idea of a new nation which in truth he helps to bring into existence, and each of them recoils from everything which, in practical terms, the creation of the new nation involved. For each of them, the past of the nation is of intense importance, but while that recovery of the past is meant to strengthen the nation in its future development, the past becomes a myth of foreboding, not so much a path to the future as an indignant repudiator of the future. And, for each of them, history becomes a continuous circling of self-destruction. (Edwards, 1979: 211)

That 'self-destruction' and 'repudiation' is remembered on the surface of the Irish land. My argument begins again, and Yeats becomes (finally) the kind of author Joyce self-fashioned for *Finnegans Wake* (1939) – incidentally (and ironically) the year Yeats dies. The modernity that Yeats forges opposes the historicisation of the English that emptied Irish land of memory and memorial tradition, nomadically and dismemorially remembering the mythical Ireland back into the land and into his poetry.

Notes

1 Another line of thought would follow Paul Delaney's research into Travelling communities in Ireland. Delaney (2001: 57) writes that in Yeats's play *Where There Is Nothing*, Yeats stages a version of a member of aristocratic Ascendancy class, Paul Ruttledge, giving up his landlordism in order to subvert the social order by becoming a tinker, a wanderer. Delaney overtly compares this to Gregory's and Yeats's own restlessness and rejection of their inheritance as representative of colonialism.
2 Its narrative is reminiscent of the Mediaeval Mystery Cycle from the pre-Reformation, centuries earlier.
3 It is important to note the different lengths of time each of these figures spends in contact with the land. I list them here in decreasing temporal amounts.
4 The concept of *Herkunft*, translated as 'descent' in *Language, Counter-memory, Practice*, is one of the constitutive ideas of Foucault's 'historical sense', which as noted above is analogous with 'counter-memory'.
5 Perhaps contrary to Foucault's use of these terms, I do not mean them wholly negatively; I praise the interest in temporality, but acknowledge

that it is reductive (and clearly tragic) to focus on such a simplistic view of the passage of time.

6 'Red Hanrahan is a character invented by Yeats, though partly modelled on a notable Gaelic poet, Eoghan Rua O Súilleabháin (Owen O'Sullivan the Red, 1748–84). Red Hanrahan is the hero of a number of short stories by Yeats. Owen O'Sullivan appears in the original titles of a few poems from *The Wind Among the Reeds* [1899]' (Edward Larrissy's editorial note in Yeats, 2001a: 492–3).

7 The difference between enforced exile and voluntary exile could also be considered, although a focus on the attendant lords would give a different reading of the nature of exile and nomadism in *As You Like It*.

8 In the F edition of *King Lear*, Edgar speaks these lines; however, in Q (1608), the Duke of Albany speaks them.

9 To draw a comparison where dancers make a sincere mark in the earth, Rory Ryan (2012: 22) writes about Yeats's introduction of the Faculties in *A Vision* through a poem that describes dancers marking the Great Wheel in the sand.

10 In *After Theory*, Docherty describes how 'Dance, quite literally, becomes *ungrounded*, and is, almost by definition, an art of deterritorialization, an art concerned with movements to and from the earth, with the relation of the human body for the space around it' (Docherty, 1990: 21; emphasis in original).

11 Sir John Davies (1564/5–1618) is a critically important figure to this chapter, even if his contribution is manifestly slight. The *ODNB* records that in 1594 Davies registered *Orchestra*, the 'earliest extant edition of which is dated 1596'. Between these two years, Davies was called to the Bar. His poetry of land and his legal practice were therefore connected. Moreover, upon the new King James VI/I's ascension to the throne, Davies accompanied the king south from Scotland, ultimately being appointed solicitor-general for Ireland, a post he assumed in November 1603. He was instrumental in 'laying the legal foundations for a civil society', and in the continued policy of 'surrender and regrant' in 1606. As such, Davies emblematises the historicising of English jurisprudence, particularly in relation to civilising a barbaric Ireland reliant on memorial practices. Though *Orchestra* was not written about Ireland, and indeed I am using it to *counter* the policies that Davies and his colleagues later espoused in the sixteenth century, this overlap is more than mere coincidence. For more on Davies, see Pawlisch (1985: 4 and *passim*) who writes that 'Of the crown lawyers involved in the formulation of Irish policy and reform, the most important was Sir John Davies'.

12 As I revise this chapter, Chloe Zhao's *Nomadland* (Searchlight, 2020) has just won the Best Picture award at the 2021 Academy Awards, and

this description by Braidotti seems most apt to describe the life that Frances McDormand's Fern begins to enjoy.

13 This contrasts with T. S. Eliot's 'dead sound on the final stroke of nine' ('The Waste Land' in Eliot, 2015: i. The Burial of the Dead, l. 68), in which there is little hope for escaping the malaise of the modern world; Longley also draws attention to the parallels between the poems (Longley, 2013: 50–3).

14 Here I refer to *A Vision B*, the second version of Yeats's theosophical treatise.

7

'[D]ithering, blathering': Seamus Heaney, the diseased word-hoard, and the Historian

MÁIRE Sweet smell! Sweet smell! Every year at this time somebody comes back with stories of the sweet smell. Sweet God, did the potatoes ever fail in Baile Beag? Well, did they ever – ever? Never! There was never a blight here. Never. Never. But we're always sniffing about for it, aren't we? – looking for disaster.

– from *Translations* by Brian Friel

Our literature and our history have given us, more than any other people, the desire to dig down into the soil we stand on, and this digging is our intensity, and it may yet give us an answer to the riddle.

– from 'If I were four-and-twenty' by W. B. Yeats
(alternative ending)

Introduction

Where I investigated Yeats's poems for their interest in the *surface* of the land, I instead investigate Heaney's poems for their investment in the *subterranean* aspect of the land. That underground nature also functions in the territorial text of the poems: what becomes embedded in the poems is as important as the land's figuration in language. This interest in depths and the underground is also connected to memory, archaeology, and the archive in Heaney's writing. I call this practice 'counter-history', with Heaney becoming a proper-noun Historian.

Heaney's 1980 collection of essays, *Preoccupations*, largely discussed other writers in whom Heaney was interested, including Irish poets Patrick Kavanagh, John Hewitt, and Paul Muldoon. Heaney's title displays his *pre*-occupation with these writers, a temporal interest antecedent to his own poetry. Additionally, his 2002 *Finders Keepers*, an edited collection of prose, is given the title for very specific reasons: 'In the playground the phrase "finders keepers" probably still expresses glee and stakes a claim, so in that sense it can apply as well to the experience of a reader of poetry: the first encounter with work that excites and connects will induce in the reader a similar urge to celebrate and take possession of it' (Heaney, 2003: ix). Though similar, the notion of 'finders keepers' departs from 'preoccupations' in the idea of possession: uncovering or discovering[1] something is only completed when it is taken care of and claimed as one's own. *Preoccupation* becomes *possession* – but a possession conditioned by the original discovery of the object. In terms of memory, the accessed memory is known – remembered fully – by virtue of taking ownership of it. We have already seen a version of this in Beckett's *Malone Dies*. However, these ideas operate in Heaney's mnemopoetics through the ideas of archaeology – both the historical, Foucauldian category, and its mundane, material activity – and the archive – especially after Derrida's 'Archive Fever' updated by historian Carolyn Steedman. Heaney's poetry, when thought through these ideas, will show him to be both an archaeo-poet, insisting on digging up past memories, and an *arkhe*-poet, investing in storing the unearthed memories in his poems: the latter become his archive. But this is not the archive that Ricoeur describes: 'The moment of the archive is the moment of the entry into writing of the historiographical operation. ... In archives, the professional historian is a reader' (Ricoeur, 2006: 166). In Heaney's archive, by contrast, the professional historian is superseded by a reader of poetry. By supplanting the more traditional archive found in the *corpus juris* and in the land as inherited object, Heaney's counter-history is yet another instance of dismemory.

The land–memory nexus is easy to establish in Heaney's poems. From the earliest poem 'Digging' in *Death of a Naturalist* (1966), the land featured heavily as the go-to memorial *locus*. In *North's* (1975) title poem 'memory incubat[es] the spilled blood' (Heaney, 1998: l. 28) before instructing to 'Lie down / in the word-hoard' (ll. 29–30). This is but one signal that Heaney's poetry is concerned with roots and being rooted in the land. This land also encloses the nation within it and connecting with those tendrils allows Heaney

to become a modern, national poet. In order to explicate this position, I will explore his poetry's continuous relationship to disease
and thereafter to a secular modernity that is conditioned and signified by muddiness, rather than characterised through a sacred
Edenism.

This muddiness is dismemorial counter-history – invoking
Foucault – through which Heaney in part excavates Shakespeare's
Hamlet, and also memorialises through the 'enabl[er] memor[y]'
of Shakespeare (Homem, 2018: 41). Without the memory of
Shakespeare, Heaney's trajectory of development cannot take place.
Thus, in Heaney's 'Viking Dublin: Trial Pieces', the persona explicitly 'follow[s] into the mud', confidently declaring 'I am Hamlet
the Dane, / skull handler, parablist, / smeller of rot // in the state'
who comes 'to consciousness / by jumping into graves, / dithering,
blathering' (Heaney, 1998: iv, ll. 11–16). Becoming in this poem is
intimately linked to the muddy, modern land – that which is often
thought of as backward and rotten. I will show, via *Hamlet*, how
Heaney's archaeo- and *arkhe*-poetry open the possibility of becoming a modern, national poet in the muddiness and unruliness of the
land. This involves exploring Heaney's word-hoard: the words and
images he retrieves from the Irish land and memorial archive. But
it also considers how Heaney deploys these terms and images in his
poetry, through which his poetic oeuvre substitutes for a narrative
history, becoming instead *another* Irish archive. Heaney's engagement with Shakespeare, especially in his evocation of Hamlet's
'dithering' and 'blathering', is at the heart of this counter-historical
practice.

Archaeology and the archive

I explained above Ricoeur's conception of the trajectory from the
eikon that is impressed as a *tupos* to become a memory. When
these memories enter language, they become testimony that, in
turn, becomes archivable and thereafter accessible by historians for
their own narrative process. This process obtains in this chapter.
However, I employ two further terms to help explicate Heaney's
position as a national poet of memory. The first of these terms
is 'archaeology'. This material branch of history has long been

recognised as central to understanding the past: by dusting or digging, past objects emerge from the earth. Archaeology is traditionally a vertical procedure, delving down into the sedimented past, layer by layer. Consider Charlotte Smith's 'Beachy Head' (1807), in which the recent science of archaeological fossil discoveries is romanticised:

> Or did this range of chalky mountains, once
> Form a vast bason, where the Ocean waves
> Swell'd fathomless? What time these fossil shells,
> Buoy'd on their native element, were thrown
> Among the imbedding calx: when the huge hill
> Its giant bulk heaved, and in strange ferment
>
> Grew up a guardian barrier, 'twixt the sea
> And the green level of the sylvan weald.
> Ah! very vain is Science' proudest boast,
> And but a little light its flame yet lends
> To its most ardent votaries[.] (Smith, 1993: ll. 382–92)

Smith continues to diminish the importance of the new science and its fossils because they impact little on the lives of the peasant, hidden as the fossils are in the depths of the chalky land. Nonetheless, this is an important moment in poetry's development as Smith sees in the land the possibility of time travel: 'What time these fossil shells ... were thrown' is known in the now of poetic creation. In her note to these lines, Smith comments that 'The appearance of sea-shells so far from the sea excited my surprise' (l. 375n), evidencing the diachronic nature of objects – inanimate and formerly animate – that burst through the land's surface and find their way into a poetry that becomes another kind of storage space. This moment in Smith's poem enacts *archaeological* poetry, which derives and records poetic inspiration from what is memorialised in the land's depths.

For Foucault, archaeology is 'The never completed, never wholly achieved uncovering of the archive', and whilst it 'does not relate analysis to geological excavation' (Foucault, 2002: 148), I am employing it in relation to Heaney, a poet of depth, to reveal his own relation to the land's archive. Furthermore, archaeology may not be strictly to do with excavation, but it does involve 'pierc[ing]' the 'unfortunate opacity' of the object under inquiry 'if one is to reach at last the depth of the essential in the place in which it is held in reserve; it is concerned with discourse in its own volume, as a *monument*. It is not an interpretive discipline: it does not seek another, better-hidden discourse' (Foucault, 2002: 155; emphasis in original). This notion of piercing the opaque object suggests memories in the archive that have hitherto been unavailable to historical description can now be discursively examined, albeit in piecemeal: this is counter-history. This counter-history shares in the molecular – as opposed to the molar – focus of Deleuze and Braidotti, and to this end shares a theoretical *locus* with my analysis of Yeats's poetry.

This counter-historical archaeology requires an equally robust understanding of the archive. For Derrida, after Foucault, the archive is a place and a commandment: the *arkheion* (ἀρχεῖον) was the home of the municipal archive, overseen and administered by the *archon* (ἀρχον), a public official. *Arkhe* (ἀρχή) signalled the *locus* of the archive, but also the commandment *to archive*: law and space interweave inextricably at this juncture. The 'nomological principle' of the *arkhe* stems from the impulse to store and to use the store as a constructed origin of the law. Equally, the archons, the archive's guardians, are also impelled to interpret the archive, but this happens in synchrony with the archive's construction: the archons are not the same as archaeologists. Moreover, just as with Foucault's calls to recognise and respect heterogeneity, Derrida warns of the 'archival violence' (Derrida, 1995a: 9, 12) of creating homogeneity in the construction of the archive, much like the early modern English discourse of *corpus juris* that sought to exert a unifying, homogeneous power over English territories. Clearly, Derrida needs an archaeologist of the order of Foucault in order to treat the archive and its contents properly.

Derrida, however, also explores another, more modern conception of the archive through Freud's psychoanalysis. Freud argues that everything that the psyche undergoes, witnesses, and experiences must be 'stored' somewhere: in the unconscious or preconscious (in the first topology), or in the recesses of the *id* and *superego* (in the second). In either case, there is a metaphorical memory system at work, best described in Freud's analysis of the 'mystic writing-pad' (1924). There Freud explains that 'our mental apparatus ... has an unlimited receptive capacity for new perceptions and nevertheless lays down permanent ... memory-traces of them' (Freud, 2001a: 228). The Mystic Writing-Pad was a children's toy that allowed for permanent and short-term traces of exterior stimuli, recording them in grades of impressions on wax. Not only does Freud's memorial metaphor repeat that of the ancients' theories of memory, involving impressions in wax, but it also considers memory as something to do with depth: the shallow, receptive *surface* of the pad retains only what are now called short-term memories, while the deeper wax slab retains long-term memories. The greater the depth, the more permanent the memorial trace.

Against these ideas, Derrida calls to mind Freud's theories of the death-drive. Derrida notes that the death-drive eludes perception in the archive, instead seeking to destroy any traces of its action: 'It leaves no monument, it bequeaths no document of its own' (Derrida, 1995a: 14). Not only does the death-drive – *Thanatos* – seek dissolution of all the life-drive – *Eros* – pursues, it also seeks to maintain its invisibility: it is *unarchivable*. This is not wholly antithetical to the work of the psychoanalytic archive, suggests Derrida, but is complementary and necessary to the archival process. Derrida contends that 'There would indeed be no archive desire without the radical finitude, without the possibility of a forgetfulness which does not limit itself to repression' (Derrida, 1995a: 19).[2] Inasmuch as the archive contains only what remains after the inscrutable actions of the death-drive, the archived material also acknowledges the absence of what the death-drive has destroyed, and acknowledges the work of the death-drive which is also absent. These twin absences also represent archival violence.

Given Foucault's insistence that archaeology 'is not a return to the innermost secret of the origin' (Foucault, 2002: 146), and Derrida's argument that the psychoanalytical archive is always already a marker of destruction, it seems that the archaeologist's job is always destined to fail – or at least, to find difficulty. There needs to be another figure who can make creative sense of those absences. I want to fashion that figure in the mould of Seamus Heaney, as an archaeo- and *arkhe*-poet. These two actions of writing describe how archiving and re-archiving – dismemorialising – constitute his poetics. Moreover, Shakespeare is at the heart of his own archive of development that appears via memory in his poems. Hamlet, whom Heaney's persona considers himself resembling, is at the core of these Shakespearean memories that, *pace* Homem (2018), allow the poet to develop and to chart his own development.

To give a unifying name to this figure who achieves both the archaeological and archiving processes, let me call him a Historian. Not an amorphous figure who 'writes histories' or narrativises history into chronological order (as I accuse the early modern English of doing), but instead a Historian according to Carolyn Steedman's analysis. In *Dust* (2001), Steedman updates Freud, Foucault, and Derrida, and relates her own experiences as a social historian of entering the archive and writing about what she finds there. Ultimately, she concludes, 'history gives a habitation and a name to all the fragments' (2001: 149). This, of course, intertextually participates (in Lachmann's terms) in Theseus's words from *A Midsummer Night's Dream*, previously referenced in my section on bodies:

> And as imagination bodies forth
> The forms of things unknown, the poet's pen
> Turns them to shapes, and gives to airy nothing
> A local habitation and a name. (V.i.14–17)

Steedman's Historian does what Shakespeare's Theseus asserted about poets 400 years previously, archaeologically describing the heterogeneous archive in more localised terms, using both the *locus* and nomological principle of the archive as a template. Steedman's Historian is my archaeo- and *arkhe*-poet, transferring the molecular characteristic of nomadism from the becoming writer to the archive in its becoming. By becoming a Historian, Heaney resists narratives of alien territorialisation, instead dismemorially exploring how the Irish land can continually grant its archivist a new identity.

Modern Hamlet

Not only is *Hamlet* a play of memory, as I discussed at length above, but it is also a modern play. De Grazia argues cogently that *Hamlet* is a modern play not just because of its eponymous hero but because of his introspective soliloquies. De Grazia notes that to be called 'modern' in early modern England was a slight because it directly opposed 'ancient': 'For two centuries, Shakespeare's drama had been deemed *unruly* and *wild* by the biases of the ancients' (de Grazia, 2007: 18). De Grazia suggests that the notion of unruliness had to be thrown off before *Hamlet*'s true greatness could be appreciated. If, however, we take unruliness as a positive attribute – a resistance to sovereign appropriation – then *Hamlet* becomes a discourse of resistance to territorialisation, offering itself to anti-colonial and postcolonial literatures. *Hamlet* offers an unruly counter-history.

Furthermore, de Grazia has noted that 'The critical tradition that has identified *Hamlet* with the onset of the modern period has ignored the centrality of land':

> The play dramatizes one conflict over land after another: Fortinbras I and Hamlet I over crown lands, Hamlet I and Claudius over the garden kingdom, Gonzago and Lucianus over the 'bank of flowers' or 'estate', Norway and Poland over a 'patch of ground', the boy and adult companies over the commercial stage, the Crown and the Church over the churchyard, Laertes and Hamlet over Ophelia's flowered body, and the actor who plays Hamlet and any actor whose role challenges Hamlet's command over the stage. (de Grazia, 2007: 43)

Clearly land in *Hamlet* is as much about sovereignty and sovereign territory – 'rights of memory' – as it is about the inert soil. In terms of territorialisation, there is a tendency to appropriate the surface of the land (just as with the texts I analysed previously). This is not only true of sovereigns – the kings who choose to have this land called 'Denmark' or 'Norway' – but also of those who amass land as a means of wealth: 'This sequence of hypothetical persons [in the graveyard scene] – statesmen, courtiers, landlords, lawyers – now disintegrating into earth, in life strove to acquire and retain tracts of land' (de Grazia, 2007: 32). In this sense land is something available for appropriation, particularly as it elevates in social terms those who appropriate. De Grazia also describes how the question of land and law – and by extension sovereignty – are intimately tied together in *Hamlet*'s history, with Q1's 'landless' becoming 'lawless' in F (I.i.101). Similarly, in the graveyard scene, de Grazia wonders whether 'Hamlet [is] supposed to handle one skull (the lawyer/landlord's) or two (the lawyer's and the landlord's)?' (de Grazia, 2007: 141). The salient points for my argument are that *Hamlet*'s counter-historical unruliness – its resistance to territorialisation and appropriation – is inextricable from its land discourse.

But de Grazia's analysis proceeds a step further in this, for at the heart of her reading is the label that Hamlet gives the Ghost upon the latter's insistence on Horatio's and Marcellus's sworn secrecy. Hamlet thanks the Ghost: 'Well said, old mole, canst work i'th' earth so fast?' (I.v.161). Correcting later deployments of the teleological mole that burrows to the surface like the *Geist* (Hegel) or like the workers' revolution (Marx), de Grazia instead observes the indistinguishability between the mole and its etymological cognate 'mold' – the earth – which it throws up in looking for food. This embeddedness is a feature of the land throughout *Hamlet*: the mole, the Ghost's descent into the beneath-the-stage space, the skulls that the clown surfaces, Ophelia's death (albeit in water), and Ophelia's burial. The territorial battle – the sovereign contest *over land* – thus appears to be preoccupied with rooting *in the land*, and the subsequent resurfacing or *rupture*: the Ghost returns, skulls are thrown up. The modern unruliness of *Hamlet* concerns what is memorially archived in the land, and what dismemorially returns from beneath the surface through processes of archaeology. This is yet another way, albeit more material and landed, of describing hauntology.

Rather than holy burials – 'What ceremony else?', asks Laertes during Ophelia's burial; the Priest replies that Ophelia's burial in the churchyard is more than Ophelia is due since 'She should in ground unsanctified been lodged' (V.i.214–18) – there is instead 'a violent rivalry' contested in 'units of acreage' (de Grazia, 2007: 150) with two men wrestling in a hole in the ground. This is the kind of muddiness that exemplifies *Hamlet*'s modernity, and it relies not on the surface of the land, but on what is held in its bosom; that is, it calls on memories that have hitherto not entered narrative and colonial history. Moreover, this land is no longer sacred but now secular, having been driven away from the holiness of the church. This, in part, provokes Hamlet's soliloquising, not least when he despairs over Fortinbras going 'to gain a little patch of ground / That hath in it no profit but the name' (IV.iv.17–18). Hamlet laments that

I see
The imminent death of twenty thousand men
That for a fantasy and trick of fame
Go to their graves like beds, fight for a plot
Whereon the numbers cannot try the cause,

Which is not tomb enough and continent
To hide the slain[.][3] (IV.iv.58–64)

These bodies that will rupture the land represent counter-historical
unruliness – sovereign appropriations of territory cannot be fully
accomplished in *Hamlet* without resistance. This, too, constitutes
Hamlet's secularised modernity.

Given Heaney's explicit turn to *Hamlet* in 'Viking Dublin', it is
no surprise that his poetry is also interested in land, and in what
remains in its bowels. Susan Shaw Sailer reminds us that in Heaney's
early poetry 'bogs preserve centuries-old artifacts and corpses and
then yield them to the present' (Sailer, 1991: 54–5).[4] The land is
coordinated with time, which also coordinates it with modernity:

> [T]he rootedness of the present in the past and the presentness of
> the past names a world which seems to operate independent of time:
> corpses yielded up by the bog have been preserved by it; farmers
> might be planting their potatoes in the fourteenth as well as in the
> twentieth centuries. ... The world of these poems teems with forces
> that constantly threaten to overwhelm it. (Sailer, 1991: 56)

As these memorial bog-bodies emerge from the land's depths,
Heaney's poetry records and archives them in language, taking
part metaphysically in the history housed in Ireland's land. This
joins him with modernity, since 'By going down into the bog and
backwards in time Heaney has found an identity for Ireland'
(Brown, 1981: 293). Heaney's archaeo-poetry uncovers the bodies and archives them in his poems; this entails, in its own way,
Heaney's critical figuration as an archaeologist and, ultimately, as
a Historian.

However, there are moments when, far from describing the
archive, Heaney's persona enters the archive and commingles with
it. In an early poem, 'North', Heaney writes about the word-hoard:

The longship's swimming tongue

was buoyant with hindsight –
...

It said, 'Lie down
in the word-hoard, burrow

the coil and gleam
of your furrowed brain.

Compose in darkness'. (Heaney, 1998: ll. 20–33)

This 'word-hoard' is the archive and becomes part of Heaney's poems since 'it is not possible for us to describe our own archive, since it is from within these rules that we speak, since it is that which gives to what we can say' (Foucault, 2002: 146) – therefore the archaeo- and *arkhe*-poetic positions are interrelated. The 'word-hoard' operates in two ways in Heaney's poetry. First, the instruction to the poet-speaker is not only to connect with the land, but also to 'burrow' into the land and to 'compose in darkness': poetry is found beneath. The second is that the underground changes the poet into a poet of land – of *this* land in fact. The land precedes the poet as the poet turns the land into poetry. The Gaelic name for the study of place lore is *dinnseanchas*; the role is a pre-modern one, described by Foster as 'the celebration of place-names, [and] a feature of this poetic topography; what endured was the mythic landscape, providing escape and inspiration' (Foster, 1989: 5). This endurance testifies to the memorialisation of the land in itself, to which the *dinnseanchas* poet allies himself. This poetic sensibility, like the lifestyle that turns to the bogs each winter to fuel the fire, has been incubated in the land and is taken up by Heaney in his poetry. The word-hoard hibernates underground where the poet can burrow to find it, but equally, in the burrowing, the poet is writing the land anew in the present. Here is the counter-historical Historian who, by unearthing the vocabulary, is disremembering the land's memories, and dismemorialising them in the poetry. This capital-H Historian natively disremembers.

The word-hoard is notably reified in Heaney's poetry, emerging on to his page in words that point to the poet's earthwork. Words such as digging, roots, opened ground, irruption, vowel, wound, sore, fault, the underground, and earthworm all appear and demonstrate the poet's 'burrowing'. Sophie Hillan writes that 'In the many-layered language that we all share ... we have to dig, sometimes quite deeply, to find our buried treasure' (Hillan, 2005: 88) – where the buried treasure is hidden is where Heaney can 'solve the riddle' (in Yeats's terms) of Ireland. Like the found objects that, in Sailer's terms, 'overwhelm' the poetry, the poet becomes modern by disremembering the word-hoard and dismemorialising the land anew in those reified terms. By becoming Steedman's counter-historical Historian, and through archiving the memories in the land in his poems, memory is Heaney's fodder.

Disease

And yet much of Heaney's writing is contaminated by disease: the archive has a fever. In the early 'At a Potato Digging', a poem about the Famine of the 1840s, oblique links tie the health of the nation to that of its food supply – a food supply, importantly for my argument, that is deeply settled in the ground, albeit rootlessly: 'The new potato, sound as stone, / putrefied when it had lain three days in the long clay pit. / Millions rotted along with it' (Heaney, 2006a: ll. 34–7). The rotten land, manifest in the potato plight, is matched by those who farmed and fed off the land: they too are rotten. A tension emerges between the *dinnseanchas* poet, who elevates the land to mythical status by venerating its places and place names, and a poet who writes about rot, disease, and death. As Máire declares in Friel's *Translations*, quoted in my epigraph, there remains an element of Irish tradition that *looks for* the blight, even when it has never taken place – this signifies the archival violence of the death-drive that erases the Irish land's memories.

For Heaney, the question is posed as to whether any positive memories remain beneath the Irish surface. The diseased land is secularised and removed from myth and religious discourse – except, of course, if you are using the rotten land as a measure of the people's proximity to God, their civility, and their intelligence:

> [A] most ritch and plentifull Countrye, full of Corne and Cattell that yow would have thought they would have beene able to stande longe, yett err one yeare and a half, they were brought to such wretchedness, as that any stonie harte would haue rewed the same … [and] in shorte space there were none almost left and a most populous and plentyfull Countrye suddenlie lefte voyde of man or beast, yet sure in all that warr there perished not manye by the sworde, but all by the extremitye of famyne, which they themselues had wrought[.] (Spenser, 1934: 135)

Here Spenser accuses the Irish of immorality because of the way they farmed the land. Spenser's role in admonishing the place of the bards in Irish culture stands in opposition to the *dinnseanchas* tradition. A question emerges: why would Heaney align his ethics with Spenser's, when Spenser is clearly anti-Irish independence (such as 'independence' was figured in early modern Ireland)? Furthermore, in his essay 'Feeling into Words', Heaney shows that he keenly understands the easy transition from debate about a piece of land to sovereignty, commenting that in the contemporary land question, the land's 'sovereignty has been temporarily usurped or infringed ... What we have is the tail-end of a struggle in a province between territorial piety and imperial power' (Heaney, 1984: 42, 57). In this latter opposition, however, Heaney's words express his frustration at the return of the land to a sacred discourse – at least imperial power removes that and accuses those involved of de-sacralisation (or indeed of secularisation). This crucial link between disease/rot and secularisation provides Heaney with the opportunity to turn Irish land into his modern Ireland; and this modern Ireland will, in turn, engender Heaney an Irish national poet, a poet of *dinnseanchas*. Therefore, by archaeologically excavating the diseased rottenness beneath the surface, Heaney can archive it in his poetry and convert the land to his own: disremembered and dismemorialised disease provides entry to modernity.

Unruly counter-history is also disease. *Hamlet*, Heaney's reference for 'dithering' and 'blathering' and 'coming into consciousness' in the dirt, also contains a narrative of rot and disease,[5] and Hamlet, it turns out, is coeval if not identical with disease. First, Horatio explains that the Ghost's return 'bodes some strange eruption to our state' (I.i.68). Inasmuch as the Ghost has come from purgatory and returns to the symbolically demonic space of the cellar, this is a material description by Horatio: the Ghost has erupted out of the cellar beneath and irrupted on to the stage above. This is also an unruliness, as by rupturing the surface of the land the memorial Ghost who commands to 'remember me' is challenging whoever politically lays claim to the land, resisting the sovereign control currently in place. The Ghost's unruliness is matched by Fortinbras's traipsing to claim the 'little patch of ground' explored above. In Horatio's concerns here, and Hamlet's concerns having spoken to the Norwegian Captain, the task of the sovereign is not merely to control the surface of the land, but to stop the disremembered resurfacing of those things that ought to be housed in the land's depths. Memories must stay below, stored inaccessibly and certainly not available to archaeological revelation.

For this reason, Horatio's 'strange eruption' represents a modern, counter-historical unruliness that troubles present sovereignty, but also makes the land secular: religious discourse has no hold here. There is one other use of the phrase 'strange eruption' in Shakespeare's writing. In *1 Henry IV* Hotspur responds to Owen Glendower's tale of his mythical birth:

> GLENDOWER   At my nativity
> The front of heaven was full of fiery shapes,
> Of burning cressets; and at my birth
> The frame and huge foundation of the earth
> Shaked like a coward.
>
> ...
>
> HOTSPUR [T]he earth shook to see the heavens on fire,
> And not in fear of your nativity.
> Diseasèd nature oftentimes breaks forth
> In strange eruptions[.] (III.i.12–27)

For Hotspur 'strange eruption' implies 'disease'. Turning back to Hamlet, Marcellus's 'something's rotten in the state of Denmark' (I.iv.90) springs to mind alongside Horatio's 'strange eruption'. To tie into this story of diseased eruptions, it is important to recall that Hamlet was born on the day that King Hamlet won the Norwegian lands from King Fortinbras (V.i.138–9). De Grazia writes:

> The annexing of [Norwegian] land and the birth of a prince are a dynastic dream-come-true. One event complements the other. Indeed the legal instruments drawn up at the time of the combat seem designed to assure that the territorial gain will be passed on to the victor's descendants. ... On the very day that Denmark won these inheritable lands, a prince to inherit them was born. Like a happy astrological convergence, the coincidence seems prophetic: Hamlet was born to rule. (de Grazia, 2007: 1–2)

Like Glendower, Hamlet was born *out of the land*. As John of Gaunt says of England in *Richard II*, the land in *Hamlet* seems to be a 'teeming womb of royal kings' (II.i.51), and Hamlet is the baby

bursting forth at a crucial point of established sovereignty. The battle between the two kings, an unruly battle that was unseating one
of the kings from their land, gave birth to Hamlet. Strange eruptions are diseases; Hamlet, too, can be considered diseased, if not
the disease itself. Unruliness and disease are two sides of the same
coin. And so, when considering Heaney's turn to the diseased and
rotten land, it is essential to remember his turn to Hamlet's 'coming
to consciousness', even if it is attended by 'dithering, blathering'; the
latter would now appear as direct responses to the 'murders and pie-
ties' (Heaney, 1998: l. 13) that closely resemble Heaney's complaint
about 'territorial piety'. To dither, to blather, to follow the worm into
the mud: all of these may well lead to disease (or be symptoms of
disease), but they are also a counter-historical modernity emerging
from the land in a non-sacred, 'strange' modernity.

The unruliness of disease in *Hamlet* is cemented finally by
Horatio's discussion about King Hamlet's victory against King
Fortinbras that made the latter 'forfeit with his life all these his
lands / Which he stood seized of' (I.i.87–8) to King Hamlet. De
Grazia reminds us that if to be 'seized' is to have legal possession
of land, then to be 'diseased' is 'to be illegitimately dispossessed of
lands' (de Grazia, 2007: 157).[6] Thereafter disease can be thought
both a medical and legal ailment, and in *Hamlet* both connect to the
land. Moreover, the legal iteration accords with a modern idea of
unruliness. To be diseased, or at least to be in the bosom of the land
– dismemorially recovering the archive – or divesting others of territorial possession of that land, now becomes desirable; to be holy or
to aspire to divinity is dismissed as a pre-modern, anti-progressive
idea. Rather than Brown's narrow reading of Heaney's persona pre-
ferring Hercules over Antaeus – 'To be a man is to act, and if your
form of action is to create let it be the art of direct political statement' (Brown, 1981: 295) – Antaeus (from the poem of the same
name), 'cradled in the dark that wombed me' (Heaney, 1998: l. 10)
and (from 'Hercules and Antaeus') the 'mould-hugger' (1998: l. 8),
comes much closer to the ethic of poetry and its medium of creating political messages. The archive becomes the generative *locus* of
poetry, and that archive is buried deep in the land. Through archaeological 'Description' – which according to Heaney in 'Fosterage'
from 'Singing School' is adequate with 'revelation!' (Heaney, 1998:
l. 1)[7] – Heaney accommodates himself in the land metaphorically
just as his poetry accommodates the land.

There are, of course, many other underground, diseased elements in Heaney's poetry and, having established the twisting of
the negative disease to a positive, I now turn to its other diseased
underground elements. In 'Veteran's Dream', the poem enacts
a shift between body and land for the First World War veteran
whose wound becomes contaminated: 'Where he lies / On cankered
ground, / A scatter of maggots, busy / In the trench of his wound'
(Heaney, 1993: ll. 13–16). The displaced trench in which the veteran, Mr Dickson, would have fought finds its place on the body.
In this instance the land–memory coordinate shifts on to the body,
such that the memory of the land is what fills Mr Dickson's dream.
In 1990's *The Cure at Troy*, Heaney's heavily politicised translation
of Sophocles's *Philoctetes*, Philoctetes is himself afflicted by a cursed
snake bite which becomes a weeping sore that leads him 'astray'
(Heaney, 1990: 63) and becomes a narcissistic and self-indulgent
excuse. The Chorus tells Philoctetes that 'Your wound is what you
feed on … / … / Stop eating yourself up with hate' (Heaney, 1990:
61). This wound for Philoctetes is, nevertheless, a sign of his own
abjection, his 'being forgotten', that will linger as a scar signifying
the past (Heaney, 1990: 73).

Another disease is evident in 'Augury', in which

The fish faced into the current,
Its mouth agape,
Its whole head opened like a valve.
You said 'It's diseased.'

A pale crusted sore
Turned like a coin
And wound to the bottom,
Unsettling silt off a weed. (Heaney, 1993: ll. 1–8)

Here it is the fish that has been caught in the depths of the river,
whose diseased body is itself given depth and interiority through the
sore that pierces the skin. The shift from body to land (here, water)
is important in asserting the positive value of sores and disease and,
ultimately, of plumbing the depths of water or burrowing into the
ground – of going *à la recherche de mémoire*. In Heaney's poetry,
modern Ireland's emergence is contingent upon the associative
qualities of bodies and/in land that form memories and, later, the

archive legacy. Thus, in 'Augury', the fish's corporal disease allows the speaker and his friend to look to the future, and no longer resort to the past that was previously ossified in the ground, while Philoctetes commits, when he leaves Lemnos, to being 'like a fossil that's being carried away' (Heaney, 1990: 80). Memory remembers forward, an idea certainly available when Hamlet accepts his own mortality in the graveyard in Act Five Scene One, as well as in Derrida's ideas, since

> the question of the archive is not, we repeat, a question of the past. ... It is a question of the future, the question of the future itself, the question of a response, of a promise and of a responsibility for tomorrow. The archive: if we want to know what this will have meant, we will only know in the times to come. (Derrida, 1995a: 27)

The *in-augurating* fish that is plucked from the depths of the water remembers so as to look forward. Modernity emerges from diseased dismemories – linking again with the becoming consciousness of the nomad, the ruptured surface enacts that process of modernity.

To understand how the veteran's wound is similarly positive, it is valuable to examine other wounds in Heaney's poems. One of the most famous wounds is in 'The Grauballe Man', one of Heaney's many bog bodies. The bog bodies are the paradigmatic version of the memorial archive that Heaney reveals. Although they have already been unearthed and exhibited by the time he reads about them in P. V. Glob's *The Bog People* (1965), Heaney's treatment of them in his poems, by describing their stories – giving them a *local* habitation and a name – proves him to be Steedman's archaeological Historian and archiving poet. The 'cured wound' of 'The Grauballe Man' 'opens inwards to a dark / elderberry place' (Heaney, 1998: ll. 22–4). I understand this wound as working in two ways. First, it opens up to ambiguity and imagination as the Grauballe Man cannot be determined exactly: 'Who will say "corpse" / to his vivid cast? / Who will say "body" / to his opaque repose?' (ll. 25–8). This molecular indeterminacy is also a feature of Hamlet in the land 'dithering and blathering', as well as the indeterminacy that heralded modernity in Yeats's poetry, above. Second, the wound enacts a fractal spatiality, in which the bog body – itself a wound in the opened, ruptured bogland – becomes Irish land. Archaeology thus becomes the archive. The interchange described above between bodies and land here reaches its apotheosis when the wounded body is the wounded Irish land.[8] That wound is both injured and sexualised: disease leads to desire. Modernity happens perversely – it is unruly – and is completely secularised in its muddy disease.

The twin possibilities of that wound wend their way into 'Kinship' in which, contra Yeats, the poet-speaker digs a spade into the land and discovers that 'This centre holds / and spreads' (Heaney, 1998: iv, ll. 1–2). Raphaël Ingelbien is astounded by Heaney's assertion here, writing that

> Few contemporary poets have dared to contradict the opening of 'The Second Coming' … so boldly. Heaney fuses a vision of origins with the vowel of primeval Irishness and offers the rough beast of his Celtic primitivism as the center that holds *North* together. Heaney's synthesis reverts to a full-blown organicist nationalism and also consecrates the naturalization of language that is a hallmark of his early poetry. (Ingelbien, 1999: 649)

The 'centre' is the place where a spade has been pushed into the bogland by the speaker. Instead of dissolving, this is a stabilising modern world: it is the generative *locus* of poetry where the poet grasps sovereignty, and where the nation becomes. By archaeologically searching for memory, Heaney's poetry seeks to expedite counter-historical modernity. The sexualised crack in the earth is suitably fruitful. 'This', the speaker continues,

> is the vowel of earth
> dreaming its root
> in flowers and snow,
>
> mutation of weathers
> and seasons,
> a windfall composing
> the floor it rots into.
>
> I grew out of all this
> like a weeping willow
> inclined to
> the appetites of gravity. (Heaney, 1998: iv, ll. 14–24)

As in the first of my conclusions about the Grauballe Man's wound, that which is rotten and rooted in the earth – and linked to dreams, such as the veteran's – is nomadically indeterminate, becoming:

imagination. Diseased memories are ripe for archive in poetry. From this, the speaker tells us that 'I grew'. In 'Kinship' 'vowel' becomes one of those words from the 'word-hoard' that describes the ruptured and embedded earth, the 'vowel, springing from the earth of Heaney's native landscape, [that] is crucial to his vision of Ireland' (Ingelbien, 1999: 636).

With this in mind, 'The Grauballe Man' becomes an archaeologically excavated source of imagination with its roots firmly in the earth. But the imagination is dependent not upon anything emanating from the earth, but something that 'lies / perfected in my memory', 'tanned and toughened' (Heaney, 1998: ll. 37–8, 21). Here at last is the central intersection between what is embedded in the land and part of Heaney's poetic memory. These are at once archived as objects in the poetry. Like the Viking Dublin pieces, this is an ossified past on which the speaker is calling. Whereas Yeats sought the tradition that was memorially impressed upon the land, Heaney's poetry seeks roots that are preserved and conserved in the earth on which to build his poetic imagination, and through which to make counter-history happen. Heaney's speaker uncovers that which Prospero buried in *The Tempest* (1610–11): 'I'll break my staff, / Bury it certain fathoms in the earth, / And deeper than did ever plummet sound / I'll drown my book' (V.i.54–7). Counter-historical becoming is enacted when archaeology takes place in poetry. In turning burial in the land – normally left only to those who have died – into a space for dwelling (as in Antaeus), Heaney's poetry repeats the motion already identified in Yeats: the location under the land's surface is turned into a site by the presence of bodies and unruly disease makes it a dwelling space. What was a site of sacred burial is now a modern, but secular, land. The Heaney Historian gives Irish history a new *locus* for burial.

Opened ground

Heaney's collected poems in the late 1990s were subtitled *Opened Ground*. This phrase, which appears severally in Heaney's poetry, is sourced from the underground word-hoard. It is also the phrase that most readily connects the poetic with the political. It first appears in *North*'s 'Act of Union', the poem that exemplifies the connection between the sexualised body and the sexualised land: 'No treaty / I foresee will salve completely your tracked / And stretchmarked body, the big pain / That leaves you raw, like opened ground, again' (Heaney, 1998: II, ll. 11–14). Heaney's aversion to the political union between Great Britain and Ireland that formed the United Kingdom in 1801 connects both the land metaphor – 'opened ground' – and the body to which it refers to the political metanarrative. If read in relation to 'At a Potato Digging', in which the health of the Irish nation is reflected in the blight that afflicted the food embedded in the land, then the phrase 'opened ground' can be read as not only a metaphor, but also as a direct signifier of the land's rupture and the rupture of the island itself. It is the sign that dismemory is at work. Indeed, just as Heaney did, Brown writes that the land is Erin herself in *North*, or 'Mother Ireland, Kathleen Ní Houlihann [*sic*], the terrain itself; but she is also a subject people and by association the Irish Catholic consciousness' (Brown, 1981: 293). Kathleen Ní Houlihan is the memory that Heaney continually reveals and describes – dismemorially archives – in his poems.

'Act of Union' consists of two sonnets in which the male first-person narrator talks to his lover about the child they have conceived who is growing in the lover's womb. The speaker is cast as the coloniser, an idea cemented at the beginning of the second sonnet: 'And I am still imperially / Male, leaving you with the pain' (Heaney, 1998: II, ll. 1–2). That the poem ends with a proclamation that no political treaty could repair the land, and that the body of the lover – as the land of Ireland – will be irreparably open, is suggestive. It implies that Ireland *is* 'opened ground' as long as the nation is 'half-independent'. Along with the intimations of messianism – the birth pangs of 'the big pain / That leaves you raw' (II, ll. 13–14) – this poeticised colonisation structures an Irish revolution through the coming messiah out of the body that is Irish land: a 'strange eruption'. But now this body is not the Judeo-Christian messiah, but instead a secular, diseased body whose unruliness threatens to break the Act of Union. Apart from anything else, all this demonstrates the political responsibility of Heaney's disremembered digging through Ireland's memorial archive.

In Heaney's poetry modern Ireland gives birth to an unruly/diseased body. This unruliness is in itself secular as it threatens the stable control of religious discourse, just as that discourse manifests in colonial and imperial discourses of power. I have established that Heaney's preferred hero was Antaeus, and not Hercules, particularly because of the former's birth in the land. But we also see what happens when, like Antaeus, or indeed like Hamlet having to resort to the duel, deracination takes place in Heaney's poetry. Hamlet's removal to the duel-hall is accompanied by his famous resignation that 'the readiness is all' and 'Let be' (V.ii.200–2); removed from the scuffle in the grave in Act Five Scene One, Hamlet knows he is less likely to win in a courtly duel where socialised laws apply. Heaney's poetry shows a similar reluctance to being taken out of the land. For this reason, by archiving in his poems, by figuring the depths of land in language, Heaney calms that anxiety. *At* root, Heaney remains *in* the roots.

In *District and Circle* (2006) Heaney returns to one of the bog bodies about which he writes in *Wintering Out* (1972). In 'The Tollund Man in Springtime', the speaker takes home from Jutland some Tollund rushes, hoping to keep them alive so as to plant them back in Ireland.

> Through every check and scan I carried with me
> A bunch of Tollund rushes – roots and all –
> Bagged in their own bogged-damp. In an old stairwell
> Broom cupboard where I had hoped they'd stay
> Damp until transplanted, they went musty.
> Every green-skinned stork turned friable,
> The drowned-mouse fibres withered and the whole
> Limp, soggy cluster lost its frank bouquet
> Of weed leaf and turf mould. (Heaney, 2006b: ll. 71–9)

Out of their environment and context, deracinated from the land, the plants die; this is tragedy. This danger awaits in Heaney's conception of sovereign Ireland if it fails to recognise the power of that which is rooted and underground. This advocacy of the underground is also why Heaney's poetry promotes a secular and memorial return to Station Island (in *Station Island* (1984)), in which the poet-speaker encounters figures of the past, held in the no-space of St Patrick's entrance to purgatory (a space of no-time, as well). As he leaves Station Island, the speaker is urged by Joyce – 'wintered hard and sharp as a blackthorn', i.e. immortally preserved – to '"write / for the joy of it. Cultivate a work-lust"'

(Heaney, 1998: XII, ll. 22–4). As if completing the task of writing, in *Human Chain* (2010), Heaney's final collection, 'Herbal' ends with this declaration that the history of the speaker's relationship with the land resulted in 'Me in place and the place in me' (Heaney, 2010: 142). This is what Heaney's poetry cultivated throughout his career. This intimacy with place is catalysed by Heaney's engagement with Shakespeare. Homem writes that Heaney's 'use of Shakespeare is exceptional for its regularity and for its role in repeatedly signposting the poet's personal, civic and literary development' (Homem, 2018: 36). The two trajectories – relationships with the land and with Shakespeare – not only run parallel, but they are mutually constructed and catalysed by one another. It is the 'dithering' and 'blathering' of Hamlet in 'Viking Dublin', the becoming that happens when the land is pierced, and the ossified bodies that provide the dismemorial platform for future modernising that Heaney archaeologically uncovered and wrote into his poetry. In doing so, Heaney's poetry both harnesses *Hamlet*'s modernities, but also departs by learning a lesson. Land provides both the moment of nomadic becoming and the link between early modern England and modern Irish literature.

In *Hamlet* this concentration on what is in the land serves a different topology of sovereignty: instead of being from above – from God in heaven – this is sovereignty from below. In instituting this type of sovereignty, Shakespeare's *Hamlet* advocates a great common sovereignty, or authority wielded not by divinely appointed monarchs, but instead something that ascends from those working on the land. The Clown becomes the prime representative of this, as his dismemorial knowledge of the bodies in the earth and the history of Danish sovereignty are intimately linked together. But this is not a pure elevation of the lower social classes, for what the Clown talks about is purely the monarchy and the upper echelons of Elsinore's society. In this way, the Clown is seen as elevated to the level of intimate relations with the *locus* of power. Helgerson writes that Shakespeare's histories worked in a similar way, by rejecting 'the ruled'; however, by 'Identifying [Shakespeare] himself, his plays, his company, and his audience with the problematics of early modern kingship, he left out of consideration the no less pressing problematics of subjecthood'. This strategy 'was designed to elevate Shakespeare and his art out of the company of the base mechanicals with whom playwriting had inevitably associated him' (Helgerson, 1992: 239, 240). Read in this way, the ruptured land's sovereignty is emblematic of the author's growing 'authority' in early modern culture, a representation of the secularisation of modern power. It concerns a changing dynamic between the land, the ruler and ruled – with the latter also being populated by those who script the ruler and the land. Bursting forth from the land, both Shakespeare and Hamlet challenge that authority whilst never fully escaping its relationship with the land. In Heaney's poetry, the writer who wanted to escape the binary of 'territorial piety and imperial power' does so by harnessing the power of the diseased, underground memories in *Hamlet*. Heaney's poetry also follows Shakespeare's play in making the poet one of place and space, related to the land but, crucially, never leaving its 'darkness'. Heaney becomes the poet of *dinnseanchas*, the 'writer of poems and tales which relate the original meanings of place names and constitute a form of mythological etymology' (Heaney, 1984: 131). Heaney's lying down in the word-hoard allows him to reconstitute these places through the counter-historical 'mythological etymology' as he becomes the poet of place that elevates him to author of Ireland. Ireland is archived 'in' him. But Heaney's is an unruly, muddy and diseased (de-seized), counter-historical modernity. That Heaney does so out of the land, rather than from on top of its surface, indicates not only his deep understanding of Ireland's (sedimented) past but also how his poetry can dismemorially structure the future – and how Hamlet could have avoided tragedy.

Conclusion

The language of internal occupation – of being inside, beneath, contained within – structures much of Heaney's poetry. It is Heaney's subject, and Heaney's mode of writing. The land is the paradigmatic version of this interior logic, but in terms of what is planted in it, what is unearthed from its depths, and what can be set down to lay foundations. Crucially, this idea of rootedness is intimately connected to that of memory: *Death of a Naturalist* starts with 'Digging' in which the poet's chosen tool, the pen, is used to dig beneath the surface. He does so because he sees himself remembering his father's subterranean activity in himself, storing it not in the land, but in his poetry. The pattern started in Heaney's first collected poem sets the model for his poetic career. Heaney archaeologically reveals the trove of treasure that the land contains – trial pieces, bog bodies, potatoes – and describes their fragments, localising them and using them to explain Ireland's due process: its law. The poetry becomes the archive. His poetry is both archaeological, in Foucault's terms, and archiving, in Derrida's sense of the word. Heaney becomes the *dinnseanchas* Historian.

And this is all enabled by an enduring fascination with Shakespeare. Hamlet is the paradigmatic delver into the deep, defying etiquette and morality as he jumps confusedly into the grave. He wants to revive Ophelia, and to keep her alive with him, much as the Ghost of his father has stayed with him after his death. Sadly for Hamlet, it is not to be. His 'dithering' and 'blathering' in the grave is the beginning of his tragic end. He fails to keep Ophelia's ghost alive; he fails to keep Yorick's skull safely stored underground. However, when Heaney engages with Shakespeare, such as in 'The Real Names', he considers 'memory like mitigation' (2001: l. 139). Through Shakespeare's ghosts, who are kept alive in memory before and as they are harnessed and written '*into* his lines' (Homem, 2018: 44; emphasis in original), Heaney uses Shakespeare positively. 'Shakespeare, in this regard', continues Homem, 'emerges in his writing less as daunting precedent than as enabling verbal force'. Shakespeare *is* Heaney's archive, but also catalyses Heaney's dismemorial research of Ireland's land and his archival poetry.

*

To recapitulate, 'counter-memory' constitutes a 'transformation of history into a totally different form of time' (Foucault, 1980: 160), while counter-history is practised by the Historian, who 'gives a habitation and a name to all the fragments' (Steedman, 2001: 149), but without making those fragments cohere. I argue that Yeats is a proponent of the former, and Heaney of the latter.

These writing activities take place in relation or reaction to a crude, colonial historicisation that was indexed with power, the net result of which was to evacuate Irish land of its autochthonic memories, leaving only 'empty homogeneous time' in its wake. The

English planters and governors engendered it in the late sixteenth and early seventeenth centuries; famine also wrought it in the mid-nineteenth century; and the War of Independence finally overcame it in 1921. In various ways, each of these events was historicised as part of an English (or latterly British) national narrative that inexorably produced Empire. In the earlier instances, Edward Coke's emphasis on English *corpus juris* found a willing participant in Sir John Davies in Ireland; during the Famine, Charles Trevelyan, the civil servant who oversaw Famine relief and financial aid to Ireland during the crisis, saw the period as the logical answer to a Malthusian equation. He noted with glee that 'the case of Ireland is at last understood. Irish affairs are no longer a craft and mystery. The abyss has been fathomed. The Famine has acted with a force which nothing could resist, and has exposed to view the real state of the country, so that he who runs may read' (Trevelyan, 1848: 187–8). For Trevelyan, the story of Famine was a British one, revelling in the possible improvements that could now be made to the British civil service thanks to the learning process the Famine had enacted. In both these instances, English/British history supersedes Ireland in importance and priority. The Whiggish narrative of progress lends the British modern colonial project an importance that the land troubles to the west could not overshadow. The historicisation of the British narrative of Irish land was to the fore.

However, counter-memory and counter-history restore a *milieu de mémoire* in Irish land, thereby producing the nation-state built on and out of the land's heritage. The emphasis in both poets on a kind of mythopoetics, where mythic truth is unsteadily remembered or re-instituted in the now, lends the Irish modernity a different character to the English/British one. Ireland's modernity is nomadic, transitory, rooted in memory; it is muddy, diseased, produced in and through poetry. Ireland's modernity, through the writing of these two Nobel laureates, is dismemorial, and not chronological.

Notes

1 Two words that are interchangeable in early modern English.
2 This inherent destructiveness leads Derrida to label this process a *mal d'archive*: 'archive fever' or 'archive sickness'.

3 A large part of Act Four Scene Four is absent from Q1 (which appears as Scene Twelve in the Ard³ edition of Q1), almost as if the notion of bodies rupturing the land's surface, and its subsequent treatment, could not be permitted initially. Instead, the scene irrupted into the play's fuller second version, poking its own body above the land of Q1's nine lines that were not 'tomb enough and continent / To hide the slain'. There is no equivalent passage in F.

4 Potatoes are tubers, and therefore rootless in the ground; potatoes are nomadic in this vein, but also in owing to their history of travel from the New World to Ireland. This journey took place in the early modern period (q.v. Tomás O'Riordan, 2001).

5 It is worth also reminding that Scarry establishes the fact of the body as *locus* for memory through the concept of disease and immunity (Scarry, 1987: 110).

6 De Grazia also confirms that 'Until the eighteenth century, diseased shared both spelling and pronunciation with diseized' (de Grazia, 2007: 157).

7 In 'Fosterage', a poem dedicated to Heaney's mentor and former employer, Michael McLaverty, the McLaverty speaker also urges the persona to '"Go your own way"' (l. 5) and to write history from below; or, that is, counter-history: 'Remember / Katherine Mansfield – *I will tell / How the laundry basket squeaked … that note of exile*' (ll. 6–8; emphasis in original).

8 Another instance of this is in 'Sibyl', the second of the 'Triptych' poems:

> The ground we kept our ear to for so long
> Is flayed or calloused, and its entrails
> Tented by an impious augury.
> Our island is full of comfortless noises. (Heaney, 1998: ll. 17–20)

These lines also mix intertextual memories of *Hamlet* (V.ii.197) and *The Tempest* (III.ii.135).

Conclusion: 'I disremember'

THE COVEY Freedom! What's th' use o' freedom, if it's not economic freedom?

ROSIE (emphasizing with extended arm and moving finger) I used them very words just before you come in. 'A lot o' thricksters', says I, 'that wouldn't know what freedom was if they got it from their mother' ... (*To Barman*) Didn't I, Tommy?

BARMAN I disremember.

ROSIE No, you don't disremember. Remember you said, yourself, it was all 'only a flash in th' pan'. Well, 'flash in the pan, or no flash in th' pan', says I, 'they're not goin' to get Rosie Redmond', says I, 'to fight for freedom that wouldn't be worth winnin' in a raffle!'

– from *The Plough and the Stars* by Sean O'Casey

In the summer of 2016, two centenaries were celebrated on either side of the Irish Sea. The Easter Rising had had its exact centenary on Easter of that year, but commemorations and celebrations were ongoing; the 400th anniversary of Shakespeare's death had also had its commemorations in April but were still ongoing. Two of those commemorations shared a memorial *locus* at the National Theatre on London's Southbank.

At the National's Lyttelton Theatre, co-directors Jeremy Herrin and Howard Davies staged Sean O'Casey's 1926 play *The Plough and the Stars*. In the programme accompanying the production, an explicit effort was made to highlight how O'Casey's drama was representative of the Irish revolution. First, Senia Pašeta's article '"There'll be blood yet": paths to the Easter Rising of 1916' elaborated on the formation of the Ulster Volunteers, the Irish Volunteers, the Irish Citizens Army, the women's-only Cumann na mBan, and

briefly explained the story of the Easter Rising. She connected
O'Casey to the Irish Volunteers, and then noted his distancing from
the group, before remarking that O'Casey's play reflected negatively
on some of the revolutionary action. This was because 'O'Casey
wrote mainly from the perspective of civilians, of ordinary people
and of flawed participants'. Pašeta proceeded to assert that 'The
Easter Rising was in many ways a highly intimate and parochial
event, but its implications and legacies have been experienced and
analysed over the last hundred years across the country and the
world' (Pašeta in National Theatre, 2016: n.p.).

Second, James Moran's history of O'Casey as a playwright
began with the telling statement, 'Sean O'Casey did not fight during the Easter Rising of 1916.' He proceeded to narrate the changing responses at the Abbey Theatre to O'Casey's drama, the first
theatre that produced his plays, including *The Plough and the Stars*.
Critically, only the second half of the play is set during the Rising,
with the first half set six months before; nevertheless, the play gar-
nered criticism from 'a group of republican women' since O'Casey
'particularly singled out Patrick Pearse for mockery' in the play
(James Moran in National Theatre, 2016: n.p.). Moran's commentary is of course accurate, but lends his focus to the production's
commemorative aspect by writing about the Easter Rising, rather
than, for example, the history of the Dublin tenement.

Finally, intersecting these two brief critical essays was a timeline
of key dates of the revolutionary period in Ireland. Starting with the
date of the third Home Rule Bill in April 1912, it ends with Roger
Casement's execution in London in August 1916. Combining the
academics' histories of O'Casey's relationship to the Rising with
the historical chronology of events cements the commemorative element of the production.

Outside the theatre in the Lyttelton Lounge was the commemoration for Shakespeare. The *5 Hamlets* exhibition was part of
the National Theatre's larger *Commemorating Shakespeare*, and
(according to the press release) featured 'recordings, props, designs,
costume and more from the NT's five productions of Hamlet –
which opened the NT in 1963, our South Bank building in 1976,
and has been produced more than any other Shakespeare play'. The
emphasis in this exhibition was not only on Shakespeare but on

how Shakespeare had been remembered and produced over the past fifty years of the National Theatre. Situated next to each other, this production and this exhibition sat uneasily without a single note of sympathy between them. And yet they spoke eloquently to me of the way that intertextual memories of Shakespeare in modern Irish literature construct a productive dialogue.

These two represent the current practice of commemoration. On the one hand, partial histories are the focus as 1916 is prioritised over other 'memories' of O'Casey's life and of his play; on the other, commemoration is narrativised, in which the present is allied to the far past through a nearer one. That the two take place in the same *locus* of memory – a theatre of memory, no less – seems to coordinate my argument: intertextual memory forges useful, if disruptive connections.

This idea is too fortuitous; of course, the timings of the centenary of the Easter Rising and the quatercentenary of Shakespeare's death are simply coincidental.[1] I have shown that there is a link between the two: memory. Part I on ghosts showed that the ghost who lives *in memory* is able to intervene in chronological, mortal temporality at any moment, and affect and shape the future at that time. It was *Hamlet*'s Ghost that modelled this behaviour as it was borne out in Synge's *Playboy*, with Old Mahon worryingly resurrecting twice; in 'Hades' when Bloom found the anachronistic ghost of his son more compelling than the annoying ghost of his father; and in Banville's *Ghosts* when Freddie, a father, adopted the spectral temporality to live outside the mortal world, in a mode of spectral temporality.

In Part II on bodies, I demonstrated how the question of the Irish Republic is a fraught one. Beckett's bodies in the *Three Novels* convey the testimonial brunt of colonialism, and respond with an increasingly monadic theatricality, in which Coriolanus's experience as a theatregoer is mimicked by Molloy, and Volpone's dissembling is echoed by the Unnamable. O'Brien's Caithleen also memorialises a failed nationalism in her reduction to a depthless, wombless woman, *à la* Hermione in *The Winter's Tale*, but she also becomes a figure able to stymie the falsified narratives of women's nationalist conscription.

Finally, Part III on land was about counter-memory and counter-history. Yeats's counter-memorial strategy of restoring Ireland's mythic and memorial history was added to by Heaney's counter-historical strategy, in which, like Steedman's Historian, he gave a name and *locus* to fragmented memories, maintaining them *as* memories. For Yeats, the Shakespearean model shifted from Lear, who too readily privileged chronology over propriety, to Spenser's Colin Clout and Shakespeare's Duke Senior from *As You Like It*, both of whom privileged the dance as signifier of a nomadic home-coming. Whereas for Heaney, Hamlet was the starting point for his personae's journeys from being *in the land* to the Shakespeare-enabled transition into having the Irish land invested in the poetry and even in the personae themselves. These different temporalities, privileging genealogy and counter-memory over history in the for-mer, and archaeological/archival counter-history in the latter, prove the insufficiency of a taut, linear 'continuous trajectory' (Ricoeur, 2006: 166) of intertextual memory.

The kind of intertextual memories I have described here deline-ate a greater concern with the *future* over the *past*. Moreover, they are not pure or generative memories, in which we might expect Shakespeare's frames or language to *help* shape the new Irish nation. Rather they demonstrate a literary and political disruptive-ness: Synge's revolution takes place offstage; Bloom looks to and hopes for his dead son's spectral return; Freddie Montgomery slides into the shadows; the Unnamable reluctantly returns to the stage; Caithleen Brady has an elective hysterectomy; Yeats focuses on the scarred landscape; and Heaney (re)stores memories of violence in his diseased and wounded poetry. However, in that focus on the future, these dismemories are also aligned with the nationalist strat-egy of creating a promise of Ireland to the future. Much as Derrida explains the American Declaration of Independence as pre-emptive, declaratively creating an American nation to come (*à venir*) in the future (*avenir*), so did Padraic Pearse in 1916 promise an Irish Republic to the future. More relevantly still, the 'very moment of foundation or institution' of Justice (read: a new nation), 'is never a moment inscribed in the homogeneous fabric [*tissu*] of a story or history, since it rips it apart with one decision' (Derrida, 2002: 241). As that rip in time, modern Ireland offers a space for scripting a new nation – not Spenser's kingdom of English, but Irish writers' independent republic. To this Irish future are these writers turned, via intertextually remembering a sort of *arche* or origin of English literature (viz., literature of a nation called 'England'): William Shakespeare.

The counter-intuitiveness of this approach is plain. And yet the evidence in the preceding pages demonstrates the value of imagining Shakespeare's oeuvre as an *arkhe* – or an archive – that can supply Irish writers with the vocabulary to voice their thoughts on the page about themselves and Ireland. Therefore, the dismemories I have identified appear not only through an exploration of literary intertextuality, but effectively restate the significance of Shakespeare to literature in English, regardless of locale. I am clearly firm in the belief that Shakespeare is a significant literary figure, though my aim is not to underscore that, especially in the midst of a febrile literary-critical debate about the importance – in which I firmly believe – of re-evaluating who and what constitutes the canon. Nevertheless, I have shown Shakespeare and his contemporaries to be significant to Irish writing, because these (white, mostly male) Irish writers also viewed Shakespeare and his contemporaries as significant figures in English letters. However, the way in which they have engaged has varied: Anglo-Irish Yeats knowingly venerated Shakespeare's drama; global Heaney dared to talk with Shakespeare; Beckett suppressed and diffused the significance of Shakespeare; to O'Brien, Shakespeare is a constant companion, and mainstay of her literary, if not political, hinterland. Taken together, the *different* ways in which these writers have intertextually remembered Shakespeare also constitute a sense of a heterogeneous *dis*memory. One of my conclusions is that Shakespeare may be a privileged example of how intertextuality goes beyond mere quotation, with or without marks of acknowledgement. Perhaps, that is, only intertextual memories of Shakespeare make dismemory possible: perhaps only through remembering Shakespeare can these Irish writers shape their nation.

Sean O'Casey was another dramatist whose explicit focus was the modern Irish nation and its birth pangs. In *The Plough and the Stars* (1926), a play set in the run-up to and during the 1916 Easter Rising, Rosie is talkatively trying to sell her wares to the drinkers in the pub. When the Barman dismissively replies to Rosie, 'I disremember', he accepts Rosie's premise that there is *something* to remember, but rejects defining exactly what that is. It is a cloaking device that the Barman uses so as not to commit to Rosie's ruse of talking up to the punters in a bid to make a sale of her body for the next half-hour or so (The Covey, in this regard, being an unlucky choice on her part). To disremember is to acknowledge that acts of memory are taking place and are being recorded, but refuses to specify and locate the memories of recall, nor how the memories are being reframed in the now. Critically, to disremember is not 'to misremember', and is certainly not 'to forget'; it is also more than 'pretending to forget', as Beiner framed it. Dismemory is using the pretence to forget – a privileged literary memorial form called intertextuality – as a way of disrupting political hegemony in an attempt to shape the future.

And so, as we approach the end of the decade of centenaries, this especially privileged moment of commemoration with its intense pressure on processes and acts of memory, there remains a task for literary critics: to find those moments of disremembering when texts recall others, are enhanced in remembering them, and when they use these memories to launch free of either Malvolio's 'whirligig of time' (V.i.370) or Yeats's ever 'widening gyre' (1997b: l. 1). In this, the way that Shakespeare is remembered in modern and contemporary Irish literature is paradigmatic of a truer epistemology of literary memory, of intertextuality.

Note

1 It is also coincidental that the summer of 2016 witnessed the largest sundering of Britain from Ireland since the Anglo-Irish war: the Brexit referendum. This, too, was driven by dismemories that constructed an imagined utopia called 'Britain'; Shakespeare, too, was brought in to serve the agenda (see, for example, Stephen O'Neill (2019)). Whilst I have not fully considered this dimension of the Shakespeare–Ireland connection, the time is ripe for a study of Brexit-era Ireland and the new meaning of Shakespeare in this context.

References

Note: Works by the same author are listed chronologically, except works of Shakespeare, which are listed by title.

'Bunreacht na hÉireann (Constutition of Ireland)' (n.d.), www. irishstatutebook.ie/eli/cons/en/html [accessed 20 April 2021]

Adams, R. M. (1974), 'Hades', in *James Joyce's 'Ulysses': Critical Essays*, ed. by C. Hart and D. Hayman (Berkeley, CA: University of California Press), pp. 91–114

Agamben, G. (1998), *Homo Sacer: Sovereign Power and Bare Life* (Stanford, CA: Stanford University Press)

—— (2002 [1999]), *Remnants of Auschwitz: The Witness and the Archive* (New York, NY: Zone Books)

—— (2015 [2014]), *The Use of Bodies*, trans. by A. Kotsko, vol. IV, 2 (Stanford, CA: Stanford University Press)

Allison, J. (1997), 'W. B. Yeats and Shakespearean Character', in *Shakespeare and Ireland: History, Politics, Culture*, ed. by M. Thornton Burnett and R. Wray (Houndmills: Macmillan), pp. 114–35

Anderson, B. (2006 [1983]), *Imagined Communities: Reflections on the Origin and Spread of Nationalism*, revised edn (London: Virago)

Anon. (2000), 'Oblique Dreamer: Interview with John Banville', *Observer*, 17 September https://theguardian.com/books/2000/sep/17/fiction.john banville [accessed 25 September 2015]

—— (30 October 2015), 'Shakespeare Lives in 2016', www.culturenort hernireland.org/features/drama/shakespeare-lives-2016 [accessed 10 October 2018]

Arendt, H. (1998 [1958]), *The Human Condition* (Chicago, IL: Chicago University Press)

Aristotle (2011 [?340 BCE]), *Aristotle's Nichomachean Ethics*, trans. by R. C. Bartlett and S. D. Collins (Chicago, IL: Chicago University Press)

Assmann, J. (1997), *Moses the Egyptian: The Memory of Egypt in Western Monotheism* (Cambridge, MA: Harvard University Press)

Augusteijn, J. (2010), *Patrick Pearse: The Making of a Revolutionary* (Basingstoke: Palgrave Macmillan)

Balme, C. B. (2014), *The Theatrical Public Sphere* (Cambridge: Cambridge University Press), doi: 10.1017/CBO9781139051668

Banville, J. (1998a [1989]), *The Book of Evidence* (London: Picador)

—— (1998b [1993]), *Ghosts* (Basingstoke: Picador)

—— (2000), 'Oblique Dreamer', *Observer*, 17 September www.theguardian.com/books/2000/sep/17/fiction.johnbanville [accessed 3 October 2020]

—— (2006 [2005]), *The Sea* (London: Picador)

—— (2016), *Time Pieces: A Dublin Memoir* (Dublin: Hachette Books Ireland)

Barish, J. (1985 [1981]), *The Antitheatrical Prejudice* (Berkeley, CA: University of California Press)

Barthes, R. (1977), *Image Music Text*, trans. by S. Heath (London: Fontana)

—— (2000 [1980]), *Camera Lucida*, trans. by R. Howard (London: Vintage)

Beckett, S. (2006), *The Complete Dramatic Works* (London: Faber & Faber)

—— (2009 [1951–3]), *Three Novels: Molloy, Malone Dies, The Unnamable* (New York, NY: Grove Press)

Beiner, G. (2018), Forgetful Remembrance: Social Forgetting and Vernacular Historiography of a Rebellion in Ulster (Oxford: Oxford University Press)

Benjamin, W. (1999), *Illuminations*, trans. by H. Zorn, ed. by H. Arendt (London: Pimlico)

Benstock, S. (1975), 'Ulysses as Ghoststory', *James Joyce Quarterly*, 12.4, 396–413

Beplate, J. (2014), 'Weaving the Wind: Joyce's Uses and Abuses of Memory', *James Joyce and Cultural Memory*, ed. by O. Frawley and K. O'Callaghan, 4 vols, vol. 3, *Memory Ireland* (New York, NY: Syracuse University Press), pp. 157–71

Bergson, H. (1991 [1910]), *Matter and Memory* (New York, NY: Zone Books)

Blanchot, M. (1968 [1955]), *L'éspace Littéraire* (Paris: Éditions Gallimard)

Boland, E. (2016), *A Poet's Dublin*, ed. by P. Meehan and J. Allen Randolph (New York, NY: W.W. Norton)

Boose, L. E. (1975), 'Othello's Handkerchief: "The Recognizance and Pledge of Love"', *English Literary Renaissance*, 5.3, 360–74

Braidotti, R. (1994), *Nomadic Subjects: Embodiment and Sexual Difference in Contemporary Feminist Theory* (New York, NY: Columbia University Press)

—— (2011), *Nomadic Theory: The Portable Rosi Braidotti* (New York, NY: Columbia University Press)

Brown, M. P. (1981), 'Seamus Heaney and *North*', *Studies: An Irish Quarterly Review*, 70.280, 289–98

Buse, P., and A. Stott (1999), 'Introduction: a Future for Haunting', in *Ghosts: Deconstruction, Psychoanalysis, History*, ed. by P. Buse and A. Stott (Basingstoke: Macmillan), pp. 1–20

Butler, C., and W. Maley (2013), '"Bringing rebellion broachèd on his sword": Essex and Ireland', in *Essex: The Cultural Impact of an Elizabethan Courtier*, ed. by A. Connolly and L. Hopkins (Manchester: Manchester University Press), pp. 133–52

Butler, J. (2011 [1993]), *Bodies That Matter: On the Discursive Limits of 'Sex'* (London: Routledge)

Carson, C. (1989), *Belfast Confetti* (Winston-Salem, NC: Wake Forest University Press)

Cheng, V. J. (2014), 'Amnesia, Forgetting, and the Nation in James Joyce's *Ulysses*', in *James Joyce and Cultural Memory*, ed. by O. Frawley and K. O'Callaghan, 4 vols, vol. 3, *Memory Ireland* (New York, NY: Syracuse University Press), pp. 10–26

—— (2018), *Amnesia and the Nation: History, Forgetting, and James Joyce* (Basingstoke: Palgrave Macmillan), doi: 10.1007/978 -3-319-71818-7

Cicero (2001 [55 BCE]), *On the Ideal Orator (De Oratore)*, trans. by J. M. May and J. Wisse (New York, NY: Oxford University Press)

Collins, C., and M. P. Caulfield (2014), *Introduction: The Rest Is History* (Basingstoke: Palgrave Macmillan)

Collins, N. (2015), '"This Prison Where I Live": Ireland Takes Centre Stage', *Cahiers Elisabéthains*, 88.1, 125–38, doi: 10.7227/CE.88.1.9

Connor, S. (2009), 'Beckett and Sartre: The Nauseous Character of All Flesh', in *Beckett and Phenomenology*, ed. by U. Maude and M. Feldman (London: Continuum), pp. 56–76

Cooper, D. E. (1974), 'Memories, Bodies and Persons', *Philosophy*, 49.189, 255–63

Costello, E. (2015), 'Post-Medieval Upland Settlement and the Decline of Transhumance: A Case-Study from the Galtee Mountains, Ireland', *Landscape History*, 36.1, 47–69, doi: 10.1080/01433768.2015.1044283

Crawford, N. (2008), 'Synge's *Playboy* and the Eugenics of Language', *Modern Drama*, 51.4, 482–500, doi: 10.1353/mrd.0.0075

Crispi, L. (2012), 'The Genesis of Leopold Bloom: Writing the Lives of Rudolph Virag and Ellen Higgins in "Ulysses"', *Journal of Modern Literature*, 35.4, 13–31

Crotty, P. (1992), 'Fathers and Sons', *New Welsh Review*, 17, 12–23

D'Hoker, E. (2018), 'Performing Prospero: Intertextual Strategies in John Banville's *Ghosts*', in *Shakespeare and Contemporary Irish Literature*, ed. by N. Taylor-Collins and S. van der Ziel (Basingstoke: Palgrave Macmillan), pp. 223–42, doi: 10.1007/978-3-319-95924-5_10

Darlington, J. (1913), 'Mr Trench on Hamlet', *Studies: An Irish Quarterly Review*, 2.8, 476–84

Davies, J. (1596), *Orchestra or A Poeme of Dauncing Judicially Proouing the True Obseruation of Time and Measure, in the Authenticall and Laudable Vse of Dauncing*, 2nd edn (London: I. Robarts)

Davison, N. R. (1996), *James Joyce, 'Ulysses', and the Construction of Jewish Identity: Culture, Biography, and 'the Jew' in Modernist Europe* (Cambridge: Cambridge University Press)

Delaney, P. (2001), 'Representations of the Travellers in the 1880s and 1900s', *Irish Studies Review*, 9.1, 53–68

Deleuze, G. (1993 [1988]), *Fold: Leibniz and the Baroque*, trans. by T. Conley (London: The Athlone Press)

Deleuze, G., and F. Guattari (2005 [1980]), *A Thousand Plateaus: Capitalism and Schizophrenia*, trans. by B. Massumi (London: Continuum)

Derrida, J. (1984 [1976]), *Signéponge=Signsponge*, trans. by R. Rand (New York, NY: Columbia University Press)

——— (1987), *The Truth in Painting*, trans. by G. Bennington and I. McLeod (Chicago, IL: The University of Chicago Press)

——— (1994 [1993]), *Specters of Marx: The State of the Debt, the Work of Mourning, and the New International*, trans. by P. Camuf (New York, NY: Routledge)

——— (1995a), 'Archive Fever: A Freudian Impression', *Diacritics*, 25.2, 9–63

——— (1995b [1993]), *On the Name*, trans. by D. Wood, J. P. Leavey, Jr, and I. McLeod (Stanford, CA: Stanford University Press)

——— (2000), *Demeure: Fiction and Testimony*, trans. by E. Rottenberg (Stanford, CA: Stanford University Press)

——— (2002), *Acts of Religion*, trans. and ed. by G. Anidjar (New York, NY: Routledge)

Dobbins, G. (2009), 'Synge and Irish Modernism', in *The Cambridge Companion to J. M. Synge*, ed. by J. P. Mathews (Cambridge: Cambridge University Press), pp. 132–45

Docherty, T. (1990), *After Theory: Postmodernism/Post Marxism* (London: Routledge)

——— (2013 [2012]), *Confessions: The Philosophy of Transparency* (London: Bloomsbury)

Doggett, R. (2013), 'Shakespeare and Transnational Heritage in Dowden and Yeats', in *Celtic Shakespeare: The Bard and the Borderers*, ed. by W. Maley and R. Loughnane (Farnham: Ashgate), pp. 217–29

Donne, J. (1991), *The Complete English Poems of John Donne* (London: Everyman's Library, 1991)

Dowd, G. (2007), *Abstract Machines: Samuel Beckett and Philosophy after Deleuze and Guattari* (Amsterdam: Rodopi)

Dunne, D. (2016), *Shakespeare, Revenge Tragedy and Early Modern Law: Vindictive Justice* (Basingstoke: Palgrave Macmillan)

Eagleton, T. (1995), *Heathcliff and the Great Hunger: Studies in Irish Culture* (London: Verso)

Eckley, G. (1974), *Edna O'Brien* (Lewisburg, PA: Bucknell University Press)

Edelman, L. (2004), *No Future: Queer Theory and the Death Drive* (Durham, NC: Duke University Press)

Edwards, P. (1979), *Threshold of a Nation: A Study in English and Irish Drama* (Cambridge: Cambridge University Press)

Elden, S. (2013), *The Birth of Territory* (Chicago, IL: The University of Chicago Press)

Eliot, T. S. (1950 [1920]), *The Sacred Wood: Essays on Poetry and Criticism*, 7th edn (London: Methuen)

——— (2015), *The Poems of T. S. Eliot*, ed. by C. Ricks and J. McCue, 2 vols, vol. 1 (London: Faber & Faber)

Ellmann, M. (2004), 'The Ghosts of *Ulysses*', in *James Joyce's 'Ulysses': A Casebook*, ed. by D. Attridge (Oxford: Oxford University Press), pp. 83–101

Ellmann, R. (1968 [1954]), *The Identity of Yeats*, 2nd edn (London: Faber)

——— (1969 [1949]), *Yeats: The Man and the Masks* (London: Faber)

Ferriter, D. (2015), *A Nation and Not a Rabble: The Irish Revolution 1913–1923* (London: Profile Books)

Foster, R. F. (1989), *Modern Ireland: 1600–1972* (London: Penguin)

——— (2015 [2014]), *Vivid Faces: The Revolutionary Generation in Ireland 1890–1923* (London: Penguin)

Foucault, M. (1980), *Language, Counter-Memory, Practice: Selected Essays and Interviews*, trans. by D. F. Bouchard and S. Simon, ed. by D. F. Bouchard (Ithaca, NY: Cornell University Press)

——— (1990 [1976]), *The History of Sexuality: Volume One, An Introduction*, trans. by R. Hurley (London: Penguin)

——— (2002), *The Archaeology of Knowledge*, trans. by A. M. Sheridan (London: Routledge)

Frawley, O. (2011), 'Introduction', in *History and Modernity*, ed. by O. Frawley, 4 vols, vol. 1, *Memory Ireland* (New York, NY: Syracuse University Press), pp. xiii–xxiv

Frazier, A. (1987), 'The Making of Meaning: Yeats and *The Countess Cathleen*', *The Sewanee Review*, 95.3, 451–69

Freeman, J. (2015), *Remaking Memory: Autoethnography, the Memoir and Ethics of the Self* (Faringdon: Libri)

Freud, S. (2001a), 'A Note Upon the "Mystic Writing-Pad"', in *The Ego and the Id and Other Works*, trans. by J. Strachey, 24 vols, vol. 19, *The Standard Edition of the Complete Psychological Works of Sigmund Freud* (London: Vintage), pp. 225–32

—— (2001b), 'On the History of the Post Psychoanalytic Movement', '*Papers on Metapsychology*' and *Other Works*, trans. by J. Strachey, in *The Standard Edition of the Complete Psychological Works of Sigmund Freud*, ed. by J. Strachey, 24 vols, vol. 14 (London: Vintage)

Friberg, H. (2007), 'Waters and Memories Always Divide: Sites of Memory in John Banville's *The Sea*', in *Recovering Memory: Irish Representations of Past and Present*, ed. by H. Friberg, I. G. Nordin, and L. Y. Pedesen (Newcastle: Cambridge Scholars Publishing), pp. 244–62

Friberg-Harnesk, H. (2018), *Reading John Banville Through Jean Baudrillard* (Amherst, NY: Cambria Press)

Friel, B. (2000 [1981]), *Translations* (London: Faber & Faber)

Frow, J. (1997), 'Toute la mémoire du monde: Repetition and Forgetting', in *Time and Commodity Culture: Essays in Cultural Theory and Postmodernity* (Oxford: Clarendon Press), pp. 218–46

Fukuyama, F. (1992), *The End of History and the Last Man* (New York, NY: Macmillan)

Garber, M. (2010), *Shakespeare's Ghost Writers* (New York, NY: Routledge)

Garrison, A. E. (2009), '"Faintly Struggling Things": Trauma, Testimony, and Inscrutable Life in Beckett's *The Unnamable*', in *Samuel Beckett: History, Memory, Archive*, ed. by S. Kennedy and K. Weiss (New York, NY: Palgrave Macmillan), pp. 89–109

Gibbons, L. (2014), '"Old Haunts": Joyce, the Republic, and Photographic Memory', in *James Joyce and Cultural Memory*, ed. by O. Frawley and K. O'Callaghan, 4 vols, vol. 3, *Memory Ireland* (New York, NY: Syracuse University Press), pp. 187–201

—— (2015), *Joyce's Ghosts: Ireland, Modernism, and Memory* (Chicago, IL: The University of Chicago Press)

—— (2016), 'Time Transfixed: Photography, Ruins, and the Easter Rising' (Highlanes Gallery and Drogheda Arts Festival)

Gibson, A. (2010), *Samuel Beckett* (London: Reaktion Books)

Godwin, J. (1979), *Robert Fludd: Hermetic Philosopher and Surveyor of Two Worlds* (London: Thames and Hudson)

de Grazia, M. (2007), '*Hamlet*' *Without Hamlet* (Cambridge: Cambridge University Press)

Greenblatt, S. (1984 [1980]), *Renaissance Self-Fashioning: From More to Shakespeare* (Chicago, IL: Chicago University Press)

—— (2013 [2001]), *Hamlet in Purgatory* (Princeton, NJ: Princeton University Press)

Greenwood, A. (2003), *Edna O'Brien* (Horndon, Tavistock: Northcote House Publishers)

Grene, N. (1971), *The Synge Manuscripts in the Library of Trinity College, Dublin* (Dublin: The Dolmen Press)

Hadfield, A. (1997), *Edmund Spenser's Irish Experience: Wilde Fruit and Salvage Soyl* (Oxford: Clarendon Press), doi: 10.1093/acprof:oso/9 780198183457.001.0001

Halbwachs, M. (1980 [1950]), *The Collective Memory*, trans. by F. J. Ditter and V. Y. Ditter (New York, NY: Harper Colophon Books)

—— (1992), *On Collective Memory*, trans. and ed. by L. A. Coser (Chicago, IL: The University of Chicago Press)

Harney-Mahajan, T. (2015), 'Refashioning the Wedding Dress as the "Future Anterior" in Marina Carr and Edna O'Brien', *Women's Studies*, 44.7, 996–1021, doi: 10.1080/00497878.2015.1071617

Hartman, G. H. (1961), 'Maurice Blanchot: Philosopher-Novelist', *Chicago Review*, 15.2, 1–18

Heaney, S. (1984 [1980]), *Preoccupations: Selected Prose 1968–1978* (London: Faber & Faber)

—— (1990), *The Cure at Troy* (London: Faber & Faber)

—— (1993 [1972]), *Wintering Out* (London: Faber & Faber)

—— (1998), *Opened Ground: Poems 1966–1996* (London: Faber & Faber)

—— (2001), *Electric Light* (London: Faber & Faber)

—— (2003 [2002]), *Finders Keepers: Selected Prose, 1971–2001* (London: Faber & Faber)

—— (2006a [1966]), *Death of a Naturalist* (London: Faber & Faber)

—— (2006b), *District and Circle* (London: Faber & Faber)

—— (2010), *Human Chain* (London: Faber & Faber)

Heidegger, M. (2008 [1927]), *Being and Time*, trans. by J. Macquarrie and E. Robinson (New York, NY: Harper Perennial)

Helgerson, R. (1992), *Forms of Nationhood: The Elizabethan Writing of England* (Chicago, IL: University of Chicago Press)

Her Majesty's Stationery Office (1899), Calendar of the State Papers Relating to Ireland, of the reigns of Henry VIII., Edward VI., Mary, and Elizabeth, 1509–[1603], ed. by E. G. Atkinson, vol. 8 (London)

Herren, G. (2012), 'Mourning Becomes Electric: Mediating Loss in *Eh Joe*', *Samuel Beckett and Pain*, ed. by M. H. Tanaka, Y. Tajiri, and M. Tsushima (Amsterdam: Rodopi), pp. 43–65

Hewitt, S. (2021), *J.M. Synge: Nature, Politics, Modernism* (Oxford: Oxford University Press)

Hezser, C. (2005), '"Are You Protestant Jews or Roman Catholic Jews?" Literary Representations of Being Jewish in Ireland', *Modern Judaism*, 25.2, 159–88

Hillan, S. (2005), 'Wintered into Wisdom: Michael McLaverty, Seamus Heaney, and the Northern Word-Hoard', *New Hibernia Review*, 9.3, 86–106

Hirsch, M. (1997), *Family Frames: Photography, Narrative, and Postmemory* (Cambridge, MA: Harvard University Press)

Homem, R. C. (2018), '"Memory Like Mitigation": Heaney, Shakespeare and Ireland', in *Shakespeare and Contemporary Irish Literature*, ed. by N. Taylor-Collins and S. van der Ziel (Basingstoke: Palgrave Macmillan), pp. 27–48

Hutson, L. (2008), *The Invention of Suspicion: Law and Mimesis in Shakespeare and Renaissance Drama* (Oxford: Oxford University Press)

Ingelbien, R. (1999), 'Mapping the Misreadings: Ted Hughes, Seamus Heaney, and Nationhood', *Contemporary Literature*, 40.4, 627–58

James, H. (2008), *The Turn of the Screw and Other Stories* (Oxford: Oxford University Press)

Johnstone, N. (2006), *The Devil and Demonism in Early Modern England* (Cambridge: Cambridge University Press)

Jones, D. H. (2012), 'Strange Pain: Archive, Trauma and Testimony in Samuel Beckett and Christian Boltanski', in *Samuel Beckett and Pain*, ed. by M. H. Tanaka, Y. Tajiri, and M. Tsushima (Amsterdam: Rodopi), pp. 135–50

Jones, E. C. (2010), 'History's Ghosts: Joyce and the Politics of Public Memory', *Journal of Irish Studies*, 25, 3–17

—— (2014), 'Ghosts through Absence', in *James Joyce and Cultural Memory*, ed. by O. Frawley and K. O'Callaghan, 4 vols, vol. 3, *Memory Ireland* (New York, NY: Syracuse University Press), pp. 125–44

Jonson, B. (1966 [1607]), 'Volpone, or the Fox', in *Three Comedies: 'Volpone', 'The Alchemist', 'Bartholomew Fair'*, trans. by M. Jamieson (Harmondsworth, Middlesex: Penguin), pp. 34–171

—— (1970), *Ben Jonson: Selected Masques*, ed. by S. Orgel (New Haven, CT: Yale University Press)

Joyce, J. (1986 [1922]), *Ulysses*, ed. by H. W. Gabler (London: The Bodley Head)

—— (1998 [1922]), *Ulysses*, ed. by J. Johnson, *Oxford World's Classics* (Oxford: Oxford University Press)

—— (2008a [1914]), *Dubliners* (Oxford: Oxford World's Classics)

—— (2008b [1916]), *A Portrait of the Artist as a Young Man* (Oxford: Oxford World's Classics)

Kantorowicz, E. H. (1957), *The King's Two Bodies: A Study in Mediaeval Political Theology* (Princeton, NJ: Princeton University Press)

Kavanagh, P. (1977), *Collected Poems* (London: Martin Brian & O'Keefe)

Kennedy, S. (2009), 'Does Beckett Studies Require a Subject? Mourning Ireland in the *Texts for Nothing*', in *Samuel Beckett: History, Memory,*

Archive, ed. by S. Kennedy and K. Weiss (New York, NY: Palgrave Macmillan), pp. 11–29

——, ed. (2010), *Beckett and Ireland* (Oxford: Oxford University Press)

Kennedy, S., and K. Weiss, eds (2009), *Samuel Beckett: History, Memory, Archive* (New York, NY: Palgrave Macmillan)

Kenner, H. (1952), 'Joyce's *Ulysses*: Homer and Hamlet', *Essays in Criticism*, 2.1, 85–104, doi: 10.1093/eic/II.1.85

Kersnowski, A. H., ed., (2018), *Conversations with Edna O'Brien* (Jackson, MS: University Press of Mississippi)

Kiberd, D. (1996 [1995]), *Inventing Ireland: The Literature of the Modern Nation* (London: Vintage)

—— (2009), *Ulysses and Us* (London: Faber & Faber)

—— (2017), *After Ireland: Writing the Nation from Beckett to the Present* (London: Head of Zeus)

Kierkegaard, S. (2000), *The Essential Kierkegaard*, trans. and ed. by H. V. Hong and E. H. Hong (Princeton, NJ: Princeton University Press)

Kilroy, J. F. (1971), *The 'Playboy' Riots* (Dublin: Dolmen Press)

Kinahan, F. (1988), *Yeats, Folklore, and Occultism: Contexts of the Early Work and Thought* (Boston, MA: Unwin Hyman)

Knecht, R. (2015), '"Shapes of Grief": Hamlet's Grammar School Passions', *English Literary History*, 82.1, 35–58

Kott, J. (1964 [1961]), *Shakespeare Our Contemporary*, trans. by B. Taborski (New York, NY: Doubleday)

Kristeva, J. (1986), *The Kristeva Reader*, ed. by T. Moi (New York, NY: Columbia University Press)

Lachmann, R. (2008), 'Mnemonic and Intertextual Aspects of Literature', in *Cultural Memory Studies: An International and Interdisciplinary Handbook*, ed. by A. Erll and A. Nünning (Berlin: Walter de Gruyter), pp. 301–10

Laqueur, T. W. (1992), *Making Sex: Body and Gender from the Greeks to Freud* (Cambridge, MA: Harvard University Press)

—— (2015), *The Work of the Dead: A Cultural History of Mortal Remains* (Princeton, NJ: Princeton University Press)

Lawrence, W. J. (1916), 'Dublin and the Sinn Féin Rising' (Dublin), doi: drs1.ivrla_30574

Leerssen, J. (2001), 'Monument and Trauma: Varieties of Remembrance', *History and Memory in Modern Ireland*, ed. by I. McBride (Cambridge: Cambridge University Press), pp. 204–22

Leggatt, A. (1969), 'The Suicide of Volpone', *UTQ*, 39.1, 19–32

Lehnhof, K. R. (2000), '"Rather Say I Play the Man I Am'" Shakespeare's *Coriolanus* and Elizabethan Anti-Theatricality', *Shakespeare and Renaissance Association Selected Papers*, 23, 34–41

──── (2013), 'Acting, Integrity, and Gender in Coriolanus', *Shakespeare Bulletin*, 31.3, 353–73, doi: 10.1353/shb.2013.0055

Lesser, Z. (2015), *'Hamlet' after Q1: An Uncanny History of the Shakespearean Text* (Philadelphia, PA: University of Pennsylvania Press)

Levinas, E. (2006 [1991]), *Entre Nous: On Thinking-of-the-Other*, trans. by M. B. Smith and B. Harshav (London: Continuum)

Lloyd, D. (2010), 'Frames of *Referrance*: Samuel Beckett as an Irish Question', in *Beckett and Ireland*, ed. by S. Kennedy (Oxford: Oxford University Press), pp. 31–55

Longley, E. (2001), 'Northern Ireland: Commemoration, Elegy, Forgetting', in *History and Memory in Modern Ireland*, ed. by I. McBride (Cambridge: Cambridge University Press), pp. 223–53

──── (2013), *Yeats and Modern Poetry* (New York, NY: Cambridge University Press)

Mann, N. (2012), '"Everywhere That Antinomy of the One and the Many": The Foundations of *A Vision*', in *W. B. Yeats' 'A Vision': Explications and Contexts*, ed. by N. Mann, M. Gibson, and C. V. Nally (Clemson, SC: Clemson University Digital Press), pp. 1–21

Maples, H. (2011), 'Producing Memory: A History of Commemoration and the Abbey Theatre', in *History and Modernity*, ed. by O. Frawley, 4 vols, vol. 1, *Memory Ireland* (New York, NY: Syracuse University Press), pp. 172–83

Marshall, D. G. (1985), 'The Necessity of Writing Death and Imagination in Maurice Blanchot's L'Espace Littéraire', *boundary 2*, 14.1/2, 225–36

Martin, F. X. (1967), '1916: Myth, Fact, and Mystery', *Studia Hibernica*, 7, 7–126

Martin, M. W. (2016), *Memoir Ethics: Good Lives and the Virtues* (Lanham, MD: Lexington Books)

McBride, I. (2001), 'Introduction: Memory and National Identity in Modern Ireland', in *History and Memory in Modern Ireland*, ed. by I. McBride (Cambridge: Cambridge University Press), pp. 1–42

McCabe, R. A. (2002), *Spenser's Monstrous Regiment: Elizabethan Ireland and the Poetics of Difference* (Oxford: Oxford University Press)

McCarthy, B. (2011), 'W.B. Yeats, John Ruskin and the "Lidless Eye"', *Irish University Review*, 41.2, 25–41

McFeaters, A. V. (2010), 'How the Irish Ended History: Postmodern Writings of James Joyce, Flann O'Brien, and Samuel Beckett' (unpublished doctoral dissertation, Florida State University)

McGahern, J. (2008 [1990]), *Amongst Women* (London: Faber & Faber)

McMinn, J. (1988), 'An Exalted Naming: The Poetical Fictions of John Banville', *The Canadian Journal of Irish Studies*, 14.1, 17–27

McNaughton, J. (2010), 'The Politics of Aftermath: Beckett, Modernism, and the Irish Free State', in *Beckett and Ireland*, ed. by S. Kennedy (Oxford: Oxford University Press), pp. 56–77

McWilliams, E. (2013), *Women and Exile in Contemporary Irish Fiction* (Basingstoke: Palgrave Macmillan)

Merleau-Ponty, M. (1988), *In Praise of Philosophy and Other Essays*, trans. by J. Wild and J. E. John (Evanston, IL: Northwestern University Press)

—— (2008 [1948]), *The World of Perception*, trans. by O. Davis (London: Routledge Classics)

Mooney, S. (2006), '"Sacramental Sleeves": Fashioning the Female Subject in the Fiction of Edna O'Brien', in *Edna O'Brien: New Critical Perspectives*, ed. by K. Laing, S. Mooney, and M. O'Connor (Dublin: Carysfort Press), pp. 196–218

Morash, C. (1995), *Writing the Irish Famine* (Oxford: Oxford University Press)

Murphy, A. (2015), 'Shakespeare's Rising: Ireland and the 1916 Tercentenary', in *Celebrating Shakespeare*, ed. by C. Calvo and K. Coppélia (Cambridge: Cambridge University Press), pp. 161–81, doi: 10.1017/CBO9781107337466.009

Murphy, N. (2020), 'The Poetics of Pure Invention: John Banville's *Ghosts*', ed. by L. P. Zuntini de Izarra, H. Schwall, and N. Taylor-Collins, *Word upon World: Half a Century of John Banville's Universes (= Brazilian Journal of Irish Studies (ABEI)*, 22.1, 109–20, doi: 10.37389/abei.v22i1.3851

Murray, C. (1997), *Twentieth-Century Irish Drama: Mirror up to Nation* (Manchester: Manchester University Press)

National Theatre (2016), *Sean O'Casey's 'The Plough and the Stars'*, ed. by J. Herrin and H. Davies (London: Sean O'Casey)

Neville, G. (2012), 'Remembering and Forgetting the Great Famine in France and Ireland', *New Hibernia Review*, 16.4, 80–94

Noble, L. (2004), 'The *Fille Vièrge* as Pharmakon: The Therapeutic Value of Desdemona's Corpse', in *Disease, Diagnosis, and Cure on the Early Modern Stage*, ed. by S. Moss and K. L. Peterson (London: Routledge), pp. 135–50

Nora, P. (1996 [1992]), 'Between Memory and History', in *Realms of Memory: Rethinking the French Past*, trans. by A. Goldhammer, 3 vols, vol. 1 (New York, NY: Columbia University Press), pp. 1–21

Nunes, C. (2007), 'Return to the Lonely Self: Autonomy, Desire and the Evolution of Identity in *The Country Girls Trilogy*', *Canadian Journal of Irish Studies*, 33.2, 39–47

Ó Ciosáin, N. (2001), 'Famine Memory and the Popular Representation of Scarcity', in *History and Memory in Modern Ireland*, ed. by I. McBride (Cambridge: Cambridge University Press), pp. 95–117

O'Brien, (1963), 'The Wedding Dress', *John McGrath Collection*, British Film Institute, London, ITM-17689, Box 8, Item 1

—— (1978 [1976]), *Mother Ireland* (Middlesex, England: Penguin)

—— (1986), *The Beckett Country: Samuel Beckett's Ireland* (Monkstown: Black Cat)

—— (1987 [1960–86]), *The Country Girls Trilogy and Epilogue* (London: Jonathan Cape)

—— (2001 [1972]), *Night* (Boston, MA: Mariner)

—— (2006), *The Light of Evening* (Boston, MA: Houghton Mifflin)

—— (2010), *Haunted* (London: Faber & Faber)

—— (2013 [2012]), *Country Girl: A Memoir* (London: Faber & Faber)

O'Casey, S. (1998), *Plays Two* (London: Faber & Faber)

O'Connell, M. (2011), 'On Not Being Found: A Winnicottian Reading of John Banville's *Ghosts* and *Athena*', *Studies in the Novel*, 43.3, 328–42

—— (2013), *John Banville's Narcissistic Fictions* (Basingstoke: Palgrave Macmillan)

O'Connor, B. (2013), *The Irish Dancing: Cultural Politics and Identities, 1900–2000* (Cork: Cork University Press)

O'Hagan, A. (2014), 'Edna O'Brien's *Night* Is All Passion, All Mind', *Guardian*, 22 August www.theguardian.com/books/2014/aug/22/edna -obrien-night-all-passion-all-mind [accessed 10 August 2020]

O'Neill, S. (2018), 'Beyond Shakespeare's Land of Ire: Revisiting Ireland in English Renaissance Drama', *Literature Compass*, 15.10, n.p., doi: 10.1111/lic3.12491

—— (2019), 'Finding Refuge in *King Lear*: From Brexit to Shakespeare's European Value', *Multicultural Shakespeare: Translation, Appropriation and Performance*, 19.1, 119–38

O'Riordan, T. (2001), 'The Introduction of the Potato into Ireland', *History Ireland*, 9.1, 27–31

O'Toole, F. (2013), 'Art Is the Way to the Heart When Commemorating a Centenary', *The Irish Times*, 27 July www.irishtimes.com/culture/art -is-the-way-to-the-heart-when-commemorating-a-centenary-1.1476289 [accessed 19 July 2016]

Ong, W. (1958), *Ramus, Method, and the Decay of Dialogue: From the Art of Discourse to the Art of Reason* (Cambridge, MA: Harvard University Press)

Ormsby, R. (2008), '*Coriolanus*, Antitheatricalism, and Audience Response', *Shakespeare Bulletin*, 26.1, 43–62, doi: 10.1353/shb.2008.0035

Orr, A. D. (2003), 'From a *View* to a *Discovery*: Edmund Spenser, Sir John Davies, and the Defects of Law in the Realm of Ireland', *Canadian Journal of History*, 38.3, 395–408, doi: 10.3138/cjh.38.3.409

Paster, G. K. (1993), *The Body Embarrassed: Drama and the Disciplines of Shame in Early Modern England* (Ithaca, NY: Cornell University Press)

Pawlisch, H. S. (1985), *Sir John Davies and the Conquest of Ireland: A Study in Legal Imperialism* (Cambridge: Cambridge University Press)

Pearse, P. (1980), *A Significant Irish Educationalist: The Educational Writings of P. H. Pearse*, ed. by S. Ó Buachalla (Dublin: The Mercier Press)

Pedretti, M. (2013), 'Late Modern Rigmarole: Boredom as Form in Samuel Beckett's *Trilogy*', *Samuel Beckett Today / Aujourd'hui*, 45.4, 583–602

Pelan, R. (1996), 'Edna O'Brien's "World of Nora Barnacle"', *Canadian Journal of Irish Studies*, 22.2, 49–61

Peterson, K. L. (2010), Popular Medicine, Hysterical Disease, and Social Controversy in Shakespeare's England (Farnham: Ashgate)

Peterson, S. (2006), '"Meaniacs" and Martyrs: Sadomasochistic Desire in Edna O'Brien's *The Country Girls Trilogy*', in *Edna O'Brien: New Critical Perspectives*, ed. by K. Laing, S. Mooney, and M. O'Connor (Dublin: Carysfort Press), pp. 151–70

Pine, E. (2011), *The Politics of Irish Memory: Performing Remembrance in Contemporary Irish Culture* (Basingstoke: Palgrave Macmillan)

Plato (1978), 'Symposium', in *The Portable Plato*, trans. by B. Jowett, ed. by S. Buchanan (Harmondsworth, Middlesex: Penguin), pp. 121–87

—— (2013 [1929]), *'Timaeus' and 'Critias'*, trans. by A. E. Taylor, *Routledge Library Editions: Plato* (London: Routledge)

—— (2015), *'Theaetetus' and 'Sophist'*, trans. and ed. by C. Rowe (Cambridge: Cambridge University Press), doi: 10.1017/CBO9781139047036

Plowden, A. (1980), *Elizabeth Regina: The Age of Triumph, 1588–1603* (London: Macmillan)

Pollard, T., ed., (2004), *Shakespeare's Theater: A Sourcebook* (Malden, MA: Blackwell Publishing)

Putz, A. (2013), *The Celtic Revival in Shakespeare's Wake: Appropriation and Cultural Politics in Ireland, 1867–1922* (Basingstoke: Palgrave Macmillan)

Rainolds, J. (1599), *Th'Overthrow of Stage-Playes, Early English Books Online Text Creation Partnership* (Alberico: D. Gentiles)

Ramus, P. (1966 [1574]), *The Logike*, trans. by R. M'Kilwein (Leeds: The Scolar Press)

Ranelagh, J. O. B. (1983), *A Short History of Ireland* (Cambridge: Cambridge University Press)

Rayner, A. (2006), *Ghosts: Death's Double and the Phenomenon of Theatre* (Minneapolis, MN: University of Minnesota Press)

Renan, E. (1990), 'What Is a Nation?', in *Nation and Narration*, ed. by H. K. Bhabha (London: Routledge), pp. 8–22

Rich, B. (1609), *A Short Survey of Ireland, Truely Discovering Who It Is That Hath So Armed the Hearts of That People, with Disobedience to their Princes. With a Description of the Countrey, and the Condition of the People, etc* (London: Printed by N. O.)

Richards, S. (2009), 'The Playboy of the Western World', in *The Cambridge Companion to J. M. Synge*, ed. by J. P. Mathews (Cambridge: Cambridge University Press), pp. 28–40

Ricoeur, P. (2006 [2000]),*Memory, History, Forgetting*, trans. by K. Blamey and D. Pellauer (Chicago, IL: University of Chicago Press)

Ritschel, N. O. C. (2002), *Synge and Irish Nationalism: The Precursor to Revolution* (Westport, CT: Greenwood Press)

Roche, A. (2015), '"Mirror up to Nation": Synge and Shakespeare', *Irish University Review*, 45.1, 9–24

Royle, N. (2003), *The Uncanny* (New York, NY: Routledge)

Rutter, C. C. (2001), *Enter the Body: Women and Representation on Shakespeare's Stage* (London: Routledge)

Ryan, R. (2012), 'The Is and the Ought, the Knower and the Known: An Analysis of the Four *Faculties* in Yeats's System', in *W. B. Yeats's 'A Vision': Explications and Contexts*, ed. by N. Mann, M. Gibson, and C. V. Nally (Clemson, SC: Clemson University Digital Press), pp. 22–54

Sailer, S. S. (1991), 'Myth in the Poetry of Yeats and Heaney', *Canadian Journal of Irish Studies*, 17.2, 54–63

Sallis, J. (1999), *Chorology: On Beginning in Plato's 'Timaeus'* (Bloomington, IN: Indiana University Press)

Sanders, E. R. (2006), 'The Body of the Actor in Coriolanus', *Shakespeare Quarterly*, 57.4, 387–412, doi: 10.1353/shq.2006.095

Sartre, J.-P. (2003 [1943]), *Being and Nothingness: An Essay on Phenomenological Ontology*, trans. by H. E. Barnes (London: Routledge)

Scarry, E. (1987), *The Body in Pain: The Making and Unmaking of the World* (New York, NY: Oxford University Press)

Schoenfeldt, M. C. (1999), *Bodies and Selves in Early Modern England: Physiology and Inwardness in Spenser, Shakespeare, Herbert, and Milton* (Cambridge: Cambridge University Press)

Schwall, H. (1997),'Banville's Caliban as a Prestidigitator', in *Constellation Caliban: Figurations of a Character*, ed. by N. Lie and T. D'haen (Amsterdam: Rodopi), pp. 291–311

——— (2006), '"Mirror on Mirror Mirrored is all the Show": Aspects of the Uncanny in Banville's Work with a Focus on *Eclipse*', *Irish University Review*, 36.1, 116–33

Selleck, N. (2008), *The Interpersonal Idiom in Shakespeare, Donne, and Early Modern Culture* (Basingstoke: Palgrave Macmillan)

Senn, F. (1992), *Annotations to James Joyce: Hades ein Kapitel aus dem 'Ulysses' Englisch–Deutsch* (Mainz: Dieterich)

Shakespeare, W. (2006a), *As You Like It*, ed. by J. Dusinberre, *The Arden Shakespeare Third Series* (London: Thomson)

—— (2016a), *Hamlet*, ed. by A. Thompson and N. Taylor, revised edn, *The Arden Shakespeare Third Series* (London: Bloomsbury)

—— (2006b), *Hamlet: the First Quarto (1603)*, ed. by A. Thompson and N. Taylor, *The Arden Shakespeare Third Series* (London: Bloomsbury, 2006b)

—— (2015a), *King Henry IV, Part 1*, ed. by D. S. Kastan, *The Arden Shakespeare Third Series* (London: Bloomsbury)

—— (2002a), *King Lear*, ed. by R. A. Foakes, *The Arden Shakespeare Third Series* (London: Thomson)

—— (2002b), *King Richard II*, ed. by C. R. Forker, *The Arden Shakespeare Third Series* (London: Bloomsbury)

—— (2015b), *Macbeth*, ed. by S. Clark and P. Mason, *The Arden Shakespeare Third Series* (London: Bloomsbury)

—— (2017), *A Midsummer Night's Dream*, ed. by S. Chaudhuri, *The Arden Shakespeare Third Series* (London: Bloomsbury)

—— (2001), *Othello*, ed. by E. A. Honigmann, *The Arden Shakespeare Third Series* (London: Bloomsbury)

—— (2004), *Pericles*, ed. by S. Gossett, *The Arden Shakespeare Third Series* (London: Bloomsbury, 2004)

—— (2010), *The Taming of the Shrew*, ed. by B. Hodgdon, *The Arden Shakespeare Third Series* (London: Bloomsbury)

—— (2003), *The Tempest*, ed. by V. M. Vaughan and A. T. Vaughan, *The Arden Shakespeare Third Series* (London: Thomson)

—— (2016b), *Twelfth Night, or What You Will*, ed. by K. Elam, *The Arden Shakespeare Third Series* (London: Bloomsbury)

—— (2016c), *The Winter's Tale*, ed. by J. Pitcher, *The Arden Shakespeare Third Series* (London: Bloomsbury)

Sharp, J. (1671), *The Midwives Book, or, The Whole Art of Midwifery Discovered* (London)

Sheehan, P. (2009), 'Beckett's Ghost Dramas: Monitoring a Phenomenology of Sleep', in *Beckett and Phenomenology*, ed. by U. Maude and A. Feldman (London: Continuum), pp. 158–76

Shelley, P. B. (2009), *The Major Works*, ed. by Z. Leader (Oxford: Oxford University Press)

Smith, C. (1993), *The Poems of Charlotte Smith*, ed. by S. Curran (New York, NY: Oxford University Press)

Speaight, G. (1970 [1955]), *Punch & Judy: A History by George Speaight*, revised edn (London: Studio Vista)

Spenser, E. (1934 [1596]), *A View of the Present State of Ireland*, ed. by W. L. Renwick (London: Eric Partridge)

—— (1970), *Poetical Works*, ed. by J. C. Smith and E. de Selincourt (Oxford: Oxford University Press)

—— (1987 [1590–1609]), *The Faerie Queene*, ed. by T. P. Roche and C. P. O'Donnell (London: Penguin Classics)

Spivak, G. C. (1995), 'Ghostwriting', *Diacritics*, 25.2, 64–84

Steedman, C. (2001), *Dust* (Manchester: Manchester University Press)

Steinberg, E. R., ed., (1979), *The Stream-of-Consciousness Technique in the Modern Novel* (Port Washington, NY: National University Publications)

Stern, T. (2007), *Rehearsal from Shakespeare to Sheridan* (Oxford: Clarendon Press)

Sullivan, G. A. (2005), *Memory and Forgetting in English Renaissance Drama* (Cambridge: Cambridge University Press)

Syme, H. S. (2012), *Theatre and Testimony in Shakespeare's England: A Culture of Mediation* (Cambridge: Cambridge University Press)

Synge, J. M. (1995), *The Playboy of the Western World and Other Plays*, ed. by A. Saddlemeyer (Oxford: Oxford University Press)

Taylor-Collins, N. (2018), 'Moving the Statue: Myths of Motherhood in Eavan Boland, Shakespeare and Early Modern Culture', in *Shakespeare and Contemporary Irish Literature*, ed. by N. Taylor-Collins and S. van der Ziel (Basingstoke: Palgrave Macmillan), pp. 71–95, doi: 10.1007/978-3-319-95924-5_4

———— (2020a), 'Ageing John Banville: from Einstein to Bergson', ed. by L. P. Zuntini de Izarra, H. Schwall, and N. Taylor-Collins, *Word upon World: Half a Century of John Banville's Universes* (= *Brazilian Journal of Irish Studies (ABEI)*, 22.1, 159–72, doi: 10.37389/abei.v22i1.3855

———— (2020b), 'The City's Hostile Bodies: Coriolanus's Rome and Carson's Belfast', *Modern Language Review*, 115.1, 17–45, doi: 10.5699/modelangrevi.115.1.0017

Taylor-Collins, N., and S. van der Ziel (2018), 'Introduction: Shakespeare, Ireland and the Contemporary', in *Shakespeare and Contemporary Irish Literature*, ed. by N. Taylor-Collins and S. van der Ziel (Basingstoke: Palgrave Macmillan), pp. 1–25, doi: 10.1007/978-3-319-95924-5_1

Thompson, H. (2010), *The Role of Irish Women in the Writings of Edna O'Brien: Mothering the Continuation of the Irish Nation* (Lewiston, NY: The Edwin Mellen Press)

Tóibín, C. (2016), 'After I Am Hanged My Portrait Will Be Interesting', *London Review of Books*, 31 March, pp. 11–23

Trevelyan, C. E. (1848), *The Irish Crisis* (London: Longman, Brown, Green & Longmans)

Ure, P. (1963), *Yeats the Playwright: A Commentary on Character and Design in the Major Plays* (London: Routledge and Kegan Paul)

Valente, J. (2011), *The Myth of Manliness in Irish National Culture, 1880–1922* (Urbana, Chicago, Springfield, IL: University of Illinois Press)

———— (2014), 'Ethnostalgia: *Irish Hunger* and Traumatic Memory', in *The Famine and the Troubles*, ed. by O. Frawley, 4 vols, vol. 3, *Memory Ireland* (New York, NY: Syracuse University Press), pp. 174–92 van der Ziel, S. (2018), 'Shakespeare in *Purgatory*: "A Scene of Tragic Intensity"', *Yeats Annual*, 21, 355–90, doi: 10.11647/OBP.0135.10

—— (2019), '*Godot*'s Shakespeare', *Irish Studies Review*, 27.1, 38–55, doi: 10.1080/09670882.2018.1555401

Weimann, R. (1978), *Shakespeare and the Popular Tradition in the Theater: Studies in the Social Dimension of Dramatic Form and Function*, ed. by R. Schwarz (Baltimore, MD: Johns Hopkins University Press)

Welch, R. (1999), *Book The Abbey Theatre, 1899–1999: Form and Pressure* (Oxford: Oxford University Press), doi: 10.1093/acprof:oso/9780198121879.001.0001

Wheatley, D. (2010), '"Nothing Will Come of Nothing": Zero-Sum Games in Shakespeare's King Lear and Beckett's Endgame', in *Shakespeare and the Irish Writer*, ed. by J. Clare and S. O'Neill (Dublin: University College Dublin Press), pp. 166–78

Williams, R. (1977), *Marxism and Literature* (Oxford: Oxford University Press)

—— (2011 [1961]), *The Long Revolution*, revised edn (Cardigan: Parthian)

—— (2015 [1979]), *Politics and Letters: Interviews with 'New Left Review'*, ed. by G. Dwyer (London: Verso)

Wilson, R. (1993), *Will Power: Essays on Shakespearean Authority* (Hemel Hempstead: Harvester Wheatsheaf)

Yates, F. A. (2005 [1966]), *The Art of Memory* (London: Pimlico)

Yates, W. B. (1923), 'William Butler Yeats – Nobel Lecture', www.nobelprize .org/nobel_prizes/literature/laureates/1923/yeats-lecture.html [accessed 1 June 2012]

—— (1986 [1937]), *A Vision* (London: PAPERMAC)

—— (1994), 'Later Essays', ed. by W. H. O'Donnell, in *The Collected Works of W. B. Yeats*, ed. by R. J. Finneran and G. Mills Harper, 14 vols, vol. 5 (New York, NY: Scribner)

—— (1997a), 'Early Essays', ed. by G. Bornstein and R. J. Finneran, 2nd edn, in *The Collected Works of W. B. Yeats*, ed. by R. J. Finneran and G. Mills Harper, 14 vols, vol. 4 (New York, NY: Scribner)

—— (1997b), 'The Poems', ed. by R. J. Finneran, 2nd edn, in *The Collected Works of W. B. Yeats*, ed. by R. J. Finneran and G. Mills Harper, 14 vols, vol. 1 (New York, NY: Scribner)

—— (2001a), *The Major Works*, ed. by E. Larrissy (Oxford: Oxford University Press)

—— (2001b), 'The Plays', ed. by D. R. Clark and R. E. Clark, 2nd edn, in *The Collected Works of W. B. Yeats*, ed. by R. J. Finneran and G. Mills Harper, 14 vols, vol. 2 (New York, NY: Scribner)

Index

Note: Literary works can be found under authors' names. 'n.' after a page reference indicates the number of a note on that page.

Abbey Theatre 23–4, 26, 34n.21, 50, 52, 110, 279
actor 30, 34n.20, 50, 126, 128, 138, 139, 146, 147, 152, 158, 160, 161, 164–6, 259
Ad Herennium 20
Agamben, Giorgio
  Homo Sacer 98, 116
  Remnants of Auschwitz 126, 128, 133
  Use of Bodies, The 115, 154
amnesia 3, 8, 20, 30, 50, 53, 116–17, 119, 138–41, 144, 145, 151, 155, 157, 158, 161–2, 164, 166, 167, 200, 206, 234, 240, 245, 257
  see also Yeats, W. B., *Wanderings of Oisin, The*
anachrony *see* Derrida, Jacques, hauntology
anamnesis 1–2, 9, 18, 21, 25, 29, 48, 66, 117, 143–5, 181, 206, 242, 246, 248
Anderson, Benedict 23, 205
Anglo-Irish Treaty 33n.10, 231, 271
Anglo-Irish War (1919–21) 4, 15, 22, 207, 245, 276, 283n.1
antitheatricality 20, 30, 58, 138, 140, 146–9, 152, 154, 155–63 *passim*, 166, 167, 198–9, 201n.10

archaeology 78, 208, 218, 248, 252–3, 254–8 *passim*, 260, 261, 264–6, 268–70, 273, 275, 281
  see also Heaney, Seamus
archive 87, 97, 127, 134, 166, 208, 217, 232, 243, 252–8 *passim*, 260, 261–4, 266, 268, 270–2, 274–5, 276n.2, 281, 282
  see also Heaney, Seamus
Arendt, Hannah 89
Aristotle 92n.22, 94, 136n.8
arkhe (ἀρχή) 253–8 *passim*, 262
art of memory, the 17–19, 21–2, 25, 28, 29, 34n.14, 232
Ascendancy, the 225–6, 249n.1
Augustine of Hippo 127–8
authority 19, 20, 32, 43, 51, 52, 56, 61, 64, 66, 74–5, 79, 81, 85, 87, 103, 107–8, 120, 208, 211, 214–15, 217, 230, 273–4

Banville, John 6, 35n.20, 46, 48, 112n.7
  Athena 109
  Book of Evidence, The 94, 101–2, 109
  Ghosts 9, 29, 39, 41–2, 46, 93–112 *passim*, 112n.8, 280

Sea, The 107, 111n.1
Time Pieces: A Memoir 42, 117
Barthes, Roland
  Camera Lucida 87
  Image Music Text 2
Battle of the Somme (1916) 4
Beckett, Samuel
  Eh Joe 137
  Malone Dies 123, 139, 146–57
    passim, 167, 253
  Mercier and Camier 163
  Molloy 30, 125, 127–8, 133–4,
    136n.5, 138–9, 142–6
    passim, 158, 167, 199, 200,
    201n.10, 280
  Three Novels 9, 12, 30, 116,
    127–8, 133–5, 138, 143,
    146, 164, 167, 198, 280
    see also individual volumes
  Unnamable, The 30, 31, 119,
    125, 127–8, 133–4, 139,
    146, 157–66 *passim*, 167,
    200, 280, 281
  Waiting for Godot 137–8, 163
Benjamin, Walter 205
  'Work of Art in the Age of
    Mechanical Reproduction,
    The' 24, 85–6
Bergson, Henri 105, 112n.7
  Matter and Memory 115, 143,
    164
biopolitics 29, 30, 116–17, 171
  see also Agamben, Giorgio;
    Foucault, Michel
Blanchot, Maurice 102, 103, 107
  Instant of My Death, The 93,
    112n.5
  L'éspace littéraire 98–100, 108
blood sacrifice 171–2, 207
  see also Easter Rising (1916)
body 6, 9, 29–30, 40, 53, 67, 74,
    76, 84, 115–201 *passim*,
    205, 207–8, 238, 239,
    240–1, 242, 243, 246,
    250n.10, 258, 259, 261,
    267–8, 270–3, 277n.3,
    277n.5, 280, 282
Boland, Eavan 11, 200n.4

Braidotti, Rosi 230, 250–1n.12,
    256
  Nomadic Subjects 216, 222,
    231, 245
  Nomadic Theory 217–18, 221,
    233, 236, 238, 245
Brando, Marlon 174–6, 178
Brehon Law 209, 212
Brexit 283n.1
Bruno, Giordano 19, 34n.14
Bunreacht na hEireann
  (*Constitution of the Irish
  Republic*) 171, 200n.2,
  245
Burton, Richard 174, 200n.5

Camillo, Giulio 19
Carson, Ciaran
  Belfast Confetti 9–10, 32
Catholicism 45, 54, 69n.6, 182–3,
    245, 271
chora see khôra (χώρα)
Christology 149, 183, 197, 238
Cicero 92n.15
coenæsthesia 139, 142–4
Coke, Edward 212–13, 276
collective memory 15–16, 27, 88,
    90, 105, 118, 150
  see also Halbwachs, Maurice
Collins, Lindsay 47
colonialism 3, 7, 26, 28, 29, 31,
    52, 87, 111, 128, 139, 158,
    199, 208, 214, 215, 242,
    249n.1, 250, 272, 275, 276,
    280
counter-history 31, 207–8, 218,
    252–4, 256–76 *passim*,
    277n.7, 280–1
  see also Heaney, Seamus
counter-memory 31, 207–8, 218,
    220–49, 249n.4, 275–6,
    280–1
  see also Yeats, W. B.
Cuchulain 27, 247
  see also Pearse, Pádraig; Yeats,
    W. B., *On Baile's Strand*
cultural memory 1, 25, 42, 83, 199,
    220

dance 30, 104, 207–8, 218, 220–1,
    226, 228–43 *passim*, 244,
    245–6, 247, 248, 250n.9,
    250n.10, 281
Darlington, Joseph 19, 26, 43
Davies, Sir John 250n.11
    Discovery, A 213
    Orchestra 30, 242–3
Deane, Seamus
    Reading in the Dark 6
decade of centenaries 3–4, 10,
    33n.5, 33n.6, 283
Deleuze, Gilles 256
    Fold 152–3
    Thousand Plateaus, A 246–7
Deleuze, Gilles and Félix
    Guattari
    Thousand Plateaus, A 246–7
demythologisation *see* myth
Derrida, Jacques
    Acts of Religion 158n.5, 281
    'Archive Fever' 253, 256–8, 268,
    275, 276n.2
    Demeure 112n.5
    hauntology 47, 71, 71–8 *passim*
    On the Name 132
    Signéponge=Signsponge 106–7,
    112n.8
    Specters of Marx 46, 47, 49n.4,
    56, 84, 86, 91n.3, 91n.5,
    95, 101, 104
    Truth in Painting, The 106, 107
Descartes, Réné 115, 136n.8, 140,
    198
diabology 55–6, 58
dialectic 18, 21, 43–5, 52, 64–5,
    207, 216
    see also Hegel, Georg Wilhelm
    Friedrich; Ramus, Peter
dinnseanchas 262–4, 274–5
disease 141, 190, 191, 201n.11,
    208, 215, 218n.1, 254,
    263–71 *passim*, 274, 275,
    277n.5, 277n.6, 281
    see also Heaney, Seamus;
    Shakespeare, William,
    works, *Hamlet*
dismemory *see* disremember

disremember 2–3, 6, 9, 24, 29–31,
    48, 61, 67–8, 73, 80, 83–5,
    87, 90, 93–5, 97–9, 103,
    105, 106, 108–9, 111, 135,
    157, 160, 162, 164–7,
    168n.5, 172, 197, 199,
    217–18, 222, 238, 242,
    246, 248–9, 253, 254,
    257–8, 260, 262–6, 268,
    271, 273–6, 278, 281–3,
    283n.1
Donne, John
    'Extasie, The' 118–19
double, the 97, 100–8 *passim*,
    112n.6, 112n.8
Dublin Lockout (1913–14) 3–5,
    15

Eagleton, Terry
    Heathcliff and the Great Hunger
    205
Easter Rising (1916) 3–6 *passim*,
    10–12, 15, 22–3, 25–9
    passim, 33n.5, 207,
    278–80, 282
ego see Freud, Sigmund
eikon (εἰκών) 16–17, 21, 22, 24, 40,
    47, 66, 80, 107, 171, 254
Eliot, T. S. 2–3, 33n.3
    Waste Land, The 251n.13
Elizabeth I 119–20, 139, 210–11,
    215, 219n.6
Ellmann, Maud 86, 87
Ellmann, Richard 227, 229, 241–2,
    245, 246
English Civil War, the (1642–51) 19
epistemology 55, 172, 205, 283
eschatology 73, 183, 186, 188, 206

Famine, the 205–7, 209, 218n.1,
    224–6, 263, 276
    see also Kavanagh, Patrick
father(s) 29, 31, 39, 41, 42, 44,
    45–6, 48, 51, 52, 54, 56,
    60–8 *passim*, 71, 72–5
    passim, 78–85 *passim*,
    93–4, 99, 100–1, 110–11,
    112n.6, 129, 133, 173, 177,

179–80, 222–4, 226, 247,
274–5, 280
see also son(s)
Ferriter, Diarmaid 4, 12, 16, 17, 22
Ficino, Marsilio 19
filiality 46, 101, 111, 224
see also father(s); son(s)
Fludd, Robert 19–20
forgetfulness *see* amnesia
Foster, R. F. 10, 11, 16, 22–4,
24n.19, 200n.3, 209–10,
218n.1, 225, 227, 262
Foucault, Michel 31, 49n.6, 116,
133, 231, 246, 249n.4,
249n.5, 254, 258
Archaeology of Knowledge, The
255–7, 262
History of Sexuality, The (vol. 1)
171, 191
'Nietzsche, Genealogy, History'
221–2, 227, 229–30, 275
see also counter-history;
counter-memory
Freud, Sigmund 47, 83, 202, 258
ego 102–3
id 102–3, 256
'Mourning and Melancholia' 14,
34n.12
'A Note Upon "The Mystic
Writing-Pad"' 256–7
superego 256
and trauma 63
and the uncanny 8
Friel, Brian 99
Translations 252, 263
Fukuyama, Francis 91n.4
future, the 2, 21, 22, 25, 29, 30,
41–2, 47, 52, 59, 61–8
passim, 72–3, 79–80, 82–3,
87, 89, 90, 93, 97, 99–100,
105–6, 109–11, 123–5,
144, 149, 157, 159–67
passim, 168n.5, 172,
181–4, 208, 216, 218, 220,
226, 235, 243, 248–9, 268,
273–4, 280, 281, 283

Garber, Marjorie 8, 29, 37, 39, 42,
56, 60, 73, 105, 112n.6

genealogy 39, 46–8, 64, 100, 197,
218, 224–6, 229, 281
General Post Office (GPO) 5, 14,
22, 24, 26, 33n.5
ghost 6, 8, 9, 29, 39–112 *passim*,
116, 148, 200, 224, 260,
264, 275, 280
Gibbons, Luke 34n.14, 47, 83–7,
91n.12, 92n.14, 92n.17
Glasnevin Cemetery 41, 71, 72, 78,
85, 93
see also Joyce, James, *Ulysses*,
'Hades'
Globe Theatre 20, 121, 148
GPO *see* General Post Office
Grazia, Margreta de 258–60,
265–6, 277n.6
Greenblatt, Stephen 46, 55–7, 109,
139–40
Greene, John 56–7
Gregory, Lady Augusta 24, 171,
183, 200n.7, 229, 249n.1
and Yeats, W. B., *Cathleen ni
Houlihan* 25–6, 170, 198

Halbwachs, Maurice 16, 72, 83,
118, 150
see also collective memory
handkerchief, the *see* Brando,
Marlon; O'Brien, Edna,
Country Girl: A Memoir,
Country Girls, The;
Shakespeare, William,
works, *Othello*
hauntology *see* Derrida, Jacques
Heaney, Seamus 6, 9, 30–1, 207–8,
216–17
'Act of Union' 32, 270–1
'Antaeus' 266, 270, 272
'At a Potato Digging' 263, 271
'Augury' 267–8
bog bodies 261, 268, 272, 275
Cure at Troy, The 267–8
Death of a Naturalist 253, 274
and depth 31, 252, 255–6, 261,
265, 267–8, 272, 274
'Digging' 253, 274
District and Circle 272
'Feeling into Words' 264, 266

Finders Keepers 253
'Fosterage' 266, 277n.7
'Grauballe Man, The' 268–70
'Herbal' 273
'Hercules and Antaeus' 266,
    270, 272
Human Chain 273
'Kinship' 269–70
and muddiness 208, 218, 254,
    269, 274, 276
North 6, 75, 253, 269, 271
'North' 253, 261–2, 270
Opened Ground 270–1
'Personal Helicon' 107
Preoccupations 252–3
'Real Names, The' 275
'Sibyl' 277n.8
'Singing School' 266
Station Island 272–3
'Tollund Man in Springtime,
    The' 272
'Triptych' 277n.8
'Veteran's Dream' 267–8
'Viking Dublin: Trial Pieces' 208,
    254, 261, 264, 266, 268,
    270, 273, 275
Wintering Out 272
word-hoard 253–4, 261–3, 270,
    274
see also archaeology; archive;
    counter-history; disease
Hegel, Georg Wilhelm Friedrich 64,
    69n.8, 260
Heidegger, Martin 98, 235, 245
Helgerson, Richard 1–2, 212–13,
    273–4
hermetic-cabalism 18, 19, 21
Hewitt, John 33n.7, 252
Heywood, Thomas 56, 158
Historian, the *see* Steedman,
    Carolyn
history 1, 8, 12, 13, 15–17, 21,
    24, 33n.8, 34n.16, 48, 51,
    52, 60, 62, 67, 73, 91n.4,
    98, 109, 111, 135, 205–17
    passim, 221, 225–6, 227,
    229, 235, 239–40, 244,
    245, 249, 254, 258, 260,

261, 270, 275, 276, 277n.7,
    280, 281
see also counter-history
Holinshed, Raphael 34n.16
homelessness 216, 221–2, 233, 236
    see also nomadism
Homer 229
Odyssey, The 72, 88
Home Rule 207, 227, 279
hospitality 32, 216
Houlihan, Kathleen ní *see* Mother
    Ireland
humanism 18–19, 21, 27, 42–3
hysterectomy *see* womb
hysterica passio 189–99 *passim*
    see also womb

id see Freud, Sigmund
imagination 17, 27, 40, 53, 64, 70,
    94, 96–7, 100, 105, 112n.2,
    116–17, 123, 124, 129,
    142, 149–50, 152, 153,
    158, 172, 175–6, 218, 225,
    229, 231–2, 234, 237, 258,
    268, 270
interior monologue 70
    see also soliloquy
intertextuality 2–3, 7–8, 30–2,
    33n.3, 51, 111, 136n.9,
    137, 149–50, 166, 173,
    183, 198, 200, 258, 277n.8,
    280–3 *passim*
    see also Barthes, Roland;
    Kristeva, Julia; Lachmann,
    Renate
involuntary memory 78, 83,
    92n.18
    see also Proust, Marcel
Irish Civil War (1922–3) 3, 15, 19,
    207, 226, 231, 232
Irish Free State 4, 12, 33n.10, 90,
    163, 199
    see also Republic of Ireland
Irish National Theatre, The *see*
    Abbey Theatre
Irish Times, The 4–5, 11, 26, 51
Irish War of Independence *see*
    Anglo-Irish War (1919–21)

James, Henry
  Turn of the Screw, The 111n.1
James VI/I 19, 250n.11
Jonson, Ben 30, 135n.1, 146, 198
  Bartholomew Fair 162–3
  Hymenaie 162
  Volpone 139, 159–67 *passim*
Jorden, Edward 191
Joyce, James 6, 34n.12, 46, 48,
    229, 272
  Dubliners 92n.13
  Finnegans Wake 249
  *Portrait of the Artist as a Young
    Man, A* 26–7
  Ulysses 17, 39, 72–3, 79, 82, 84,
    87, 89, 91n.12, 95, 100
  'Circe' 70, 79–82, 84, 89–90,
    92n.17, 92n.19
  'Cyclops' 70, 81, 91n.10, 93
  'Eumaeus' 81, 91n.9
  'Hades' 9, 29, 41, 46, 70–92
    passim, 94, 98, 110, 280
  'Ithaca' 91n.9
  'Nestor' 91n.2
  'Scylla and Charybdis' 70–1,
    82
Judaism 81, 103, 271

Kantorowicz, Ernst
  King's Two Bodies, The 139
katabasis (καταβασις) *see nekuya*
    (νέκυια)
Kavanagh, Patrick 252
  'Great Hunger, The' 206
khôra (χώρα) 131–2, 190, 195, 197,
    200
Kiberd, Declan 25–7, 65–7, 70–1,
    101, 129, 136n.5, 170, 186,
    196
Kierkegaard, Søren
  'Either/Or' 88
Kott, Jan 1, 35n.24, 137
Kristeva, Julia 2, 7–8, 132, 136n.9,
    190
  see also intertextuality; *khôra*
    (χώρα)
Kyd, Thomas
  Spanish Tragedy, The 59

Lachmann, Renate 7–8, 29, 30, 48,
    72, 139, 149, 166, 173, 258
land 9, 29, 30–1, 51, 61–2, 64, 67,
    88, 110, 151, 187, 200,
    203–77 *passim*, 280–1
  depth *see* Heaney, Seamus
  Land Wars, the 207, 224–5,
    227–8, 247
  surface *see* surface; Yeats, W. B.
  see also territory
Land League, the 225, 227–8
Laqueur, Thomas 55, 85, 191,
    201n.9
law 13, 29, 42, 53, 57, 60, 62, 64,
    66, 74–7, 80, 81, 90, 103,
    108, 119, 126, 168n.5, 207,
    209, 212–14, 216, 236,
    248, 250n.11, 256, 258,
    259, 272, 275
  see also Brehon Law
Lawless, Emily
  'Fontenoy, 1745' 197
lethargy 30, 133, 138–41, 155,
    157, 163, 166–7, 201n.10
  see also amnesia
Levinas, Emmanuel 91–2n.12,
    167n.2
lieux de mémoire see Nora, Pierre
Longley, Edna 232–5, 240, 251n.13

McAleese, Mary 171
McBride, Sean 172
MacDonagh, Thomas 22
McGahern, John 128
  Amongst Women 136n.5
Markievicz, Constance 171
Martyn, Edward 24
  see also Abbey Theatre
Marx, Karl 46, 260
masculinity 30, 128, 170–1, 174–5
Massinger, Philip 33n.3
maternity 47, 91n.6, 98, 131, 131,
    134, 142, 146–8, 150, 154,
    171, 172, 177, 182, 187,
    190–4 *passim*, 196, 197,
    223, 226
  see also khôra (χώρα); Mother
    Ireland

melancholy 14–15, 34n.12
  see also Freud, Sigmund,
    'Mourning and
    Melancholia'; mourning
memoir 6, 30, 42, 117, 126, 128–
  33 passim, 172–6 passim,
  181–2, 187, 195, 197
  see also khôra (χώρα); O'Brien,
    Edna; testimony
Merleau-Ponty, Maurice 118, 155
method 18–19, 21, 22, 43–6, 49n.4
  see also Ramus, Peter
metrocolonial 52, 64, 69n.5, 110
milieux de mémoire see Nora,
  Pierre
mnemohistory 8
modern Ireland 1–3, 6, 9–10, 15,
  28–9, 31, 32, 51, 53, 67,
  68, 73, 82, 111, 132, 135,
  139, 191–2, 198, 200, 213,
  221–2, 225, 234–5, 242,
  244, 245, 247, 264, 267,
  271, 281
modernism 65, 68, 88, 166
modernity 12, 17, 21, 52–3, 56, 62,
  64–5, 68, 85, 88, 97, 116,
  120, 208, 212–13, 216,
  221, 225, 227–8, 235, 236,
  238, 240, 245, 249, 254,
  260–1, 264, 266, 268–9,
  273, 274, 276
More, Sir Thomas 139
motherhood see maternity
Mother Ireland 30, 119, 125, 134,
  170–2, 181–2, 189–91, 196,
  198–200, 203, 245, 271
  see also O'Brien, Edna
mourning 14, 34n.12, 42, 70, 74,
  76–80, 82, 84, 88–9, 91n.6,
  110, 135, 217
  see also melancholy
Muldoon, Paul 11, 252
murder 41, 46, 50–1, 57, 60,
  61–5 passim, 76–7, 94,
  98, 101–2, 109, 144, 148,
  223–4, 266
myth 17, 19, 31, 60, 64, 68, 74, 77,
  90, 178, 198, 200n.4, 208,

  227–9, 239–40, 248–9,
  262, 263, 265, 274, 276,
  280–1

National Library of Ireland 4, 70
National Theatre, UK 278–80
nekuya (νέκυια) 72, 88, 90n.1
Nobel Prize 31, 207, 229, 276
nomadism 207, 211, 216–18, 220–
  2, 230, 231, 233, 234–6,
  238, 240–5 passim, 246,
  248–9, 250n.7, 250–1n.12,
  258, 268–9, 273, 276,
  277n.4, 281
Nora, Pierre
  lieux de mémoire 150, 206
  milieux de mémoire 21, 71–2,
    276
Northbrooke, John 57
novel, the 129, 132–3, 195
  see also memoir

O'Brien, Edna 169, 191–2, 198,
  207
  Country Girl: A Memoir 129,
    132–4, 172–6
  Country Girls, The 133, 173,
    176, 178, 180
  Country Girls Trilogy, The 9,
    30, 125, 129, 132, 134,
    169–204 passim
    see also individual volumes
  Epilogue 196–7
  Girls in Their Married Bliss 133,
    182, 186, 194
  Haunted 170, 200n.1
  Light of Evening, The 169
  Lonely Girl, The 173, 180–6
  Mother Ireland 134, 170, 203
    see also Mother Ireland
  Night 176
  Wedding Dress, The 200n.1
O'Casey, Sean 279–80
  Plough and the Stars, The
    282–3
offstage 41, 52, 54, 55, 59–68
  passim, 90, 93, 95, 97, 100,
  108–11, 193, 281

ontology 73–4, 76–7, 86, 96,
126–8, 153
see also Derrida, Jacques,
hauntology

pain 78, 88, 119, 124–5, 140,
142–4, 182, 187, 189, 198,
271
Paster, Gail Kern 140, 190–2, 194
patriarchy 48, 182, 191, 194
Pearse, Pádraig 5–6, 22–3, 27, 171,
279, 281
phenomenology 15–16, 105, 119,
121–4, 135–6n.2, 136n.3,
153, 155, 198
see also Heidegger, Martin;
Merleau-Ponty, Maurice;
Ricoeur, Paul; Sartre,
Jean-Paul
phonograph *see* technology
photograph *see* technology
Pine, Emilie 11, 13, 28, 32, 73, 90
platea 158, 168n.3
Plato 96
Symposium 89, 92n.21
Theaetetus 86, 131
Timaeus 129–32, 136n.8, 195
Plunkett, Joseph 22
poiesis (ποίησις) 73, 89–90, 92n.21,
93, 108, 110, 116, 129,
132
postmemory 150
postmodernism 27, 94, 109–11
potentiality 73, 75, 88–9, 93, 111,
117
private sphere 19, 21, 22, 29
see also public sphere
propriety 18, 121, 134, 151–4
passim, 209, 222, 223, 229,
236, 259, 261, 281
of memory 12, 15, 150–3 *passim*
Prospect Cemetery *see* Glasnevin
Cemetery
Protestantism 10, 19–20, 42, 45,
54–7 *passim*, 139, 226
Proust, Marcel 83, 91n.7
Prynne, William 161
public sphere 19–21, 23, 29, 151
see also private sphere

Punch and Judy 149, 156–8, 162,
165, 167
puppets 157–8, 160, 162–3, 165–7

Rainolds, John 146, 148, 154,
161–2, 166
Ramus, Peter 18–21, 26, 42–6,
49n.4
Reformation, the 3, 19, 54, 56,
69n.6, 249n.2
see also Protestantism
Renan, Ernest 13
representation 3, 40, 44, 60, 86,
89, 119–21, 124, 135, 165,
193–4, 199, 210, 215, 217,
245, 274
Republic of Ireland 3–5, 33n.5,
128, 139, 163, 171, 280,
281
see also Irish Free State
revenge 46, 51, 59–60, 62, 69n.10,
75–7, 101, 126–7
Revival, the 52, 62, 67, 73, 90,
216
revivification 192–4, 196–7,
201n.9
see also Christology; *hysterica
passio*
Rich, Barnabe 54, 58–60
Ricoeur, Paul 14–17 *passim*, 21,
33n.4, 76, 94, 96, 97, 105,
117–18, 126–7, 150, 253,
281
Robinson, Mary 171
romance 65, 138, 182–3, 186, 193,
194
Royle, Nicholas 47–8, 91n.5, 107,
108

Sartre, Jean-Paul 105, 125,
135–6n.2
Being and Nothingness 121–4,
142–4, 167, 198
satire 8, 30, 146
see also Jonson, Ben
Scarry, Elaine 119, 124–5, 142–3,
182, 188–9, 198, 277n.5
self-fashioning 55, 62, 109, 139–40
see also Greenblatt, Stephen

Shakespeare, William
  First Folio 147, 250n.8
  quatercentenary 4, 6, 13, 280
  tercentenary 26–7
  works
    Antony and Cleopatra 174
    As You Like It 30–1, 138, 175,
      216, 220–2, 235–8 *passim*,
      242, 245, 250n.7, 281
    Coriolanus 20, 30, 32, 139–
      43 *passim*, 146–54 *passim*,
      163–4, 166–7, 167n.1, 174,
      199, 201n.10, 223, 280
    Hamlet 19, 20, 26–7, 29, 31,
      33n.8, 40, 42–7 *passim*,
      48–9n.3, 50–68 *passim*,
      69n.10, 70–82 *passim*,
      84–9 *passim*, 91n.5, 91n.6,
      93–111 *passim*, 112n.6,
      120, 127, 137, 148, 174,
      196, 216, 221–2, 223–4,
      254, 257, 258–61 *passim*,
      264–6, 268, 272–5, 277n.8,
      279–81
    1 Henry IV 174, 265
    2 Henry IV 174
    Henry V 34n.16, 137, 174,
      223
    Julius Caesar 55, 58–9, 174
    King John 174
    King Lear 30, 51, 137,
      168n.3, 216, 220–3,
      229–32, 234, 236, 247,
      250n.8, 281
    Love's Labour's Lost 137
    Macbeth 55, 58–9, 149–50,
      152, 153, 172
    Measure for Measure 13
    Merchant of Venice, The 51
    Midsummer Night's Dream, A
      32, 113, 116, 137–8, 258
    Othello 30, 149–50, 152,
      172, 174, 176–83 *passim*,
      185–6, 189, 192, 199
    Pericles 172, 189, 196–7, 199
    Richard III 55, 168n.3
    Taming of the Shrew, The 30,
      137, 172, 174, 176, 183–7
      passim, 192, 199, 201n.8

    Tempest, The 94, 112n.2,
      137–8, 169, 174, 270,
      277n.8
    Timon of Athens 223, 234
    Twelfth Night 137, 174
    Winter's Tale, The 30, 137,
      170, 172, 189, 192–3, 196,
      223, 280
    see also Globe Theatre
Shelley, Percy Bysshe
  'Ozymandias' 234–5
skulls 53, 61, 67–8, 76, 224, 254,
  259–60, 275
Smith, Charlotte
  'Beachy Head' 255
soliloquy 43, 55, 127, 138, 149,
  153, 184, 258, 260
  see also interior monologue
son(s) 29, 39, 41–2, 46–8, 64–5,
  67, 71, 72, 75, 78–80, 82,
  84, 89, 93, 94, 97–101,
  103, 108, 110–11, 143,
  148, 149, 154, 172, 187,
  193, 200n.7, 223–4, 226,
  247, 280–1
  see also father(s); filiality
Sophocles 267
spectrality 29, 46, 54–62, 65–6, 68,
  78, 94, 96–7, 110
Spenser, Edmund 1–2, 207
  Colin Clouts Come Home Again
    208, 210–11, 216, 281
  Faerie Queene, The 208,
    212–16, 220, 242
  'Shepheardes Calender, The' 220
  *View of the Present State of
    Ireland, A* 208, 211–15,
    263–4
Spivak, Gayatri Chakravorty
  104–5
Steedman, Carolyn 208, 252–3,
  258, 261–3, 268, 270, 275,
  281
surface 30, 130, 165, 178, 194–5,
  197, 215, 220, 224,
  227–9, 233, 235, 239–40,
  246, 249, 252, 255, 257,
  259–60, 263–5, 268, 270,
  274, 277n.3

see also Heaney, Seamus;
O'Brien, Edna, *Epilogue*,
*Girls in Their Married
Bliss*; Shakespeare, William,
works, *Winter's Tale, The*;
Yeats, W. B.
Syme, Holger 119–21, 125, 127,
198
Synge, J. M. 6, 48, 69n.8, 71, 134,
229, 241, 281
*Playboy of the Western World,
The* 9, 29, 39, 41, 46,
50–69 *passim*, 90, 93–5,
98, 100, 103, 110, 149, 280
Playboy riots 52, 68n.1
Well of the Saints, The 51, 58,
69n.3

technology 72–3, 84–90, 92n.20,
116
phonograph 71, 86–7, 89
photograph 11, 71, 86–7, 89,
92n.17
see also Barthes, Roland
tekhnè (τέχνη) 89, 132
territory 6, 29–31, 47, 95, 207,
208, 221, 224–6, 230–1,
234, 235, 238, 240, 246–7,
252, 256, 259–61, 264–6,
274
deterritorialisation 208, 211,
221, 225, 230, 233, 242,
247, 250n.10
reterritorialisation 211, 220–2,
225, 227, 231, 236, 242
territorialisation 207, 216, 222,
229, 231, 235, 240, 242,
246, 258, 259
testimony 15, 16, 30, 119, 126–8,
131–3, 135, 142–4, 155,
163–5, 172, 198, 209, 254,
280
see also memoir
theatre of memory 22, 26, 28–9,
280
theatricality 20, 21, 22–5 *passim*,
28, 30, 39, 50, 52, 55,
58, 119–23 *passim*, 125,
126–7, 128, 137, 138–9,

145–8 *passim*, 151–2,
155–7, 158–60, 161–2,
164–6, 198, 280
see also antitheatricality
Tone, Wolfe 10
transhumance 211, 218
see also nomadism
Troubles, The 9, 207
tupos (τύπος) 15, 17, 40, 66, 86,
107, 228, 235, 254
Tyrone Rebellion (1594–1603)
208–10

Virgil 59
Aeneid 72, 88

West Britain 69n.5
Wilder, Thornton 175
Williams, Raymond
structure of feeling 1–2, 7
witness 16, 22, 106, 120, 126–7,
131, 135, 146, 148, 155,
256
see also testimony
womb 30, 119, 125, 132, 170–1,
186–200 *passim*, 201n.8,
201n.11, 265, 266, 271,
280, 281
see also hysterica passio
wound-man, the 151
Wyatt, Thomas 140

Yates, Frances *see* art of memory,
the
Yeats, W. B. 6, 9, 24–6, 27–8,
30–1, 48n.1, 48n.2, 49n.6,
183, 198, 207–8, 216–18,
220–51 *passim*, 252, 256,
268–70, 275, 280–2
'Acre of Grass, An' 234
Anima Mundi 41, 50, 99, 232,
241
'At Stratford-on-Avon' 222–3
Cathleen ni Houlihan see
Gregory, Lady Augusta
'Celtic Element in Literature,
The' 241
'Certain Noble Plays of Japan'
241

'Coole Park, 1929' 234–5, 238–9
Countess Cathleen, The 225–6
'Discoveries' 242
'Double Vision of Michael Robartes, The' 246, 248
'General Introduction for My Work, A' 241
Green Helmet and Other Poems, The 228
'If I were four-and-twenty' 252, 262
'Irish Airman Foresees His Death, An' 200n.7
'Meditations in a Time of Civil War' 226–7, 232
'My Descendants' 226–7, 233
'My House' 226
'Nineteen Hundred and Nineteen' 245–6
On Baile's Strand 247

Per Amica Silentia Lunae 40
Purgatory 223–4
'Sailing to Byzantium' 89
'Second Coming, The' 269, 283
'Solomon and the Witch' 228–9
'Tower, The' 228, 231–4, 239, 248
'Under Ben Bulben' 235, 240
'Upon a House Shaken by the Land Agitation' 226–8, 234
Vision, A 41, 243, 244, 246, 248, 250n.9, 251n.14
Wanderings of Oisin, The 239–41, 244–6, 248
Where There Is Nothing 249n.1
Wind Among the Reeds, The 250n.6
see also counter-memory; dance; Nobel Prize; surface
Young Irelanders 10

9 781526 149619